THE URBAN READER

edited by **SUSAN CAHILL** and

MICHELE F. COOPER

Queens College of the City University of New York

PRENTICE-HALL, INC., ENGLEWOOD CLIFFS, NEW JERSEY

THE URBAN READER

for tom and marve

and our students and colleagues
who influenced the making of this book in any way

Our thanks to Bill Oliver, editor, Judy Winthrop, designer,
and Robb Heinemann, production editor, at Prentice-Hall.

THE URBAN READER

Edited by SUSAN CAHILL and MICHELE F. COOPER

© 1971 by PRENTICE-HALL, INC., Englewood Cliffs, New Jersey

Because acknowledgments to the publishers of the material
reprinted in this book are extensive, they appear
in detail at the end of the book.

C–13–939058–8
P–13–939041–3

Library of Congress Catalog Card Number: 75–137898

Current Printing (last number):
10 9 8 7 6 5 4 3 2

Printed in the United States of America

PRENTICE-HALL INTERNATIONAL, *London*
PRENTICE-HALL OF AUSTRALIA, PTY. LTD., *Sydney*
PRENTICE-HALL OF CANADA, LTD., *Toronto*
PRENTICE-HALL OF INDIA PRIVATE LIMITED, *New Delhi*
PRENTICE-HALL OF JAPAN, INC., *Tokyo*

INTRODUCTION

Anyone who has ever lived or worked in a big city will be in touch with the deadly and vigorous crosscurrents of urban life moving through this book. Its contents represent this urban experience of contradictory forces: the relentless pull toward ugliness and tedium and the thrusts toward new possibilities and life. The duality exists, unmistakably. Paradox is the fact of urban, as well as of any other, life. It is obvious, then, why the city has often been used as a symbol of the whole range of human experience, of man himself.

It has not been hard to find materials that echo the death rattle heard in city schools, streets, ghettos, and subways. The many descriptions of educational, social, political, and economic systems that no longer work but refuse to retire are depressingly familiar. The reasons for their collapse are familiarly controversial. Is it lack of money or lack of manhood? Big business or citizen indifference? Do the systems sicken the people, who in turn stagnate the city? Urban stagnation, the cold repression of a culture against man—whose only movement is to send city dwellers in growing numbers to country, commune, and suburb—seems to some irreversible. Their theme song might be, "We Gotta Get out of This Place."

Lively and compassionate alternatives there are. Many selections— both written and visual—reflect the insights and innovations alive or possible among students, educators, artists, and people in the streets. In their defiance and creativity, we see the other side of the duality, the city as a culture *for* man. Which side bears the seeds of the future is an open question. This book contains the omens of the here and now, good and bad.

If, however, the reader gets from this book only a negative impression of city life, he should look more closely at its written and visual contents. The selections perform no whitewash of the negative side of city life, but in most cases, even as they expose the problems, they are equally urgent in suggesting or embodying alternatives. We see the selections about workers for change—VISTA Volunteers, Young Lords, Black Panthers, Chicanos, Chinese-American youth, teachers in mini-schools, volunteers in local projects, Saul Alinsky's organizers from the middle class—as beacons of hope on the urban horizon. Throughout the book and especially in the section

"The Artists at Work," it is clear that artists—poets, painters, writers, sculptors, architects, photographers, and musicians—have been inspired by the city. Surely to show the city as a rich source of artistic inspiration is to give a strong sense of the city's health. Having looked more closely, then, and having seen the springs of hope under the hard, dry surface of urban life, the reader will better understand what Richard Wright meant when he wrote about his life in Chicago: "There in that self-conscious city, that city so deadly dramatic and stimulating, we caught whispers of the meanings that life could have, and we were pushed and pounded by facts much too big for us." This book does not compromise his vision of urban possibilities and defeat.

Neither does it soften the powerful facts of American life in the seventies, facts relevant to the experience and interests of urban college students: Southeast Asia, the Black revolution, student rebellion, pollution, poverty, ineffective schools, blight. Whether in poem or photograph, song, essay, or story, *The Urban Reader* encompasses these urgent issues and the gamut of controversial responses to them: community control, power to the people, drugs, welfare, population control, riots, free schools, urban "renewal," and the revolution of many minorities. It also shows that local people—in contrast to Federal agencies—are organizing in growing numbers to save the city in their own neighborhoods. Such local responses signal a new and hopeful way of creating rather than accepting the facts of urban life.

Because the selections focus on such real situations, verifiable through the reader's own experience any day in any city, we believe this book can contribute to the search for more meaningful forms of learning. Its vistas go far beyond the walls of classrooms and lecture halls into the complex life of the city itself. Thinking and arguing, reading and writing about what one finds *out there*—and the book should compel the reader to start walking and looking and asking questions in his own city—has a lot to do with making college education part of the urban solution instead of another problem. It has everything to do with making it more personal. Working as an apprentice to the city itself may have some nightmarish qualities, but these are real and streaked with promise.

About the book's organization: In choosing and arranging the contents, we have been mainly concerned with those selections which expose both the problems besetting the cities and the alternatives being chosen or suggested by the imaginative and undefeated. Part I, "Preliminaries," has two entries. "The City, Pro & Con" is a sequence of quotations which reflects the stagnation and energy that is the paradox of the urban experience. "An Urban Dictionary" supplies a few essential definitions. Part II, "Crosscurrents of City Life" presents nine ways of looking at the city. Each of the nine sections in Part II, in a wide variety of styles and media, treats a different aspect of city life, such as politics, art, education, economics, cultural diversity, and the psychology of the city dweller, in the light of their problems and possible solutions. Part III, a visual essay of "City People," presents the photographer's response to the people whose voices have been heard in many preceding selections.

All the writers and artists included have lived and, with few exceptions, are still working in an American city. Several have left for Europe or Africa or nowhere in particular to hide or write or wander. Some have never returned. Most have come home. *The Urban Reader* makes both decisions understandable.

Susan Cahill
Michele F. Cooper

New York

CONTENTS

2

4

5

6

POLITICS AND POWER STRUGGLES   249

7

EDUCATION: Up Against the Classroom Wall   281

8

9

THE FUTURE: A Bad Trip? 359

PART

III

CITY PEOPLE: A Photographic Essay 385

PRELIMINARIES

THE CITY,
PRO AND CON,
IN 75 WORDS OR LESS

The mobs of great cities add just so much to
the support of pure government, as sores do to
the strength of the human body.

> THOMAS JEFFERSON
> *Notes on Virginia*

Cities force growth and make men talkative and
entertaining, but they make them artificial.

> RALPH WALDO EMERSON
> *"Farming"*

What absurdity can be imagined greater than
the institution of cities. Cities originated not in
love but in war. It was war that drove men
together in multitudes and compelled them
to stand so close and build walls around them.

> ELIZABETH PEABODY
> of Brook Farm

Whatever had been my taste for solitude and
natural scenery, yet the thick, foggy, stifled
elements of cities, the entangled life of so many
men together, sordid as it was, and empty of
the beautiful, took quite a strenuous hold upon
my mind. I felt as if there could never be
enough of it.

> NATHANIEL HAWTHORNE
> *The Blithedale Romance*

. . . the courage, the heaven-scaling audacity of it all, and
the lightness withal, as if there was nothing that was not
easy, and the great pulses and bounds of progress,
so many in directions all simultaneous that the coordination is indefinitely future, give a kind of *drumming
background* of life that I have never felt before. I'm sure
that once in that movement, and at home, all other places
would seem insipid.

> WILLIAM JAMES
> Letter to Henry James

I knew then and there that I loved Chicago. It was
so strong, so rough, so shabby and yet so vital and
determined. It seemed more like a young giant afraid of
nothing, and that it was that appealed to me.

> THEODORE DREISER
> *Dawn*

Internationalism engendered in the immigrant quarters
of American cities might be recognized as an effective
instrument in the cause of peace.

> JANE ADDAMS
> *Twenty Years at Hull House*

The city seen from the Queensboro Bridge is always
the city seen for the first time, in its first wild promise of
all the mystery and the beauty in the world.

> F. SCOTT FITZGERALD
> *The Great Gatsby*

New York lays hand upon a man's bowels; he grows drunk
with ecstasy; he grows young and full of glory; he feels
that he can never die.

THOMAS WOLFE

Physical nearness coupled with social distance makes it
necessary for urbanites to cultivate reserve and to disguise
inner feelings.

E. GORDON ERICKSEN
Urban Behavior

The contemporary urban region represents an ingenious
device for vastly enlarging the range of human
communication and widening the scope of individual
choice. Urbanization thus contributes to the freedom
of man.

HARVEY COX
The Secular City

Cityside rigidity and unfreedom force severe limitations
upon intelligence—the houses all look alike.

WARREN TALLMAN
New American Story

Nature watching is quite as easy in the city as in
the country; all one has to do is accept Man as a part
of Nature.

EDGAR ANDERSON
Landscape

Billy:
> . . . Where you from man?

Stranger:
> (sighs) A City.

Billy:
> Just a city?

Stranger:
> Mmm-mmm. It doesn't make any difference what
> city. All cities are alike. That's why I'm out
> here now.

Billy:
> Yeah, why?

Stranger:
> 'Cause I'm from the city, a long way from the city—
> and that's where I want to be right now.

PETER FONDA, DENNIS HOPPER,
TERRY SOUTHERN
Easy Rider

It is in the streets that we will make our struggle.
The streets belong to the people! Long live the flower-cong
of the gutters!

ABBIE HOFFMAN
Revolution For The Hell Of It

Being human is itself difficult, and therefore all kinds of
settlements (except dream cities) have problems. Big cities
have difficulties in abundance, because they have people
in abundance. But vital cities are not helpless to combat
even the most difficult of problems.

JANE JACOBS
*The Death and Life of
Great American Cities*

AN URBAN DICTIONARY

bu·reauc·ra·cy (byoo-rok′rə-si, byoo-rō′krə-si), *n.* [*pl.* BUREAUCRA-CIES (-siz)], [Fr. *bureaucratie* < *bureau* + Gr. *kratia* < *kratein*, to be strong], 1. the administration of government through departments and sub-divisions managed by sets of officials following an inflexible routine. 2. the officials collectively. 3. governmental officialism or inflexible routine: see also RED TAPE. 4. the concentration of authority in administrative bureaus.

boss·ism (bôs′iz′m, bos′iz′m), *n.* domination or control by bosses, especially of a political machine or party.

central city, the principal municipality of a metropolitan area, surrounded by suburbs and smaller towns; esp., the crowded, industrial, often blighted area.

cit·i·fied (sit′i-fid′), *adj.* having the manners, dress, etc. attributed to city people.

cit·y (sit′i), *n.* [*pl.* CITIES (-iz)], [ME. & OFr. *cite, citet;* L. *civitas* (< *civis,* citizen), orig., citizenship, community of citizens, hence one of the Gaulish states, chief town in such a state], 1. a large, important town. 2. in the United States, an incorporated municipality whose boundaries and powers of self-government are defined by a charter from the State in which it is located: abbreviated *c.* 3. in Canada, a municipality of the highest rank. 4. in Great Britain, a borough or town with a royal charter, usually a town that has been or is an episcopal see. 5. all the people of a city. 6. in ancient Greece, a city-state. *adj.* of or in a city.

city father, any of the important officials of a city; councilman, alderman, etc.

city hall, 1. a building which houses the offices of a municipal government. 2. a municipal government —*to fight city hall* [Colloq.] to take up the apparently futile fight against petty or impersonal bureaucratic authority.

city manager, an administrator appointed by a city council or similar body to act as manager of the city.

cit·y·scape (-skāp′), *n.* [CITY + (LAND)SCAPE], 1. a painting, photograph, etc. representing a view of a section of a city. 2. a view of a section of a city, esp. of buildings silhouetted against the horizon.

city slicker, [Colloq.] a city dweller regarded, esp. by rural people, as a smooth, tricky person.

civ·ic (siv′ik), *adj.* [L. *civicus,* civil < *civis,* citizen], 1. of a city. 2. of citizens. 3. of citizenship.

con·gest (kən-jest′), *v.t.* [< L. *congestus,* pp. of *congerere,* to bring together, pile up < *com-,* together + *gerere,* to carry, perform], 1.

7

to cause too much blood to accumulate in (a part of the body). 2. to overcrowd; fill to excess: as, the shopping district was *congested*. *v.i.* to become congested.

con·ges·tion (kən-jes′chən), *n.* 1. an excessive accumulation of blood in a part of the body. 2. a congesting or congested condition: as of population or traffic.

cos·mo·pol·i·tan (koz′mə-pol′ə-t′n), *adj.* [*cosmopolite* + *-an*], 1. belonging to the whole world; not national or local. 2. not bound by local or national habits or prejudices; at home in all countries or places. *n.* a cosmopolitan person or thing; cosmopolite.

de·cen·tral·i·za·tion (dē-sen′trəl-i-zā′shən, dē′sen-trəl-i-zā′shən), *n.* a decentralizing or being decentralized.

de·cen·tral·ize (dē-sen′trəl-iz′), *v.t.* to break up the centralization of authority, as in a government or industry, and distribute among more places, local authorities, etc.

down·town (doun′toun′, doun′-toun′), *adj.* 1. of or in the geographically lower part of a city or town: opposed to *uptown*. 2. of, in, or like the main business section of a city or town. *adv.* to, toward, or in the geographically lower part or main business section of a city or town. *n.* the main business section of a city or town.

e·col·o·gy (ē-kol′ə-ji), *n.* [< Gr. *oikos*, house; + *-logy*], 1. the branch of biology that deals with the relations between living organisms and their environment. 2. in *sociology*, the relationship between the distribution of human groups with reference to material resources, and the consequent social and cultural patterns. Abbreviated *ecol.*

ghet·to (get′ō), *n.* [*pl.* GHETTOS (-ōz)], [It.], 1. in certain European cities, a section to which Jews are, or were, restricted: the word is also applied, often in an unfriendly sense, to any section (of a city) in which many Jews live; hence, 2. any section of a city in which many members of some national or racial group live, or to which they are restricted.

graf·fi·to (grə-fē′tō), *n.* [*pl.* GRAFFITI (-ti)], [It., a scribbling < *graffio*, a scratch], an inscription, slogan, drawing, etc. crudely scratched or scribbled on a wall or other public surface.

lead poisoning, an acute or chronic poisoning caused by the absorption of lead or any of its salts into the body: it may result in anemia, constipation, colic, paralysis, or muscular cramps.

may·or (mā′ẽr, mâr), *n.* [ME. & OFr. *maire* < L. *major*, compar. of *magnus*, great], the chief administrative official of a city, town, or other municipality.

meg·a·lop·o·lis (meg′ə-lop′ə-lis), *n.* [Gr. *megalopolis*, great city], an extensive, heavily populated, continuously urban area, including any number of cities.

melting pot, 1. a container in which metals or other substances are melted; crucible. 2. a country, place, etc. in which immigrants of various nationalities and races are assimilated.

me·trop·o·lis (mə-trop′′l-is), *n.* [*pl.* METROPOLISES (-iz)], [L.; Gr. *mētropolis* < *mētēr*, a mother + *polis*, a state, city], 1. the main city, often the capital, of a country, state, or region. 2. any large city or center of population, culture, etc. 3. in ancient Greece, the mother city or state of a colony.

4. the seat, or see, of a metropolitan bishop; main diocese of an ecclesiastical province.

met·ro·pol·i·tan (met′rə-pol′ə-t'n), *adj*. [LL. *metropolitanus*], 1. of or constituting a metropolis. 2. designating or of a metropolitan or metropolis. *n*. 1. a person who lives in and knows a metropolis or one who has the characteristic attitudes and manners of such a person. 2. *a*) an archbishop having authority over the bishops of a church province. *b*) in the *Orthodox Eastern Church*, a bishop ranking just below Patriarch. 3. in ancient Greece, a citizen of a metropolis. Abbreviated *met., metrop.*

mu·nic·i·pal (mū-nis′ə-p'l), *adj*. [L. *municipalis* < *municipium*, a town subject to Rome but governed by its own laws < *municeps*, inhabitant of a free town, free citizen < *munia*, official duties, functions + *capere*, to take], 1. *a*) of or characteristic of a city, town, etc. or its local government. *b*) having self-government locally. 2. of the internal, as distinguished from the international, affairs of a state or nation. Abbreviated *mun.*

mu·nic·i·pal·i·ty (mū-nis′ə-pal′ə-ti), *n*. [*pl*. MUNICIPALITIES (-tiz)], [Fr. *municipalité* < *municipal*; L. *municipalis*; see MUNICIPAL], 1. a city, town, etc. having its own incorporated government. 2. the officials governing such a community.

nar·co·tic (när-kät′ik), *n*. [*ME*. narcotyke < OFr. *narcotique*, orig. adj. < ML. *narcoticus* < Gr. *narkoun*, to benumb < *narkē*, numbness, stupor < I.E. *nerk- < base *(*s*)*ner*-, to twist, entwine, whence SNARE, NARROW], 1. a drug, as opium or any of its derivatives (morphine, heroin, codeine, etc.), used to relieve pain and induce sleep: narcotics are often addictive and in excessive doses can cause stupor, coma, or death. 2. anything that has a soothing, lulling, or dulling effect —*adj*. 1. of, like, or capable of producing narcosis. 2. of, by, or for narcotic addicts.

pol·lute (pə-lōōt′), *v.t.* [POLLUTED (-id), POLLUTING], [ME. *poluten* < L. *pollutus*, pp. of *polluere*, to pollute], to make unclean, impure, or corrupt; desecrate; defile; contaminate; dirty.—*SYN*. see CONTAMINATE.

pol·lu·tion (pə-lōō′shən), *n*. [ME. *poluccion*; LL. *polutio*], a polluting or being polluted.

rapid transit, a system of rapid public transportation in an urban area, using electric trains running along an unimpeded right of way, as in a subway.

re·new (ri-nōō′, ri-nū′), *v.t.* [ME. *renewen* < *re-* + *newe* (see NEW), after L. *renovare* (see RENOVATE)], 1. to make new or as if new again; make young, fresh, or strong again; bring back into good condition. 2. to give new spiritual strength to; make better in spirit. 3. to cause to exist again; re-establish. 4. to begin again; take up again; resume. 5. to go over again; say again; repeat: as, *renew* one's objections, *renew* a promise. 6. to replace by something new of the same kind; put in a fresh supply of: as, *renew* provisions. 7. to refill with a fresh supply. 8. to give or get an extension of: as, *renew* a lease. *v.i.* 1. to become new again; be renewed. 2. to begin again; start over.

re·new·al (ri-nōō′əl, ri-nū′əl), *n*. a renewing or being renewed.

ren·o·vate (ren′ə-vāt′), *v.t.* [RENOVATED (-id), RENOVATING], [< L.

renovatus, pp. of *renovare*, to renew; *re-*, again + *novare*, to make
new < *novus*, new], 1. to make
new or like new; clean up, replace
worn and broken parts in, repair,
etc. 2. to refresh; revive. *adj.*
[Archaic], renovated.—*SYN.* see
RENEW.

ren·o·va·tion   (ren'ə-vā'shən), *n.* a
renovating or being renovated.

slum   (slum), *n.* [c. 1800 < cant;
orig. sense, a room; ? cant perver-
sion of the word *room*], a heavily
populated area in which housing
and other living conditions are
extremely poor. *v.i.* [SLUMMED
(slumd), SLUMMING], to visit
slums: as, they *slummed* out of
curiosity.

smog   (smog), *n.* [*sm*oke + f*og*], a
mixture of fog and smoke.—*SYN.*
see MIST.

social work,   any service or activity
designed to promote the welfare
of the community and the individual, as through health and psychology clinics, recreation halls
and playgrounds, aid for the needy,
the aged, the physically handicapped, etc.

social worker,   a person who does
social work.

ten·e·ment   (ten'ə-mənt), *n.* [ME.;
OFr., a holding; ML. *tenementum*
< L. *tenere*, to hold], 1. in *law*,
land, buildings, offices, franchises,
etc. held of another by tenure. 2.
a dwelling house. 3. a room or
set of rooms tenanted as a separate dwelling. 4. a tenement house.
5. [Poetic], a dwelling place; abode.

tenement house,   a building divided into tenements, or apartments, especially one that is in the
poorer section of a city and is overcrowded, dirty, or deteriorated.

town house,   a city residence, especially as distinguished from a
country residence of the same
owner.

up·town   (up'toun'), *adj.* of, going
toward, or in the upper part of a
city or town, or the part away from
the main business district. *adv.* in
or toward the upper part of a city
or town. *n.* the upper part of a
city or town. Cf. DOWNTOWN.

ur·ban   (ūr'bən), *adj.* [L. *urbanus*
< *urbs*, a city], 1. of, in, con-
stituting, or comprising a city or
town. 2. characteristic of the city
as distinguished from the country;
citified. Opposed to *rural*.

ur·ban·ism   (ūr'bən-iz'm), *n.* 1. a)
the character of life in the cities;
urban life, organization, problems,
etc. *b*) the study of this. 2. movement of the population to, or concentration of the population in, the
cities—ur'ban·ist *n., adj.*—ur'ban·
is'tic *adj.*

ur·ban·ite   (-īt'), *n.* a person living
in a city.

ur·ban·i·za·tion   (ūr'bən-i-zā'shən,
ūr'bən-ī-zā'shən), *n.* an urbanizing or being urbanized.

ur·ban·ized   (-nīzd'), *adj.* 1. made
urban in character. 2. in U.S.
census use, designating or of a
population area that includes one
or more cities and adjoining
densely settled urban places,
whether incorporated or unincor-
porated, at least one of the cities
having a population of 50,000 or
more.

ur·ban·ol·o·gist   (ūr'bə-näl'ə-jist),
n. [URBAN + *-o-* + -LOG(Y) +
-IST], a student of, or specialist in,
urban problems.

urban renewal,   rehabilitation of
deteriorated or distressed urban

areas, as by slum clearance and redevelopment construction in housing and public facilities.

welfare (wel′fâr′), *n*. [ME. *wel*, well + *fare* < AS. *faru*, lit., a journey < *faran*, to fare, go; cf. FARE], 1. the state of being or doing well; condition of health, happiness, and prosperity; well-being. 2. welfare work.

welfare work, the organized effort of a community or organization to improve the living conditions and standards of its members.

zone (zōn), *n*. [Fr. < L. *zona* < Gr. *zōnē*, a belt < *zōnnynai*, to gird < IE. **yosmen-* < base **yos-*, to grid, whence OSlav. *pojasǫ*, to grid], —*v.t.* [ZONED, ZON′ING]. 1. to mark off or divde into zones; specif., *a*) to divide (a city, etc.) into areas determined by specific restrictions on types of construction, as into residential and business areas, *b*) to limit to a certain use by designating as or placing in a zone. 2. to surround with or as with a belt or zone; encircle. 3. to mark with bands or stripes.

CROSSCURRENTS OF CITY LIFE

THE CITY,
MUST FIND ITS MEANING IN ITS PEOPLE,
ITS LIFE IN THEIR RELATIONSHIPS.

1

LIFE STYLES
AND
CITY PSYCHES

A look at the photography throughout *The Urban Reader* provides the best introduction to this first section. From the great variety of images comes the impression of the city as a place where many different kinds of people live to the sounds of their different drummers. A sense of the human variety—of so many people shaping their lives in widely contrasting styles—can be acquired in the course of any day or hour spent people-watching on a city street corner. Life flows by in waves of ever-changing faces, gestures, gaits, and fashions, born out of the currents of psychic life running beneath the surface. The title of this section, then, describes its contents. Psyche, a Greek word meaning soul, spirit, or mind, refers to the many human souls and spirits, people of many minds, who make the psychology of the American city what it is—a rich conglomerate of energy, boredom, despair, and joy.

About the individual selections and their connection to each other: The first seven writers have seven different views toward life in the city and write in the subjective "I" of the first person, a voice so often unheard in the urban mass. Their moods are as various as the written forms they use to express themselves: loneliness in Kenneth Patchen's poem, liberation in Paul Simon's song and Eldridge Cleaver's vignette, humor in Shirley Jackson's story, serious commitment and self-scrutiny in Byron Rushing's and Genevieve Ray's autobiographical pieces, and a restless energy in the narrative of Cal, a Hell's Angel.

By means of this chorus of contrasting voices a central point is made early in the book: No one mood, writer, or event can convey the whole truth of life in the city. If a particular writer is to communicate even a fragment of that truth, he must be in touch with his own feelings and let us hear his private voice.

The next three selections focus on the death of feelings through apathy and materialism. The news article by Martin Gansberg about the Kitty Genovese murder case treats perhaps the most corrosive aspect of the city psyche—the apathy that permits 38 city dwellers to witness a murder and then go back to bed, doing nothing to help the victim. "Outside of a Small Circle of Friends," a song by Phil Ochs, describes this same event in a different mood and form and adds other such incidents, showing that common to all is a locked-in life style of that urban personality which considers its survival dependent on noninvolvement in other people's disasters. The lack of compassion of city people devoted only to their material possessions, the "self-protective cunning" of the cultural elite, are major themes in J. Krishnamurti's "Life in a City," a short philosophical essay with observations about a symbolic urban couple.

All these failures to sympathize, responsible for much of the revulsion toward the modern city, leave human wrecks in their wake. The article by Joseph Lelyveld and Charlayne Hunter, "Obituary of a Heroin User Who Died at 12," and the Stephen Sondheim lyrics, "Gee, Officer Krupke," record attempts to escape or challenge this compassionless tide. Drugs, gangs, and crime can be seen as responses to the pathology of indifference.

Paradoxically, the anonymity of city people offers a kind of freedom unavailable in small towns. The chance for wider horizons—cultural, sexual, and economic—explains the influx of single women to the city, an immigration analyzed by Caroline Bird in "The Single Girls of the City: Why They Don't Want to Be Wives." The reasons why a big city tolerates many different life styles in the first place are probed in the final article of this section, "Deviance and Democracy in San Francisco" by Howard Becker and Irving Horowitz. The cultural open-mindedness of this city manifests the healthiness of the city psyche, the natural dynamism of a human environment.

IN THE FIRST PERSON

I WENT TO THE CITY

Kenneth Patchen

And there I did weep,
Men a-crowin' like asses,
And livin' like sheep.
Oh, can't hold the han' of my love!
Can't hold her little white han'!
Yes, I went to the city,
And there I did bitterly cry,
Men out of touch with the earth,
And with never a glance at the sky.
Oh, can't hold the han' of my love!
Can't hold her pure little han'!

THE 59TH STREET BRIDGE SONG
(FEELIN' GROOVY)

Paul Simon
Simon and Garfunkel

Slow down,
You move too fast.
You got to make the morning last.
Just kickin' down the cobble stones,
Lookin' for fun and feelin' Groovy.

Hello lamppost,
What-cha knowin'
I've come to watch your flowers growin'.
Ain't-cha got no rhymes for me?
Doot'in' doo-doo, feelin' Groovy.

Got no deeds to do,
No promises to keep.
I'm dappled and drowsy and ready to sleep.
Let the morningtime drop all its petals on me.
Life, I love you.
All is Groovy.

ON WATTS

FOLSOM PRISON
AUGUST 16, 1965

Eldridge Cleaver

As we left the Mess Hall Sunday morning and milled around in the prison yard, after four days of abortive uprising in Watts, a group of low riders[1] from Watts assembled on the basketball court. They were wearing jubilant, triumphant smiles, animated by a vicarious spirit by which they, too, were in the thick of the uprising taking place hundreds of miles away to the south in the Watts ghetto.

"Man," said one, "what they doing out there? Break it down for me, Baby."

They slapped each other's outstretched palms in a cool salute and burst out laughing with joy.

"Home boy, them Brothers is taking care of Business!" shrieked another ecstatically.

Then one low rider, stepping into the center of the circle formed by the others, rared back on his legs and swaggered, hunching his belt up with his forearms as he'd seen James Cagney and George Raft do in too many gangster movies. I joined the circle. Sensing a creative moment in the offing, we all got very quiet, very still, and others passing by joined the circle and did likewise.

"Baby," he said, "They walking in fours and kicking in doors; dropping Reds[2] and busting heads; drinking wine and committing crime, shooting and looting; high-siding[3] and low-riding, setting fires and slashing tires; turning over cars and burning down bars; making Parker mad and making me glad; putting an end to that 'go slow' crap and putting sweet Watts on the map—my black ass is in Folsom this morning but my black heart is in Watts!" Tears of joy were rolling from his eyes.

It was a cleansing, revolutionary laugh we all shared, something we have not often had occasion for.

1 *Low Rider*. A Los Angeles nickname for ghetto youth. Originally the term was coined to describe the youth who had lowered the bodies of their cars so that they rode low, close to the ground; also implied was the style of driving that these youngsters perfected. Sitting behind the steering wheel and slumped low down in the seat, all that could be seen of them was from their eyes up, which used to be the cool way of driving. When these youthful hipsters alighted from their vehicles, the term *low rider* stuck with them, evolving to the point where all black ghetto youth—but *never* the soft offspring of the black bourgeoisie—are referred to as low riders.

2 *Reds*. A barbiturate, called Red Devils; so called because of the color of the capsule and because they are reputed to possess a vicious kick.

3 *High-siding*. Cutting up. Having fun at the expense of another.

Watts was a place of shame. We used to use Watts as an epithet in much the same way as city boys used "country" as a term of derision. To deride one as a "lame," who did not know what was happening (a rustic bumpkin), the "in-crowd" of the time from L.A. would bring a cat down by saying that he had just left Watts, that he ought to go back to Watts until he had learned what was happening, or that he had just stolen enough money to move out of Watts and was already trying to play a cool part. But now, blacks are seen in Folsom saying, "I'm from Watts, Baby!"— whether true or no, but I think their meaning is clear. Confession: I, too, have participated in this game, saying, I'm from Watts. In fact, I did live there for a time, and I'm *proud* of it, the tired lamentations of Whitney Young, Roy Wilkins, and The Preacher notwithstanding.

MY LIFE WITH R. H. MACY

Shirley Jackson

And the first thing they did was segregate me. They segregated me from the only person in the place I had even a speaking acquaintance with; that was a girl I had met going down the hall who said to me: "Are you as scared as I am?" And when I said, "Yes," she said, "I'm in lingerie, what are you in?" and I thought for a while and then said, "Spun glass," which was as good an answer as I could think of, and she said, "Oh. Well, I'll meet you here in a sec." And she went away and was segregated and I never saw her again.

Then they kept calling my name and I kept trotting over to wherever they called it and they would say ("They" all this time being startlingly beautiful young women in tailored suits and with short-clipped hair), "Go with Miss Cooper, here. She'll tell you what to do." All the women I met my first day were named Miss Cooper. And Miss Cooper would say to me: "What are you in?" and I had learned by that time to say, "Books," and she would say, "Oh, well, then, you belong with Miss Cooper here," and then she would call "Miss Cooper?" and another young woman would come and the first one would say, "13-3138 here belongs with you," and Miss Cooper would say, "What is she in?" and Miss Cooper would answer, "Books," and I would go away and be segregated again.

Then they taught me. They finally got me segregated into a classroom, and I sat there for a while all by myself (that's how far segregated I was) and then a few other girls came in, all wearing tailored suits (I was wearing a red velvet afternoon frock) and we sat down and they taught us. They gave us each a big book with R. H. Macy written on it, and inside this book were pads of little sheets saying (from left to right): "Comp. keep for ref. cust. d.a. no. or c.t. no. salesbook no. salescheck no. clerk no. dept. date M." After M there was a long line for Mr. or Mrs. and the name, and then it began again with "No. item. class. at price. total." And down at the bottom was written ORIGINAL and then again, "Comp. keep for ref.," and "Paste yellow gift stamp here." I read all this very carefully. Pretty soon a Miss Cooper came, who talked for a little while on the advantages we had in working at Macy's, and she talked about the salesbooks, which it seems came apart into a sort of road map and carbons and things. I listened for a while, and when Miss Cooper wanted us to write on the little pieces of paper, I copied from the girl next to me. That was training.

Finally someone said we were going on the floor, and we descended from the sixteenth floor to the first. We were in groups of six by then, all following Miss Cooper doggedly and wearing little tags saying BOOK INFORMATION. I never did find out what that meant. Miss Cooper said I had to work on the special sale counter, and showed me a little book called *The Stage-Struck Seal*, which it seemed I would be selling. I had gotten about halfway through it before she came back to tell me I had to stay with my unit.

I enjoyed meeting the time clock, and spent a pleasant half-hour punching various cards standing around, and then someone came in and said I couldn't punch the clock with my hat on. So I had to leave, bowing timidly at the time clock and its prophet, and I went and found out my locker number, which was 1773, and my time-clock number, which was 712, and my cash-box number, which was 1336, and my cash-register number, which was 253, and my cash-register-drawer number, which was K, and my cash-register-drawer-key number, which was 872, and my department number, which was 13. I wrote all these numbers down. And that was my first day.

My second day was better. I was officially on the floor. I stood in a corner of a counter, with one hand possessively on *The Stage-Struck Seal*, waiting for customers. The counter head was named 13-2246, and she was very kind to me. She sent me to lunch three times, because she got me confused with 13-6454 and 13-3141. It was after lunch that a customer came. She came over and took one of my stage-struck seals, and said "How much is this?" I opened my mouth and the customer said "I have a D.A. and I will have this sent to my aunt in Ohio. Part of that D.A. I will pay for with a book dividend of 32 cents, and the rest of course will be on my account. Is this book price-fixed?" That's as near as I can remember what she said. I smiled confidently, and said, "Certainly; will you wait just one moment?" I found a little piece of paper in a drawer under the counter: it had "Duplicate Triplicate" printed across the front in big letters. I took down the customer's name and address, her aunt's name and address, and wrote carefully across the front of the duplicate triplicate "I Stg. Strk. Sl." Then I smiled at the customer again and said carelessly: "That will be seventy-five cents." She said "But I have a D.A." I told her that all D.A.'s were suspended for the Christmas rush, and she gave me seventy-five cents, which I kept. Then I rang up a "No Sale" on the cash register and I tore up the duplicate triplicate because I didn't know what else to do with it.

Later on another customer came and said, "Where would I find a copy of Ann Rutherford Gwynn's *He Came Like Thunder?*" and I said "In medical books, right across the way," but 13-2246 came and said "That's philosophy, isn't it?" and the customer said it was, and 13-2246 said "Right down this aisle, in dictionaries." The customer went away, and I said to 13–2246 that her guess was as good as mine, anyway, and she stared at me and explained that philosophy, social sciences and Bertrand Russell were all kept in dictionaries.

So far I haven't been back to Macy's for my third day, because that night when I started to leave the store, I fell down the stairs and tore my stockings and the doorman said that if I went to my department head Macy's would give me a new pair of stockings and I went back and I found Miss Cooper and she said, "Go to the adjuster on the seventh floor and give him this," and she handed me a little slip of pink paper and on the bottom of it was printed "Comp. keep for ref. cust. d.a. no. or c.t. no. salesbook no. salescheck no. clerk no. dept. date M." And after M, instead of a name, she had written 13-3138. I took the little pink slip and threw it away and went up to the fourth floor and bought myself a pair of stockings for $.69 and then I came down and went out the customers' entrance.

I wrote Macy's a long letter, and I signed it with all my numbers added together and divided by 11,700, which is the number of employees in Macy's. I wonder if they miss me.

I WAS BORN

Byron Rushing

I was born July 29, 1942.

On July 29, 1962, I pedaled my bicycle across the Massachusetts Avenue bridge from Cambridge to Boston and Roxbury to hear Elijah Muhammad speak at a Muslim rally in the Boston Arena. Mr. Muhammad was sick; Malcolm X was the main speaker.

For two quick hours Malcolm told the truth. He raised only one contradiction—discussion of the response of the Nation to murder of one of its members by a white cop outside the Mosque in Los Angeles. A murder with no retaliation. The freedom of cops to murder like that and get away with it haunts me still, and still raises the question of the Nation's seriousness. Yet, I was born on July 29th.

Leo. I realize that birth now as I did not then. I pedaled my bike to Harvard where I was making up a physics course I had flunked during the year. I majored in linguistics. Planned to go to med school. Later that summer I attended the Ninth International Congress of Linguistics.

The argument against infant baptism is that the infant doesn't know what's going on. I was baptized by the Rev. Edler Hawkins, June 13, 1943, at St. Augustine Presbyterian Church in the Bronx. I didn't know what was going on. *June 1963*: After a completely useless year at school, I returned home to work as a surgical technician in Syracuse Memorial Hospital before going to work for SNCC in the South for the next academic year.

WE CAN STOP URBAN RENEWAL (NEGRO REMOVAL)

if the city continues to relocate Negroes into:
—segregated areas of the city
—areas that will be doomed by urban renewal in the next 5 years
—houses that are worse than those Negroes are being forced to move from

Negroes must refuse to be forced into unsatisfactory housing. CORE DIRECT ACTION has stopped Urban Renewal at Madison and Townsend. CORE sitins drove the wreckers off the lot!

The issue is Housing Discrimination. We want a better deal for Negroes who have to relocate! We plan to hold this lot and take other action until positive steps are taken to *desegregate* housing!

MEET WITH CORE THURSDAY, 8 P.M. PEOPLE'S A.M.E.

Zion Church
711 E. Fayette St.
Help us plan further action.

I never went South. I began doing volunteer work in Syracuse CORE. Instead of going on the March on Washington, a few of us sat in on an urban renewal site and blocked the demolition of a gas station—Pelnick's Construction firm wasn't tearing down any houses that day—in what was quickly becoming the ex-black community. No one came out to persuade us to get off the site—almost the entire local urban renewal staff had gone on the March.

I stayed in Syracuse working for CORE at $25 a week.

While I was at Harvard, I went to Muhammad's Mosque on Interval St. in Roxbury one Sunday afternoon. Minister Louis X gave the address. More truth. But still that contradiction: notwithstanding his persuasive arguments against the white devil and his innate brutality, the only people he encouraged his listeners to take into back alleys and whip were Negro pimps. One of the brothers gave me a ride back to Cambridge. He told me I was lucky to be at Harvard and "if you'd combine that Harvard thing with Mr. Muhammad's program, brother, nothing could beat you." It is very tempting.

I don't know how to deal with a prophet or a saint; I didn't know how to deal with Malcolm. It was a struggle to understand that I had to struggle—with the truth, with the prophets and the saints, with the devil. And then there was Jesus. And the truth was my slavery, my death, my escape, my ambivalance, my cowardice. My brother. My enemy.

In the winter of 1963 I came closest to committing suicide. In that immense, frozen, *white* despair, I discovered that if God was real, he was *black* and I sought a nappy-haired, thick-lipped Jesus.

FIGHT INJUSTICE IN SYRACUSE

1. All of CORE's charges in the Presley case have been substantiated by the report of the Mayor's Commission on Human Rights. The Mayor said that CORE was lying. Now the Mayor's Commission has said that the charges by CORE were true. Will Mayor Walsh apologize to CORE and the Negro community?

2. CORE pressure has improved the city jail. People are no longer kept in Willow Street Jail for more than one night. Last fall Negroes were kept in that jail for two, three, and four weeks. Negroes will only get equal treatment if they KEEP THE PRESSURE ON.

3. The case of Marine Private Joseph Brooks is still in the courts. As you remember, Brooks claimed that he was beaten by a policeman. Brooks took his complaint to the police chief. For the next week he was harassed by the police and city officials. (Eleven CORE members were arrested helping Brooks obtain jus-

We are all baptized as infants. We must grow to understand the significance and implications of that sign and seal. I now know that what seemed to be the temptation to commit suicide was the beginning of the tortuous, rupturing experience of dying/borning. And it didn't last for only one night, or one week, but on and on. The slow destruction of the old, the sinful, the white self. I was lying and I had to admit the truth. I thought I was safe; I had to be insulted; I had to Tom for some dumb, white cop. And watch myself again and again and not be able to help myself. It was the cops who taught me that we black folk are a formidable community, they knew our potential better than I did. Although I usually saw the police as the guardians of the city's enforcement of segregation, I soon experienced them as the occupation troops in the black colony, free to beat, insult, shoot black natives with the total, defensive, calculated,

tice.) After Brooks was beaten, he was charged and convicted of public intoxication. *He was not drunk.* But there is NO JUSTICE FOR NE- GROES IN SYRACUSE CITY COURTS. These cases are being ap- pealed. JOIN CORE AND FIGHT INJUSTICE IN SYRACUSE.

paranoiac support of the white ad- ministrators. The administrator was the power, and he enforced that power through his alter ego, the cop. Want to know what the mayor, governor, president, bishop, think of black peo- ple? Look in the face of some dumb cop.

Paul wasn't struck blind on the road to Damascus; he was struck with the realization that he was already blind. At Harvard I had the fantasy that somewhere, deep in the stacks of Widener, there was the book, ignored, unnoticed, that, upon my reading it, would make my life right. Would give me the shocking bright light of discerning truth from irrelevance. *Get your ass up off the ground and go to the city. Get out of the stacks, there ain't nothing there for you.* I was blind and blind I rode my bike across the Charles and Ananias spoke to me and the scales dropped from my eyes.

Malcolm was smooth. Outside the arena, NAACP members were pass- ing out leaflets: Go in and listen, but here's a program that *can* get you into the mainstream. . . . I was talking to the two brothers in front of me: about Jack Johnson (and how they wouldn't let him sail on the Titanic) and about some talented local boys out of some gym on Washington Street.

I have heard Malcolm so much since that day; I can't remember what he said. Just his description of Ronald Stokes' murder and the humiliation of the Muslims in L.A. Stokes' widow was on the platform and told that when she had heard, several months later, that two of the white cops involved in the murder had been killed in an auto crash, she cried, "All praise is due to Allah!"

I went up and shook Malcolm's hand; I didn't ask him anything. A black father introduced his daughter to him. The father had sent her to Moscow to get a decent education. Malcolm replied, "When I talk about the white man I mean the white devil in America." A white woman walked up to him and began talking—quickly, asking rhetorical questions. She held in her hand a white plastic crucifix on an opened Bible. Strange satanic talisman.

RUSHING OUTLINES CORE TACTICS

"To change the status quo, you have to be willing to do the unpopular," Byron Rushing, Executive Secretary of the Syracuse chapter of the Con- gress of Racial Equality (CORE), told

I grew up in Syracuse. When I re- turned to work for CORE, white people would always ask me "What do you know about our city? Where are you from?"

I believed in the integration goal and the nonviolence method. I wanted a heavily attended session of the Catholic Neighbor Training Council last night.

Rushing, speaking to more than 700 persons at Bishop Ludden High School, explained the aims and operations of Syracuse CORE as part of a survey of interracial and civil rights groups. Last night's fifth meeting of the eight-part series drew the largest audience to date.

"Negotiation is always first," Rushing declared as he outlined CORE tactics, "but when it fails there are other means." He described these as picketing or sitting-in or its variations.

The object of such actions is "direct confrontation of the public with the problem," Rushing noted, but he stressed that CORE advocates only nonviolent action.

"Action outside the usual channels of redress is necessary," he added, "because our society is so structured as to keep the Negro in a subordinate position."

He said the Negro's difficulty is different from other minority groups in the past, because the Negro's "inferiority" was written directly into the Constitution in three places.

"You can win court battles but lose the war," Rushing asserted, "because the majority of the people are not in the court room, don't hear the case, and thus do not learn about the crimes of racial injustice."

Results are realized "when you leave the court-room and go downtown and confront the people when and where they are not used to it," he said.

Rushing reviewed the housing demonstrations downtown last fall, and remarked, "The whole community was aroused by these demonstrations—not necessarily in favor of us, but at least

to love white people, openly, brotherly, sexually. I sat on that urban renewal site, scared in my gut, as a white crane operator dropped a demolition ball closer and closer toward me. I led mass meetings of blacks and whites singing, "Black and white together."

I cannot pinpoint the day when the idea of integration, of confronting this white society's conscience and nonviolently forcing it to respond with humane acts, all became irrelevant. Birth. Baptism. The old life lingers, lingers. Malcolm sank into me slowly; yet he had already laid his hands on me. There was the response of the white dominions and principalities to two police harassment cases we were handling. There was the frustrating CORE demonstration at the World's Fair and ACT's stall-in which never materialized. And after each draining act, all we could say as we analyzed our loss was: "Next time bigger and better demonstrations."

Inside I knew that there were two movements and I had been sucked into the wrong one. That one was the movement to free white folks' consciences, to make white folks human. And so you invent demonstration-dramas to confront them, and they organize fair housing groups or Equality Projects and get homes for thirty-five Negro families in the suburbs or stop their church from buying from a firm that discriminates, and, by their standards, they have put their bodies on the line, they have suffered courageously. Yet their acts do not affect the other movement one bit. Black people continue to be murdered in increasing numbers, housed in increasing squalor, supported by increasing unemployment, made more powerless, they were aroused, which in itself is good."

He said the tangible results of the demonstrations were non-existent, however, and promised demonstrations of a new type in the future here, in which "more than 100 persons will be arrested," but he did not elaborate.

Dear Neighbor,

Plans are being made to move the Greyhound Bus Station into the Loblows store building on East Adams Street.

If this happens it will mean:

YOUR CHILDREN WILL BE IN DANGER OF BEING HIT BY BUSES entering and leaving the station;

NOISE from the buses entering and leaving the station DAY AND NIGHT;

FUMES from the buses in your backyards and in your houses.

We know of no other city that has a LARGE BUS STATION IN A RESIDENTIAL AREA. There are about 700 residential units in this area. Most of the families that live here are Negro. Is that why City Hall doesn't think they have to ask us before they put a bus station in our neighborhood?

City Hall and Urban Renewal say that this bus station is only "temporary"—BUT THAT COULD MEAN YEARS OF THESE DANGERS!

Plans to place the bus station next to the Pioneer Homes only show how City Hall feels about us. The city has again and again demolished areas of the Negro community for projects that no other community would stand for. The city has repeatedly placed things in the Negro community because they know that Negroes "never complain." Well, all that has got to end. WE MUST SERVE NOTICE ON THE

and the gap between white and black grows greater and greater. In my haste to express my birth, I had not listened, I was duped by the white conspiracy in myself, I had forsaken the movement for black freedom and power.

I met Malcolm five years ago. I left Syracuse three years ago. I never returned to Harvard.

I am scared. And even with my lucky, easy life I am sick and tired. I want to join a monastery in Ethiopia and tend Abyssinian cats and the mummies of long gone emperors. But he has turned me around. Sell your coats and buy swords.

Like most black people I have spent my life being both an obedient child and a responsible parent to white people. That self is dead. And although I have spent too much time in preparing that carcass for burning, it is being consumed. And at my young/old age I must learn to love my true parents, learn to be obedient; I must learn to love my true children, learn to be responsible. I must learn my brother, learn my enemy. I must learn my God. Learn my devil.

I do not hate this enemy. I know him too well. He has been too close, inside me. It is not his money or his power that makes him evil, it is his godlessness, his idolatry. It is not that he is politically or economically unable to stop being racist, it is that he is psychologically and spiritually unable.

I know how I am blind. I know the devil. I am baptized. It does not make it any easier.

CITY THAT OUR COMMUNITY
WILL NO LONGER BE THE
AREAS OF LEAST RESISTANCE
WHERE THE CITY CAN EX-
ECUTE PROJECTS THAT IN NO
WAY ADD TO THE WELFARE OF
OUR COMMUNITY. This is a petition to show the city and tell the
mayor that you are protesting the use
of the Loblows building as a bus station. Please sign this petition: this is
the *first* step in keeping our neighborhood *safe*.

> Yours truly,
>
> Inez Heard,
> Citizens of Pioneer
> Byron Rushing,
> Syracuse CORE

Once you have been baptized you are born again. No matter what you do from then on, you *are* different. And that difference will save you or destroy you.

AN ANGLO'S BARRIO

Genevieve Ray

"Hey, Teacher, Teacher! You work in my brother's school?" I turned to see three brown little faces looking at me. "You're my brother's teacher?" "Nope, it must be somebody else," I said. "I'm not a teacher." As I walked on down the street I chuckled to myself, "All of us white people look the same."

It was my first day as a VISTA in East Harlem, and I was on my way to meet my supervisor. I walked past what seemed like millions of people, all rattling away in Spanish, jostling each other to get closest to the side-walk clothing shops, the fruit stalls, the record stores blaring Pete Rodriguez and Joe Bataan, and the lunch counters advertising *cerveza fria* and *arroz con pollo*. If anyone else noticed me in that crush of people, they must have known that I was from another world and was trying hard not to act like I was scared.

In fact, I was scared. I had always thought of myself as working with black people. Many of my college friends were black, and I felt that I had some understanding of their culture. I knew something about their dancing and their humor. I knew them. I knew how to act. But Puerto Ricans were different. I knew very little Spanish. I didn't like their music. But it was something even more basic. I had a strong gut reaction that they were *too* different. How would I act? What would I say? How would I start? I wanted to run. But I reassured myself that "Maybe this is just a small part of the community. I'll get to the black section later."

It was months before I allowed myself to realize that my initial reaction had been nothing but prejudice. I had only thought of prejudice in terms of black and white, not recognizing that in Colorado, where I grew up, there is actually stronger feeling against brown people. Folks back home shake their heads over the tensions in Newark and Selma, and thank the heavens that they do not have racial problems. Yet they unthinkingly refer to Chicanos as "dirty Mexicans," and steer clear of them because they know that "90 percent of them carry switchblades."

I had not been raised this way. I was taught that discrimination is ugly and wrong. But prejudice hangs in the air, and the most "liberal" people can be touched by it. It touched me. I was afraid to work with Puerto Ricans because of a general feeling against people with a Spanish background.

I was to learn, throughout my year, that East Harlem may have taught me just as much about what it means to be white and middle-class in America as it taught me about being poor and a minority.

When I met my VISTA supervisor that first day, he said, "I don't want you sitting around this office. I want you to walk. Get acquainted with the neighborhood. Talk to people. Learn something about the housing. Get a feel for the place. In two weeks come back, and we'll talk about what you think you want to do." He introduced me to the other VISTAS assigned to the project, and they gave me a tour of our part of East Harlem. I felt like somebody's 8-year-old sister, tagging along behind the Volunteers. They seemed so busy and at home, stopping every half block to chat with someone: "How is Mrs. Rivera's baby?" or "Are you coming to the block meeting tomorrow?" or "Did you hear that José's wife finally left him?"

I kept thinking, "How do they know all these people? I'll never be able to do this." I wanted to be friendly and have them like me, but I felt strange intruding on their conversations. So I smiled a lot, shifted from one foot to another, and felt utterly useless and incredibly foolish.

As I explored the neighborhood, I found that although the flavor is Spanish, East Harlem is mixed—Italian, Puerto Rican, and black. The area was once entirely Italian, but now the other groups have taken over most of the white section and have left one narrow strip near the East River as pure Italian territory. The other VISTAS told me that although I could see a shop selling Italian ices sandwiched between a Spanish *bodega* (grocery store) and a "Soul Sound" record store, this was not friendly integration. There are sharp lines of animosity drawn between the three groups. This division makes the job of a VISTA doubly hard. We were not only outsiders, but were identified by many blacks and Puerto Ricans as Italians. We were not only trying to get people working together —difficult enough with a homogeneous group—but were trying to get three very prejudiced groups working together.

For two weeks I walked, and when I went back to talk with my supervisor I had no more idea of what I wanted to do than I had when I left his office. There were so many problems—rotten plumbing, broken windows, dope addicts, homes with no fathers and too many kids, eviction notices, furniture repossessed, decayed teeth, falling plaster, not enough money, no jobs, no job training, 16-year-old teenagers who couldn't read, no social security payments, stolen welfare checks, rat bites, knifings, no food for supper, hospitals that wouldn't take your case, teachers that didn't care, agencies that told you to come back next week, housing inspectors who got paid off by the landlord, and the memory of a thousand white college kids who had been there before, had made promises, broken them, and gone back to school in the fall.

How could I possibly do anything substantial? Where would I start? Which one of these things could be a beginning? Why was I bewildered? Weren't VISTA volunteers supposed to *do* something? In VISTA training I had learned to teach remedial reading, but I felt massively ill-equipped to deal with any of these problems.

Finally I decided to start a tutoring center for grade school children. I really preferred working with teenagers and didn't particularly want to tutor, but out of the desperation to do something, to fit the VISTA image, I went ahead.

One of the VISTAS mentioned that a local church had a storefront on 119th Street, but wasn't using it. So I went to the priest and got permission to fix it up and use it, at least until the church got the money to start its own program.

From the first day I opened the doors and started sweeping up the rubble, I knew I would have no problem meeting people. Countless children appeared to ask, "What's this going to be? A school? Are you a teacher?" The second day the priest sent two Neighborhood Youth Corps boys to help me clean, and the next day they brought ten of their friends.

The following day more appeared, until we had about 15 boys and 5 girls, most of them Puerto Rican, a few black. They ranged in age from 15 to 19.

They all wanted to help clean and fix up the storefront for their own center. They planned a program including job counseling, discussions, movies, karate demonstrations, dances, and (at my insistence) tutoring and homework help. I happily gave up my idea of a tutoring center for grade-schoolers.

A perfect situation had fallen right into my lap. I had a project! I was *doing* something. I could think and worry about "my kids." I was a VISTA volunteer!

Most of my first three months was spent with these teenagers. We spent hours sitting on tables and boxes in the storefront, or walking around East Harlem. The kids enjoyed shocking me with gory stories about gang fights, teaching me the latest dances, asking questions about my home ("Do you have Halloween in Colorado?"), and instructing me in the basics of street life. They were experts, and candidly pointed out to me that in spite of my college degree, I had a lot to learn. They were willing and delightful tutors, and I soaked up my lessons.

My first big shock came when we were discussing the riots. I had read all of the accounts of the various riots around the country and felt that they were an expression of anger and hatred toward the white community. The people, I thought, believed that the only way to get change is to force it. They were rioting and looting to get changes made.

But the kids talked about the riots in East Harlem the summer before in a much different manner. "Oh, you should have been here for the riots—man, they were *fun*! Everybody along First Avenue had guns, people were throwing bottles out of windows—and dumb George almost got shot!" The tone was one of general hilarity, and it hardly fit my image of a down-trodden people struggling for their rights against unimaginable odds. They were just kids having fun. Later, the day after Martin Luther King was shot, George and Alfred stopped by my apartment. They were on their way to the major looting area and wanted to know if I wanted anything. "You want a stereo? A transistor? We'll get you anything you want." When I refused their offer, George said peevishly, "Oh, I thought you'd say that. You country hicks don't even know what fun is!"

I learned that the addicts always start the looting. Junkies seize a fruitful situation when they see one. Once the stores are broken into, everyone joins in the free-for-all.

Because I sympathize so strongly with the struggle of poor people, I had over-sentimentalized my view of the looting. I had to readjust my thinking. The riots were not a conscious statement of anger; they were manifestations of a frustration which runs much deeper. The riots were not a protest against social injustice, they were the unconscious result of social injustice.

After several months of "tutoring" from the teenagers, I began to be able to put things into some perspective. Just before Christmas, I wrote in my journal:

People back home told me that Harlem is a terrifying place, with rats and roaches, killing and dope addicts. It is true—Harlem is terrifying—but not because of the roaches (at the most, a nuisance) and the rats, murders, and junkies. All of these are facts of one's life here. And Harlem is terrifying because these things have existed here so long that they are facts of life—and there is no real belief that change is possible.

Facts of life, then: the welfare mother who told us in training, "You kids come into our communities and are shocked by the garbage and the rats. You want to start clean-up campaigns and get rid of the rats. I have lived with them for 40 years, and unless one bites my daughter, rats are the least of my problems. You find out what *I* am concerned about, even if it's a broken door hinge, and start to work on that." A fact of life that the storefront I originally wanted to rent is owned by members of the Mafia, who would not appreciate me or my 20 Puerto Rican teenagers as renters. A year ago a man was killed there by the racketeers, his body, armless and decapitated, was found in the river. The kids are completely matter-of-fact about this violence.

A fact of life that the kids fell all over themselves with laughter when they learned that I had never seen a rat: "We'll bring you one! You can see them jumping around all night in the store across the street."

A fact of life in Harlem that people laughed at my shock at seeing a policeman walk into a little corner grocery, ask for a cigar, and then walk out without paying. As they say, "Baby, you ain't seen nothin' yet. This is kid stuff." Corruption spreads throughout the system . . . the foot patrolman is paid off by the numbers man, the prostitute, the pusher, the racketeer, and he keeps paying right on up the ladder. And people back home cannot understand why people here do not have respect for the law.

And it's another fact of life that these kids who are so great and have so much potential are sniffing cocaine. One of these days I will hear that one of them has died from an overdose of heroin, or has gotten hepatitis from shooting dope with a dirty needle. Tito (an ex-addict who is now a community worker) tells me that there is nothing I can do about it: "They will come to you with a sob story and try to get money. But all you can do is be tough and not let them con you. You can't preach to them about the dangers of experimenting with hard drugs. You are from the outside world and you have never been a junkie. They know better than you do what is likely to happen if they play around with dope. There is not an addict in Harlem who has not sworn he would never be a junkie."

All of these things which were foreign to me four months ago have become facts of my life too. I will look at them differently, but I have to understand how people here think about them. I wonder what else I will discover?

The kids taught me that VISTA volunteers do not have instant understanding just because we care. We bring to a community our own backgrounds, our own ways of looking at things, our own sympathies, our own hangups. Our work is often critically affected by the fact that we see what we want to see, what we are able to see.

We never did get the storefront. The church's money didn't come through, the rent was too high for us to pay, and by January all the lights had been turned off and the landlord would not let us stay. We tried to get foundation money but couldn't. The kids gradually drifted away from the block and went separate ways. Bert, Willie, Isaac, and Mustafa are in their first year of college. George is in the Army. Others are still in high school or are working. Some continued with drugs. Robert, Elvin, and Frankie have already had hepatitis. Paco, Alex, and Harry are in jail for drug use. Every once in a while I see Chino on the corner, nodding and scratching—a bona fide junkie. No one has died yet.

By January I had started working with Mercedes, a community woman who worked as an organizer on what is considered the worst block in East Harlem. The housing is wretched, many buildings are abandoned and swarm with addicts, and every crime imaginable centers in this area. Shootings and knifings are commonplace, and it is not unusual to see fire engines appear on the block four times in one night. People who make changes here are not well-liked by the criminal element, and through Mercedes I learned that sometimes community organization is not just a problem of motivating apathetic people to speak for themselves. The people here were scared stiff and wouldn't even leave their apartments for a meeting, for fear of robbery. Asking someone to join a tenant organization on this block was literally asking him to risk his life. At first I was hopeful and wrote in my journal:

Today I made visits with Mercedes—she is beautiful—a *real* fighter! Her life has been threatened, but she stays. She has gotten some support for change in the block, ironically enough from the numbers-runner. He says he is willing to try to make it a better place. The numbers racket will never stop, I know, and this man is surely not likely to give up his own livelihood, but he can still be helpful in ridding the block of its more dangerous aspects. It's going to take a long time, but one has to believe that it can be done. Of course, the frustration comes in the knowledge that even if the junkies and the car-stealers are ousted from the block, they'll just move on to another. So we put band-aids on gaping wounds.

We had to give up. Mercedes finally had to move from the block. A man was killed trying to defend her, and she had started getting threats on the lives of her children. This was one of the hardest things for me to accept, because I couldn't lose that insane belief that somehow a VISTA is invested with magical powers. If you work hard enough, something will change. But this block was not ready yet.

This, plus the failure of the storefront project, brought me into the traditional VISTA volunteer disease, the four-month slump. I spent hours staring into the TV my roommate had found, and in my journal alternately wallowed in self-pity and berated myself:

I don't think I can stay in this work. I become too frustrated at the immensity of the problems, how little is done, how many workers are here with nothing being accomplished. So stupid, what do you think *you're* doing? You aren't so great either. You are too satisfied with tokens of Good Deeds, and are too impressed with yourself when you do one little good thing. You are 90 percent jive and 10 percent production. So what if you got Skipper to come for reading lessons twice in a row? What good does that do when his sisters and brothers are cramped in that stinking apartment house? And they won't learn to read either. You haven't fought hard enough. You have got to stop retreating from what you're supposed to be doing. O.K. Tomorrow I *will* get up, I *will* begin my day right. I will *not* turn on the TV.

For a couple of months I worked at various projects—sponsoring a teenage newspaper, assisting welfare clients, tutoring some of the teenagers in their reading, and helping various groups write proposals for funding. But my heart wasn't really in any of the things I was doing, and I flitted from project to project, hoping that I could finally dedicate myself to something. About this time a VISTA evaluator visited our project, and I overheard our supervisor talking about us: "Oh, Frieda is working with the buying club, Sandy has started a drama group, Bill is doing a fine job with his legal projects, and Gennie . . . well, Gennie has had a hard time settling down to one thing." Truer words were never spoken.

I escaped to Colorado toward the end of March, and among my family and friends I suddenly forgot that I had been confused and frustrated in New York. I magically became the Expert on All Ghettos. I had been down there in the streets, and I knew "where it was at." It took me a couple of days to calm down, but after the glamour had worn off I was able to think about my work in East Harlem with some semblance of sanity. My older brothers probed me with questions, and I finally had to admit to myself that I honestly had not fought hard enough. I had rationalized my own shortcomings by saying the problems were too hard. I wasn't lying; the problems are too hard for one person to solve in one year, but I used that as an excuse for not working. I had never really had to work before. Like many young people of my background, I had been raised in relative comfort, had made decent grades with a minimum of effort, and had gotten most of the things I wanted. I was one of the golden children of the middle class who wanted to become Involved. Finally I understood what the black community organizer had meant when he spoke to us in VISTA training: "If you want to help us, you get yourself together first. You may be living in our community, but until you work out your own problems, you will be of no use to us. Poor people have enough problems of their own without adding your hangups on top."

When I got back to East Harlem, I began working on two projects and was determined to stick to them. I did. For the rest of my year, and for the six months I lived there after my year ended, I was finally a real VISTA. I worked with the block association on 119th St., where the storefront is. The members of the group are strong, hard-working and dedicated people who are taking their lives into their own hands. They have written their own proposal and have rented that same storefront where I started out and are remodeling it as a neighborhood center. They do not need me. My other project was a training program in electronics. I got together with an engineer who wanted to do something, we wrote a proposal and got money for a summer program. I am pleased.

It was hard to leave East Harlem. It is now a part of my life, and I suppose I am a part of some of the lives there. But my job lies in other directions, possibly in trying to help change the attitudes of people back home. I first started realizing this when I was flying back to New York from Colorado after the mid-year trip home. On the plane I wrote in my journal:

> Coming home was good for me because it gave me one of the keys to what being a VISTA is all about. When most of us get into the field, we want desperately to see things as they really are, to be a part of what is happening, to be trusted. Many Volunteers make the mistake of trying too hard to be accepted. They learn all the "jive talk" and try to cover up the fact that they are educated and come from comfortable homes. They end up losing the respect of the very people they want to reach. They try to out-poor the poor. This is a gross mistake. Community people are not stupid. They see us first as symbols

of the affluent white society which is keeping them down. They test us constantly to see if we are for real, and if we pass the tests we will be accepted. But we are different, and we will always be different, as long as this society is split. The poor people know it, and the Volunteer is lost if he doesn't recognize it. The difference is that we are here by choice and they are here by necessity. When our year is up, we can leave. We can go home.

MEETING THE ANGELS

Cal

I was in the Straight Satans. I had the Straight Satan colors. That's why I did this, man. See, because they thought that just because they were fuckin' Angels they could fuck with me, you hip to it? And, you know, I'm sort of like a junior Hell's Angel. My club means just as much to me as his club does you know? Because I was in this club for a long time, too, the Straight Satans. Not the Satan's Slaves, the Straight Satans, different club. That's why I fucked over those two guys, Angels. I got this new scooter, see? I just got this new Triumph, you know, and I already broke it in and everything. I just got through gunkin' it down and everything, polishing it up. 'Cause it's brand, spankin' new. Breakin' it in. And so, after I get through polishing it, I decided to take a little putt with my scooter. And I'm trippin' along on the freeway, you know, mindin' my own business, drivin' slow like I usually drive, sixty-five, just puttin' along, staying up with the traffic. 'Cause in town on the freeways, in town in Los Angeles, man, they go sixty-five, not forty-five, thirty-five. You know this freeway, the Dan Ryan? You hip to it? You know the mileage you have to go? Forty-five miles an hour. They hold that as a minimum, that's your minimum speed, forty-five on the freeways in California. But anyhow, I'm trippin' along, way out, man, I'm out about Pomona, and these two dudes come up to me in the back. And I'm puttin' along, just minding my own business. And one of them pushes my handlebar just like that, you know? And, man, I'm in a panic. I'm going off the freeway into this ice plant. I don't know if you know what an ice plant is, but if you're ever in California, look alongside the freeway and stop if you want. It's just like watermelon, things. That's why it's called ice plant. And I'm going off at sixty-five miles an hour about. 'Cause he pushed my handlebars pretty good. I goes off into this ice plant and it's real slippery and everything, man. And like they cranked on and split, see? And so I'm hassling this ice plant, I'm really slipping all around, I'm going down is what it is, see? So I drops it down into second gear. By this time I'm just about stopped and almost falling, man. And I cranks it on. And I just, I sort of like—I'm flat-tracking out of that place now, you hip to it? I'm comin' up back on the freeway. I'm shootin' right straight up for the freeway. And I gets on the freeway, man, and I start chasing these dudes. And I really turn that goddam Triumph on, you hip to it? And then it was hardly broke in. And I come up to 'em and they didn't see me. They figured, you know, well, this dude, he's had it. So I'm coming up on 'em and they don't hear me, see? And I just come right up in between both of 'em and push both their handlebars, see? And then I cranked on, and I split for a while. And what I would do, man, is I knew, see, I didn't push their handlebars hard enough to do any damage to them—to knock 'em one way or another. Just more or less just disturbed their driving. 'Cause you don't have that much leverage when you're using both hands, alongside. And so, anyhow, I'd wait for 'em. I had a brand new Bonneville, see? This is about '59. You know who built it? A guy named Kulan. He's in Jacksonville, Florida. And that fucker could really go, you hip to it? I had all the best cams in it and everything from Kulan. We put cams in it. And Kulan pistons and what not. And I'd just wait for these guys, you know? To pull up on my tail, man, about ten feet away, and then I'd turn it on and I'd split. And then I'd wait for 'em. I was playing with these people, man. I played with 'em for fifteen miles. And this was blowin' their minds, see? So I said, well, I'm tired of this little game, 'cause I didn't want them two to catch me. So I turned it on. I really turned it on and I just split out of sight. I sees this cafe comin' up, so I pull over to the cafe, you know, and I decide to get me a cup of coffee. I put my bike on the center stand and all that jazz, went inside, ordered me a cup of coffee. And by the time like the waitress got to me and served me with my coffee, I heard these two bikes comin' in like. They caught me. You hip to it? So they park their bikes, put 'em on the kick stand and as they're walkin'—they parked their bikes behind my bike, in other words, I couldn't get out, see? And as they're walkin' by my bike one of them starts to sit on it. And so I come out of my tree. I figure, what these dudes gonna do? Fuck up my new bike? Like kick in the carburetors? And spokes and whatnot? Gonna play some games? So I come out the door and I says, I hope you guys don't get no ideas about that bike. You know, like I'd get salty. In other words, I told 'em how it is. And so this guy, man, they called him Jesus 'cause he looked just like Jesus Christ. The fucker had long hair, way down here, man. And it was combed straight and beautiful hair, man, you know, for a dude. Anyhow, he acted like God, too. That's another thing. Every time we'd go on a run he'd find the highest place and he'd pray. You hip to it? The dude was a hypnotist, too, man. He used mass hypnosis. A whole group. Are you hip to this now? The dude was an artist and here he was a Hell's Angel. And he spent some time in prison, man, with a hypnotist, that's how come, see, the hypnotist was in there for doin' some illegal scene. But anyhow, he was the one sittin' on my bike. And the other guy, man, was just—he wasn't too big. This guy, this Jesus, man he was about six four, see, and about 230 pounds, big mother. That's why he acted like God. He was big and bad. And this other guy was just, you know, a dude like Funny Sonny. And so they ain't said a word to me. They're bummering my mind now, see, they ain't talking one way or another. They ain't even talking to each other. While we were outside, there was a span of maybe about three or four minutes. And three or four minutes is a long time when you don't know if you're gonna get hassled or not. And so the guy got off the bike and he says, let's go have a cup of coffee. You know? In other words, he hung it up. They decided not to hassle me, right there. So anyhow, we're having a cup of coffee and we're talking about each other's clubs. And it happened to be that I was straight, too, you know? In other words, I turned them on to some dope and they turned me on. Like we had a mutual scene right there, you hip to it? And so we went outside, we did up a couple of numbers. This is before we split from the restaurant. And we started talking about each other's clubs. And they invited me over to their meeting. 'Cause this is where they were going. See, when they started hassling. They were going to their meeting, I hasseled their mind so bad they hung up their meeting, man, to catch me and fuck me up. 'Cause you don't fuck with Angels unless you want to be fucked with. See, in California. Anyhow, so they invited me to their meeting. Then after we got through smoking the joints, we split off to the meeting and we played tag going there. You ever play tag on a bike?

---

38 WHO SAW MURDER DIDN'T CALL THE POLICE

Martin Gansberg

For more than half an hour 38 respectable, law-abiding citizens in Queens watched a killer stalk and stab a woman in three separate attacks in Kew Gardens.

Twice their chatter and the sudden glow of their bedroom lights interrupted him and frightened him off. Each time he returned, sought her out, and stabbed her again. Not one person telephoned the police during the assault; one witness called after the woman was dead.

That was two weeks ago today.

Still shocked is Assistant Chief Inspector Frederick M. Lussen, in charge of the borough's detectives and a veteran of 25 years of homicide investigations. He can give a matter-of-fact recitation on many murders. But the Kew Gardens slaying baffles him—not because it is a murder, but because the "good people" failed to call the police.

"As we have reconstructed the crime," he said, "the assailant had three chances to kill this woman during a 35-minute period. He returned twice to complete the job. If we had been called when he first attacked, the woman might not be dead now."

This is what the police say happened beginning at 3:20 A.M. in the staid, middle-class, tree-lined Austin Street area:

Twenty-eight-year-old Catherine Genovese, who was called Kitty by almost everyone in the neighborhood, was returning home from her job as manager of a bar in Hollis. She parked her red Fiat in a lot adjacent to the Kew Gardens Long Island Rail Road Station, facing Mowbray Place. Like many residents of the neighborhood, she had parked there day after day since her arrival from Connecticut a year ago, although the railroad frowns on the practice.

She turned off the lights of her car, locked the door, and started to walk the 100 feet to the entrance of her apartment at 82–70 Austin Street, which is in a Tudor building, with stores on the first floor and apartments on the second.

The entrance to the apartment is in the rear of the building because the front is rented to retail stores. At night the quiet neighborhood is shrouded in the slumbering darkness that marks most residential areas.

Miss Genovese noticed a man at the far end of the lot, near a seven-story apartment house at 82–40 Austin Street. She halted. Then, nervously, she headed up Austin Street toward Lefferts Boulevard, where there is a call box to the 102nd Police Precinct in nearby Richmond Hill.

She got as far as a street light in front of a bookstore before the man grabbed her. She screamed. Lights went on in the 10-story apartment house at 82–67 Austin Street, which faces the bookstore. Windows slid open and voices punctuated the early-morning stillness.

Miss Genovese screamed: "Oh, my God, he stabbed me! Please help me! Please help me!"

From one of the upper windows in the apartment house, a man called down: "Let that girl alone!"

The assailant looked up at him, shrugged, and walked down Austin

Street toward a white sedan parked a short distance away. Miss Genovese struggled to her feet.

Lights went out. The killer returned to Miss Genovese, now trying to make her way around the side of the building by the parking lot to get to her apartment. The assailant stabbed her again.

"I'm dying!" she shrieked. "I'm dying!'

Windows were opened again, and lights went on in many apartments. The assailant got into his car and drove away. Miss Genovese staggered to her feet. A city bus, O-10, the Lefferts Boulevard line to Kennedy International Airport, passed. It was 3:35 A.M.

The assailant returned. By then, Miss Genovese had crawled to the back of the building, where the freshly painted brown doors to the apartment house held out hope for safety. The killer tried the first door; she wasn't there. At the second door, 82–62 Austin Street, he saw her slumped on the floor at the foot of the stairs. He stabbed her a third time—fatally.

It was 3:50 by the time the police received their first call, from a man who was a neighbor of Miss Genovese. In two minutes they were at the scene. The neighbor, a 70-year-old woman, and another woman were the only persons on the street. Nobody else came forward.

The man explained that he had called the police after much deliberation. He had phoned a friend in Nassau County for advice and then he had crossed the roof of the building to the apartment of the elderly woman to get her to make the call.

"I didn't want to get involved," he sheepishly told the police.

Six days later, the police arrested Winston Moseley, a 29-year-old business-machine operator, and charged him with the homicide. Moseley had no previous record. He is married, has two children and owns a home at 133–19 Sutter Avenue, South Ozone Park, Queens. On Wednesday, a court committed him to Kings County Hospital for psychiatric observation.

When questioned by the police, Moseley also said that he had slain Mrs. Annie May Johnson, 24, of 146–12 133d Avenue, Jamaica, on Feb. 29 and Barbara Kralik, 15, of 174–17 140th Avenue, Springfield Gardens, last July. In the Kralik case, the police are holding Alvin L. Mitchell, who is said to have confessed that slaying.

The police stressed how simple it would have been to have gotten in touch with them. "A phone call," said one of the detectives, "would have done it." The police may be reached by dialing "O" for operator or SPring 7-3100.

Today witnesses from the neighborhood, which is made up of one-family homes in the $35,000 to $60,000 range with the exception of the two apartment houses near the railroad station, find it difficult to explain why they didn't call the police.

A housewife, knowingly if quite casual, said, "We thought it was a lover's quarrel." A husband and wife both said, "Frankly, we were afraid." They seemed aware of the fact that events might have been different. A distraught woman, wiping her hands in her apron, said, "I didn't want my husband to get involved."

One couple, now willing to talk about that night, said they heard the first screams. The husband looked thoughtfully at the bookstore where the killer first grabbed Miss Genovese.

"We went to the window to see what was happening," he said, "but the light from our bedroom made it difficult to see the street." The wife, still apprehensive, added: "I put out the light and we were able to see better."

Asked why they hadn't called the police, she shrugged and replied: "I don't know."

A man peeked out from a slight opening in the doorway to his apartment and rattled off an account of the killer's second attack. Why hadn't he called the police at the time? "I was tired," he said without emotion. "I went back to bed."

It was 4:25 A.M. when the ambulance arrived to take the body of Miss Genovese. It drove off. "Then," a solemn police detective said, "the people came out."

OUTSIDE OF A SMALL CIRCLE OF FRIENDS

Phil Ochs

Brightly

Look out-side the win - dow, there's a wo-man be-ing grabbed. — They dragged her to the bush - es, and now she's be-ing stabbed.— May-be we should call the cops— and

try to stop the pain,—— But Mo - nop - o - ly—— is
so much fun,— I'd hate to blow the game,—— And I'm
sure it would- n't in - ter- est—— an - y - bod - y
out - side of a small cir - cle of friends.

2. Riding down the highway, yes, my back is getting stiff.
Thirteen cars have piled up—they're hanging on a cliff.
Maybe we should pull them back with our
    towing-chain,
But we gotta move, and we might get sued, and it looks
    like it's gonna rain.
And I'm sure it wouldn't interest anybody outside
    of a small circle of friends.

3. Sweating in the ghetto with the Panthers and the poor.
The rats have joined the babies who are sleeping
    on the floor.
Now, wouldn't it be a riot if they really blew their tops,
But they got too much already, and besides
    we got the cops.
And I'm sure it wouldn't interest anybody outside
    of a small circle of friends.

4. There's a dirty paper using sex to make a sale.
The Supreme Court was so upset they sent him off
    to jail.
Maybe we should help the fiend and take away his fine,
But we're busy reading *Playboy* and *The Sunday
    New York Times.*
And I'm sure it wouldn't interest anybody outside
    of a small circle of friends.

5. Smoking marijuana is more fun than drinking beer,
   But a friend of ours was captured; and they gave him
         thirty years.
   Maybe we should raise our voices, ask somebody why;
   But demonstrations are a drag, besides we're much
         too high.
   And I'm sure it wouldn't interest anybody outside
         of a small circle of friends.

6. Look outside the window, there's a woman
         being grabbed.
   They dragged her to the bushes, and now she's
         being stabbed.
   Maybe we should call the cops and try to stop the pain,
   But Monopoly is so much fun, I'd hate to blow
         the game.
   And I'm sure it wouldn't interest anybody outside
         of a small circle of friends.

LIFE IN A CITY

J. Krishnamurti

It was a well-proportioned room, quiet and restful. The furniture was elegant and in very good taste; the carpet was thick and soft. There was a marble fireplace, with a fire in it. There were old vases from different parts of the world, and on the walls were modern paintings as well as some by the old masters. Considerable thought and care had been spent on the beauty and comfort of the room, which reflected wealth and taste. The room overlooked a small garden, with a lawn that must have been mowed and rolled for many, many years.

Life in a city is strangely cut off from the universe; man-made buildings have taken the place of valleys and mountains, and the roar of traffic has been substituted for that of boisterous streams. At night one hardly ever sees the stars, even if one wishes to, for the city lights are too bright; and during the day the sky is limited and held. Something definitely happens to the city-dwellers; they are brittle and polished, they have churches and museums, drinks and theatres, beautiful clothes and endless shops. There are people everywhere, on the streets, in the buildings, in the rooms. A cloud passes across the sky, and so few look up. There is rush and turmoil.

But in this room there was quiet and sustained dignity. It had that atmosphere peculiar to the rich, the feeling of aloof security and assurance, and the long freedom from want. He was saying that he was interested in philosophy, both of the East and of the West, and how absurd it was to begin with the Greeks, as though nothing existed before them; and presently he began to talk of his problem: how to give, and to whom to give. The problem of having money, with its many responsibilities, was somewhat disturbing him. Why was he making a problem of it? Did it matter to whom he gave, and with what spirit? Why had it become a problem?

His wife came in, smart, bright and curious. Both of them seemed well read, sophisticated and worldly wise; they were clever and interested in many things. They were the product of both town and country, but mostly their hearts were in the town. That one thing, compassion, seemed so far away. The qualities of the mind were deeply cultivated; there was a sharpness, a brutal approach, but it did not go very far. She wrote a little, and he was some kind of politician; and how easily and confidently they spoke. Hesitancy is so essential to discovery, to further understanding; but how can there be hesitancy when you know so much, when the self-protective armour is so highly polished and all the cracks are sealed from within? Line and form become extraordinarily important to those who are in bondage to the sensate; then beauty is sensation, goodness a feeling, and truth a matter of intellection. When sensations dominate, comfort becomes essential, not only to the body, but also to the psyche; and comfort, especially that of the mind, is corroding, leading to illusion.

We *are* the things we possess, we *are* that to which we are attached. Attachment has no nobility. Attachment to knowledge is not different from any other gratifying addiction. Attachment is self-absorption, whether at the lowest or at the highest level. Attachment is self-deception, it is an escape from the hollowness of the self. The things to which we are attached —property, people, ideas—become all-important, for without the many things which fill its emptiness, the self is not. The fear of not being makes for possession; and fear breeds illusion, the bondage to conclusions. Conclusions, material or ideational, prevent the fruition of intelligence, the freedom in which alone reality can come into being; and without this freedom, cunning is taken for intelligence. The ways of cunning are always complex and destructive. It is this self-protective cunning that makes for attachment; and when attachment causes pain, it is this same cunning that seeks detachment and finds pleasure in the pride and vanity of renunciation. The understanding of the ways of cunning, the ways of the self, is the beginning of intelligence.

OBITUARY OF A HEROIN USER WHO DIED AT 12

Joseph Lelyveld and Charlayne Hunter

Walter Vandermeer—the youngest person ever to be reported dead of an overdose of heroin here—had been identified by many of the city's leading social service agencies as a child in desperate need of care long before his body was discovered in the common bathroom of a Harlem tenement on Dec. 14, two weeks after his twelfth birthday.

For most of these agencies he never became more than one case among thousands passing through their revolving doors. Others tried to fit him into their programs but lacked the manpower or resources to focus on him effectively. Eventually he would be shunted off to yet another institution.

It was not heartlessness or malfeasance that explain why he usually went unnoticed, just overwhelming numbers. As one school official expressed it, "There are thousands of Walter Vandermeers out there."

Along the way his case was handled by Family Court, the Society for the Prevention of Cruelty to Children, the Department of Social Services and its Bureau of Child Welfare, the Board of Education's Bureau of Attendance and Bureau for the Education of Socially Maladjusted Children, the Wiltwyck School for Boys and the Office of Probation.

Most of these agencies have refused to discuss their actions in the case on the ground that their relationship with the boy was confidential.

But interviews with neighbors, relatives and individuals in the schools and agencies through which he passed have made it possible to retrace the course of his short life and his efforts to find a foothold in a world that always seemed to him on the verge of collapse.

The agencies had exhausted their routine procedures before he died; only his file continued to move. For his last 14 months he was left to himself, with no consistent supervision or counseling of any kind, on the decaying block where he lived most of his life and died—117th Street between Eighth and Manhattan Avenues.

There he was in intimate daily contact with addicts and pushers, as if none of the overstrained agencies had heard of him or even existed. After his death, one of the block's junkies paid him this discerning tribute: "Walter lived to be 30 in 12 years. There was nothing about the street he didn't know."

CUPCAKES AND COCA-COLA

In those months he slept at home only sporadically and attended school for a total of two and a half days.

Walter would be out late at night hawking newspapers in bars or begging for coins at the corner of Eighth Avenue. In the daytime, when most children were in school, he would station himself near a radiator in a grocery store for warmth until chased or borrow a couch to catch up on the sleep he had missed.

His diet was made up of Yankee Doodle cupcakes, Coca-Cola and, when he had the change, fish 'n' chips.

It was a life of frightening emptiness and real dangers. The only regular thing about it was a daily struggle for survival.

"Walter didn't do too bad," a junkie on the block remarked when he was dead.

"He didn't do too good," retorted a black youth, full of bitterness over what heroin has done to Harlem. "He won't see his 13th birthday."

"He didn't do too bad," the junkie repeated. "He looked after himself."

The one thing the court and the various agencies to which it referred his case never knew was that he was experimenting with drugs. But even this probably wouldn't have mattered, for no treatment centers have yet been authorized for narcotics users under the age of 16, although youths under 16 in the city are dying of heroin overdoses at the rate of one a week.

ANGER AND FEAR

Two sides of Walter Vandermeer are remembered on his block.

One was the apprentice hustler, an angry, mistrustful youth given to violent rages in which he hurled bottles and flayed about with iron pipes.

The other was the small child who cried easily and searched continually for adult protection and warmth. Some of the older addicts, into whose orbit he gravitated in the last months of his life, say he would sometimes call them "Mommy" or "Daddy" and fantasy a household into which he could move as their child.

"Walter wanted a lot of attention," said his oldest sister, Regina Price. And there were those in his family and neighborhood who tried to extend it, when they could. Given the stress of their lives, that was only now and then and never for long.

Survival on 117th Street is a hard proposition at best, and Walter's circumstances were already far from the best when he was born Dec. 1, 1957.

His mother, Mrs. Lillian Price, had come to New York from Charleston, S.C., with her husband, Cyril, in 1947, when she was 22. Her schooling had never got beyond the third grade and she was on welfare within a year—(21 years later, she is still there).

In 1949, Mrs. Price had her first children—twins—and her husband moved out.

By 1957 she was, in social-work jargon, the nominal head of a growing, desperately disorganized "multiproblem" family. Walter was her sixth child; there had been four fathers. Five more children (one of whom died in infancy) were to be born in the next seven years to Mrs. Price and a Liberian immigrant named Sunday Togbah.

FATHER DEPORTED

Walter's father, known variously as Robert or Willie Vandermeer, entered the country illegally from Surinam, having jumped ship here in 1947. Six months after Walter was born, he was found by immigration authorities while he was working as a counterman at a mid-town pharmacy and deported.

But by then, it appears, Mr. Vandermeer and Mrs. Price had separated, for hardly six months after he left the country she gave birth to the first of the children she was to have with Mr. Togbah.

Only one other Vandermeer was left in the family, a brother, Anthony, three years older than Walter.

In those days, Mrs. Price and six of her children were squeezed into one room of a three-room apartment at 305 West 117th Street they somehow shared with a couple with two children of their own. (Another of Mrs. Price's children, a daughter named Beverly, was being raised by a friend.)

According to the recollection of neighbors, Walter was sniffing airplane glue by the time he was 6 and sitting in on card games on the stoops when he was 8. In school he was marked as a disruptive child who could not be contained within a classroom's four walls unless permitted to fall asleep, which he did regularly, a sign to his teachers that he was staying out nights.

Public School 76 on West 121st Street gave up on him in early 1967, when he was in the third grade, soon after his ninth birthday. Walter had been out of school more days than not that year. When he was there he seemed locked in an aggressive pattern, roaming the halls and throwing punches at teachers who sought to restrain him.

Sometimes his violence could be seen as a stifled cry for attention and help. On one occasion he stormed out of an art class, only to fly into a rage because his teacher had not pursued him.

Walter was repeatedly warned to behave better, then suspended on March 2, 1967. It does not appear that the school ever attempted to arrange psychological consultations for him or his mother with the Board of Education's Bureau of Child Guidance.

After Walter's death, Assemblyman Hulan E. Jack was to charge that the school had "put the child out onto the street."

In fact, it did just the opposite by referring his case to the Society for the Prevention of Cruelty to Children, which then brought it up in Family Court on a neglect petition.

PLACED IN QUEENS SHELTER

On March 14, both Walter and his brother Tony—the two Vandermeers—were placed in the Society's Children Shelter in Queens. Later they were shifted from there to the Children's Center at Fifth Avenue and 104th Street.

An attendance teacher, as truant officers are now called, had singled out the older boy as a youth of unusual intelligence and promise. Six months later, Tony was assigned to a home operated by a private agency in Yonkers, where he has made what is regarded as a highly successful adjustment.

But Walter got lost in the judicial maze. While one branch of Family Court found Mrs. Price unable to care for Tony, another decided in August to release Walter—the younger and more disturbed of the two boys —to her care.

He had been classified as a "person in need of supervision" rather than a "neglected" child—a narrow legal distinction that has the effect of blaming the child and not the parent for his difficulties.

The fact that the law forces the judge in such cases to an implicit finding of blame, a court officer said, places a tremendous psychological pressure on parents to resist help for their children: It does not seem to be offered as help but as punishment for having failed them.

Releasing Walter to Mrs. Price was tantamount to releasing him to the street (by now the family had shifted to a top-floor apartment at 2124 Eighth Avenue, near 115th Street).

The court expected Walter to go to Public School 148, a special school for disturbed and socially maladjusted children at West End Avenue and 82d Street. But there was no response to repeated notices sent by the school to the boy and his mother.

Meantime, members of the family recall, Tony was attempting, without success, to interest the agency that looked after him in his younger brother's plight.

Stranded, Walter at 10 was reaching for his own solutions.

One involved Mrs. Barbara Banks, who had regarded him as a godchild ever since she accompanied Mrs. Price to the hospital at the time of his birth. Around Christmas, 1967, she said, she told Walter he could move in with her and three of her children, since her eldest son was going into the Army.

"A whole lot of people told me, 'Ain't no hope for that boy,' " she said. "But I believed I could save him. He was so inquisitive, he could have been anything."

Although Walter eagerly seized the invitation, she said, she was soon forced to withdraw it, for her son was never inducted. Walter felt rejected.

Late one night he made that clear in his own way by climbing to the roof of a tenement across 117th Street and hurling a bottle through Mrs. Banks's window, raining glass on her bed.

The boy spent most of his time on the streets until April, 1968, when the Family Court assigned him to the Wiltwyck School for Boys, a treatment center for disturbed youths from the slums that had enjoyed the patronage of Mrs. Eleanor Roosevelt.

The idea was to place Walter at the school's main center at York-town Heights in Westchester County, but the center was full and cutting down on its staff because of a budget crisis. As a temporary alternative—to get Walter off the streets—he was put in Patterson House, at 208 East 18th Street, a "halfway house" run by the school for youths returning to their communities from the main center.

PUT ON TRANQUILIZERS

Dr. Howard A. Weiner, a psychiatrist who was then in charge of Patterson House, remembers that Walter was "extremely bright verbally" but says he was "as disturbed as any kid we had."

Like many maladjusted children from the poorest, most disorganized families, he would erupt into towering rages when he felt himself under pressure and he had to be held till he regained control. Usually that took at least an hour, so it was decided to give him 50 milligrams of the tranquilizer Thorazene four times a day.

At first, Walter showed his suspicions about his new surroundings by taking food from the table in a napkin and hiding it under his bed.

After his wariness subsided, he permitted himself to draw close to his child-care counselor, John Schoonbeck, a recent graduate of the University of Michigan. Learning that they both had Dutch names, Walter eagerly proclaimed that they were "soul brothers."

Mr. Schoonbeck, who now is on the staff of Time magazine, says Walter was "a great little kid." Dr. Weiner credits him with giving Walter the warm, reliable affection he had rarely found in an adult.

Encouraged by his counselor, Walter finally put in an appearance at P.S. 148. In fact, in May he went to school there regularly—his first stretch of steady school attendance in more than a year and the last in his life.

Flora Boyd, a teacher at the school, says Walter had never learned to read beyond the first-grade level but thought he could catch up. "He was an intelligent little boy," she recalls. "Of course, he had a lot of problems. But he could learn."

Every afternoon when he returned to Patterson House, he would insist on doing his homework before anything else, according to Mr. Schoonbeck.

In the evenings and on weekends, he regularly made quick, unauthorized expeditions to Harlem to check on his family and block, but always returned to Patterson House.

A NEED FOR ROOTS

Children like Walter, Dr. Weiner said, need to go back regularly to their home environments, however disturbed these may appear, "because their identities are bound to their communities—they need to re-establish who they are."

Finally a place opened for him at Wiltwyck's pastoral upstate campus, and on June 20, Mr. Schoonbeck accompanied him to Yorktown Heights —the fifth separate institutional setting in which he had been lodged in 15 months.

Walter felt that he had been betrayed and trapped. He had never been told that his stay at Patterson House would be temporary. It was a repetition of his experience with Mrs. Banks and, predictably, he flew into a fit of anger on his first afternoon at the school.

Wiltwyck's troubles, meantime, had gone from bad to worse. In May, a third of its staff had been suspended after protesting that students were receiving inadequate clothing and food in the wake of the economy drive.

In the next two months, Walter ran away at least four times. As justification, he told his family he had been beaten at the school. Wiltwyck concluded that it could not hold Walter without his mother's cooperation and that this was unavailable.

On Oct. 10, 1968, Wiltwyck turned Walter back to Family Court, which meant he was where he had been more than a year earlier, only more frustrated and "street-wise."

His involvement with institutions was now nearly ended.

It took warrants to bring him and his mother to court so that he could be ordered to go to school, or to Harlem Hospital for psychiatric counseling, or to one of Haryou-Act's "self-help teams."

Asked why the court had not placed him in a state institution—a training school or mental hospital—in order to take him off the street, a judge replied that Walter, who was too disturbed for Wiltwyck, did not seem disturbed enough.

In fact, the probation officer assigned to the case recommended last spring that he be detained in a training school. But Walter's sister Regina insisted that her mother oppose the recommendation in court. In the back of her mind were recollections of the state institutions in which she was placed after she became pregnant at the age of 12.

QUESTION OF SURVIVAL

She knew that a youth in detention had to "stay by himself" to survive, she said, for there were always homosexual fellow inmates threatening to "mess up his mind." Regina wanted Walter to receive care, but she thought the probation officer only wanted to "criticize him" and "lock him up." In her view, state institutions were no less dangerous than the streets.

On his own, Walter continued to search out adults he felt he could trust.

In November, he went down to East Sixth Street to call on John Schoonbeck, who had quit Patterson House in discouragement and was packing for a trip to Africa. Walter asked plaintively if he could come along.

On the block he had a half-dozen households where he dropped in regularly at unpredictable hours to cadge food, coins, an undemanding hour in front of a television set.

One addict said Walter tagged along after a gang that called itself Bonnie and the Seven Clydes. The gang specialized in auto thefts and shoplifting, and he accompanied it on several forays downtown.

He also teamed up, it was said, with some older youths who conducted raids into Morningside Heights and learned to snatch purses.

According to Regina, he bought most of his own food and clothes and sometimes had as much as $50 in his pockets. But it is doubtful that he had any regular income as a drug courier, as has been alleged, for he continued until his last days to hustle for small change, selling newspapers and delivering groceries.

In his last month, Walter's already disastrous family situation deteriorated sharply.

Last summer, Mrs. Price was living most of the time on 117th Street, although her younger children were still in the apartment on Eighth Avenue. Walter stayed on the block, too, although not with her, sometimes sleeping on a fire escape above a warehouse. When his mother saw him, she would shout, "Go home!" Walter would shout back, "Go home yourself!"

Sometimes, neighbors say, she would call the police on her son.

In September, an 18-year-old half-brother, Reggie Brooks, was arrested for robbery. Five days before Walter's death, he was sent to the Rikers Island reformatory.

In October, another half-brother, Eugene Price, 19, was shipped back to Vietnam, where he had already served a year, for an involuntary second tour of duty.

In November, the whole family was evicted from the Eighth Avenue apartment because Mrs. Price had not paid the $73.10 monthly rent for seven months out of her $412-a-month welfare checks.

She said she was holding the money in escrow because the toilet hadn't worked for a year and a half, but never got to Rent Court to explain this to the judge, perhaps because she no longer had the money.

Tony Vandermeer became distraught when he heard the news and got permission to come down from Yonkers for a day. It was not only the eviction that alarmed him—word had also reached him that Walter had started to take drugs.

The chances are negligible that any child on 117th Street could retain much innocence about narcotics, for the block is wide open to the traffic.

"I can go to my window any morning and see a man hand somebody some money and get his little package in return," a resident said. The fact that the police regularly manage not to see the same thing convinces the residents that they are indifferent, at best.

Walter's brother Reggie had long been using narcotics. Sometimes he would show his "works"—the eyedropper, needle, cord and bottle cap that are the tools of the addict's vocation—to his younger brothers. Once Walter found an empty glassine envelope on their tenement stairway, filled it with salt and sold it to Reggie as a $3 bag of heroin.

ADDICT RECALLS HIM

Interviewed briefly after Walter's death, when he was brought to the funeral home from Rikers Island, Reggie said he knew who had first given drugs to his brother and named a 17-year-old addict on 117th Street, who shall be called Theresa here.

When she was visited the next day, Theresa was sitting next to a stove with all its burners on, the only warm corner in an apartment that had been without heat all winter. She readily acknowledged that she had been on drugs for two years, had been close to Walter and had known him to be using them.

Although she denied ever having given him any herself, Theresa said she had often seen him "skin" (inject the drug beneath the surface of his skin) but had never known him to "main" (inject it directly into a vein). Usually, she said, he skinned at the top of the stairs at 303 West 117th Street or in an apartment next door at 301 shared by two of her fellow addicts.

At 301, the two addicts—call them Mary Lou and Lizzie—also denied ever having sold or given drugs to Walter, but Mary Lou said he would often ask for them. She said that she had seen him "snort" (inhale heroin) and that she had occasionally allowed him to watch while she "mained."

Sometimes she would think of Walter as "a little man," Lizzie said. At other times she would see him as an abandoned child and haul him to the bathroom to scrub him in the tub. Treated like a child, he would behave like one, she said.

The two addicts said they found it hard to imagine his locking himself in the bathroom across the street to "shoot up" by himself.

"Walter was scared of the needle," Lizzie said, laughing indulgently as one might in recalling a baby's first steps. "He'd always say, 'Wait. Don't hurt me. Let me get myself together. Please Wait!' "

It was their expert speculation that he might have tried to "find the hole" where he had been "hit" earlier in the evening.

BROTHER'S ANGER ERUPTS

After the funeral, Tony Vandermeer rushed Lizzie, overturning a floral wreath and shouting, "You killed my brother!" He had heard stories on the block that Lizzie and Theresa had dragged his brother's body on the morning of Dec. 14 from 301 and across 117th Street to 310, where it was found.

Lizzie acknowledged that she had a loud argument with Walter the night before he died over $9—the change left from $25 he had given her to buy him some clothes—but insisted she had not seen him after that.

"Tony really didn't know me at all," she said. "He just had nobody else to blame."

Another addict—known here as Sugar—moved off the block as soon as the body was found. Walter had been especially close to him since the summer, it was said, and sometimes called him "Daddy."

A lanky, good-looking youth who now works at two jobs to keep up with the "Jones" (his habit), Sugar still returns to the block late at night to make his connection.

The other night at about 12:30 A.M. he came ambling into Mary Lou's apartment on the heels of two pushers—one wearing a leather tunic, the other done out in a frilly shirt with lace cuffs like an 18th-century gentleman.

After an interlude in a bedroom, Sugar appeared rolling down his sleeve and adjusting his cuff link. Behind his dark glasses his eyelids were drooping. His only response to a question about Walter was a perfunctory expression of "shock" over his death.

"But something had to happen," Sugar drawled sleepily. "He was always hanging around."

Dr. Michael Baden, an assistant medical examiner, who examined the body at the scene, said it looked to him like "a typical overdose case." But he cautioned that his office never classified narcotics overdoses as homicides, suicides or accidents, for medical evidence on this point is invariably moot.

Curiously, chemical tests failed to reveal any trace of heroin in the eyedropper found next to Walter in the sink—a hint, by no means conclusive, that it might have been planted.

The autopsy proved that Walter had been using drugs for at least three months—possibly longer—but the absence of any track marks on his arms indicated he had probably yet to become a full-fledged addict.

He had also yet to give up on himself. About a month before he died, Walter received a new pair of shoes from Mrs. Carletha Morrison, one of the women on the block whom he would allow to mother him. He said he would save them for going back to school.

A SCHOOL DROP-IN

According to both Regina and Mrs. Morrison, he seemed to think he could not go to school until his mother took him to court. No one seemed to realize that he was still enrolled at P.S. 148, where he had appeared only three times the previous year.

When the school reminded the Bureau of Attendance of his truancy, it was told to stop sending in reports on the boy because Family Court had his case "under advisement"—a bureaucratic formula that seemed to have no specific application.

Occasionally last fall, Walter would drop into the class of his younger brother "Doe" at P.S. 76 and would be allowed by the teacher to stay. He even asked his brother to teach him reading.

"I gave him my book and any words he didn't know I told him," said "Doe," who is 11.

He was also looking forward to Christmas. Regina had promised to buy him a pair of expensive alligator shoes and a blue pullover. In addition, she said she would treat him to ice skating in Central Park and a movie downtown, probably "The Ten Commandments."

Everyone noticed a macabre touch in a legend stamped on the cheap "Snoopy" sweatshirt Walter was wearing when he died.

"I wish I could bite somebody," it said. "I need to relieve my inner tensions."

"When I heard that I broke down," Regina said. "That was him. That was the way he felt."

GEE, OFFICER KRUPKE

FROM "WEST SIDE STORY"

Stephen Sondheim

1. Dear kindly Sergeant Krupke, You gotta understand,
   It's just our bringin' up-ke that gets us out of hand.
   Our mothers all are junkies, Our fathers all are drunks.
   Golly Moses, natcherlly we're punks!

   Gee! Officer Krupke, we're very upset;
   We never had the love that ev'ry child oughta get.
   We ain't no delinquents, We're misunderstood.
   Deep down inside us there is good!

   There is good! There is good, There is good,
   There is untapped good. Like inside, the worst of us
       is good!

2. Dear kindly Judge, your Honor, My parents treat me
       rough.
   With all their marijuana, They won't give me a puff.
   They didn't wanna have me, But somehow I was had.
   Leapin' lizards, that's why I'm so bad.

   Right! Officer Krupke, you're really a square;
   This boy don't need a judge, he needs a analyst's care!
   It's just his neurosis that oughta be curbed.
   He's psychologically disturbed!

   I'm disturbed! We're disturbed, we're disturbed,
   We're the most disturbed, Like we're psychologically
       disturbed.

3. My father is a bastard, My ma's an S. O. B.
   My grandpa's always plastered, My grandma
            pushes tea.
   My sister wears a mustache, My brother wears a dress.
   Goodness gracious, that's why I'm a mess.

   Yes! Officer Krupke, you're really a slob.
   This boy don't need a doctor, just a good honest job.
   Society's played him a terrible trick,
   And sociologically he's sick!

   I am sick! We are sick, We are sick,
   We are sick, sick, sick, Like we're sociologically sick!

4. Dear kindly social worker, They say go earn a buck,
   Like be a soda jerker, Which means like be a schmuck.
   It's not I'm antisocial, I'm only anti-work.
   Gloryosky, that's why I'm a jerk.

   Eek! Officer Krupke, you've done it again.
   This boy don't need a job, he needs a year in the pen.
   It ain't just a question of misunderstood;
   Deep down inside him he's no good!

   I'm no good! We're no good, We're no good,
   We're no earthly good, Like the best of us is
            no damn good!

Judge:
      The trouble is he's crazy.
Psych:
      The trouble is he drinks.
Social worker:
      The trouble is he's lazy.
Judge:
      The trouble is he stinks.
Psych:
      The trouble is he's growing.
Social worker:
      The trouble is he's grown!
All:
      Krupke, we got troubles of our own!

Gee, Officer Krupke, We're down on our knees,
'Cause no one wants a fellow with a social disease.
Gee, Officer Krupke, What are we to do?
Gee, Officer Krupke, krup you!

THE SINGLE GIRLS OF THE CITY:
WHY THEY DON'T WANT TO BE WIVES

Caroline Bird

New York City probably has more nubile women running around loose than any other spot on earth. There were, to be exact, 68,366 more single females than males aged 20 to 34 at the Census of 1960, when there was still a comfortable surplus of single men of marriageable age in the country as a whole. You don't have to go to the library to prove that there were more single girls in 1968, when the deficit of eligible males has become national: You can see them any fine day, striding along in their interesting clothes on the streets of the girl ghetto on the Upper East Side.

"What's to become of them?" a bachelor friend asked rhetorically. "They're smart. They earned the money to buy those clothes themselves. They're attractive. They're desperately willing. And some of them are damned nice girls. . . ." He spoke as if they were a civic blight, like starlings, for which a solution, preferably scientific, should be sought.

"What's to become of *you?*" I snapped. "You're not married yourself at the moment!"

"Me? Well, I've thought of marrying again," he confessed, picking his way carefully through the novel concept that single *men* could be a problem. "I'm tired of entertaining in restaurants, and I've come to the point in my career where I need a hostess, and she has to be a wife."

"Men in single state should tarry, but women, I suggest, should marry!" I chanted. But why should it be so? Maybe, as a matter of fact, it wasn't so.

Because my companion seemed intolerably smug, I reminded him of all the ways in which single men are worse off than single women. They are, for instance, more apt to die young—by their own hand as well as from other causes. They are more apt to be sick, and especially more apt to be *mentally* sick (judging by the sex ratio of admission to mental institutions). So far as happiness can be measured, they turn out to be the unhappiest of mortals. On the happiness scale devised by Norman

Bradburn of the National Opinion Research Center of the University of Chicago, for instance, the married are happier than the single, but single women are happier than single men.

"Maybe it's really very simple," I suggested. "Maybe the girls of New York don't get married because they don't want to be wives. Maybe they came to New York to save themselves from being like their mothers. They want a different kind of marriage, but when it comes right down to it they are afraid that being a wife means being a sort of domestic convenience, like a comfortable chair you fall into at night without looking at it. New York is full of attractive single girls who like men—but do they really want marriage?"

"They sure say they do," he shouted back at me. "Why else do they take beach houses at Fire Island? What do you think all those smart girls are doing at night school? Improving their minds? What about all those cruises, singles bars, dating agencies, ski resorts? Why do they ask how many single men they'll meet when they go on job interviews? They'll do anything to catch a man's eye. Some of them buy dogs to attract attention on the street. They'll do anything to get a man except go to Alaska. And they *talk* about doing that."

"Exactly," I interrupted. "They don't go to Alaska. They just talk about it. Maybe that's a clue. Maybe they are protesting too much. Maybe they don't want to get married—and settle for the life their mothers are leading—but they don't dare admit even to themselves that they don't want to get married. They're afraid you'll think there's something wrong with them."

"Sure is!" my friend answered cheerfully. "Only you haven't explained just *what* it is."

It's hard for men to grasp the notion that women don't always want to be wives. If a girl is attractive but single, they figure that she may be hung up on men or sex, or the victim of a terrible love affair or a hereditary disease or unspeakable social disadvantages.

When I was researching my book *Born Female*, a magazine editor who conceded that he discriminated against married women maintained that single women didn't get ahead because they weren't as competent as the men competing with them. He held this to be a self-evident truth requiring no proof. "After all, it's got to be," he argued. "The *best* women aren't out working. They've been hauled off to the suburbs to raise families. Only the duller ones who lose out in the marriage market are left on the job market. They don't have what it takes, so they don't get promoted."

I didn't bother to cite careful civil service studies confirming the common observation that women have to be "twice as good" as men to get the same job. Instead, I countered with what I regarded to be a self-evident truth: As long as women try to marry men better than themselves, the *best* women will be precisely those who will lose out on the marriage market and have to enter the job market. If the gods distribute their gifts equally among men and women, then there should be enough high-I.Q. men to marry high-I.Q. women. But we all know that women try to marry up, while men may—and, considering their need for admiration, often do —reach down the scale to marry a girl who would have been just as happy looking up to a man with less on the ball. The losers in this game of musical chairs are the top women and the bottom men, so bachelors are apt to be the stupidest, poorest, least competent jerks from the wrong side of the railroad tracks, while single women are apt to be bright, beautiful, wellborn creatures who literally can't find men good enough for them.

This is the marriage gradient. Men see it when you point it out, but they keep forgetting about it. Some frankly admit as much. "I know men and women are equal," one man told me impatiently during one of the many arguments I've had about equal opportunity for women. "I just don't like to hear a lot of *talk* about it."

Girls don't talk about the marriage gradient. It's not good to be better or taller or sexier than men. But every single girl in New York understands the marriage gradient only too well, for New York is where the top women come when they are leftover at home.

Girls who can't find husbands they can look up to come to New York in hopes of finding something better than what happened to Mother. They aren't sure, at first, whether they're looking for a new set of men, hopefully "better" than the ones at home, or whether they're looking for "an interesting job," or both. Men who want something better than the prospects at home come to New York, too. Both the girls and the men get started in interesting beginner jobs. The girls discover, very quickly, that they are a more sharply selected group than the men. (The average girl stays home and marries up, but quite average boys will seek their fortunes afar.)

The new girls have new problems. At home, there simply were no jobs or men worth the trouble. In New York, there are a few, but the competition for them is fierce, and there's a sort of whipsaw between husband-hunt and career. On the job, the invisible bar limits the promotion of a woman on the theory that she won't be permanent. The average girls are stymied and may go back home, to be replaced by younger girls seeking their fortunes. Meanwhile, the average men move up the promotion ladder as a matter of course.

The selective process feeds on itself. New leftover women keep coming to town from all over the U.S. (and, indeed, the whole world). Some of them find men to marry in New York—often on the second round (divorced men remarry more frequently than divorced women)—and the best of those who don't, settle down to compete for the jobs open to women and to hammer out a style of life that turns out to be better than Mother's even if it *doesn't* include marriage. The way the system works, the single girls of New York increase steadily in numbers and caliber.

The single girls of New York complain, but the loudest complaints don't come from girls who could be described as wallflowers. "It's the least confident girls who marry as soon as they get out of college," a public relations counselor in her early 30s said. "When you first come to New York there's so much to do and see, and there's plenty of time. If you've been at all competent with guys, you don't think you have to rush. But then when you start pushing thirty you look around and discover that the eligible men have all been snapped up by desperate little girls who were afraid they'd get left. By the time you're thirty, all the men in your life are either married, divorced, or crazy, so what the hell. You make out." She was, as a matter of fact, making out well financially, and did not look under-privileged socially either.

The single girls I interviewed were single for different reasons, but all of them seemed, in one way or another, to be wary of the kind of life they would lead as wives. The stumbling block in many cases was often the unspoken assumptions about marriage as an institution—either their own assumptions, or the assumptions they feared were being made by the men in their lives. Consider these stories:

Joanna had been married right out of high school to a boy she divorced a year later. She came to New York, got a job, plotted to meet eligible men. "There's a time in the life of every man when he's ripe to be married," she reasoned. "All I have to do is to be there at the right time." She met a young lawyer in the elevator of the apartment house in which she was living, and kept up with him when he left New York to set up a practice of his own in a small town where the girls were less interesting and less accommodating. But when he proposed—by mail and flying visits —she wasn't sure that she was willing to give up her stimulating job to follow him to a place where she'd be wholly dependent on him for money and fun. To help make up her mind, she is consulting a psychiatrist.

Discuss: Does she really love this man? Does love mean what it used to mean?

Angie had not married when the rest of her high-school crowd paired off because she wanted to go to college. Small, athletic and good at her studies, she found all sorts of things she wanted to do. She learned to scuba-dive. She bought a wet suit and swam all winter in the ocean.

She earned enough money to buy a sports car. She took flying lessons and got a pilot's license. All this while she was dating a quiet older man who said he'd wait until she felt like marrying. "He never made any demands on me, and he was understanding," she says. "So it was awfully hard to get rid of him. But I finally managed it. I realized that it would be wrong to marry him. He was—how shall I put it?—not as quick as I. He had not been to college. I would have been bored with him, and I liked him too much to do that to him." She expects to marry, sometime, but she now finds that the men around are a bit young and flabby.

"I come on strong and scare them," she says. "And I'll tell you something worse: If they don't scare easily, then I just try harder to scare them. I don't want a man unless he's got it all over me."

Discuss: Is Angie spoiled? How could her parents and guidance counselors have directed her energy into more constructive channels?

Bette is married now, but you'd never know it. Her husband invents things and stays home, where he is an inspired father to their three children, while Bette lives an intense career life as an executive in a competitive industry requiring extensive travel. Even when she is in New York her hours are long and erratic. She married following a six-year psychoanalysis during which she discovered that she wanted to make money of her own so she wouldn't have to ask a husband for money and be turned down, as her mother often was.

Discuss: Is Bette happy? Was her psychoanalysis a success? Will her children suffer? Is there anything wrong with her husband?

Linda was in love with a married man who was a devout Roman Catholic and wouldn't divorce his wife. At least, that's what Linda told all her girl friends. For years she talked about her great love and the happy times she had with him when he was able to stay with her in her midtown apartment, where she lived on a small inheritance and genteel odd jobs of research. None of us ever met him, and eventually she stopped talking about him and began having an unattached literary critic around to her apartment as a more or less regular dinner guest. The literary man was good fun and people invited him along with her to parties. She is a pretty and vivacious girl who is popular with a wide circle of friends, and although she talks about her great disappointment in not marrying and having a family, she seems to be enjoying herself.

Discuss: Did Linda really have a lover? If so, did she really want him to divorce his wife and marry her? Would she have been happier if he had?

Francie was one of the few girls whose married man actually did divorce his wife. To his amazement, she refused to marry him. "It's all right to divorce your wife, but your divorce has nothing to do with me," she explained. "I won't marry you if you got a divorce to marry me. Only if you would have gotten a divorce anyway." They had a terrible quarrel and he threatened to strangle her and bury her in the woods where the body would never be found.

After a decent interval, they made up and she married him, largely because, as she put it, there wasn't any good reason *not* to do it. But the night they were married they had their first quarrel about sex. He wanted it and she didn't feel like it.

"But we're *married* now," he insisted.

"What difference does that make?" she demanded.

"But don't you want to be a wife—my wife? All the religions of the world say . . ."

It was, as she pointed out, the first time in their five years of sleeping together that they had ever talked about religion. She sat up in bed and sobbed with anger, "How did I ever get myself into a spot like this?" When she stopped crying, she put on her clothes and left.

Discuss: What was wrong with this man?

Now you may think that these girls are simply nuts, but if you met them at a party (and you probably have) you'd remark that they were smarter and healthier than the men escorting them and that they looked better and were clearly having more fun out of life than most of the married women in the room. They've got problems, all right, and one of them is that their married women friends privately envy them while publicly pitying them. Women sense that their single status is the consequence rather than the cause of an authentic personal style, and in New York bachelor girls are a special threat because the city attracts the leftover women at the top from all over the country, and, indeed, the whole world.

The marriage gradient is especially steep for them not only because the superior men who would be their natural mates are snapped up early by marriage-bound younger girls who don't mind dropping out of college, but because superior men are more willing than superior women to tolerate a bad marriage. If they become bored with their wives, they simply brighten the lives of the superior single women in New York and further spoil them for the much less exciting men who are available for them to marry. With superior women it's the other way around. Those who took their mothers' advice and lowered their sights to the boy across the street are apt to turn up in New York, a few years later, as divorcees out for a new start. Meanwhile, the men they divorce stay home and marry local girls who can honestly bolster their badly damaged self-esteem.

But the marriage gradient isn't the whole answer. Because they are an elite in all other ways, the leftover women are also more demanding. They are confident enough to ask themselves, "Why marry *Jim*?" as well as "Why *marry* Jim?" and, ultimately, though this takes guts, "*Why* marry anyone?"

"Sure, I'd like to have someone to relax with when I get home from work," a recent divorcee told me. "But it depends on what goes with it."

"You sound just like a wary bachelor," I pointed out. And it's true. In the central city, where men and women get up in the morning and do much the same thing all day, they want the same, rather than complementary, things from each other. "I hate to talk when I first get into the house at night," another girl explained of an affair she had recently broken off. "It's a relief to have the place to myself." Many husbands feel the same way, but this girl is hardly the one to bring a man his slippers and drink.

Once you have the courage to ask, "Why get married?" you discover to your discomfort that in the central city, marriage is no longer the only way to fulfill *any* basic personal need. Marriage is still the most satisfactory as well as the cheapest and easiest way to engage in many important activities, such as rearing children, but it is no longer the *only* way to make a success even of that.

Wives can no longer do as good a job of catering, cooking, baking, butchering, nursing, teaching, sewing, child training or decorating as the specialists their husband's money can buy—nor can they expect to be as good a dancer, hostess, sounding board, business adviser, sexual partner, or showpiece as some woman he can find to specialize in one of these feminine roles. So women who are modestly affluent through their own nonbedroom efforts are finding that one man is not necessarily the best partner for chess, sex, camping, partygiving, investing, talking, plumbing, vacationing, gallery-going, and all the other activities which the city offers. No husband or wife can supply the full satisfaction a single person may derive from a love affair, a sex affair, a job, friends, a psychiatrist, or even, at the end, a top-flight trained nurse.

Traditionalists who subscribe to the sex-for-support theory assume that marriage will break down if women can support themselves. One sociologist thinks the sex-support deal can be salvaged as long as "working in the bedroom" is easier for women than jobholding. But what happens when sex is divorced from pregnancy and women want it as much as men? What happens when sexual intercourse occupies the same role in the life of a woman as it does in the life of a man?

This is, of course, what is happening. Vance Packard, like most men, finds it upsetting, a "sexual wilderness." In spite of the sly stories men have always told about the responsiveness of some women they've had, men in general—and Vance Packard speaks well of them—are threatened by the sexual demands of women *in marriage*. The sex-for-support theory to which some sociologists subscribe assumes that men are willing to pay heavily in money for nice, comfortable, undemanding, wordless, hot-and-cold-running sex they can turn on (or off) like a tap. As Francie discovered, single girls get more consideration in bed than wives, and I once heard a speaker convulse an audience of married women by referring to sexual intercourse as "what we did before we were married."

When an institution fails for the brightest, the most ambitious, the most energetic—as my editor friend liked to put it, "the best"—when this same institution fails for half the people who enter it (we now have 50 percent as many divorces as marriages), then I agree with Vance Packard that it is time to psychoanalyze, not the people who can't make it work, but the deal which is causing so many so much trouble.

The single girls of New York are acting out the dissatisfactions all women feel with traditional marriage. They are trying out new styles of marriage and non-marital man-woman relationships. This is as it should be, for they are an aristocracy—the brightest, the best, the most aspiring girls from everywhere.

THE CULTURE OF CIVILITY:
DEVIANCE AND DEMOCRACY IN SAN FRANCISCO

Howard S. Becker and Irving Louis Horowitz

Deviants of many kinds live well in San Francisco—natives and tourists alike make that observation. The city's apparently casual and easygoing response to "sex, dope and cheap thrills" (to crib the suppressed full title of Janis Joplin's famous album—itself a San Francisco product) astounds visitors from other parts of the country who can scarcely credit either what they see happening or the way natives stroll by those same events unconcerned.

☐ Walking in the Tenderloin on a summer evening, a block from the Hilton, you hear a black whore cursing at a policeman: "I wasn't either blocking the sidewalk! Why don't you motherfucking fuzz mind your own goddamn business!" The visiting New Yorker expects to see her arrested, if not shot, but the cop smiles good-naturedly and moves on, having got her back into the doorway where she is supposed to be.

☐ You enter one of the famous rock ballrooms and, as you stand getting used to the noise and lights, someone puts a lit joint of marijuana in your hand. The tourist looks for someplace to hide, not wishing to be caught in the mass arrest he expects to follow. No need to worry. The police will not come in, knowing that if they do they will have to arrest people and create disorder.

☐ Candidates for the city's Board of Supervisors make their pitch for the homosexual vote, estimated by some at 90,000. They will not be run out of town; the candidates' remarks are dutifully reported in the daily paper, as are the evaluations of them by representatives of SIR, the Society for Individual Rights.

☐ The media report (tongue in cheek) the annual Halloween Drag Ball, for which hundreds of homosexuals turn out at one of the city's major hotels in full regalia, unharassed by police.

□ One sees long-haired, bearded hippies all over the city, not just in a few preserves set aside for them. Straight citizens do not remark their presence, either by gawking, hostility or flight.

□ Nudie movies, frank enough to satisfy anyone's curiosity, are exhibited in what must be the largest number of specialty movie houses per capita in the country. Periodic police attempts to close them down (one of the few occasions when repression has been attempted) fail.

The items can be multiplied indefinitely, and their multiplicity demands explanation. Most cities in the United States refuse to let deviants indulge themselves publicly, let alone tolerate candidates who seek their bloc votes. Quite the contrary. Other cities, New York and Chicago being good examples, would see events like these as signs of serious trouble, omens of a real breakdown in law enforcement and deviance control, the forerunner of saturnalia and barbarian take-over. Because its politicians and police allow and can live with activities that would freak out their opposite numbers elsewhere, San Francisco is a natural experiment in the consequences of tolerating deviance. . . .

We can summarize this low-key approach to deviance in the phrase "a culture of civility." What are its components, and how does it maintain itself?

San Francisco prides itself on its sophistication, on being the most European of American cities, on its picturesque cosmopolitanism. The picturesque quality, indeed the quaintness, rests in part on physical beauty. As the filling of the Bay and the destruction of the skyline by high-rise buildings proceeds to destroy that beauty, the city has come to depend even more on the presence of undigested ethnic minorities. It is as though San Francisco did not wish its Italians, Chinese or Russians to assimilate and become standard Americans, preferring instead to maintain a panoply of ethnic differences: religious, cultural and culinary (especially culinary). A sophisticated, livable city, on this view, contains people, colonies and societies of all kinds. Their differences create a mosaic of life styles, the very difference of whose sight and smell give pleasure.

Like ethnic minorities, deviant minorities create enclaves whose differences add to the pleasure of city life. Natives enjoy the presence of hippies and take tourists to see their areas, just as they take them to see the gay area of Polk Street. Deviance, like difference, is a civic resource, enjoyed by tourist and resident alike. . . .

Because of that tolerance, deviants find it possible to live somewhat more openly in San Francisco than elsewhere. People do not try so hard to catch them at their deviant activities and are less likely to punish them when caught. Because they live more openly, what they do is more visible to straight members of the community. An established canon of social psychology tells us that we find it harder to maintain negative stereotypes when our personal experience belies them. We see more clearly and believe more deeply that hippies or homosexuals are not dangerous when we confront them on the street day after day or live alongside them and realize that beard plus long hair does not equal a drug-crazed maniac, that limp wrist plus lisp does not equal child-molester.

When such notions become embodied in a culture of civility, the citizenry begins to sense that "everyone" feels that way. We cannot say at what critical point a population senses that sophistication about deviance is the norm, rather than a liberal fad. But San Francisco clearly has that critical mass. To come on as an anti-deviant, in a way that would probably win friends and influence voters in more parochial areas, risks being greeted by laughter and ridicule in San Francisco. Conservatives who believe in law and order are thus inclined to keep their beliefs to themselves. The more people keep moralistic notions to themselves, the more everyone believes that tolerance is widespread. The culture maintains itself by convincing the populace that it is indeed the culture.

It gets help from public pronouncements of civic officials, who enunciate what will be taken as the collective sentiment of the city. San Francisco officials occasionally angle for the conservative vote that disapproves licentiousness. But they more frequently take the side of liberty, if not license. When the police, several years ago, felt compelled to close the first of the "topless joints," the judge threw the case out. He reasoned that Supreme Court decisions required him to take into account contemporary community standards. In his judgment San Francisco was not a prudish community; the case dismissed. The city's major paper, the *Chronicle*, approved. Few protested.

Similarly, when California's leading Yahoo, Superintendent of Public Instruction Max Rafferty, threatened to revoke the teaching credentials of any San Francisco teacher who used the obscene materials listed in the standard high school curriculum (Eldridge Cleaver's *Soul on Ice* and LeRoi Jones' *Dutchman*), the City did not remove the offending books from its curriculum. Instead, it successfully sued to have Rafferty enjoined from interfering in its operation.

In short, San Franciscans know that they are supposed to be sophisticated and let that knowledge guide their public actions, whatever their private feelings. According to another well-known law of social psychology, their private feelings often come to resemble their public actions, and they learn to delight in what frightens citizens of less civil cities.

We do not suggest that all kinds of deviation are tolerated endlessly. The police try, in San Francisco as elsewhere, to stamp out some vices and keep a ceiling on others. Some deviance frightens San Franciscans too, because it seems to portend worse to come (most recently, users and purveyors of methedrine—"speed merchants" and "speed freaks"—whose drug use is popularly thought to result in violence and crime). But the line is drawn much farther over on the side of "toleration" in San Francisco than elsewhere. A vastly wider range of activities is publicly acceptable. Despite the wide range of visible freakiness, the citizenry takes it all in stride, without the fear and madness that permeates the conventional sectors of cities like Detroit, Chicago, New York, Washington, D.C., and similar centers of undaunted virtue.

How does a culture of civility arise? Here we can only speculate, and then fragmentarily, since so few cities in the United States have one that we cannot make the comparisons that might uncover the crucial conditions. San Francisco's history suggests a number of possibilities.

It has, for one thing, a Latin heritage. Always a major seaport, it has long tolerated the vice that caters to sailors typical of such ports. It grew at the time of the gold rush in an explosive way that burst through conventional social controls. It ceded to its ethnic minorities, particularly the Chinese, the right to engage in prostitution, gambling and other activities. Wickedness and high living form part of the prized past every "tourist" city constructs for itself; some minor downtown streets in San Francisco, for instance, are named for famous madames of the gold rush era.

Perhaps more important, a major potential source of repressive action—the working class—is in San Francisco more libertarian and politically sophisticated than one might expect. Harry Bridges' longshoremen act as bellwethers. It should be remembered that San Francisco is one of the few major American cities ever to experience a general strike. The event still reverberates, and working people who might support repression of others know by personal experience that the policeman may not be their friend. Trade unionism has a left-wing, honest base which gives the city a working-class democracy and even eccentricity, rather than the customary pattern of authoritarianism.

Finally, San Francisco is a town of single people. Whatever actual proportion of the adult population is married, the city's culture is oriented toward and organized for single people. As a consequence, citizens worry less about what public deviance will do to their children, for they don't have any and don't intend to, or they move from the city when they do. (Since there are, of course, plenty of families in the city, it may be more accurate to say that there are fewer white middle-class families, that being the stratum that would, if family-based, provide the greatest number of complaints about deviance. Black, chicano and oriental populations ordinarily have enough to worry about without becoming guardians of public morality.) . . .

The example of San Francisco's handling of moral deviance may not provide the blueprint one would like for settling urban problems generally. Its requirements include a day-to-day working agreement among parties on the value of compromise and a procedure by which their immediate interests can be openly communicated and effectively adjusted. Those requirements are difficult to meet. Yet it may be that they are capable of being met in more places than we think, that even some of the knottier racial and political problems contain possibilities of accommodation, no more visible to us than the casual tolerance of deviance in San Francisco was thinkable to some of our prudish forebears.

2

THE PHYSICAL ENVIRONMENT
Urban Ecology

For many writers and artists of the past and present, the sounds, smells, sights, and sensations of the city have never been as inviting as those of the countryside. As the place where industrial life first grew strong, the city is damned on two counts. First, it is not the country and is therefore neither quiet, fragrant, nor green; second, it is the scene of the irreversible crime of the industrial revolution. For romantics, such a setting kills the imagination of people and artists. According to Irish dramatist John Millington Synge, art, for example, could only be pallid and joyless in a place where "the springtime of local life has been forgotten, and the harvest is a memory only and the straw has been turned into bricks." For such writers, bricks are bad, grass is good, and the noise of cars, not cows, will drive metropolitan man to his madness in the grand concrete canyons. Some would disagree, finding the urban environment a source of great excitement and stimulation. In the selections which follow, city people of different backgrounds and professions express their points of view on the controversial question of whether the city is a human or an inhuman environment.

The first selection deals with an obvious fact of urban life, the juxtaposition of the rich and the poor in city neighborhoods. In a pair of contrasting interviews called "Two Blocks Apart," Peter Quinn and Juan Gonzáles, two urban teenagers, talk about life in their respective neighborhoods, so different though so close.

Following these interviews are a song and two poems that continue the focus on the nature of the city's physical environment. In the first, Leonard Cohen watches the theater of the city streets from his hotel window and sings of the bad show in "Stories of the Street." Mitchell Goodman, however, finds beauty and a sense of holiness in his poem "Snow on the City Three Days Before Christmas." The third poem is by Allen Ginsberg, "By Air, Albany–Baltimore." In it, the poet takes an aerial view of snow-covered megalopolis, the huge string of central cities and their suburbs that stretches along the eastern coast from Boston to Washington, and reflects on the causes of the city's destruction.

Next is "The Physical City: A Photographic Montage" whose pictorial images complement those re-created in words by the writers in this section. They exemplify the physical scenes which have fired the imagination and outrage of sensitive city-dwellers, artists, and urban professionals.

The ecology movement is concerned with winning the war on polluted cities in a variety of controversial ways. Several of its programs are included here under the title "Eco-tactics." To evaluate them just after experiencing the powerful vision of environmental poets and photographers is to apply a difficult test; nevertheless, these and many other programs are at least being tried. The next four selections in this section move toward the positive and defend the basic faith of city lovers, evidence once again of the duality of the urban scene that envelopes us all in its ambivalent experience of pollution and promise.

In the essay "The Sounds of the City," James Tuite takes a unique and positive approach to urban noise, finding it not a pollutant but rather a celebration of the city's vitality. In "Chicago—August 24–29," Norman Mailer also feels the physical vibrations of a big city and calls them good; he finds Chicago "the last of the great American cities." Jane Jacobs explores the problems and potentialities of the city street in "The Uses of

Sidewalks: Safety." To her the streets are the city's physical arteries and should be helped to sustain their traffic of life in only positive ways. The final selection by Arthur Tress is a photographic essay "Open Spaces in the Inner City." In a creative way it contributes visual proof to the case in favor of the city as a human, dynamic environment by finding sources that can offer peace and privacy usually missed or condemned. Only city lovers with the eyes to see and the minds to imagine the possibilities could have written and photographed these four selections.

TWO BLOCKS APART

Charlotte Leon Mayerson

Juan Gonzales and Peter Quinn, two seventeen-year-old boys, live in the same New York City neighborhood. They are both high school seniors in the same school district, both Catholics in the same parish, both ballplayers with the same parks and school yards at their disposal. That they do not know each other is an urban commonplace; that they are utter strangers in the conditions of their lives, in their vision of what they themselves are, seems a personal illustration of the apparent failure of the American melting pot. . . .

The area in which these boys live contains some of the most beautiful streets in New York and also some of the ugliest. It has a large park, playgrounds and ball fields, a library, a museum, and a narcotics-addiction center. Houses scattered throughout the neighborhood are, from time to time, "raided for dope" or for prostitution. These raids take place around the corner from the many well-kept and sometimes expensive apartment houses of the area. The crime rate here is relatively low for this borough of New York City, although burglaries, muggings, and juvenile complaints have vastly increased over the neighborhood's own formerly low rate. About 30 percent of the population is classified as "nonwhite."

Juan lives in a New York Housing Authority Low Income Project, which faces on a particularly unattractive commercial area. More than nineteen hundred families live in the nine buildings that comprise the project. To qualify for residence, a family with two children can earn no more than $5,080 a year. Family income is closely checked by Housing Authority employees, who also may inspect individual apartments at will to ascertain that building rules are being complied with.

The area formerly contained small "old law tenements" and "single-room occupancy" dwellings that were condemned for bad repair, dirt, disease, and crime. Juan lived in one of these houses until it was demolished, moved to another neighborhood for a few years, and returned when the project was completed.

Peter lives in a well-kept apartment house that was built on a fairly luxurious scale in the nineteen twenties. The building is on one of the nicer streets of the neighborhood, overlooking a large park. One hundred families live in the house. A doorman is always in attendance in the front lobby and the whole atmosphere seems remarkably friendly and intimate.

JUAN GONZALES

Man, I hate where I live, the projects. I've been living in a project for the past few years and I can't stand it. First of all, no pets. I've been offered so many times dogs and cats and I can't have them because of the Housing. Then there's a watch out for the walls. Don't staple anything to the walls because then you have to pay for it. Don't hang a picture. There's a fine. And they come and they check to make sure.

Don't make too much noise. The people upstairs and the people downstairs and the people on the side of you can hear every word and they've got to get some sleep. In the project grounds you can't play ball. In the project grounds you can't stay out late. About ten o'clock they tell you to go in or to get out. Then . . . there's trouble because they don't want you to hang around in the lobby. They're right about that one thing, because like in good houses, the lobby should be sort of like a show place, I think. You know, then you could have something special.

The elevators smell and they always break and you see even very old people tracking up and down the stairs. That's when the worst thing comes. People are grabbed on the stairs and held up or raped. There was this girl on the seventh floor who was raped and there was a girl on the fourth who was raped and robbed. There was an old man who was hit over the head—about fifty years old—he was hit over the head on the stairs and beat up bad. I don't know, maybe it's not always the people who live there. Maybe there's a party going on in the next-door and there are strangers in the party. You know how it is, not everybody is a relative. And those people come out and they start fights and arguments. Or they go around banging on the doors when they are drunk.

Before, when things happened in the halls, nobody would come out for nothing. When there were muggings, nobody wanted to come out in the halls and maybe have to face a guy with a knife or a gun. Lately, though, it's a little bit more friendly. Like my mother might have some-body come into our house to learn how to make rice and beans and then I tell my mother to go with them and learn how to make some American foods for a change. So now people are beginning to see on our floor that it's better to have someone help you if you are in trouble than to be alone and face the guy.

I guess in some ways the projects are better. Like when we used to live here before the projects, there were rats and holes and the building was falling apart. It was condemned so many times and so many times the landlords fought and won. The building wasn't torn down until finally it was the last building standing. And you know what that is, the last building . . . there's no place for those rats to go, or those bugs, or no place for the bums to sleep at night except in the one building still standing. It was terrible. The junkies and the drunks would all sleep in the halls at night and my mother was real scared. That was the same time she was out of work and it didn't look to us like anything was ever going to get better.

Then they were going to tear the house down. When I was about eleven or so we moved to another neighborhood. Down there I met one of the leaders of a gang called the Athletes, and the funny thing is that even though this boy was the leader, he didn't really want to belong to a gang. He only went into it because he was alone and everybody else was belonging. What could he do? Then I got associated with him and he quit his gang and we walked along together. Finally we had a whole group of us that were on our own. We still know each other. Even now sometimes I go over there or sometimes he comes here. When I was living there, sometimes he'd go away to Puerto Rico and I was always waiting for him to come back. You know, I missed him and he missed me.

My friend kept me from that fighting gang even though he was the leader. And he lived there with us, so we didn't have any trouble on the block because other gangs were afraid to come. We all lived together— Negroes, Puerto Ricans, and Italian kids—and we got along happy before I moved.

But my mother was afraid because the gang wars near the block made the other streets dangerous. You'd have all kinds of war. The Athletes would fight the Hairies. Then the newspaper had it the Hairies were fighting somebody else. My mother wanted to transfer back here, to the old neighborhood we'd lived in before the projects came.

Well, we did. But you know, every time you move you feel like it's not right because you're leaving part of yourself back there. I used to go back down there every weekend because, when we moved back here, everything was different. The projects were up, no more small houses, all twenty-one floors. There were new kids, a new school.

That time, before I knew anyone here on the block, I would have to fight a person to get introduced, and then finally either he'd beat me or I'd beat him. That way we'd get to know each other. I was new, you know. It was my building and my neighborhood, but I was new.

I would fight one guy in front of about twenty kids and I was afraid they were going to jump me. One time I said, "Look out, one guy and all of you gonna jump me. Is that a way to fight?" The guy I was fighting said they wouldn't jump me, and we fought that day and I went home bleeding. And then the next day I didn't get anybody to help me, but I went back and we fought again, and he beat me again. Then one day, I beat him. I proved him that I had courage and that I could succeed, and then, when the other boys came, this boy I had beaten up told them to lay off me.

Like back then, when I first came back to the neighborhood, my mother didn't want me to go out with all those kids on the street. I'd say to her, "Man, what am I going to do? I don't have any friends here. All I can do is just go out and look at people. You could go crazy." There were like groups of boys around and they stuck together. There were coloreds, Puerto Ricans, and Italian boys all together. But they were all friends with each other and they didn't want anybody crashing in on them. But after those fights we shook, and that was it. From then on, I was in.

. . . White kids don't belong to gangs much. They're usually cowards. Only maybe sometimes, if one white, he lived around a colored neighborhood for a long time, and he proved he's not scared, then they take him in. Me, I'm not afraid of tough kids. It's bad when you're afraid of them. Like a Paddy boy will chicken out if he was alone. Really scared to death, you know. But not me. Oh, I was smeared a lot of times—smeared is you don't have a chance. I was jumped in the park a couple of times. I was jumped down there once by a group of guys I didn't even know. Those guys jumped on me and started beating the heck out of me, kicking, cursing, using their cigarettes. That time I went to the hospital and they patched me up and took me home. But the thing is I wasn't afraid of them. Why they did so good, what happened, was they just caught me by surprise. I mean I would have caught a couple of them and they wouldn't have been able to hurt me that badly, but the trouble was they caught me by surprise and I didn't have a chance. If I knew them I would kill them afterwards. Do you think I would come home bandaged up, and you think I'm not going to do anything about it? I get riled sometimes when a guy looks at me the wrong way. You think I'm not going to get those that got me? I'll get them one at a time if I'm alone, or all at once if I have a group with me. I'm not scared to walk down the street ever. I can handle myself and I might take on a guy, he's alone, because I've seen him act big when he's with his men and now I want to test him, like alone. But taking on a whole gang, that's another thing.

Going home from school once, there was big trouble like that. On the subway, right on the train when it was moving, some guys grabbed a couple of white school girls . . . and they raped them. I couldn't stand it, right there on the subway and they did it without interference. That's something in my life I'm not proud of.

Man, you believe me? I ran all over that train trying to find a cop. And I wouldn't have minded jumping in and stopping it, no matter what, if there was a way. I got very upset but, see, I go in there, without a knife, alone, I'm going to get my brains knocked out. Even that, I wouldn't mind so bad, if I knew the girls were going to come out all right. But I knew they were still going to be played around with.

And there was nobody else who wanted to come with me. I don't think the guys I was with, they cared at all. Nobody would help me, not old people or kids. On that whole train, nobody, nobody. I was alone.

I feel lousy about it. I mean, even now, sometimes I look at a girl and I think, "Suppose that happened again? What would I do *this* time?" And I promise myself I'll go in, no matter what. But I couldn't do anything about it that time. I'm not afraid to fight, I've been fighting all my life. But nobody would help me start a little riot and get them off those girls.

There are some times, though, when everybody in the neighborhood does get together, agrees on one thing. Like the time there was one policeman who used to tease and bother everybody around the block. It got so bad that we had to fix that policeman. So everybody got together. Nobody was on the street that day except one boy, up on a stoop. The policeman said, "Get off. Get off that stoop. You don't belong here." Well, the boy stepped quickly back and the cop came up on the stoop. Up above there on the roof, they had a garbage can and they sent it right on his head. He was in the hospital for about three or four months, something wrong with his head. And the next policeman they sent wasn't so bad; he was just bad like a regular policeman.

The police are the most crooked, the most evil. I've never seen a policeman that was fair or that was even good. All the policemen I've ever known are hanging around in the liquor store or taking money from Jim on the corner, or in the store on the avenue. They're just out to make a buck no matter how they can do it. O.K., maybe if you gave them more money they wouldn't be so crooked, but what do you need to qualify for a policeman? I mean, if you have an ounce of brain and you have sturdy shoulders and you're about six feet one, you can be a policeman. That's all.

I mean, you've got to fight them all the time. A policeman is sup-posed to be somebody that protects people. You're supposed to be able to count on them. You're supposed to look up to policemen and know that if anything goes wrong, if any boys jumped me, I can just yell and the policeman will come running and save me. Around my block, you get jumped, the police will say, "Well, that's just too bad." He just sits there.

Even the sergeants are crooked. It's the whole police force is rotten. There was a man, I don't know who he was, way out in Brooklyn some-where. He broke down a whole police station, a whole police force, the detectives, the policemen, the rookies. Everybody that was on that police force was crooked. Everybody in the precinct was crooked. He had to tell them all to go home.

Like take the Negro cop. The police towards discrimination are the same as anybody else. You have colored policemen, Italian policemen, every kind. But, you know, a Negro policeman will tend to beat up another Negro more than he would beat up anybody else, because he says to himself, "I'm a cop, and this guy is going to expect special privileges. I've got to show the other people it doesn't mean anything to me, that I'm really not going to treat them different." I think the Puerto Ricans would be just the same as the Negroes. He would tend to beat up Puerto Rican people more than he would a Negro or anybody else. Maybe you think he'd feel the Puerto Ricans were somebody he should help and he should try to solve some of their problems. But that's not the way it works.

And like I said, you think they protect you? When I lived down-town, it was a terrible neighborhood. There were so many killings, and people were being raped and murdered and all. Guys, you could see them, guys you could see jumping out of windows, running away from a robber, using a needle or something. I worked in a grocery there and I was afraid to go to work, but I guess I was lucky anyhow. I mean, I never got in any kind of real cop trouble or anything. They'd pick me up only in sort of like routine. They picked up everybody once in a while to make sure, you know, that nobody is carrying weapons and there is not going to be a fight that day. Of course, as soon as the police left, everything was the same all over again, anyhow.

That time they picked me up, I was halfway home from the grocery store where I worked and—well—I'll tell you how I felt like. I felt like the policeman was the rottenest person in the world. What would happen, see, is that I was always tall, and being tall, they think that I'm older. Then, no matter what you tell them, they believe that you're older. They were looking for a draft card and I didn't have one. I was too young and I told them I didn't have a draft card. Man, I was only twelve, thirteen or so, you know. Then they'd take me on the side and hit me a couple of times and I'd go home black and blue.

You wouldn't get picked up alone, even now. A person alone they never bother with, unless he's looking at cars or something. Whenever I get picked up, it's with a group. Like if I'm walking along and there's a group here and at the same time I'm walking, even though I don't know them, a policeman comes. They take all of us. Once I got picked up when there was a poker game going on or a crap game. They picked us up and they wanted to find out who had the money, who had the dice. They hit everybody. I think I even got hit the worst because I was a little taller than the rest of them. It happens right out on the street.

They tell you to get up against the wall of a building, and then they start searching you. And you can't talk to the policeman. Never say a word when they have you against the wall. Say anything and he thinks that you are making a false move and then he has the right to shoot you. So I would stand there and he asked my name, and I'd tell. And then he'd ask for my age and when I'd tell him twelve, thirteen, fourteen, he wouldn't believe me. They didn't think a Puerto Rican kid could be so young, so tall. Then they'd take me over the side and hit me a couple of times.

I'd be scared. Half the time I was petrified from being hit and because I was thinking of what my mother would say, you know, if I was taken down to the station. That I didn't do anything didn't make any difference to the police because I was still picked up. But I guess I was lucky because every time I was picked up I got sent home. There were a couple of boys that time that were Spanish and they didn't understand the language too well. When they tried to tell the policeman something, they got black and blue marks all over. Well, they didn't like it too much and they started trying to run away and talking back and pushing around, you know. The policeman just grabbed them, got them in the car and took them away. . . .

PETER QUINN

I've always lived in this neighborhood. My parents moved to a house up the street a few years after they got married and they lived there until we moved to this building about eleven years ago. We've lived in this same building ever since, and my aunt and uncle and cousins have lived here even longer. My grandfather still lives a few blocks away, so we Quinns really are settled in here.

The apartment house we live in has run down lately like other parts of the neighborhood. My family is afraid it's going to turn into a high-class slum. There is always something being repaired with the plumbing or the electricity, since the building is pretty old now. You have to wait a longer time to get some repairs done and my mother says the service is not nearly as good as it used to be. For example, there was always a doorman at each entrance all day and all night. Now they've taken off the doorman at the back door for a few hours during the night. Another problem is that the elevators are now self-service and it's not nearly as convenient as it used to be, when there were elevator men.

We're lucky though. There's a very funny man in the house who really does a good job about all these complaints. He organizes meetings, and gets the lawyers who live here to advise him, and the tenants to pay a yearly fee for his committee, and I don't know what else. He's really a scream. I *love* him. I think he's great when meetings are held, and he really does accomplish things. The landlord has learned by now that he can't get away with anything because we're always alert to our rights.

I don't have any complaints about our own apartment though. It's spacious and has a great view of the park and my mother and sister are really great at interior decorating. I have my own room now. I used to share it with my brother, but since he's away it's exclusively for me. His bed is still there, though, and I wouldn't be sorry to have him back using it.

Aside from my sister's room and my parent's bedroom, there's a living room, dining room, kitchen and three bathrooms. My own room is really neat, the best room I know of in the world. It's got dark brown walls and orange bedspreads. I've got a guitar on the wall, a wine bottle, my school athletic letter. I love to hang things on the wall. There are two bachelor chests in the room, one for my brother, one for myself, book-cases, and trophies on a shelf, and my own desk. My brother and I each have our own closet and we fitted them very nicely with places for shoes and athletic equipment. Then there's a great big comfortable chair in my room which is the best thing to get into when you want to be off by yourself.

Sometimes, of course, my family thinks about moving because the neighborhood, in the side streets, and over in the projects, isn't what it used to be. You hear about people being mugged now and problems with gangs and all the rest.

When I was small, I knew everybody around our street; everybody was my friend. Every day all the kids would meet out at the park—we used to call it the big park. And every day we played skully bones with bottle tops and games like that and maybe threw a ball a little bit. I had no worries then. That is, I've never fought between my own friends and there weren't so many Puerto Rican or colored kids around. Now, some-times, when I leave the house at night or have to meet off in the park somewhere, I am afraid. Or when I walk down the street and I see four Puerto Ricans—and I could tell them a mile away, not that they're Puerto Rican, but that they're that type that looks like they're going to kill any-body that steps in front of them—I am really terrified. I steer clear, I cross the street.

My friends never, never look for trouble. We don't like it. If we're coming head on to one of those gangs, we cross. I'll give them the right of way anytime if they think that makes them big. There've been a few incidents like that where these guys think that by being tough they really are getting something when it's really a laugh. Once, when I was a lot younger, a colored kid stopped me and asked me if I had any money on me. I told him I had two cents and I said, "You want it?" He answered that he did want it and that he would buy some lunch with it. I said, "Go ahead, buy all the lunch you can get with that."

Of course, not all Puerto Rican kids are like that or all colored, I guess. One guy, Fernando Gutierrez, is in our group and even he once got into trouble with them. One day we were all playing ball in the big park and he had a beautiful glove that cost his father about twenty dollars. A bunch of Puerto Rican and colored kids came out and they grabbed his glove and told him that they wouldn't give it back unless we gave them some money. Well, we chipped in and we got about fifty cents together and they sold the glove back to us for the fifty cents. They didn't even know what it was worth.

The trouble is that, living as they do, there wouldn't be much else for them to look forward to besides picking up a name for being tough. All they're looking for is a reputation, since they don't have much else to look for. I saw on a TV show once a story about a Puerto Rican boy who was really typical. That boy said that during the school year the one thing he looked forward to was lunch in the school cafeteria because it was the biggest meal he had. He kind of liked school because there isn't much for him to do otherwise except sit outside on the stoop.

Of course, they're not all like that. Two Puerto Rican boys who are with our group from our church—well, they're on our side. Because they've always gone where we've gone, they know how we think and what we like to do, and that we don't like to fight. They both go to good schools and don't have anything to do with the others. When . . . if ever there is an emergency, they're with us.

The one time we've had serious problems with those gangs was a few months ago. A group of us, about fifteen, had been up at a private pool swimming and when we came out, we were standing around saying good night. One real big kid, a friend of mine, had a soda which he was drinking and a bunch of Puerto Rican kids came along. They asked him to give them a drink out of his bottle and he wouldn't. He said that he'd just bought it and that everybody was taking a sip and that he wouldn't have anything left for himself. Well, one thing led to another, but my friend wasn't going to stand for being pushed around. He said, "I'm not going to let anyone push me or my friends around." Well, that did it. They left, but the next day the same boys came up to us, this time when we were standing in front of the gym. They gave us an ultimatum. They said that they would give us three choices: either we fight them; we back down; or we never go over onto their block. They left then and we were very worried.

Of course, there's quite a large group of us, too, who go to church, club meetings and play ball together and maybe go to dances together or date. But we are not any kind of fighting group. Nobody among us likes to fight, and we'll do anything we can to stop one. That time, it was a Saturday, and we went down to the gym in the cellar of the church and we set up chairs for the next morning's Mass. All the fellows got together there and we had a democratic meeting and a few suggestions were made. We decided that if we ever fought those boys everyone of us would be killed, really. Those Puerto Rican and colored kids from the projects can get so many others of their own kind in such a short time, it's really unbelievable. They get them from all over the city within a few hours by telephone, telling what's going on. It's sort of a chain. They're called War Lords or something like that, and they even have treaties.

We knew that, once we set up a fight, perhaps three or four hundred of them would show up. Another thing is, they'd all be armed. They have knives and chains and probably even pistols. I've never seen a Puerto Rican or a colored kid use a weapon on a white boy, though I've heard of it. What I did see was one Puerto Rican kid beat another one with a chain. That's a vicious weapon.

Well, we talked about how the incident had started, how we might have avoided it, what was going to happen that night, what the odds would be. We worked it out that it was fifteen to one against us, at the very least. The solution seemed simple. We decided to back down by saying, as we back down, that we would not go as a group into their block. We met with one or two of them and we told them that when we saw them in a gang, on the street, we wouldn't say anything, wouldn't look at them. We would just ignore them as they would ignore us. That night, a meeting was arranged, with all of us on one side of the street and all of them on the other. One of our boys went out into the middle of the street. He says he felt very frightened and could see that they had weapons with them. Well, the two leaders met in the middle and discussed the matter and it all broke up. My friend was a fast talker and got us out of this by brains and not by muscle.

The thing is that we don't have to look for reputations, we don't have to pick up a name for being good fighters. We had decided all that in our strategic meeting and we all knew that it was a stupid move to fight. All we did was to provide those fools with another notch to their guns without losing anything ourselves. When you're dealing with that type, there's nothing to be ashamed of for having more brains. I'm not sure how to say it, but I think they felt a little bigger by showing us that they could put us down, because that's how they interpreted it.

The truth of the matter is that they don't like us and we don't like them. We come from Holy Family and we're white. They either don't go to church at all or go to the other parish, and they're colored—or Puerto Rican. According to their rules, making whites ashamed, as they thought they did, was real important. Then, the next time, when they see us using the private pool, or going off to the club to play ball, or driving by in our parents' car, they could feel that they were superior. The truth is that we were smart enough not to lose our heads.

There were two policemen around that night, but they didn't do anything. The policemen just told us to walk around and go home, but they didn't interfere because there was nothing really happening. The police do step in when there's any trouble, though. For example, there's one boy who lives in the project, but he hangs around most of the time with us. One night he was cutting across the playground of the project and a bunch of kids jumped him and were beating him up pretty badly. The police came along at just the right moment and got all those kids.

In general, the police in New York do a very good job. I think all this fuss about police discrimination and so forth is not true. Perhaps, once in a while, you can get a policeman who will be too rough or dishonest, but it's that way in any large group. Another problem is that if I were a policeman and I were offered $100,000 to forget about a gambling syndicate or something like that, I'd find it very hard to refuse. And I know there must be some policemen who are weaker than I am. Even with traffic violations, if they don't jeopardize anyone's life, I think it must be very hard to resist if someone gives you some money. It doesn't matter that much.

The police are just trying to do their job and if you know your rights, you're all right. For example, a bunch of us often meet up at the luncheonette at the corner and have Cokes in the evening when there's no school. Well, the proprietor doesn't like one of my friends and one night he just pushed him out. He was buddies with the policeman on the beat and he called him. When the policeman put his hand on my friend, my friend really began shouting. He told him, "I know just who you are and what you can do to me and what you can't. If you touch me again, my father will bring suit against the whole city government. I will not be discriminated against." Well, my friend was making such a fuss and drawing such a crowd, the policeman just slunk away and we went back to drinking our Cokes.

Another time something like that happened to my best friend. He goes to Europe with his family every summer, and last year he brought back a BB gun. We went into the park to a secluded place and he was trying out his gun on some pigeons—not that he could hit them, anyhow. Well, someone must have seen us and reported us to the police. The police came into the park and as soon as my friend saw them he put the gun into his pocket. The police shouted "Stop," but when John turned around and saw them he got scared and he began to run. He ran for many blocks until finally there was a policeman in front of him and policemen on both sides and they all had their guns drawn. They shouted, "Stop, or we'll shoot." Well, John stopped and fell to the ground so he wouldn't get hit and they put handcuffs on him and took him to the police station.

By the time I saw him next day there wasn't a clean place on him. He was black and blue all over, both arms were bruised, and he was really in bad shape.

I know he shouldn't have run, but he didn't want to get caught. He knew that police regularly beat people and I know for myself that I wouldn't want to be picked up by a policeman either. If I thought I had done something wrong, I would run away as far as I could.

Well, my friend's father was out of town on business, but his mother went down to the precinct as soon as she heard. The police told her that luckily all this had taken place during the day because otherwise he might have been really hurt. They said the the ballistics report showed that the gun had only been used for BB's and so he was safe. Well, when my friend's mother saw the condition he was in, she was very angry and I think she threatened to sue. But nothing ever came of it that I heard.

The police took his gun, I guess took it home for their own kids. But, really, it was a good job they did. They didn't know what he was doing with that gun and it taught him a lesson. I'm on the law's side. After all, he could have seriously hurt somebody with those BB's which are very powerful. This way, he really learned his lesson.

In a way, it's funny that this particular boy was the one who got into trouble. He's really very smart and has very strong opinions about everything. He won a medal for the German language and I consider him one of my intellectual friends. You know, out of a large group, there are a few who are more serious-minded and perhaps who use a better vocabulary and that sort of thing.

Actually, most of my friends, my really close ones, come from the neighborhood. I know some boys at school very well, but it's not the same. Most of the kids I still see are the kids I graduated from Holy Family with. They're from this immediate area, and even though most of them are in different schools now, we still see each other. I guess you could say I belong to sort of a clique.

STORIES OF THE STREET

Leonard Cohen

The stories of the street are mine
The Spanish voices laugh
The Cadillacs go creeping down
Through the night and the poison gas
I lean from my window sill
In this old hotel I chose.
Yes, one hand on my suicide
And one hand on the rose.

I know you've heard it's over now
And war must surely come,
The cities they are broke in half
And the middle men are gone.
But let me ask you one more time
O children of the dust,
These hunters who are shrieking now
Do they speak for us?

And where do all these highways go
Now that we are free?
Why are the armies marching still
That were coming home to me?
O lady with your legs so fine
O stranger at your wheel
You are locked into your suffering
And your pleasures are the seal.

The age of lust is giving birth
But both the parents ask the nurse
To tell them fairy tales on both sides of the glass
Now the infant with his cord
Is hauled in like a kite
And one eye filled with blueprints
One eye filled with night.

O come with me my little one
And we will find that farm
And grow us grass and apples there

To keep all the animals warm
And if by chance I wake at night
And I ask you who I am
O take me to the slaughter house
I will wait there with the lamb.

With one hand on a hexagram
And one hand on a girl
I balance on a wishing well
That all men call the world
We are so small between the stars
So large against the sky
And lost among the subway crowds
I try to catch your eye.

SNOW ON THE CITY
THREE DAYS BEFORE CHRISTMAS

Mitchell Goodman

Out of a snow—
white night sky
the speaking wind
drives whiteness down
to trim grim edges of
the city, to round
them.

In the early morning,
thrust and grind
of streets is muffled, men
walk one by one, leaving
tracks to tell of their
passing. The cars are snow-
cars, and silent.

The kids who live on concrete
dig the whiteness, their hands
go into it, shape it, they
are softened by
softness.

Roofs, chimneys, bridges
are blessed with whiteness,
women return with their
shopping bags to innocence,
there is gold light on
white, there is a sense
of holiness in high places,
there is something like joy
for a morning
in the puzzled faces.

BY AIR
ALBANY–BALTIMORE
TO POE
Allen Ginsberg

Albany   throned in snow
        Hudson ribboned North ice white flats
New England's blue sky horizon'd to Space
        Age eyes: Man rides the Map,
Earth ballooned vast-bottomed . . .

It's winter, Poe, upstate New York Scythed
        into mental fields, flat arbors & hairy woods
        scattered in Pubic mounds twittering w/birds—
Nobody foresaw those wormpaths asphalted
        uphill crost bridges to small church towns, chill
        snowfields streaked with metal feces-dust.
Farmland whirlpooled into mechanic Apocalypse
        on Iron Tides!
Maelstrom roar of air-boats to Baltimore!

. . . ., Wheels drop in Sunlight, over
     Vast building-hive roofs glittering,
New York's ice agleam
    in a dying world.
        Bump down to ground
Hare Krishna Preserver!

Philadelphia smoking in Gold Sunlight, pink blue
     green Cyanide tanks sitting on hell's floor,
many chimneys Smouldering, city flats virus-linked
     along Delaware bays under horizon-smog—
airplane drifting black vapor-filaments
        above Wilmington—The iron habitations
        endless from Manhattan to the Capital.
Poe! D'jya prophesy this Smogland, this Inferno,
D'jya Dream Baltimore'd Be Seen From Heaven
by Man Poet's eyes Astounded in the Fire Haze,
                  carbon Gas aghast!
Poe! D'jya know yr prophecies' *Red Death*
would pour thru Philly's sky like Sulfurous Dreams?
Walled into Amontillado's Basement! Man
     kind led weeping drunk into the Bomb
     Shelter by Mad Secretaries of Defense!

South! from the Bearded Sleeper's Wink
at History, Hudson polluted & Susquehanna
     Brown under bridges laced with factory smoke—
Proving Grounds by Chesapeake,
        Ammunition & Artillery
Edgewood & Aberdeen
        Chemical munitions factories
hid isolate in wooden gardens, Princesses
of Industry (like Movie stars hid private in Magic
     Nauseous Mansions in Old Hollywood)—
Poe! Frankenstein! Shelley thy Prophesy,
What Demiurge assembles Matter-Factories
     to blast the Cacodemonic Planet-Mirror apart
Split atoms & Polarize Consciousness &
     let th'eternal Void leak thru the Pentagon
& cover White House with Eternal Vacuum-Dust!
Bethlehem's miles of Christ-birth Man-apocalypse

Mechano-movie Refinery along Atlantic,
Shit-brown haze worse & worse over Baltimore
    where Poe's world came to end—Red smoke,
Black water, grey sulphur clouds over Sparrows Point
    Oceanside flowing with rust, scum tide
        boiling shoreward—

Red white blue Yachts on Baltimore harbor,
    the plane bounds down above gas tanks,
gas stations, smokestacks flaring poison mist,
Superhighways razored through hairy woods,
Down to Earth Man City where Poe
    Died kidnapped by phantoms
    conspiring to win elections
        in the Deathly Gutter of the 19th Century.

THE PHYSICAL CITY:
A PHOTOGRAPHIC
MONTAGE

ECO-TACTICS

The Environmental Handbook

APPLIED ECO-TACTICS

*Boston Ecology Action distributes this leaflet at supermarkets
and large department stores.*

PACKAGING = TRASH

The packaging you take home today becomes trash tomorrow. This is costing you in terms of dollars and health. Packaging can be deceptive, disguising product contents Packaging increases the cost of the products you buy. By converting trees to paper, it upsets the forest life-cycle. You must pay high municipal taxes for trash disposal. When packaging is burned in building incinerators and city dumps, it contributes to air pollution. Burning paper gives off carbon monoxide and particulates. The new polyvinyl chloride (plastic) packaging materials, which have just been cleared by the FDA for food packaging, are even more dangerous as their incineration produces hydrochloric acid, a very toxic substance. All of these pollutants irritate your eyes, nose, throat, and lungs.

FIGHT TRASH AND POLLUTION

Carry a bag or basket with you. Don't accept unnecessary paper bags. Remove excess packaging (like boxes around bottles and toothpaste tubes) at the store and ask the sales personnel to return it to the manufacturer. PASS THIS ALONG TO A FRIEND.

Ecology Action, 925 Mass. Ave., Camb.

(For more militant action, take your own containers to the super-market, empty the products into them, and leave all commercial packaging at the counter.)

SUBWAY ACTION

*The following is a mini-leaflet that is handed out to passengers
on subway cars. It stimulates discussions and generally raises
the spirit of an otherwise dull subway ride.*

Go ahead. Read this. You don't have to watch the road the way you do when you drive the car.

CONGRATULATIONS!

By riding public transportation, you are helping to solve some of the major pollution problems plaguing Boston.

1. Air pollution.   Motor vehicles powered by internal combustion engines are responsible for over 80 percent of the deadly carbon monoxides as well as the cancer-causing benzpyrene and nitrates in the air. Eighty-nine percent of the vehicles on the road in Massachusetts are privately owned and are often operated with only one person in the car. If people would use public transportation instead of their cars, air pollution levels could be significantly lowered.

2. Space pollution.   Thirty percent of the land in downtown Boston is devoted to cars. Where there are garages, there could be gardens. Where there are highways, there should be homes and places to work and play.

3. Noise pollution.   Studies show that people today show a greater hearing loss with age than ever before. Much of this is due to honking horns, loud engines and general traffic noise.

The cost of a personal car is high to the individual. The average person pays about $2000 per car per year in depreciation, gasoline, insurance, taxes, and maintenance. *But for society as a whole, personal cars are a luxury we cannot afford.* We pay in death from auto accidents, in poor health from air pollution, in loss of hearing from noise pollution, and in the destruction of our cities by the ever increasing number of highways.

How You Can Help:

1. DO NOT DRIVE IN THE CITY.
2. Walk, whenever possible, or ride a bike.
3. Use public transportation.
4. Oppose legislation calling for more highways in the cities.
5. Support legislation for improving public transportation facilities.

SURVIVAL WALK

We have found in the closing moments of the sixties that many people are willing to make a strong commitment to new values and priorities once these values are made accessible to them. There has been enough gloom and doom, and expression of pessimism about our ability to survive the ecological crisis. However, a sinking ship cannot be abandoned without great anxiety unless everyone is confident the rescue vessel can be reached in safety, its crew friendly, and its quarters at least adequate. We want to help people get together, to help each other deal with the difficult period just ahead.

On March 21, 1970, several hundred people will begin a journey to Los Angeles, some five hundred miles to the south. We will walk all the way. We will have a few relatively smog-free vehicles with us. They will be powered by propane, electricity, and muscles. Converging walks are being planned from Santa Barbara and Irvine. Others may come from San Diego and San Bernardino. We will all gather in Los Angeles the first weekend in May to celebrate the coming of a new era—the 1970's—the Survival Decade.

We consider our passage through the towns of others a discovery process, that those individuals who share our concern, commitment and knowledge might meet one another, as well as learn of those who desire and need more information. At each town we will set up exhibits, have short plays and puppet shows, answer questions, circulate petitions. Environmental fairs will be held in at least six of the San Joaquín Valley's major cities. We plan to work closely with many people along the route of the walk—county supervisors to high school students.

We also hope to plant wildflowers along our route as well as some oak trees, to establish study plots of native grasses close to schools and colleges. We will emphasize several issues of specific interest to people living in California. Many serious problems have been created by the simplification of the Valley's diverse native ecosystems into one of the largest commercial agricultural regions on the planet.

This walk will enable all Californians, and perhaps the entire nation, to share a common experience that will address all the diverse ingredients of the survival crisis. We believe the magnitude and imminence of this crisis to be so great as to warrant a formal declaration of an international state of environmental emergency. We suggest that the first six months after calling such an emergency be devoted to *intensive* public education concerning the crisis. After that, a series of town meetings across the country should be held to accept proposals for programs, and statements of changed values and priorities. These activities would serve to develop a new consensus that would assure the emergence of values and institutions to promote environmental health. It appears that nothing short of a major cultural transformation can assure our survival.

Let us not forget our position in the world. Over three billion people are affected a little more each day by our actions. No one wants to breathe foul air, drink poisoned water or digest empty foods. We believe that no one has ever purposely decided to force this upon others. But, through our cultural practices we have given our consent to those who procure the goods and services that we feel our needs and aspirations require. When we gave this consent we were as ignorant of ecological principles as the industrialists, politicians, and businessmen. Our naive trust has resulted in widespread destruction of our life-support system. We are now withdrawing our cultural consent from them and their institutions. To do this holds uncertainties for all of us. Your personal anxiety can be reduced by facing this environmental crisis, becoming involved with the solutions and taking action rather than complaining about what someone else is or isn't doing. We must give ourselves, each other, and our surroundings the tender care we all need so much.

CLIFF AND MARY HUMPHREY

THE SOUNDS OF THE CITY

James Tuite

New York is a city of sounds: muted sounds and shrill sounds; shattering sounds and soothing sounds; urgent sounds and aimless sounds. The cliff dwellers of Manhattan—who would be racked by the silence of the lonely woods—do not hear these sounds because they are constant and eternally urban.

The visitor to the city can hear them, though, just as some animals can hear a high-pitched whistle inaudible to humans. To the casual caller to Manhattan, lying restive and sleepless in a hotel twenty or thirty floors above the street, they tell a story as fascinating as life itself. And back of the sounds broods the silence.

Night in midtown is the noise of tinseled honky-tonk and violence. Thin strains of music, usually the firm beat of rock 'n' roll or the frenzied outbursts of the discotheque, rise from ground level. This is the cacophony, the discordance of youth, and it comes on strongest when nights are hot and young blood restless.

Somewhere in the canyons below there is shrill laughter or raucous shouting. A bottle shatters against concrete. The whine of a police siren slices through the night, moving ever closer, until an eerie Doppler effect brings it to a guttural halt.

There are few sounds so exciting in Manhattan as those of fire apparatus dashing through the night. At the outset there is the tentative hint of the first-due company bullying his way through midtown traffic. Now a fire whistle from the opposite direction affirms that trouble is, indeed, afoot. In seconds, other sirens converging from other streets help the skytop listener focus on the scene of excitement.

But he can only hear and not see, and imagination takes flight. Are the flames and smoke gushing from windows not far away? Are victims trapped there, crying out for help? Is it a conflagration, or only a trash-basket fire? Or, perhaps, it is merely a false alarm.

The questions go unanswered and the urgency of the moment dissolves. Now the mind and the ear detect the snarling, arrogant bickering of automobile horns. People in a hurry. Taxicabs blaring, insisting on their checkered priority.

Even the taxi horns dwindle down to a precocious few in the gray and pink moments of dawn. Suddenly there is another sound, a morning sound that taunts the memory for recognition. The growl of a predatory monster? No, just garbage trucks that have begun a day of scavenging.

Trash cans rattle outside restaurants. Metallic jaws on sanitation trucks gulp and masticate the residue of daily living, then digest it with a satisfied groan of gears.

The sounds of the new day are businesslike. The growl of buses, so scattered and distant at night, becomes a demanding part of the traffic bedlam. An occasional jet or helicopter injects an exclamation point from an unexpected quarter. When the wind is right, the vibrant bellow of an ocean liner can be heard.

The sounds of the day are as jarring as the glare of a sun that outlines the canyons of midtown in drab relief. A pneumatic drill frays countless nerves with its rat-a-tat-tat, for dig they must to perpetuate the city's dizzy motion. After each screech of brakes there is a moment of suspension, of waiting for the thud or crash that never seems to follow.

The whistles of traffic policemen and hotel doormen chirp from all sides, like birds calling for their mates across a frenzied aviary. And all of these sounds are adult sounds, for childish laughter has no place in these canyons.

Night falls again, the cycle is complete, but there is no surcease from sound. For the beautiful dreamers, perhaps, the "sounds of the rude world heard in the day, lulled by the moonlight have all passed away," but this is not so in the city.

Too many New Yorkers accept the sounds about them as bland parts of everyday existence. They seldom stop to listen to the sounds, to think about them, to be appalled or enchanted by them. In the big city, sounds are life.

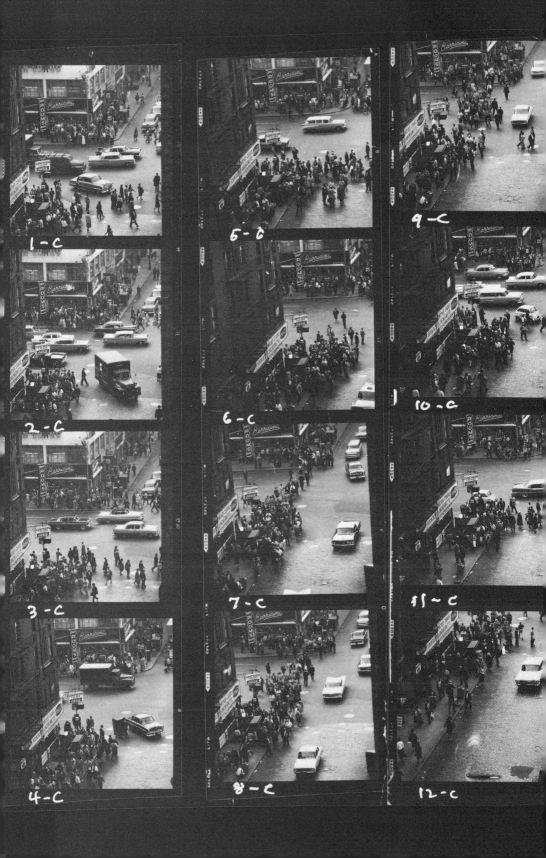

CHICAGO, AUGUST 24–29

Norman Mailer

Chicago is the great American city. New York is one of the capitals of the world and Los Angeles is a constellation of plastic, San Francisco is a lady, Boston has become Urban Renewal, Philadelphia and Baltimore and Washington wink like dull diamonds in the smog of Eastern Megalopolis, and New Orleans is unremarkable past the French Quarter. Detroit is a one-trade town, Pittsburgh has lost its golden triangle, St. Louis has become the golden arch of the corporation, and nights in Kansas City close early. The oil depletion allowance makes Houston and Dallas naught but checkerboards for this sort of game. But Chicago is a great American city. Perhaps it is the last of the great American cities.

The reporter was sentimental about the town. Since he had grown up in Brooklyn, it took him no time to recognize, whenever he was in Chicago again, that the urbanites here were like the good people of Brooklyn— they were simple, strong, warm-spirited, sly, rough, compassionate, jostling, tricky and extraordinarily good-natured because they had sex in their pockets, muscles on their back, hot eats around the corner, neighborhoods which dripped with the sauce of local legend, and real city architecture, brownstones with different windows on every floor, vistas for miles of red-brick and two-family wood-frame houses with balconies and porches, runty stunted trees rich as farmland in their promise of tenderness the first city evenings of spring, streets where kids played stick-ball and roller-hockey, lots of smoke and iron twilight. The clangor of the late nineteenth century, the very hope of greed, was in these streets. London one hundred years ago could not have looked much better.

Brooklyn, however, beautiful Brooklyn, grew beneath the skyscrapers of Manhattan, so it never became a great city, merely an asphalt herbarium for talent destined to cross the river. Chicago did not have Manhattan to preempt top branches, so it grew up from the savory of its neighborhoods to some of the best high-rise architecture in the world, and because its people were Poles and Ukrainians and Czechs as well as Irish and the rest, the city had Byzantine corners worthy of Prague or Moscow, odd tortured attractive drawbridges over the Chicago River, huge Gothic spires like the skyscraper which held the Chicago *Tribune*, curves and abutments and balconies in cylindrical structures thirty stories high twisting in and out of the curves of the river, and fine balustrades in its parks. Chicago had a North Side on Lake Shore Drive where the most elegant apartment buildings in the world could be found—Sutton Place in New York betrayed the cost analyst in the eye of the architect next to these palaces of glass and charcoal colored steel. In superb back streets behind the towers on the lake were brownstones which spoke of ironies, cupidities and intricate ambition in the fists of the robber barons who commissioned them—substantiality, hard work, heavy drinking, carnal meats of pleasure, and a Midwestern sense of how to arrive at upper-class decorum were also in the American grandeur of these few streets. If there was a fine American aristocracy of deportment, it was probably in the clean, tough, keen-eyed ladies of Chicago one saw on the streets off Lake Shore Drive on the near North Side of Chicago.

Not here for a travelogue—no need then to detail the Loop, in death like the center of every other American city, but what a dying! Old department stores, old burlesque houses, avenues, dirty avenues, the El with its nineteenth-century dialogue of iron screeching against iron about a turn, and caverns of shadow on the pavement beneath, the grand hotels with their massive lobbies, baroque ceilings, resplendent as Roman bordellos, names like Sheraton-Blackstone, Palmer House, red fields of carpet, a golden cage for elevator, the unheard crash of giant mills stamping new shapes on large and obdurate materials is always pounding in one's inner ear—Dreiser had not written about Chicago for nothing.

To the West of the Lake were factories and Ciceros, Mafia-lands and immigrant lands; to the North, the suburbs, the Evanstons; to the South were Negro ghettos of the South Side—belts of Black men amplifying each the resonance of the other's cause—the Black belt had the Blackstone Rangers, the largest gang of juvenile delinquents on earth, 2,000 by some count—one could be certain the gang had leaders as large in potential as Hannibal or Attila the Hun—how else account for the strength and wit of a stud who would try to rise so high in the Blackstone Rangers?

Further South and West were enclaves for the University of Chicago, more factories, more neighborhoods for Poles, some measure of more good hotels on the lake, and endless neighborhoods—white neighborhoods which went for miles of ubiquitous dingy wood houses with back yards, neighborhoods to hint of Eastern Europe, Ireland, Tennessee, a gathering of all the clans of the Midwest, the Indians and Scotch-Irish, Swedes, some Germans, Italians, Hungarians, Rumanians, Finns, Slovaks, Slovenes—it was only the French who did not travel. In the Midwest, land spread out; not five miles from the Loop were areas as empty, deserted, enormous and mournful by night as the outer freight yards of Omaha. Some industrial desert or marsh would lie low on the horizon, an area squalling by day, deserted by night, except for the hulking Midwestern names of the boxcars and the low sheds, the warehouse buildings, the wire fences which went along the side of unpaved roads for thousands of yards.

The stockyards were like this, the famous stockyards of Chicago were at night as empty as the railroad sidings of the moon. Long before the Democratic Convention of 1968 came to the Chicago Amphitheatre, indeed eighteen years ago when the reporter had paid his only previous visit, the area was even then deserted at night, empty as the mudholes on a battlefield after a war has passed. West of the Amphitheatre, railroad sidings seemed to continue on for miles, accompanied by those same massive low sheds larger than armories, with pens for tens of thousands of frantic beasts, cattle, sheep, and pigs, animals in an orgy of gorging and dropping and waiting and smelling blood. In the slaughterhouses, during the day, a carnage worthy of the Disasters of War took place each morning and afternoon. Endless files of animals were led through pens to be stunned on the head by hammers, and then hind legs trussed, be hoisted up on hooks to hang head down, and ride along head down on an overhead trolley which brought them to Negroes or whites, usually huge, the whites most often Polish or Hunkies (hence the etymology of Honkie— a Chicago word), the Negroes up from the South, huge men built for the shock of the work, slash of a knife on the neck of the beast and gouts of blood to bathe their torso (stripped of necessity to the waist) and blood to splash their legs. The animals passed a psychic current back along the overhead trolley—each cut throat released its scream of death into the throat not yet cut and just behind, and that penultimate throat would push the voltage up, drive the current back and further back into the screams of every animal upside down and hanging from that clanking overhead trolley, bare electric bulbs screaming into the animal eye and brain, gurglings and awesome hollows of sound coming back from the open plumbing ahead of the cut jugular as if death were indeed a rapids along some underground river, and the fear and absolute anguish of beasts dying upside down further ahead passed back along the line, back all the way to the corrals and the pens, back even to the siding with the animals still in boxcars, back, who knew—so high might be the psychic voltage of the beast—back to the farm where first they were pushed into the truck which would take them into the train. What an awful odor the fear of absolute and unavoidable death gave to the stool and stuffing and pure vomitous shit of the beasts waiting in the pens in the stockyard, what a sweat of hell-leather, and yet the odor, no, the titanic stench, which rose from the yards was not so simple as the collective diarrhetics of an hysterical army of beasts, no, for after the throats were cut and the blood ran in rich gutters, red light on the sweating backs of the red throat-cutters, the dying and some just-dead animals clanked along the overhead, arterial blood spurting like the nip-ups of a little boy urinating in public, the red-hot carcass quickly encountered another Black or Hunkie with a long knife on a long stick who would cut the belly from chest to groin and a stew and a stink of two hundred pounds of stomach, lungs, intestines, mucosities, spleen, exploded cowflop and pigshit, blood, silver lining, liver, mother-of-pearl tissue, and general gag-all would flop and slither over the floor, the man with the knife getting a good blood-splatting as he dug and twisted with his blade to liberate the roots of the organ, intestine and impedimenta still integrated into the meat and bone of the excavated existence he was working on.

Well, the smell of the entrails and that agonized blood electrified by all the outer neons of ultimate fear got right into the grit of the stockyard stench. Let us pass over into the carving and the slicing, the boiling and scraping, annealing and curing of the flesh in sugars and honeys and smoke, the cooking of the cow carcass, stamp of the inspector, singeing of the hair, boiling of hooves, grinding of gristle, the wax-papering and the packaging, the foiling and the canning, the burning of the residue, and the last slobber of the last unusable guts as it went into the stockyard furnace, and up as stockyard smoke, burnt blood and burnt bone and burnt hair to add their properties of specific stench to fresh blood, fresh entrails, fresh fecalities already all over the air. It is the smell of the stockyards, all of it taken together, a smell so bad one must go down to visit the killing of the animals or never eat meat again. Watching the animals be slaughtered, one knows the human case—no matter how close to angel we may come, the butcher is equally there. So be it. Chicago makes for hard minds. On any given night, the smell may go anywhere—down to Gary to fight with the smog and the coke, out to Cicero to quiet the gangs with their dreams of gung ho and mop-up, North to Evanston to remind the polite that *inter faeces et urinam* are we born, and East on out to Lake Michigan where the super felicities in the stench of such earth-bound miseries and corruptions might cheer the fish with the clean spermy deep waters of their fate.

Yes, Chicago was a town where nobody could ever forget how the money was made. It was picked up from floors still slippery with blood, and if one did not protest and take a vow of vegetables, one knew at least that life was hard, life was in the flesh and in the massacre of the flesh— one breathed the last agonies of beasts. So something of the entrails and the secrets of the gut got into the faces of native Chicagoans. A great city, a strong city with faces tough as leather hide and pavement, it was also a city where the faces took on the broad beastiness of ears which were dull enough to ignore the bleatings of the doomed, noses battered enough to smell no more the stench of every unhappy end, mouths—fat mouths or slit mouths—ready to taste the gravies which were the reward of every massacre, and eyes, simple pig eyes, which could look the pig truth in the face. In any other city, they would have found technologies to silence the beasts with needles, quarter them with machines, lull them with Mu-zak, and have stainless steel for floors, aluminum beds to take over the old overhead trolley—animals would be given a shot of vitamin-enrichment before they took the last ride. But in Chicago, they did it straight, they cut the animals right out of their hearts—which is why it was the last of the great American cities, and people had great faces, carnal as blood, greedy, direct, too impatient for hypocrisy, in love with honest plunder. They were big and human and their brother in heaven was the slaughtered pig—they did not ignore him. If the yowls and moans of his extinction was the broth of their strength, still they had honest guts to smell him to the end—they did not flush the city with Odorono or Pinex or No-Scent, they swilled the beer and assigned the hits and gave America its last chance at straight-out drama. Only a great city provides honest spectacle, for that is the salvation of the schizophrenic soul. Chicago may have beasts on the street, it may have a giant of fortitude for Mayor who grew into a beast—a man with the very face of Chicago—but it is an honest town, it does not look to incubate psychotics along an air-conditioned corridor with a vinyl floor.

THE USES OF SIDEWALKS: SAFETY

Jane Jacobs

Streets in cities serve many purposes besides carrying vehicles, and city sidewalks—the pedestrian parts of the streets—serve many purposes be-sides carrying pedestrians. These uses are bound up with circulation but are not identical with it and in their own right they are at least as basic as circulation to the proper workings of cities.

A city sidewalk by itself is nothing. It is an abstraction. It means something only in conjunction with the buildings and other uses that border it, or border other sidewalks very near it. The same might be said of streets, in the sense that they serve other purposes besides carrying wheeled traffic in their middles. Streets and their sidewalks, the main public places of a city, are its most vital organs. Think of a city and what comes to mind? Its streets. If a city's streets look interesting, the city looks interesting; if they look dull, the city looks dull.

More than that, and here we get down to the first problem, if a city's streets are safe from barbarism and fear, the city is thereby tolerably safe from barbarism and fear. When people say that a city, or a part of it, is dangerous or is a jungle what they mean primarily is that they do not feel safe on the sidewalks.

But sidewalks and those who use them are not passive beneficiaries of safety or helpless victims of danger. Sidewalks, their bordering uses, and their users, are active participants in the drama of civilization versus barbarism in cities. To keep the city safe is a fundamental task of a city's streets and its sidewalks.

This task is totally unlike any service that sidewalks and streets in little towns or true suburbs are called upon to do. Great cities are not like towns, only larger. They are not like suburbs, only denser. They differ from towns and suburbs in basic ways, and one of these is that cities are, by definition, full of strangers. To any one person, strangers are far more common in big cities than acquaintances. More common not just in places of public assembly, but more common at a man's own doorstep. Even residents who live near each other are strangers, and must be, because of the sheer number of people in small geographical compass.

The bedrock attribute of a successful city district is that a person must feel personally safe and secure on the street among all these strangers. He must not feel automatically menaced by them. A city district that fails in this respect also does badly in other ways and lays up for itself, and for its city at large, mountain on mountain of trouble.

Today barbarism has taken over many city streets, or people fear it has, which comes to much the same thing in the end. "I live in a lovely, quiet residential area," says a friend of mine who is hunting another place to live. "The only disturbing sound at night is the occasional scream of someone being mugged." It does not take many incidents of violence on a city street, or in a city district, to make people fear the streets. And as they fear them, they use them less, which makes the streets still more unsafe.

To be sure, there are people with hobgoblins in their heads, and such people will never feel safe no matter what the objective circumstances are. But this is a different matter from the fear that besets normally prudent, tolerant and cheerful people who show nothing more than common sense in refusing to venture after dark—or in a few places, by day—into streets where they may well be assaulted, unseen or unrescued until too late.

The barbarism and the real, not imagined, insecurity that gives rise to such fears cannot be tagged a problem of the slums. The problem is most serious, in fact, in genteel-looking "quiet residential areas" like that my friend was leaving.

It cannot be tagged as a problem of older parts of cities. The problem reaches its most baffling dimensions in some examples of rebuilt parts of cities, including supposedly the best examples of rebuilding, such as middle-income projects. The police precinct captain of a nationally admired project of this kind (admired by planners and lenders) has recently admonished residents not only about hanging around outdoors after dark but has urged them never to answer their doors without knowing the caller. Life here has much in common with life for the three little pigs or the seven little kids of the nursery thrillers. The problem of sidewalk and doorstep insecurity is as serious in cities which have made conscientious efforts at rebuilding as it is in those cities that have lagged. Nor is it illuminating to tag minority groups, or the poor, or the outcast with responsibility for city danger. There are immense variations in the degree of civilization and safety found among such groups and among the city areas where they live. Some of the safest sidewalks in New York City, for example, at any time of day or night, are those along which poor people or minority groups live. And some of the most dangerous are in streets occupied by the same kinds of people. All this can also be said of other cities.

Deep and complicated social ills must lie behind delinquency and crime, in suburbs and towns as well as in great cities. . . . It is sufficient, at this point, to say that if we are to maintain a city society that can diagnose and keep abreast of deeper social problems, the starting point must be, in any case, to strengthen whatever workable forces for maintaining safety and civilization do exist—in the cities we do have. To build city districts that are custom made for easy crime is idiotic. Yet that is what we do.

The first thing to understand is that the public peace—the sidewalk and street peace—of cities is not kept primarily by the police, necessary as police are. It is kept primarily by an intricate, almost unconscious, network of voluntary controls and standards among the people themselves, and enforced by the people themselves. In some city areas—older public housing projects and streets with very high population turnover are often conspicuous examples—the keeping of public sidewalk law and order is left almost entirely to the police and special guards. Such places are jungles. No amount of police can enforce civilization where the normal, casual enforcement of it has broken down.

The second thing to understand is that the problem of insecurity cannot be solved by spreading people out more thinly, trading the characteristics of cities for the characteristics of suburbs. If this could solve danger on the city streets, then Los Angeles should be a safe city because superficially Los Angeles is almost all suburban. It has virtually no districts compact enough to qualify as dense city areas. Yet Los Angeles cannot, any more than any other great city, evade the truth that, being a city, it *is* composed of strangers not all of whom are nice. Los Angeles' crime figures are flabbergasting. Among the seventeen standard metropolitan areas with populations over a million, Los Angeles stands so pre-eminent in crime that it is in a category by itself. And this is markedly true of crimes associated with personal attack, the crimes that make people fear the streets.

Los Angeles, for example, has a forcible rape rate (1958 figures) of 31.9 per 100,000 population, more than twice as high as either of the next two cities, which happen to be St. Louis and Philadelphia; three times as high as the rate of 10.1 for Chicago, and more than four times as high as the rate of 7.4 for New York.

In aggravated assault, Los Angeles has a rate of 185, compared with 149.5 for Baltimore and 139.2 for St. Louis (the two next highest), and with 90.9 for New York and 79 for Chicago.

The overall Los Angeles rate for major crimes is 2,507.6 per 100,000 people, far ahead of St. Louis and Houston, which come next with 1,634.5 and 1,541.1, and of New York and Chicago, which have rates of 1,145.3 and 943.5.

The reasons for Los Angeles' high crime rates are undoubtedly complex, and at least in part obscure. But of this we can be sure: thinning out a city does not insure safety from crime and fear of crime. This is one of the conclusions that can be drawn within individual cities too, where pseudosuburbs or superannuated suburbs are ideally suited to rape, muggings, beatings, hold-ups and the like.

Here we come up against an all-important question about any city street: How much easy opportunity does it offer to crime? It may be that there is some absolute amount of crime in a given city, which will find an outlet somehow (I do not believe this). Whether this is so or not, different kinds of city streets garner radically different shares of barbarism and fear of barbarism.

Some city streets afford no opportunity to street barbarism. The streets of the North End of Boston are outstanding examples. They are probably as safe as any place on earth in this respect. Although most of the North End's residents are Italian or of Italian descent, the district's streets are also heavily and constantly used by people of every race and background. Some of the strangers from outside work in or close to the district; some come to shop and stroll; many, including members of minority groups who have inherited dangerous districts previously abandoned by others, make a point of cashing their paychecks in North End stores and immediately making their big weekly purchases in streets where they know they will not be parted from their money between the getting and the spending.

Frank Havey, director of the North End Union, the local settlement house, says, "I have been here in the North End twenty-eight years, and in all that time I have never heard of a single case of rape, mugging, molestation of a child or other street crime of that sort in the district. And if there had been any, I would have heard of it even if it did not reach the papers." Half a dozen times or so in the past three decades, says Havey, would-be molesters have made an attempt at luring a child or, late at night, attacking a woman. In every such case the try was thwarted by passers-by, by kibitzers from windows, or shopkeepers.

Meantime, in the Elm Hill Avenue section of Roxbury, a part of inner Boston that is suburban in superficial character, street assaults and the ever present possibility of more street assaults with no kibitzers to protect the victims, induce prudent people to stay off the sidewalks at night. Not surprisingly, for this and other reasons that are related (dispiritedness and dullness), most of Roxbury has run down. It has become a place to leave.

I do not wish to single out Roxbury or its once fine Elm Hill Avenue section especially as a vulnerable area; its disabilities, and especially its Great Blight of Dullness, are all too common in other cities too. But differences like these in public safety within the same city are worth noting. The Elm Hill Avenue section's basic troubles are not owing to a criminal or a discriminated against or a poverty-stricken population. Its troubles stem from the fact that it is physically quite unable to function safely and with related vitality as a city district.

Even within supposedly similar parts of supposedly similar places, drastic differences in public safety exist. An incident at Washington Houses, a public housing project in New York, illustrates this point. A tenants' group at this project, struggling to establish itself, held some outdoor ceremonies in mid-December 1958, and put up three Christmas trees. The chief tree, so cumbersome it was a problem to transport, erect, and trim, went into the project's inner "street," a landscaped central mall and promenade. The other two trees, each less than six feet tall and easy to carry, went on two small fringe plots at the outer corners of the project where it abuts a busy avenue and lively cross streets of the old city. The first night, the large tree and all its trimmings were stolen. The two smaller trees remained intact, lights, ornaments and all, until they were taken down at New Year's. "The place where the tree was stolen, which is *theoretically* the most safe and sheltered place in the project, is the same place that is unsafe for people too, especially children," says a social worker who had been helping the tenants' group. "People are no safer in that mall than the Christmas tree. On the other hand, the place where the other trees were safe, where the project is just one corner out of four, happens to be safe for people."

This is something everyone already knows: A well-used city street is apt to be a safe street. A deserted city street is apt to be unsafe. But how does this work, really? And what makes a city street well used or shunned? Why is the sidewalk mall in Washington Houses, which is supposed to be an attraction, shunned? Why are the sidewalks of the old city just to its west not shunned? What about streets that are busy part of the time and then empty abruptly?

A city street equipped to handle strangers, and to make a safety asset, in itself, out of the presence of strangers, as the streets of successful city neighborhoods always do, must have three main qualities:

First, there must be a clear demarcation between what is public space and what is private space. Public and private spaces cannot ooze into each other as they do typically in suburban settings or in projects.

Second, there must be eyes upon the street, eyes belonging to those we might call the natural proprietors of the street. The buildings on a street equipped to handle strangers and to insure the safety of both residents and strangers, must be oriented to the street. They cannot turn their backs or blank sides on it and leave it blind.

And third, the sidewalk must have users on it fairly continuously, both to add to the number of effective eyes on the street and to induce the people in buildings along the street to watch the sidewalks in sufficient numbers. Nobody enjoys sitting on a stoop or looking out a window at an empty street. Almost nobody does such a thing. Large numbers of people entertain themselves, off and on, by watching street activity. . . .

OPEN SPACES IN THE INNER CITY

Photographs and Text by Arthur Tress

The enjoyable quality of urban life has not kept up with the advances of our modern life. We have put a man on the moon before we have solved the problem of collecting our cities' garbage. Our metropolitan centers daily grow more impossible to live in as millions of Americans congregate about our large urban areas. We have come up with few intelligent solutions to this crisis. Air, water, and trash pollution destroy our pleasure in the environment, while overcrowding and bad planning make it impracticable to find relaxation or escape from the cities' intense pressures. On weekends the countryside is practically out of reach because of heavy traffic on already over-congested roads. And for those without even the mobility of cars, the poor, it is certainly impossible because of inadequate public transportation facilities. According to the National Report on Civil Disorders, one of the reasons for the summer riots in the ghettos across

our country was "inadequate recreational facilities," along with unemployment, police brutality, and slum housing. "It's the youngsters who start the disturbances, the fact that our kids had no place to go was a big factor in our disorders this summer," stated one director of a summer youth program. It is from the streets where our critical disturbances erupt. Their message is the same: the American city is a cage and the smoke and ashes of civil disorder are the explosive efforts of the young to escape from its claustrophobic walls. No city today can afford a Central Park. But can cities afford to settle for the street as a substitute? Are ghetto children allergic to grass simply because they were raised on concrete? The human spirit and body needs open space in order to be a healthy and vital organism and the vistas of nature if it is to expand to its fullest and happiest capacity. City planners and urban designers have recently begun to explore the possibilities of bringing "open spaces" into the inner city "where the people are"—to meet the day to day needs of the population in their desire for a bit of quiet relaxation and peace.

Waterfront: American cities have often been located in great harbors or along rivers. They are surrounded by miles of coastal areas or river frontage, which has usually been crowded with docks, piers, factories, or railroads. People have usually been cut off from their waterfront by expressways or railroad tracks. Many planners feel it is necessary to reorient the city towards its waterfront where one can take advantage of the view and cool breezes that the water offers.

Rights of way: As transportation systems become modernized, cities find themselves with miles of abandoned aqueducts, canals, freight yards, elevated highways, and bridges. With the growth of leisure time activities such as hiking, biking, and horseback riding, many of these long narrow strips could be cleared out and made into excellent trails systems. The areas under bridges, instead of being wasted for junk lots or parking, could be made into needed recreation spaces.

3

HOUSING
Wreck and Renew

The buildings that make up the urban landscape, that tyrannize over it while they inspire our long-distance view, compel our attention in both old and new ways, because these buildings are a crucial factor in the physical environment discussed in Section 2. As a result of urbanization, brick, concrete, asphalt, glass, and steel have replaced the wood, mortar, and flagstone, the gardens and surrounding forests of the past. Our perception of this modern landscape must be in practical terms, and aesthetic terms as well—before the crumbling brick, fallen plaster, and surface soot disease our vision and destroy our few remaining fine buildings.

The housing issue is symbolized in the comparison of the skylines of towering apartments with the sprawls of congested tenements. We may look toward the sky, wondering at man's achievements, and at the same time look down to the boarded-up, burned-out places in every city, wondering at man's waste. Where and how are the great numbers of city people to live? With what accommodations? With what invisible or very visible geographic boundaries? With what response to mass relocation due to urban renewal and other building projects? Taken as a whole, this section attempts a penetrating look at being "home" in the city.

Langston Hughes' poem "Ballad of the Landlord" is the first selection focusing on housing. It is a modern ballad, and the episode it describes concerns the fate of a tenement dweller who refuses to pay his back rent to a slum landlord. Another aspect of the tenement struggle is taken up in the next selection, three articles on lead poisoning. Together these newspaper articles are a poignant social drama about a fatal problem confronted by municipal bureaucracy on the one hand and creative young activists on the other. The dates of the articles are as important as the pages they appeared on.

Third in this housing section are "Two Voices on Public Housing," an issue some feel is foremost on the urban scene. M. Stanton Evans in "Urban Dilemma" discusses the gigantic Pruitt-Igoe project in St. Louis and decides that public housing is not the answer to the ghetto but an "unqualified disaster." Walter Rybeck, however, in "The Houses Uncle Sam Builds" weighs the pros and cons of project living and sees some possibilities with appropriate expenditures.

The next selections are two poetic responses to city buildings. Herbert Woodward Martin's poem "Observation to the Empire State Building" reveals both wonderment and despair at the great building and the "semblance of life" around it. "Clark Street" is the address of a boarded-up "derelict building" waiting for the wreckers. The poet Barbara Harr muses on the defaced walls and the life they once held.

Such considerations of what man has done in building the environment that houses him lead us to some creative ideas for solving his problems. The next four selections address themselves to ideas that have been either proposed or tried in cities.

Clarence Funnyé, in "Deghettoization—Choice of the New Militancy," chooses to break up the urban ghetto for very poignant reasons. He does not romanticize ghetto life. "Harlem," a poem by Queens College student Richie Orange, however, responds to Funnyé's argument by re-creating the ghetto's life and spirit that would be lost in a move to the suburbs.

The photographic collection "Street Art," a visual essay in color, reaffirms the connection between this and the previous section on the physical environment. Street art is a highly aesthetic form of wall graffiti. Such a response to city buildings beautifies the physical and spirtual environment in a fresh way that is becoming an indigenous urban art form. Both amateur and professional artists are working on the walls of buildings, fences, storefronts, and even litter baskets and fire hydrants. These color and black and white reproductions are exciting examples.

The final selection reports one of the remaining many dramatic concepts conceived to help the housing problem. In "Slums: Instant Renewal," we see how in only 48 hours a dilapidated tenement was completely modernized to the delight of its occupants.

BALLAD OF THE LANDLORD

Langston Hughes

Landlord, landlord,
My roof has sprung a leak.
Don't you 'member I told you about it
Way last week?

Landlord, landlord,
These steps is broken down.

When you come up yourself
It's a wonder you don't fall down.

Ten Bucks you say I owe you?
Ten Bucks you say is due?
Well, that's Ten Bucks more'n I'll pay you
Till you fix this house up new.

What? You gonna get eviction orders?
You gonna cut off my heat?
You gonna take my furniture and
Throw it in the street?

Um-huh! You talking high and mighty.
Talk on—till you get through.
You ain't gonna be able to say a word
If I land my fist on you.

Police! Police!
Come and get this man!
He's trying to ruin the government
And overturn the land!

Copper's whistle!
Patrol bell!
Arrest.

Precinct Station.
Iron cell.
Headlines in press:

MAN THREATENS LANDLORD

. .

TENANT HELD NO BAIL

. .

JUDGE GIVES NEGRO 90 DAYS IN COUNTY JAIL

THE CRIME OF LEAD POISONING

LEAD POISONING: SILENT EPIDEMIC IN THE SLUMS

Jack Newfield

Except for its ironic name, Tiffany Street looks like a hundred other decaying streets in the Southeast Bronx. Mounds of uncollected garbage strewn all over. Idle young black and Puerto Rican men sitting on crumbling stoops. Mangy dogs looking through the garbage for scraps. Boarded up, burnt out houses freckled with graffiti.

At number 1051, on the fourth floor of a tenement whose dark halls stink from urine, Brenda Scurry was sitting in her clean, neat apartment telling me how her 23-month-old daughter Janet had died of lead poisoning in April.

Brenda, 23, is pretty, street smart, and black. She writes informed and angry letters to President Nixon—and gets back impersonal form letters thanking her for interest in the "New Federalism." She has two other children, four- and five-year-old boys. Her husband works in the garment center, and sometimes lives at home. That morning Brenda had gone to the local public school and discovered her five-year-old sitting in a third-grade class, and had to explain to the indifferent teacher that her child belonged in kindergarten.

"I use to live at 1113 Teller Avenue" she began quietly, but with a bittersweet edge to her voice. "Plaster from the walls started falling all over the place last November. I asked the landlord a couple times to do something about it, but he never did. Then in April one morning my daughter wouldn't eat anything. She started trembling and couldn't breathe. I got scared and she started to change colors. A neighbor called a policeman and we took her to Morisannia Hospital. A doctor looked at her and told me to go home, that she would be okay. They didn't know what it was, but they sent me home. They asked me if Janet ever ate paint or plaster, and I told them yes. I went home but her temperature kept going up and down. After five days they gave her a blood test for lead poisoning. And then she died the next day. The day after she died, the blood test came back positive. . . . Later they sent me a death certificate that said Janet died of natural causes. The doctors did an autopsy, but I still haven't got the results. I called the administrative director of the hospital twice, and they still haven't sent it to me. The hospital doesn't want to say it was lead, I guess.

"I asked welfare if they would pay for Janet's funeral, but they made me fill out a bunch of forms. So I paid for the funeral with the rent money. Then I asked welfare to pay for the rent. They said I had to fill out some other papers and that it would take a while. Then I got an eviction notice. I went to the central welfare office with it, but they still wouldn't give me any money. So I borrowed some money and moved out because I didn't want that landlord to put me on the street."

Lead poisoning is a disease endemic to the slums. The victims are hungry, unsupervised children between the ages of one and six, who get it by eating pieces of paint and plaster from flaking walls. Lead in paint was outlawed 20 years ago, but the bottom layers of walls in 800,000 run-down dwelling units in New York City still contain poisonous lead.

The city estimates that about 30,000 children each year suffer lead poisoning, but only 600 cases were reported during each of the last three years. (There are probably 300,000 victims nationally.) The early symptoms are vague—nausea, lethargy, vomiting, crankiness—and doctors and nurses are not trained to look for it since they are told that lead has been outlawed as a paint ingredient. Ghetto parents are also ignorant of the disease. In three years, Harlem Hospital has not reported a single case of lead poisoning.

But surveys by researchers and activists keep discovering thousands of undiagnosed cases living in the ghettos; lead poisoning has been called "the silent epidemic" by microbiologist Dr. Rene DuBos of Rockefeller University, a Pulitzer Prize winner last year.

According to doctors, five percent of the children who eat lead die. Of those who survive, about 40 percent suffer permanent brain damage, mental retardation, and deterioration of intelligence. A recent Chicago study of 425 children who had been treated for lead poisoning showed that 39 percent had neurological disorders years later, and 22 percent suffered from mental retardation as adults.

Two young, white, middle-class radicals have taken up the cause of lead poisoning, and for a year now have been waging a lonely crusade, bereft of money, manpower, or organizational support, to pressure the city and the health establishment, and to alert parents. One is red-haired, 30-year-old Paul Du Brul, the housing director of the University Settlement House on the Lower East Side. The other is bearded, 24-year-old Glenn Paulson, co-chairman of the Scientists' Committee for Public Information.

Du Brul met me for lunch two weeks ago. He was particularly frustrated that day over the media's failure to take an interest in lead poisoning. He had called the Post's Joe Kahn earlier that morning, and Kahn had apologized, but the city desk wasn't interested in a story without a hard news peg. The Times had printed a story a few months before, but it had been buried in the real estate section on a Sunday, "where only landlords would see it."

Mrs. Scurry had written a personal letter to the Timesman who wrote the Sunday story, telling him of her experience with her landlord, the hospital, and the Welfare Department. And he wrote back a moving lettter how he felt lead poisoning was a tragic problem, but there just wasn't a news story in her case because the hospital denied lead was the cause of her daughter's death.

And lead was a story hard to make visible or dramatic for the television networks. It didn't involve famous leaders, or exotic militants, or public violence. How do you show a *process*, how do you show indifference, how do you show invisible, institutionalized injustice, in two minutes on Huntley-Brinkley? How do you induce the news department of a television network to get outraged about nameless black babies eating tenement paint, when the public health profession, school teachers, housing experts, scientists, the NAACP, and the politicians haven't given a damn?

Du Brul then began to explore some of the ramifications of this silent epidemic.

"Look," he said, "doctors say the effect of lead poisoning is to damage the nervous system. Kids can't concentrate. They become disruptive and lose points on I.Q. tests. So I think some of Jensen's findings (geneticist Arthur Jensen) about race and chromosomes might just be the effects of environmental conditions like lead poisoning. In the last ten years, 300,000 slum kids have been sent into the New York City public school system with lead poisoning. They're not culturally inferior; they're sick. What are now considered problems of remedial education might be doctors' problems, not teachers' problems."

Two nights later Du Brul and Paulson went to Judson Church on Washington Square to speak to a meeting of about 75 doctors, nurses, interns, and radical students sponsored by Health-PAC (Policy Advisory Center). Here the discussion focused on tactics, on how to fight the problems, how to make it visible.

Du Brul proposed a "fill the hospitals" strategy, coupled with the demand that every slum child between one and six receive a free laboratory test to determine if there is lead in his system. He said Chicago and Baltimore had been using a test that has proved 90 percent effective, and the Lindsay Administration was holding back because of "bureaucratic bungling."

Some of the radical young doctors at the meeting disagreed. They said the hospitals would not, and could not, absorb the 30,000 walking cases in the city. They argued that such a tactic would collapse the already fragile hospital system. A few proposed rent strikes to force landlords to remove the paint or cover it up. Others suggested direct action at hospitals, particularly at Lincoln Hospital, which has lead on its own peeling walls. And still others urged a direct attack on the "slum system" as the root cause of lead poisoning. The meeting broke up at about 11 P.M., with even those few motivated on the issue divided over what to do first.

I spent the next few days working up an interior rage, trying to find out if anyone, with any responsibility, was doing anything about lead poisoning.

The NAACP had no program, nor any plans for any. The Department of Health, Education, and Welfare (the "good guys" in Nixonland) had no existing program and no funds allocated for any future program, but they did have a 21-page pamphlet. I could not find a copy of the pamphlet in any ghetto health office and had to acquire a copy from Glenn Paulson. The pamphlet turned out to be written in an opaque jargon that would hardly enlighten a second-year medical student, much less a welfare mother. The following is the second sentence on the first page: "Its etiology pathogenesis, patho-physiology, and epidemiology are known."

Nineteen Congressmen, including William F. Ryan, have introduced a package of three bills to provide federal funds for a mass testing program in the slums. But the bills are given no chance of emerging from the limbo of committee, or even generating public hearings.

I also called the United Federation of Teachers to see if they were doing anything to detect cases in the schools, but no one called back.

Werner Kramarsky, Mayor Lindsay's staff man in the health field, advised me to call Health Commissioner Mary McLoughlin, to find out officially what the city was doing. When I called her, I was told the commissioner was not in, so I left a message. The next day the commissioner's press secretary called me and said I couldn't under any circumstances have a direct interview with the commissioner, but that he would answer any questions. I gave him a list of four.

After three days Dr. Felicia Oliver-Smith, the department's lead specialist, called back and reported that (1) the city had tested 7,000 children last year, compared to 35,000 in Chicago; (2) the city "hoped to" have a mobile testing unit "within one year"; (3) there were 725 cases last year, and more than 7,000 already so far this year; (4) "We have no legal authority to make a landlord remove lead-based paint from tenement walls."

The only politician in the city who seems genuinely involved in the issue is Carter Burden, the Democratic-Liberal candidate for City Council in the polyglot East Harlem-Silk Stocking district. Burden has written angry letters to Lindsay, called press conferences, talked up the problem, and tried to energize grass-roots groups.

"It's terribly frustrating," Burden said last week, "The press just isn't interested at all. When I held a press conference in March on lead poisoning, not one daily paper and not one television station showed up. Just yesterday I had lunch with one of the religious leaders in East Harlem, and I tried to turn him on about lead. But he told me it was a phony issue, that *asthma* was a bigger community problem. . . . Kramarsky promised us three months ago there would be a crash program of 40,000 tests in the slums, but it didn't happen. Now I hear the city is about to start, but the summer is over, and 80 percent of the cases develop during the summer. There was no reason for the delay."

Burden also revealed that a private blood test for lead poisoning had just been conducted in his district—in the new, middle-income co-operative Franklin Plaza, which was completed *after* lead was banned from paint.

"That's a scandal," he said. "Of course there are no cases of lead poisoning in Franklin Plaza. But now they can release the results of the survey to prove lead is not a real problem in the slums." The survey was sponsored by Metropolitan Hospital and the American Cancer Society.

Some minimal testing program seems ready to be announced by the municipal bureaucracy. But it is not clear how the test will be distributed, or if it will reach the children who need it. And no one seems about to challenge the landlords to remove the deadly paint. And no one is doing anything about the hundreds of children now living in slum apartments with lead in the walls.

Today there is still lead in the walls of the apartment where Janet Scurry lived on Teller Avenue. There is lead in the two other tenements on the same block, owned by the same landlord who sent Mrs. Scurry the eviction notice. There is still lead in the crumbling walls of Lincoln Hospital, where lead victims are sent. There are still thousands of undiagnosed, lead-poisoned children walking the streets, sitting in classrooms.

As Dr. Rene DuBos said at a conference on lead poisoning earlier this year: "The problem is so well defined, so neatly packaged with both causes and cures known, that if we don't eliminate this social crime, our society deserves all the disasters that have been forecast for it."

THE VILLAGE VOICE, page 3ff., 9/18/69

CITY STARTS DRIVE ON LEAD POISONING

John Sibley

A drive against lead poisoning among slum children has been set in motion by the city Health Commissioner, Dr. Mary C. McLaughlin.

Up to now there has been virtually no enforcement of the Health Code ban against lead paint on the interior surfaces of residences. Nor has there been a major effort to find the poisoned youngsters before they suffer permanent injury.

Lead poisoning is most common among undernourished children in dilapidated apartments who eat bits of paint and plaster that fall from walls and ceilings. These youngsters develop "pica," the medical term for an unnatural craving for dirt and other nonfood materials.

In advanced stages lead poisoning destroys nerve cells, causing permanent brain damage and sometimes death.

500 CASES THIS YEAR

Last year there were 725 reported cases in the city, and health officials suspect many more were not reported. This year so far there have been approximately 500 reported cases, including two deaths.

Commissioner McLaughlin disclosed last week that she has transferred $150,000 from other health programs to the campaign against lead poisoning. The money will be used to expand the staff, which has been almost a one-man operation, and to buy needed laboratory equipment.

The staff will be increased to 15, including chemists and public-health sanitarians. It will work under the direction of Dr. Donald P. Conwell, assistant commissioner for chronic disease control.

Dr. McLaughlin said that the expansion would enable the department to identify about 2,500 more cases of lead poisoning a year. Lead poisoning usually reaches a dangerous level about three weeks before visible symptoms appear.

Measurement of the lead level in blood and urine can detect lead poisoning before permanent damage has been done.

The Health Department also expects to soon have a machine—still being developed—that can immediately measure the amount of lead in paint on a wall. This now requires a rather intricate laboratory analysis.

OVER 1 PERCENT LEAD ILLEGAL

Under the Health Code, a landlord can be required to remove any paint that contains more than 1 percent lead. But removal of the lead almost always means removing plaster behind the paint, a process that is extremely expensive. This is the main reason landlords have not been ordered to do so.

An amendment to the code, due to take effect next month, will permit landlords to cover existing walls with wallboard or other approved sheathing—a much more feasible solution and one that Commissioner McLaughlin proposes to insist upon.

"We'll give them five days to correct the situation," she said. "If they don't, we'll send in an emergency team to make repairs and bill the landlord."

Her threat drew a wince from a representative of the city's Rent and Housing Maintenance Department, who clearly did not welcome the responsibility for providing these emergency repair crews.

Dr. McLaughlin described her plans to representatives of a number of private foundations and child-care agencies whom she had called to her office to enlist their help in the drive.

Specifically, she asked their help in providing temporary quarters for poisoned children who have been treated at hospitals and released, but should not return home until their apartments are completely free of toxic paint.

The use of paint with a high proportion of lead was legal in the city until World War II. As a result many older homes still have lead paint beneath more recent coats of paint.

In a related development last week the Lead Industries Association announced the publication of a booklet describing the symptoms of lead poisoning in children and ways of preventing it. The booklet, along with a Government pamphlet on the same subject, may be obtained by writing to the association at 292 Madison Avenue.

THE NEW YORK TIMES, page 96, 10/19/69

LEAD POISONING TESTS:

YOUNG LORDS DO CITY'S WORK IN THE BARRIO

Jack Newfield

Free urine tests to detect lead poisoning were given door-to-door last Tuesday to the children who live along East 112th Street in El Barrio.

But this was accomplished only after an unpublicized three-hour sit-in at the Health Department last week by 30 members of the Young Lords Organization, health workers, nurses, and medical students forced the city to release the testing kits to the community.

In October, during the mayoralty campaign, the Health Department put out a press release announcing a crash testing program of 40,000 free tests. But the city never actually bothered to pick up any of the testing kits that were donated by the Bio-Rad Laboratories. The Health Department also never devised a method of getting the tests distributed in the slum neighborhoods where lead poisoning has reached epidemic proportions.

The Young Lords are the Latin equivalent of the Black Panthers. Like the Panthers, their motto is "Serve the People," and like the Panthers, many of their leaders discovered their politics in jail cells. They are now part of the Rainbow Coalition, which includes the Panthers, and the Young Patriots, a group of revolutionary poor white youth.

The Lords began as a Puerto Rican street gang in Chicago. Gradually, they became radicalized, and chapters began to develop in other cities, with a national leadership based in Chicago.

The Lords began to organize last summer in New York City, first around the issue of more frequent garbage collection in the ghettos; they organized several clean-ups of their own in East Harlem. Next they launched a free breakfast program for school children on the Lower East Side and in East Harlem. More recently, the Lords have gotten involved in health problems, demanding "community worker control of hospitals," and trying to educate teenagers against heroin addiction.

As part of their involvement in neighborhood health problems, they extracted a promise from Metropolitan Hospital last month for 200 free kits to test for lead poisoning. Medical authorities estimate there are 30,000 undiagnosed cases of lead poisoning each year in the city. The victims are usually children between the ages of one and three, who eat flaking or peeling paint from tenement walls. Lead poisoning can cause mental retardation, and in severe cases is fatal.

For several weeks the Lords prepared for their testing program, distributing leaflets along East 112th Street that read:

We are operating our own lead poisoning detection program with students from New York Medical College, beginning Tuesday, November 25, on 112th Street. The Young Lords and medical personnel will knock on your door Tuesday and ask to test your children for lead poison. Do not turn them away. Help save your children.

On Friday, November 21, Metropolitan Hospital suddenly reneged on its promise of free tests. Members of the Young Lords immediately called Health Commissioner Mary McLaughlin several times, but she would not take their calls.

So at 10 A.M. on Monday, November 24, a delegation of Young Lords, interns, nurses, and health workers appeared at the Health Department offices downtown to force a confrontation.

According to Gene Straus, the chief medical resident at Metropolitan Hospital, who participated in the sit-in:

We got there at 10 A.M., but none of the commissioners or assistant commissioners came to work until after 11 A.M. Finally, Dr. David Harris (an assistant commissioner) showed up at about 11 A.M. At first he said he would only see two representatives of our delegation. But we insisted he see us all. So we went into his office, which was quite spacious, and had comfortable chairs for everybody.

After we settled in, he asked us why we weren't satisfied with the city's lead poisoning program. We gave him a lot of reasons, and he seemed to be pretty up tight. At one point his secretary passed him a note she said was urgent. The note said there was a man on the phone who wanted to know what color the commissioner wanted his car. He seemed more worried about his new car than about the children dying of lead poisoning in this city. . . .

After a while he admitted the city's press release about 40,000 free tests was just a press release. When we told him we wouldn't leave unless we got the 200 tests Metropolitan Hospital promised us, he immediately sent someone right over to the laboratory (at 22 Jones Street) to pick up the tests. The tests were just sitting there for a month, while kids were getting sick all over the city. . . . When we were about to leave with the tests, Dr. Harris and Dr. Donald Conwell (another assistant commissioner) gave us a little lecture about observing proper procedures, and the proper amenities next time.

At 11:30 A.M. on Friday, November 28, I phoned Commissioner McLaughlin, who lives in Manhasset, and earns $35,000 a year. Her secretary told me she wouldn't be at work until the following Thursday because she was "attending a conference." When I said I wanted to ask her some questions about the city's lead poisoning program, she said, "Dr. Harris is in charge of that. But he's out today too. But I can switch you to his office."

Click, click, click.

"Dr. Harris's office, can I help you?"

"Yes. I'm Jack Newfield of *The Village Voice* and I'd like to talk to Dr. Harris about lead poisoning."

"Dr. Harris has nothing to do with lead poisoning. You should talk to Dr. Conwell."

"But the commissioner's office said that Dr. Harris has responsibility in this area."

"I know they always say that, I'm getting a little annoyed by it, but I'm afraid it's really Dr. Conwell who you should talk to. Shall I switch you?"

"Yes, please."

Click, click, click.

"Dr. Conwell's office."

"Is Dr. Conwell in?"

"No, he's taken today off. I think he'll be around on Monday. I'll have him call you." (He never called back.)

Later on Friday I spoke to a sales representative for Bio-Rad Laboratories, who requested anonymity because of his relationship with the city.

"It's hard to understand," he said, "but the Health Department just isn't doing anything it should be doing about this problem. Neighborhood groups keep calling us up to get the tests, but we can't give them to them. Our arrangement was to give the tests to the city. It was up to the city to tell us how and when they wanted the kits. But Dr. Harris never called us to arrange for the details. I don't think the Health Department has really thought about how you get these tests out to the people who really need them the most. . . .

"Kings County Hospital in Brooklyn is giving 200 blood tests for lead poisoning every week. If one hospital can give 200 tests each week, the city should at least be able to do that much. But they just never bothered to do any follow-up."

By Monday of this week the results of the lab tests on the first day's batch of urine samples were in. At least two positives were found among the 44 tests, including one two-year old child with a history of convulsions.

The Young Lords now plan to go out one night every week, collecting urine samples door to door in El Barrio, and then testing them over the weekend in a laboratory.

For the next few weeks, the Lords will be doing for free what some people get paid $35,000 a year by the city to do, but don't.

THE VILLAGE VOICE, page 1ff., 12/4/69

TWO VOICES ON PUBLIC HOUSING

URBAN DILEMMA

M. Stanton Evans

Slowly but surely the word is getting around that the liberal approach to problems of big-city living hasn't worked. And, interestingly enough, the realization seems to be more widespread among the liberals themselves than it is among the workaday politicians.

Take, for example, the matter of public housing. It is getting difficult these days to pick up a social science journal without coming across some new evidence, assembled by liberal professors, that public housing has proved to be a failure. The evidence shows that in New York, Washington, Chicago, Cleveland, St. Louis, etc., these projects have been unqualified disasters.

Yet the cultural lag in our society is obviously enormous. If you turn from the social science magazines to the daily press, you will find politicians urgently demanding that we "get on with" the same sort of projects which, up in the vanguard, have been tried and found wanting. It takes a while for the liberal politicians to catch up with the liberal intellectuals—although even here there are faint signs the message is seeping through.

Exhibit A in the demonstration of public housing's failure is the gigantic Pruitt-Igoe development in St. Louis, acclaimed at its inception as a major breakthrough in the field of social justice. Now the results are in, and it develops Pruitt-Igoe is a rather unseemly and even dangerous place to live. According to liberal sociologist Lee Rainwater, writing in *The Public Interest*, Pruitt-Igoe is in fact, "an embarrassment to all concerned."

Rainwater's conclusion is similar to that reached by other students of Pruitt-Igoe, including Jane Jacobs, the *Wall Street Journal*, and reporters for the St. Louis *Globe-Democrat*. What makes his verdict particularly interesting is that he backs it up by citing the comments of Pruitt-Igoe residents themselves about their federal accommodations. Concerning living conditions at Pruitt-Igoe, the respondents say, among other things:

> There are mice and cockroaches in the buildings. People use the elevators and halls to go to the bathroom. Bottles and other dangerous things get thrown out of windows and hurt people. People who don't live in the project come in and make a lot of trouble with fights, stealing, drinking, and the like. The laundry rooms aren't safe; clothes get stolen and people get attacked. People use the stairwells and laundry rooms for drinking. . . . A woman isn't safe in the halls, stairways, or elevators.

Pruitt-Igoe residents were asked to specify the kinds of behavior in the project which they felt to be most serious. Rainwater reports the following were characterized as "very frequent" by more than half of the respondents: "Holding up somebody and robbing them. Being a wino or alcoholic. Stealing from somebody. Teenagers yelling curse words at adults. Breaking windows. Drinking a lot and fooling around in the streets. Teenagers getting in fights."

All of which confirms the findings of journalists who have surveyed Pruitt-Igoe; it is a mess, no two ways about it. And all of which is also characteristic of public housing in various parts of the nation. The trouble at Pruitt-Igoe is not, as some defenders of public housing would have us believe, an "exception." It all too obviously is the rule, as becomes apparent if we inventory results attained by other investigators of such projects.

Thus Miss Jacobs, discussing the rise of crime in various big cities of the East, tells us:

> Children engaged in [street fights] turn out to be from superblock projects. . . . The highest delinquency belt in New York's Lower East Side . . . is precisely the park-like belt of public housing projects. . . . The worst girls' gang in Philadelphia has grown up on the grounds of that city's second oldest project, and the highest delinquency belt of that city corresponds with its major belt of projects.

Harrison Salisbury of *The New York Times*, discussing public housing in the New York area, says the Fort Greene project in Brooklyn is a "$20-million slum" ideal for breeding criminals. Such projects, Salisbury asserts, "are forcing centers of juvenile delinquency. They spawn teenage gangs. They incubate crime."

Salisbury quotes a housing man as saying: "The first thing that happens is the kids begin to destroy the property. Even before it is built. They steal the place blind. As soon as the windows go in they smash them. They smash them again and again. What difference does it make, it's public, ain't it? That's what they say."

In Washington, D.C., the story is the same. There, according to Haynes Johnson of the *Washington Star*, crime is particularly rampant in the eastern quadrant of the city which "contains nearly two-thirds of the public housing units in the district." He adds that "while the National Capital Housing Authority continues to talk about the long waiting lists of more than 5,000 families for public housing, in one such unit alone . . . 109 out of 350 apartments are vacant. The windows are boarded up and the entire development is as much of a slum as any group of buildings on the south side of Chicago or the west side of New York."

In short, the public housing story in various major cities of the United States resembles, point for point, the story in St. Louis. Far from being an exception, the crime, degradation and disorder which characterize the Pruitt-Igoe development represent the all-too-normal conditions in public housing units. The notion that "it's public, ain't it?" and that therefore anything goes, seems to have carried the day.

By degrees, this evidence has made its weight felt on the liberal intellectuals. Now if they can just get the word to the politicians, perhaps the nation can be spared further exercise in such federally-supported misery.

THE HOUSES UNCLE SAM BUILDS

Walter Rybeck

As if public housing did not have enough enemies, the past decade saw many liberals who once provided strongest support begin to raise questions and occasionally to denounce public housing. Perhaps it is timely to recall public housing's virtues, which include the following:

☐Even its critics must concede that public housing provides shelter that is safer and more "decent" than the slum homes in which its tenants otherwise would live.

☐The waiting lists to get into public housing are very high, on the order of 28 applicants for every vacancy, suggesting that those for whom it is designed find it appealing.

☐The vacancy rate has been very low, about half the rate of vacancies in privately rented apartments, again indicating that those in public housing find it preferable to other available housing.

☐The average turnover rate has been lower than in private housing.

□Pitifully slow as the construction of public housing has been in comparison to need, it has far surpassed other subsidized housing programs in units constructed even in recent years when other programs were heavily promoted.

□Of all forms of subsidized housing, public housing has been able to serve families farthest down the income scale.

Many Americans bring back glowing reports of public housing in Western Europe. These are difficult to evaluate. Public housing in some countries has virtually replaced private home building except in the luxury class; when slums and housing shortages persist, how does one measure the net gains? And when the poor outside public housing are subsidizing people with higher incomes to occupy better living quarters, how do the equity issues balance? But setting aside all these debatable points, one set of factors about the European experience is instructive: the quality of public housing need not be demeaning; those who live in it need not suffer social stigma on that account; and instead of being the most drab, uninspired architecture in a city, public housing may embrace the most exciting new designs for better living.

The problems with U.S. public housing must be admitted. Several "horrible examples," such as an oversized hoodlum-ridden project in St. Louis, have been publicized out of all proportion to what is typical. People who know the name Pruitt-Igoe rarely can name other projects in the same city that merit a good reputation.

An overconcentration of problem families is a major failing in many projects. The social environment ceases to be wholesome unless a portion of the residents with good behavior patterns can exert an influence.

Some public housing, on the other hand, has been so selective of the character and income of its tenants that it is fair to say that the neediest people in the community are excluded.

Probably the most neglected needy group is the large poor family, yet public housing typically does not provide units with enough bedroom space to accommodate them.

The public housing program generally has failed to develop techniques for strengthening individual, family and community life among tenants. This potential for uplift was stressed by the pioneer public housers in this country. Enough successes have been scored to show that theirs was not an idle dream, but the efforts have been the exception, not the rule.

It is reasonable to conclude, as did George Schermer after a survey of public housing for the Douglas Commission, that most of these faults could be corrected if there were much more—say ten times more—public housing, and if the operation, including social services, were more generously funded.

The year 1969 witnessed a veritable crisis in public housing which led to pressures on Congress for funding reforms. The subsidy formula for public housing is such that it covers the cost of construction while rents from tenants must cover costs of maintenance, operation, administration, and payments in lieu of local taxes. With operations and maintenance costs soaring, but with no parallel rise in the rent-paying abilities of their tenants, local public housing authorities are caught in the middle. Public housing in many cities has deteriorated at an alarming rate. Substantial subsidy of rents plus adequate funds allocated for social management are necessary if public housing is to survive. . . .

OBSERVATION TO THE EMPIRE STATE BUILDING

Herbert Woodward Martin

Stone

    on

Stone

Cemented to your diadem,

Those you house

Those around you

Create the ninth wonder

Semblance of life

Mortared together

Stone

    on

Stone

CLARK STREET

Barbara Harr

A crooked block from home, the gay boys go
past derelict buildings waiting for the wrecker

where the poignance of improvement blows about
like litter in March wind. The city's money
ends abberation, sets up family housing.

Under these steps no children play. The doors,
lockless, boarded blind eyes, stare. Stiff shades
chatter like cold teeth in broken windows.
Chalk-scrawled walls, between obscenities,
hold shredded faces of unelected men.

Before the fall, I should like to have gone inside
the flats and passageways where men have lived,
seen the turnings of their ways, and gained
the unexpected knowledge of the dead

before the swinging ball, from chain, from crane,
in its diminishing orbit, brings the end.

DEGHETTOIZATION: CHOICE OF THE NEW MILITANCY

Clarence Funnyé

When blacks were slaves on southern plantations, liberal northern whites consoled themselves with clever rationalizations about the comforts provided the "coloreds," and the happiness they enjoyed in their "own little areas watched over by (generally) benevolent white owners."

To further reconcile slavery with Christian teachings, missionaries were dispatched to obtain first-hand statement from "boss leaders" who, indeed, said in their own words that they were "carefree and contented people."

Since those early days, largely because of economic reasons, slavery and the plantation have changed form. Now we say deprived, under-privileged and disadvantaged for slaves, and ghetto or "the community" for plantation. Ghetto dwellers are supposed to have all rights of other citizens, but since blacks do not have such mobility, America, consistently Christian, has moved to salve conscience once again.

Immediately after fraudulent attempts failed to get blacks off these latter-day plantations and into the mainstream, original missionary rationalizations were updated. Black spokesmen were found who screamed into TV cameras that blacks wanted no part of the mainstream outside the ghetto. Under not-so-gentle prodding from new missionaries—now known as white liberals—some black "boss leaders" actually developed rational theories for not leaving the plantation.

One very popular theory is that confinement in all-black ghettos equals power—that allowing blacks out would deflate the power since there is a direct relationship between the number of blacks per square foot and the power enjoyed.

This theory was developed by Dr. Frances Piven, a white female from Columbia University's liberal School of Social Work who, strangely, has assumed the role of chief intellectual advocate of black manhood. Piven is usually assisted by a white male, Dr. Richard Cloward, and, as a team, they have been leaders in the ghettos-are-good-for-blacks school. One of Piven's main theses is that black men need time to develop full "manhood," and that mixing them up with whites at this point in history would be premature. They need the security of the ghetto.

The separatist line is a very popular one among
white media people.

Black "boss leaders" have outdone themselves in speaking for "the community" in furtherance of "ghettos forever." They were only supposed to back up white separatist notions and, as a spin-off, enjoy such other benefits as accrue to "leaders."

However, the new separatists have gone even further into the "militants as entertainment" bag. TV discussions on raising black armies, forcing a separate state, etc., provide a certain thrill for whites much like what the colonists got from watching Africans doing a war dance with paper spears. The white liberals appreciate this additional dividend and blacks who are suckered into such performances are rewarded with return engagements on prime TV. Their presentation is solely along the "hate whitey—we got our own bag—your house is burning down" sort of thing, much of which is true, certainly. (But does a revolutionary army leader announce detailed plans for expansion of his army over the enemy's communication lines?)

The very nature of most performances belies seriousness—they call for no program, not even an "unreasonable response," no action, and worst of all, are based on rather flimsy mandates.

There are other less sophisticated versions of the "ghettos forever" theory, but most hinge on the assumption—loudly backed up by chosen spokesmen—that blacks now regard themselves somehow as natives to the ghetto, that they really don't care much for having their own little plot of land, with green grass and fresh air, not to mention good public services, safe streets, access to jobs, etc.

Some brothers have become so caught up in mumbolistic rhetoric that even when recalling "Africa and black heritage" they forget that blacks in Africa had all the green grass, open space and pollution-free air in the world, while American whites are mostly descendents of people who came from dim, dark, damp, smelly, overcrowded European ghettos. If anyone is to "reassert his heritage" by being confined to American ghettos it should be. . . . Anyhow, once the "boss leaders" got the cue about which lines would insure maximum media coverage, they were off and running.

They pushed ghettoization with a vengeance, denouncing everyone and anyone who suggested, even indirectly, that blacks were getting the shaft in ghettos while non-ghetto areas at least enjoy some of the fruits of. . . . Attending schools with whites became a "white thing," in addition to living downtown (outside), or studying economics.

White intellectual guardians of the black boss, of course, raked the cream of this new direction. They published hundreds of articles on how whites were generally benevolent and kind and good and just and would give money for housing, welfare, etc., so long as no one "pushed integration," especially in northern cities and suburbs. Dozens of new urban alternatives poured out of universities—all justifying a sort of updated Atlanta Compromise (recall Booker T.'s separate fingers theory.)

While one can understand and even sympathize with the few brothers who are used as tools in the imprisonment game, it is less easy to excuse some of the absolutely moronic nonsense coming out of supposedly intelligent white media.

Much of it is not even vaguely camouflaged. In August of 1968, a "planner" allegedly employed at Columbia University (again Columbia) seriously suggested that blacks could be passively led into the ultimate ambush by accepting, as their "own," black new towns built on portions of U.S. Army bases. The base, according to this "planner," would also provide employment and a feeling of security (again security). In further demonstration of the inexhaustible arrogance of the new missionaries (friends of the Negro), he even outlined a budget and a development program complete with suggested black leaders.

Now the tragedy of all this is not the time and energy wasted in writing and reading, printing and distributing such obvious non-solutions. The tragedy is that the momentum of ghetto preservation is being translated into long- and short-range urban planning and development programs. The myth is becoming the method. Urban poverty programs, Model Cities, newly updated ghetto economic development programs like the new-jobs-in-the-ghetto syndrome (as reflected in the so-called CORE plan, sometime derisively called the CORE-Nixon Plan for Black Capitalists), and the Kennedy effort in Brooklyn's Bedford-Stuyvesant, are examples of ghetto preservation programs.

*All these non-solutions give the illusion of movement, cooling
the ghetto—even "involving" the militant/separatist—
while, in fact, they often aggravate the basic problem.*

A closer look is instructive. The war on poverty has all the fury of two giants dueling with powder puffs. It was supposed to divert pressure from integration of labor unions and divert blacks' attention from City Hall. Both objectives have been accomplished, and old-line civil rights activists are now establishment folk with five-foot desks, secretaries, and mimeograph machines on which to run off endless proposals for special projects.

When a few thinking brothers questioned the war on poverty, they were given Model Cities. It is supposed to involve the community in planning for its own neighborhood.

Here is the ultimate absurdity; who the hell ever heard of involving blacks in anything, much less city planning. New York City has had a City Planning Commission since 1937. No black person has ever been seriously considered for membership, yet badly-needed housing programs in at least three ghetto areas are being stalled while the City tranquilizes "the community" with illusions of power under Model Cities.

The Kennedy effort in Brooklyn is a kind of private Model Cities program. It seeks to fix up and bring industry into the ghetto, and do those other nice things necessary for "economic development." In true missionary spirit, the first large contract (that for architectural and planning services) went to a "monumental" architectural firm which is alleged to have employed its first black architect after signing the contract. Some local leaders timidly noted that the design and planning contract could have been used to develop some black A-E (Architect-Engineer) firms, which after a time would be selling services to a larger community, thus forming an economic base. The leaders observed that blacks make up an insignificantly small part of the active design industry, and that development of this economic activity was as important as allowing black trainees to participate in painting of brownstone facades.

The response was that the scale of the work required an architect-planner of stature to inspire investment, etc., so the quarter of a million dollars went for this service—while much ado was made of the employ-ment of black draftsmen or their use in minor rehabilitation work.

The Kennedy effort in Brooklyn is plodding bravely ahead even though the Senator himself is gone.

To date, they have planned a superblock, used 32 Bedford-Stuyvesant craftsmen and 272 "B-S youths" to rehabilitate 394 brownstones (exteriors only).

They are fixing up an old bottling plant (abandoned several years ago for good economic reasons) as a multiservice center, and they laud IBM's moves to construct a plant "in the community." For all the fanfare, the plant is not an economic bootstrap of the ghetto—it will provide jobs only, not investment or ownership potential. The plant is close to workers of the "B-S" ghetto, but why all the concern to bring new plants and national industries into the ghetto? That's where the least land exists, and where problems of relocation are most severe.

Neighborhood people in candid moments express grave doubts about the investment, noting that blacks can travel to jobs anywhere in the city, or city-fringe for that matter. That if the Kennedy people really wanted to be helpful, they could have bought the Brooklyn Navy Yard and turned it over to the community corporation to develop. That IBM, like Xerox in Rochester, could have built the plant and turned it over to the com-munity with a guarantee to purchase all products for the first ten or fifteen years, if they wanted to get serious. . . .

It is way past time to call a spade a spade and get on to where
we have to go. First, blacks in America do not regard
the ghetto as their special preserve.

While all get a certain special feeling from acknowledgement of African heritage, none is seriously thinking of returning to Africa—even if the African brothers wanted them to. The fact is that the black man in America is as western in values and orientation as the western white man. He has the same standards of success, moral code and gods, both secular and otherwise. He seeks access to the same system of rewards and aims to provide his family with the same modicum of security.

When helplessly trapped in a low status, he feels as frustrated and angry as any other man. And while he does not reject blackness and community (self-seeking separatists notwithstanding) he sees that a com-munity of culture and spirit is not dependent on physical confinement. Moreover, even before the planners noticed, the word was already out that manufacturing jobs in the city were going out to the suburbs. Pitifully inadequate reverse-commuter car pools have been going from Harlem to Westchester and Putnam Counties for years. NCDH (the National Committee Against Discrimination in Housing) recently documented the widespread character of this trend and predicts that it will accelerate in spite of puny efforts to the contrary. Chicago, Detroit, St. Louis, Baltimore, Philadelphia and San Francisco are just a few of the major cities experiencing rapid dispersal of jobs in manufacturing, trade, and personal services.

Blacks have tried manfully, and to little avail, to hold on by car pools and reverse commuting. NCDH studies show that reverse transportation is not available, or too time-consuming, and too expensive. The NCDH study belittles efforts to bring jobs into the ghetto and says future job creation is going to be primarily in suburban areas, but the unskilled population is going to be more and more concentrated in central city ghettos unless there is a national strategy of deghettoization and movement of many nonwhites to outlying areas.

Deghettoization—a designed and deliberate process for programmed elimination of the forced urban ghetto—was first developed by Idea Plan Associates more than four years ago. Essentially it involves a two-pronged attack on vast ghettos. Ghettos exist at least in part because of poverty—not only group poverty, but the sum total of individual poverty, and individual poverty is eliminated by a good job followed by better housing choices, usually outside the ghetto.

Cities have, over the years, developed very good mechanisms to transform relatively poor, rough people into qualified members of the middle class. Even the smallest city operates at least one junior or senior college—usually free or almost free—and a host of "special program schools." These systems worked in urbanizing the present white middle class but have been pre-empted by established "elitist" or would-be elitist fiefdoms and special interest groups to the detriment of blacks and Puerto Ricans (who ironically constitute the bulk of raw material for any new urban middle class).

New York City, because it is biggest and claims to have the worst problems, may be a good illustration of a city committing suicide with its urbanization resources. Its famed city university system contains an estimated 150,000 students, only 2 percent of whom are black and Puerto Rican. Preliminary attempts of the new underclass to cut into the action are met with all kinds of evasive delaying and diversionary mumbo jumbo cloaked in finest academic rationalization about why blacks are not qualified to participate more fully in this university of all the people.

While over half of the city's civil service workers, including its teachers, are products of the city university, its admission standards have been escalated toward keeping down the number of "undesirables." An institution which should be narrowing a very dangerous gap is, in fact, moving

full steam ahead in widening the gap and, of course, making more cata-
clysmic the eventual confrontation.

There is an alternative: Set aside at least 25 percent of all city
university seats for blacks and Puerto Ricans. One quarter of 150,000 is
37,500 seats. If after two to four years 25 percent of that figure were
graduated with A.A. or B.A. degrees, there would be nearly 10,000 new
taxpayers. Five years after the start-up period, 50,000 black and Puerto
Rican families would be subtracted from the welfare-services-consuming
class and added to the revenue-producing class. At 2.5 children per family,
this would mean 175,000 people. Given present policies, one could
expect the welfare burden to increase by 175,000 persons during the
same period.

It is not expected that professors at C.U. will welcome this kind of
cost-benefit approach to a city problem. One could, of course, question
whether their "welcome" is relevant. They are, after all, only employees
of the city—contrary to popular opinion. They do not own the system,
and their desires for an amplified status through "elitist" developments—
unrelated to requirements of real life—do not serve the city's interest. The
same kind of directed approach must be applied to all other systems
directly owned, or indirectly influenced by the city.

Deghettoization implies a political savvy not yet evidenced by ghetto
people who now only vaguely appreciate the importance of their political
weight. It will require a widely-developed system of political trade-offs and
group bargaining in City Councils and Boards of Estimate *downtown*, not
uptown fiddling around with peanuts in Model Cities or poverty programs.

Deghettoization requires that ghetto dwellers be converted
to city dwellers with city-wide concerns and involvement
at least on a political level. Ghetto dwellers must turn
outward to the larger city, not inward.

Housing policies in deghettoization must be regional. Some things
are immediately obvious: (1) Cities cannot continue to contain a dis-
proportionate share of the regional poor; (2) suburban land policies must
be thrown out or sharply brought around to the new realities, namely that
regional land and policies thereof are concerns of all the region's citizens
(states with big-city problems and uncooperative suburbs should take
back their zoning powers from the cities and suburbs and, on a state level,
zone areas to maximize opportunities and choices for all citizens); and
(3) building codes should be treated just like zoning ordinances—
abolished and/or returned to state hands with only the barest requirements

consistent with health and safety (building codes are often used to prevent the construction of low-income housing).

These requirements would be certified as met when the drawings are stamped or sealed by a registered engineer or architect. There are other impediments to the rapid production of housing required for deghettoization—such as labor shortage, or tax structures which favor unbuilt land and speculation. State zoning could fix the latter, while a halt in subsidizing of union discrimination, and nationalization of the apprentice-training programs, would fix the former.

With preliminary steps laid out, the metropolitan area that wants to plan rationally can get on with solving its ghetto (housing) problem through planned deghettoization. . . .

The city could take several internal steps to enhance the benefits from deghettoization.

Surplus in-city land, federal facilities, or closed military bases are excellent sites for in-city new towns of 50,000 to 60,000 persons for major cities; 10,000 to 20,000 for middle-sized cities. In 1967, partly at the suggestion of Idea Plan Associates, the federal government did a study of the quantity of federal land that for all practical purposes is surplus land within the city. This study has not yet been released, but this land is thought to be considerable—in one large Eastern city some 1,800 acres have been located in five government installations of various sizes, either partly or totally abandoned.

To sum up deghettoization benefits:

1. Reduction of city rents; stabilization of the housing market.
2. Better flexibility in in-city planning and development.
3. Enhancement of the city as a viable, balanced place to live should encourage return of the middle class.
4. Accelerated reduction in dependent welfare population both through increased urbanization and access to suburban-based employment.
5. Reduction in cost of city services provided to former ghetto.

To deghettoize, we must close out the present phase of
thoroughly inadequate response to city-metropolitan problems
of city-metropolitan scale.

Black separatist "entertainers" should not let themselves be used to deceive whites into believing they can solve "the problem" merely by updating old plantation techniques.

Brothers and their friends who know better should stop romanticizing Harlem and the other unsafe spirit-killing, ambition-stifling, anachronistic residential pockets of blight and neglect which "militant entertainers" now call "our community."

The crisis calls for a newer, higher form of militancy—one that avoids getting snared in the diversionary Model Cities trap and one that keeps an eye on the big ball where the power is, and that's not in a model neighborhood headquarters.

Any community which turns away from the real fight—the fight at city hall, in state capitols, and in Washington—and turns in on itself will certainly lose out to find itself out-foxed again.

Good reasonably-priced housing, access to jobs and job opportunities, fresh air and green grass—insofar as there is any left—should be shared by all equally. We are now talking about survival as men running free, not people consigned forever to modern plantations just because some men with minivisions believe it the right course, or lack the courage to try what they know to be the hard course.

Perhaps what the country needs most of all is to acknowledge that blacks are here to stay and intend to force solutions to problems of residual slavery. It is tranquil to toy with non-solutions such as community development corporations, Model Cities, or anti-poverty. If "the community," meaning black America, is to participate in planning for itself, the tools are already there on the urban scene, citywide—the city council, city planning boards and commissions, boards of education, central and local, regents, state education systems, etc. Diversionary programs sap energy and merely give a fleeting illusion of sharing in power. The new militancy will correctly assess these diversions. The momentum of the civil rights struggle has yielded far too low a return—two or three billions in urban programs is peanuts. An updated and enlightened militancy will recognize this and move toward creation of a real urban lobby at least as powerful and tenacious as the gun lobby. Blacks can form the nucleus of such a lobby.

Blacks need not reject interim diversionary programs outright. A small sub-committee in the community could be left to haggle over and amuse themselves with division of the crumbs from the tables of power. But the real thinkers will keep their eyes on where it's at.

HARLEM

(FOR TONY ORANGE)

Richie Orange

DAWN TURNS INTO DUSK/
INTO PEOPLE/
INTO ENERGY/
AS A SENSE OF MOVEMENT
A SENSE OF RHYTHM
TRANSMITS ME INTO A
WORLD OF COOL AND BEAUTY.
A SENSE OF LAUGHTER
A SENSE OF BEING
A COMING TOGETHER ON A WIDE CROWDED STREET.
WITH THE SETTING OF THE SUN
THEY COME AND/THEY COME
FROM BROOKLYN/MANHATTAN AND THE BRONX THEY COME
ALL KINDS OF PEOPLE
ALL TYPES OF PEOPLE
FREEING THEIR SOULS FROM THE CHAINS OF THEIR MINDS
IN SUPPORT OF THEIR WORLD.
PAST THE STUDS AND THE QUEERS
AND THE PIMPS DRINKING BEERS/
IN THEIR COLORFUL VINES
PASTELS AND SOLIDS AND
SOLIDLY SOLID.
ALL MOVING NOW
ALL BLENDING NOW
A COMING TOGETHER ON WIDE CROWDED STREETS.
IN PINK CADILLACS/IN SHOES THAT TALK
FROM THINGS THAT CRAWLED;
LIZARDS AND GATORS AND BOA CONSTRICTORS
MOVE TO SOUNDS FROM THE RECORD STORES
AND "I WANNA TAKE YOU HIGHER" SAYS SLY/
SLY AND THE FAMILY STONED OUT OF THEIR MINDS
AND THE MIGHTY IMPRESSIONS SAY
    "WE'RE A WINNER" AND WE "KEEP ON PUSHING"
UPTOWN ON WIDE CROWDED STREETS.
THE DANCE HAS BEGUN
AND THEY ALL COME TOGETHER AS IF THEY WERE ONE
ALL COMIN HERE/ALL COMIN DOWN
FROM WAY UPTOWN
AND HERE COME THE SISTERS
ALL KINDS OF SISTERS
IN VARIOUS SHADES OF BROWN AND BLACK
AND THEIR HIPS SWAY TO MILES AT THE BARON

AND ALL OF THE COLORS—
THE REDS, THE GREENS, THE PURPLES AND YELLOWS
IN KNITS AND DASHIKIS
IN MINIS AND GAILES
COMIN DOWN WITH BIG BAD STEPS
MOVIN AND GROOVIN
AND DANCIN AND PRANCIN
LIKE ONE HIP PARADE
WITH ALL OF THE LAUGHTER
THE ENDLESS LAUGHTER
DOWN IN THE STREETS
ON THEM WIDE CROWDED STREETS.
A HUMAN TIDAL WAVE
ENGULFS US ON OUR WAY UPTOWN/
FROM THE APOLLO AND WELLS AND
THE LITTLE RED ROOSTER.
A WAVE OF LOVE AND EMOTION
OF ACTION AND MOVEMENT.
A COOLING IT OUT YET,
YET HEATING IT IN/
OF ALL OF THE PEOPLE
AND ALL OF THE COLORS AND SMELLS
OF A WORLD WITHIN WORLDS
MIXIN AND FIXIN
AND JIVIN AND DYIN
AND MOST OF ALL LIVIN
OUR BLACK NIGGER MAGIC
"CAUSE WE OWN THE NIGHT"
AND THE STREETS AND THE SOUNDS AND THE AIR ITSELF.
AND THE LIFE IS THERE
AND THE MOVEMENT IS THERE
AND ALL OF OUR ENERGY
AND THE SPIRIT IS THERE
ON THROUGH THE NIGHT
AND RIGHT THROUGH THE DAWN
THROUGH THOSE WIDE/FUNKY/
BAD/
     BLACK/
         STREETS.

STREET ART

Allan D'Arcangelo

Roy Cato

Unsigned

Unsigned

Left by Dana Chandler   Right by Gary Rickson

SLUMS: INSTANT RENEWAL

Newsweek

At 10 o'clock one crisp morning last week, construction engineer Edward K. Rice blew a whistle outside a squalid tenement on New York's Lower East Side and the first members of a 258-man renovation crew filed into the building. Their seemingly hopeless assignment: to transform the 72-year-old slum structure into a modern dwelling in just 48 hours.

As an electronic clock ticked off the seconds in the project headquarters next door, demolition men started dumping debris into the street. Then, following a carefully plotted schedule, relays of carpenters, plumbers, electricians, painters and laborers swarmed into the buliding to race the 48-hour deadline through the day and night. "Hurry up, hurry up," the workers called to each other. Finally, as the last touch was completed, Rice stopped the clock—at exactly 47 hours, 52 minutes, and 24 seconds.

The frenetic project was staged by the U.S. Department of Housing and Urban Development to introduce a revolutionary new approach to urban renewal that it calls "instant rehabilitation." By showing that even the most wretched tenements can be remade into decent homes quickly and economically, the department hopes to foster a continuing series of similar projects in big-city slums across the country.

COST CUTTER

Instant rehabilitation is designed to telescope normal techniques that displace tenants for six months or more. It is also expected to be cheaper. Last week's well-rehearsed Lower East Side project cost $11,000 per apartment vs. an average price of $13,200 when conventional renovation methods are used and $21,000 when an entirely new building is erected.

Before beginning work at 633 East 5th Street in downtown Manhattan, government and construction officials spent a year in advance planning with New York's Carolyndale Foundation, which bought the building last year specifically for the experiment. Engineers even made trial runs on a pair of adjoining vacant buildings to develop their techniques. Once everything was ready last week, the building's 31 occupants —mostly Puerto Ricans—were moved into the nearby Broadway Central Hotel, their belongings were stored aboard moving vans and their pets were left with willing neighbors.

First, a 60-man demolition crew on leave from tearing down the old Metropolitan Opera House stripped the building to its basic walls and floors. As they progressed from the rear to the front of the house on each floor, electricians moved in right behind them to install new wiring and carpenters to put in finished fabricated walls and window units. Then, as floodlights cast an eerie shadow across the scene on the first night, a 230-foot-high crane lowered preassembled kitchen and bathroom units down three shafts in the building. Finally, all the pipes were connected, plastic-coated flooring was laid, a vermin-proof garbage chute was installed, and the corridor walls were painted a bright light blue.

DOUBTS

There are some critics who argue that the HUD renewal project is inherently futile because the ancient tenements, no matter how they are spruced up, are still flimsy in basic construction and obsolete in design. At ceremonies celebrating the completion of last week's project, HUD Secretary Robert G. Weaver conceded that "instant rehabilitation . . . is not the whole answer by any means. But it is one . . . way to get moving toward saving buildings and therefore saving neighborhoods for the people who live in them."

Certainly there were no objections from the tenants of 633 East 5th Street, who were overjoyed by the contrast between their rat-infested old apartments and their sparkling new quarters. (Although rents will go up from a current low of $42 a month to $72, no tenant will be obliged to pay more than 25 percent of his income.) Nine-year-old Miriam Davila was almost breathless with excitement as she surveyed her family's new three-bedroom unit. "It's going to be clean," she said, "with no rats and roaches and I'm going to hang a picture of Little Bo Peep on the wall and I'm going to put a statue of St. Mary on the bureau and I'm going to wash the walls all the time so they'll be clean. . . ."

4

MINORITIES
Strangers and
Cousins in
the Promised Land

"The Grim Plight of the Urban Indian" by Jerry Kamstra comes down a
little harder on "melting pot" rhetoric than do most exposures of immigrant misery, city style. Conned out of a country, concentrated in camps,
and ignored while Europeans plunged by the millions into the immigrant
hell of the port cities, the Indians are only now arriving in the promised
land of the cities beyond the reservations. They bring with them ancient
traditions as beautiful as those of the Europeans who came before them.
And they receive the same old official welcome—prejudice, unemployment, and slums.

The article by Jimmy Breslin, "The Last of the Irish Immigrants,"
suggests that the push of the hated minorities to get ahead eventually gets

them there all right, but often with their history and humanity left behind. Although Breslin writes about the present-day descendants of the 4,600,000 Irish immigrants of the nineteenth century, his criticism applies as well to several of the minority groups represented in this section.

The selections here do more than show the suffering which all immigrants to the cities have had in common at one time or another. Some show, on the one hand, the beautiful forms of strength and humanity that each group has added to the common life of the city. And others show the mockery to which these distinctive traits—whether of language, color, religion, or family tradition—have been subject. Accordingly, the short story "Ancient Gentility" by William Carlos Williams celebrates human richness amidst the material squalor of an Italian ghetto in New Jersey; and the "Letter from a Polish Immigrant," written by F. N. in 1914, expresses the determination of all minorities to learn English, to lose their foreign accent, and with it, perhaps, everything else that made them different and unwelcome. In the short story "Adam," Kurt Vonnegut, Jr., deals with both these themes—the beauty of the old world ways and the pressures to assimilate brought to bear on all foreigners.

In 1967, Martin Luther King led demonstrations for fair housing through the white ghettos of Chicago. Afterward, he said that nothing he had ever faced in Southern cities (evoked by Richard Wright in his autobiographical essay "The Ethics of Living Jim Crow") compared with the hatred hurled and spat out by the people of this Northern promised land. The immigrant pattern comes full circle. Having fulfilled the language requirement, the descendants of immigrant parents have gone on to teach their children well the city's official welcome to foreigners, the same one thrown at their own parents. In the light of the racial wars of the sixties, how ironic are the opening lines of Art Hoppe's feature column, "Take a City to Lunch": " 'We're making real progress,' said my friend, George Washington X. 'Nobody calls me "Colored" any more.' "

In one area of the racial scene, growth is in healthy evidence. The attitudes of the minorities themselves toward their oppression have changed dramatically. The last four selections tell of young men catching "whispers of the meanings that life can have," not as a result of disappearing into the mainstream, but in the process of emphasizing their distinctive identities—Puerto Rican, Mexican-American, Chinese-American, and Black. The cities have been the birthplace of this new awareness.

In the Prologue to *Down These Mean Streets*, the rage of Piri Thomas, a recent Puerto Rican immigrant, has nothing in common with the apologetic tone of the Polish immigrant's letter of 1914. In "El Paso Del Norte," John Rechy, a young experimental writer, evokes both the oppression and the beautiful traditions of Mexican-Americans in a hostile city. The short story "Food For All His Dead" by Frank Chin dramatizes a situation increasingly familiar to young minority peoples—the painful attempt of a college student (here a Chinese-American) to create a life for himself fuller than that of his parents and friends in the ghetto. And certainly the vision of manhood re-created in the final selection, Mari Evan's poem, "Vive Noir!," has little in common with the aspirations of earlier European immigrants. According to the poet, today's young stranger in the promised land will gain his freedom if it has to mean the end of New York, Chicago, and Los Angeles. These changes, then, in the consciousness of the city's latest newcomers prove Bob Dylan right—"The Times, They are A-Changin'."

THE GRIM PLIGHT OF THE URBAN INDIAN

Jerry Kamstra

Belva Cottier is an Oglalla Sioux, a grandmother, and a veteran of the Indian Alcatraz movement.[1] Articulate, and dignified, she was slightly bemused and slightly sad as she ran down the history of her people's island occupation. . . .

Question: Why did the Indian students who invaded Alcatraz this time go so ill-prepared? They lacked food, clothing, medicine. Why didn't they stock up on these supplies before they invaded the island?

Answer: Actually they didn't have anything. A lot of our students are in dire straits. They've been trying to get a good education. A lot of them have no place to stay. They live with one another, helping each other out, boarding with other Indian families in the area. They're trying to go to school. They worked hard to get an ethnic study program in the colleges.

There's a whole backlash of disappointment for many of the young Indians. They're trying to do what's right to get ahead and get a good education, but the Bureau of Indian Affairs doesn't help out much. They don't help out with educational loans of any kind. They have a few funds to take care of Indians on the reservations, but once you are off the reservation for a certain length of time you lose a lot of your Indian rights.

Question: Do they want to keep you on the reservation?

Answer: Well, they want you to either stay on it or stay off it.

Question: You can't go back and forth?

Answer: They don't like you to do that, but a lot of us do it. Like I say, the urban Indian is the forgotten Indian; he is in between.

1In Novmber, 1969, a large group of Indians seized an island in San Francisco Bay which had been deserted since the shut-down of Alcatraz Penitentiary.

Question: How many Indians live in the Bay Area, do you have any idea?

Answer: The last Bureau of Indian Affairs count was 2,500, just in the Bay Area. There are many more down in the Los Angeles area. Many Indians have relocated in the Los Angeles area. The whole idea of relocation in the first place was to get the Indian to assimilate, but it has had just the opposite effect. We have turned more Indian in the city than we were back on the reservation.

Question: Why is this?

Answer: I think it has been the touch with the outside society and the disappointments we have run into, and some subtle form of discrimination.

Question: How do you make your living? Do you get money from the Office of Economic Opportunity or from the Bureau of Indian Affairs? Do you have a job?

Answer: We all work at different kinds of jobs. When Indians are sent off the reservation on a relocation project the Bureau supposedly takes care of them for a year. That isn't always the way it works out, though. When we first leave the reservation, the Bureau gives us $600. We're supposed to live on that until we get situated in a job or a training program of some kind.

I just talked to one student who gets $61. a week from the Bureau for him and his family to live on. His rent takes $31. a week so there are a couple of days a week when they have nothing to eat. They're supposed to have food and clothing and book allowances paid out of the $600., so that doesn't leave much money to live on.

As soon as you do have a job the Bureau says, well, you have a job now and you're off our list. If you try to go back and get help through the Bureau again, you are just out of luck. There might be some instances when they help but you're considered an urban Indian now and you have to go through the state programs of poverty. . . .

Question: In other words, once the Indian leaves the reservation he becomes an urban Indian and is more or less on his own.

Answer: Yes, that's right.

Question: Why do the Indians leave the reservation?

Answer: Well, there is so much poverty on the reservation, poverty and sickness. There's nothing to do, everybody feels so useless. The outside is built up as some great big paradise. Many of the Indians leave the reservation expecting to find this paradise and when they get into the city they walk the streets.

I have seen whole families walking the streets with no place to go. We've tried to get funds from the Bureau to help with this problem, even revolving funds that we could pay back after we were situated, but it never comes to anything. The Bureau people even send sick Indians off the reservation; some of them have active tuberculosis and they send them into the city where there are no jobs, no places to stay.

The Indians aren't white people Their whole philosophy and way of life is different. Our belief is essentially one of brotherhood. We have always welcomed everyone with open arms, even from the time of the Pilgrims.

Our prophecies told us that the white man was coming. When he did come, we welcomed him. We have always believed in the light from the East. We believed in the goodness of man and have taught our children these teachings for years, long before the missionaries came and told us our beliefs were bad. . . .

THE LAST OF THE IRISH IMMIGRANTS

Jimmy Breslin

The priest had an Irish name, of course, and he got up in the pulpit of this church, a big church, a very beautiful church, Our Lady Queen of Martyrs Church in Forest Hills, and he began a sermon aimed at all the terrible people on welfare. They were together in the splendor of this church, the priest in the pulpit and the people in the pews, a fat-eyed priest and the drooping, bulging middle-aged people who seem to be the only ones to go to church anymore, and they examined, without specific mention, the Diocese of Brooklyn's ultimate vision of sin: a black woman smoking a cigarette while she opens the relief check in the morning mail.

The last thing I heard the priest talking about was the disgraceful lack of family structure of the people who go on welfare. It was depressing to hear the man talk, but I thought the worst part of the morning was that nobody else walked out of the church with me.

The stand the priest took was common for so many of the people in New York who have Irish names. How they can be this way, in the face of the history of the people who came before them, is one of the things about life which is as hard to understand as it is predictable. I was wondering, on the way home, if the priest ever had read anything like the letters written by Father John O'Sullivan and sent from Ireland to New York in 1851. At the time, over a million Irish were in the process of starving to death during the potato famine. Meanwhile, the ruling British Parliament sat and argued over allocating welfare funds because they were afraid the Irish were poor administrators and would waste and steal the relief money. And while the politicians debated, Father O'Sullivan wrote:

> I was called in to find a miserable object beside whom lay a child dead for the 24 hours previous, two others lay beside her just expiring and, horrible to relate, a famished cat got upon the bed and was about to gnaw on the corpse of the deceased infant until I prevented it.

When I got home, the people around the corner told me about St. Ann's Church, a church under the Brooklyn Bridge which has been attracting dissatisfied people, mostly young, from other parishes. The information was gladly received. For myself, you don't leave your religion. But you do start picking quarrels with the stubborn people who appear to be in church to pray *against* people.

Of the 4,600,000 Irish who immigrated to this country, the bulk of them came over during the famines. Oppression and hunger, therefore, is the true heritage of the Irish in New York. Their history in America did not begin, as they seem to feel, in the steam room of the New York Athletic Club. These Irish of New York, who march proudly up Fifth Avenue on Monday, usually can be found in similar lines, jowl to jowl, standing in opposition to much that has to do with the poor and oppressed. For each Paul O'Dwyer, who is made of whatever there is in the world that is good, there are 5,000 Irish names in New York ready to shout or vote against anything he stands for.

Now, the Irish are being singled out here because it is St. Patrick's Day, their time of year in this city. But it is anything but fair to say they are the only ethnic group in town who have learned to forget where they come from. You only had to stand in front of City Hall one afternoon last fall, with 30,000 Jewish school teachers demonstrating against black people and Mayor Lindsay, to see this. The school teachers were led by Albert Shanker, who is Mark Lane's brother. Units of the International Longshoremen's Association and the Sheetmetal Workers' Union paraded in support of the Jewish schoolteachers. The Jewish schoolteachers, in demeanor and language, were only a little more crude than the dockworkers and sheetmetal workers.

But it is the Irish we parade with, and drink with, and examine this week. With a little whiskey and a little music, the natural fun of these people takes over and the pride grows and the myths heighten and it always is one of the nicest days of the year in New York. But somewhere during the day, these Irish, who conform and restrict so much, and even obstruct, should get the chance to have a drink with somebody like Sam O'Reilly.

Sam O'Reilly is into his 70s now, which he might admit if you were to sit with him long enough over a drink and press him. He lives on Claremont Avenue in Manhattan. When they tell stories of the Easter Uprising of 1916, they almost always omit the kinds of details Sam O'Reilly remembers. Remembers very well, too. He was in the post office when it counted, on Easter Sunday, with a gun in his hand.

"You'll hear 30,000 fellows in saloons on Third Avenue saying they were in the post office," Sam O'Reilly was saying the other day, "but there are only three of us alive today in this country who were there. And you know what happened to us, don't you? When we finally had to surrender and come out, they made us march in the street between two lines of British soldiers. All the people in the city came out to watch. They were pushing against the soldiers and spittin' at us. They were mad at us because we disturbed the peace."

When they begin crying and telling stories of the glorious revolt, Sam O'Reilly always begins edging away. In Dublin in 1966, at a ceremony marking the 50th anniversary of the rebellion, they made Sam sit in the reviewing stand on the steps of the post office. When the politicians began making stirring speeches, Sam O'Reilly started to left-step down the reviewing stand and when he got to the last seat he jumped off and walked down the side street and into a saloon, which was just opening.

"Every time I hear one of our own kind over here saying something against the black fellas because they're pushing for what they want, I think of my own people spittin' on me because I was trying to push for them," Sam O'Reilly will tell you.

And on St. Patrick's Day it would be good, too, for somebody out on the town to sit down and talk to James Toner, who stands among the last of the Irish immigrants. Toner is 20, and he has been here only for a few weeks. He is one of less than 90 Irish who were admitted to the United States on a working visa last year. There is no quota for Irish immigration anymore. Toner got into the country on the last of the slim British quota. He could do this because he is from Belfast, in Northern Ireland.

The other day, James Toner sat in his white apron and chef's hat at a table in the place where he works, the John Barleycorn Restaurant on 45th Street. It was late in the afternoon, before the night rush started, and Toner had a cup of tea and talked about why he came to America.

"The religious troubles is terrible, it made me sick all the time," he said.

"He's a Catholic," Terry O'Neill, the owner, said. "Catholics in the North, they call them niggers."

"It's just like the black and white here," Toner said. "The Catholics are on the bottom, just like the blacks."

"What's it like to be on the bottom in Northern Ireland?" Toner was asked.

"You can't get a job. You go for a job, my brother got offered a job on the docks, and he went all through it with the man and the man said my brother had the job, and then the man said, oh, by the way, what school did you go to? That's how they get you. The name of the school. So the brother says St. Teresa's school and the man says to him, oh, I'm not hiring you, I have somebody who's more experienced."

"What did you do over there?"

"Me. I was lucky, I got a job in the kitchen of a restaurant. They got to needin' me, so they didn't fire me."

"What did you get paid?"

"Nineteen pound."

"Would you get more if you weren't a Catholic?"

"Oh sure, you would. You see, the whole thing is the jobs. The Catholics come last."

"What do the Catholics do for work?"

"Go on the brew. You know the *stayet*. The Relief. Then they hang around the bars and the bookie shops. There's nothin' else they can do."

"Where does a Catholic have the trouble outside of getting jobs?"

"Oh, everywhere. The Protestants don't talk to you. There's people I knew, McCombs, they lived on a byroad and I went there one day to see them and all these kids of theirs, I knew them all, and they wouldn't talk to me."

"Who else wouldn't talk to you?"

"Anybody who knew I was Catholic. They spend time tryin' to find out if you're Catholic. They're always askin', what school did you go to, what church do you go to. There's a place, Shankill Road, I never went there. They'd beat you if you was Catholic. They got signs sayin' 'No Pope Here.' "

"How do the police treat you?"

"Oh, they arrest a Catholic first. In the court, you get a bigger fine if you're a Catholic. All the legal things is that way. The brother got to be over 21 and they still don't give him the vote. There's Protestants votin' at 18."

Somebody had newspaper clippings of the Catholic Civil Rights demonstrations around Derry. The police, assigned to march with the protestors, had led the Catholics into a waiting mob of Protestant followers of the Rev. Ian Paisley. Paisley lists himself as having attended Bob Jones College in Greenville, South Carolina, which is some kind of an Elmer Gantry college. He is the George Wallace of Northern Ireland. One of his major points is that the people must support their police in the fight against the lazy, slovenly, relief-role Catholics.

"It'll come to shootin', it will," Toner said.

"Don't you think there's a better way than that?"

"There's always a better way. I hated fights myself and I never went dancin' at Protestant places because of that. But they can put you in jail for no reason, just for bein' a Catholic, and they'll never give anything to Catholics. So I guess they got to get up and start takin' what they want. There's only one way to do that. Fight."

"I guess you were good and happy to get over here," a waitress said.

"Every Catholic in the North dreams of coming here. The Protestants is glad to see you go, too."

"Do you hate the Protestants?"

"Oh, you have to," he said softly.

He got up to go back into the kitchen. He is a thin, fair-skinned young man with large, dark eyes. He came here on a Tuesday, in an Irish Airlines jet, but he had the same qualities of the ones who came long before him, on old crowded boats. James Toner had a job and was working his first full day at the John Barleycorn Restaurant on Friday night. He also brought with him something that too many of the Irish in New York today have forgotten or never knew: an understanding of what it is to be one of the jobless oppressed.

There is, because of this understanding, a permanent sadness in people like James Toner. He was saying that he liked the songs of Jesse Owens, the fine Irish ballad singer who appears at the John Barleycorn.

"He knows all the songs," Toner said. "Not just the popular ones. He keeps lookin' them up through history. Jesse does one I like the best. It's about this fella, the redcoats come and cut his head off and his girl is lyin' on the grave and weepin'. I like sentimental songs."

ANCIENT GENTILITY

William Carlos Williams

In those days I was about the only doctor they would have on Guinea Hill. Nowadays some of the kids I delivered then may be practicing medicine in the neighborhood. But in those days I had them all. I got to love those people, they were all right. Italian peasants from the region just south of Naples, most of them, living in small jerry-built houses—doing whatever they could find to do for a living and getting by, somehow.

Among the others, there was a little frame building, or box, you might almost say, which had always interested me but into which I had never gone. It stood in the center of the usual small garden patch and sometimes there would be an old man at the gate, just standing there, with a big curved and silver-capped pipe in his mouth, puffing away at his leisure.

Sure enough, one day I landed in that house also.

I had been seeing a child at the Petrello's or Albino's or whoever it was when, as often happened, the woman of the house stopped me with a smile at the door just as I was leaving.

Doc, I want you to visit the old people next door. The old lady's sick. She don't want to call nobody, but you go just the same. I'll fix it up with you sometime. Will you do it—for me?

Would I! It was a June morning. I had only to go twenty feet or so up the street—with a view of all New York City spread out before me over the meadows just beginning to turn green—and push back the low gate to the little vegetable garden.

The old man opened the house door for me before I could knock. He smiled and bowed his head several times out of respect for a physician and pointed upstairs. He couldn't speak a word of English and I knew practically no Italian, so he let it go at that.

He was wonderful. A gentle, kindly creature, big as the house itself, almost, with long pure white hair and big white moustache. Every movement he made showed a sort of ancient gentility. Finally he said a few words as if to let me know he was sorry he couldn't talk English and pointed upstairs again.

Where I stood at that moment it was just one room, everything combined: you cooked in one corner, ate close by, and sat yourself down to talk with your friends and relatives over beyond. Everything was immaculately clean and smelt just tinged with that faint odor of garlic, peppers and olive oil which one gets to expect in all these peasant houses.

There was one other room, immediately above. To it there ascended a removable ladder. At this moment the trap was open and the ladder in place. I went up. The old man remained below.

What a thrill I got! There was an enormous bed that almost filled the place, it seemed, perhaps a chair or two besides, but no other furniture, and in the bed sinking into the feather mattress and covered with a great feather quilt was the woman I had been summoned to attend.

Her face was dry and seamed with wrinkles, as old peasant faces will finally become, but it had the same patient smile upon it as shone from that of her old husband. White hair framing her face with silvery abundance, she didn't look at all sick to me.

She said a few words, smiling the while, by which I understood that after all it wasn't much and that she knew she didn't need a doctor and would have been up long since—or words to that effect—if the others hadn't insisted. After listening to her heart and palpating her abdomen I told her she could get up if she wanted to, and as I backed down the ladder after saying good-bye, she had already begun to do so.

The old man was waiting for me as I arrived below.

We walked to the door together, I trying to explain to him what I had found and he bowing and saying a word or two of Italian in reply. I could make out that he was thanking me for my trouble and that he was sorry he had no money, and so forth and so on.

At the gate we paused in one of those embarrassed moments which sometimes arrive during any conversation between relative strangers who wish to make a good impression on each other. Then as we stood there, slightly ill at ease, I saw him reach into his vest pocket and take something into his hand which he held out toward me.

It was a small silver box, about an inch and a quarter along the sides and half an inch thick. On the cover of it was the embossed figure of a woman reclining among flowers. I took it in my hand but couldn't imagine what he wanted me to do with it. He couldn't be giving it to me?

Seeing that I was puzzled, he reached for it, ever so gently, and I returned it to him. As he took it in his hand he opened it. It seemed to contain a sort of brown powder. Then I saw him pick some of it up between the thumb and finger of his right hand, place it at the base of his left thumb and . . .

Why snuff! Of course. I was delighted.

As he whiffed the powder into one generous nostril and then the other, he handed the box back to me—in all, one of the most gracious, kindly proceedings I had ever taken part in.

Imitating him as best I could, I shared his snuff with him, and that was about the end of me for a moment or two. I couldn't stop sneezing. I suppose I had gone at it a little too vigorously. Finally, with tears in my eyes, I felt the old man standing there, smiling, an experience the like of which I shall never, in all probability, have again in my life on this mundane sphere.

LETTER FROM A POLISH IMMIGRANT[1]

F.N.

I'm in this country four months (from 14 Mai 1913–Noniton–Antverpen).

I am polish man. I want be american citizen—and took here first paper in 12 June N 625. But my friends are polish people—I must live with them—I work in the shoes-shop with polish people—I stay all the time with them—at home—in the shop—anywhere.

I want live with american people, but I do not know anybody of american. I go 4 times to teacher and must pay $2 weekly. I wanted take board in english house, but I could not, for I earn only $5 or 6 in a week, and when I pay teacher $2, I have only $4-$3—and now english board

1 "Letter of an Anonymous Polish Immigrant to the Massachusetts Commission on Immigration, August, 1914," *Report of the Commission on the Problem of Immigration in Massachusetts* (Boston, 1914), 134.

house is too dear for me. Better job to get is very hard for me because I do not speak well english and I cannot understand what they say to me. The teacher teach me—but when I come home—I must speak polish and in the shop also. In this way I can live in your country many years—like my friends—and never speak—write well english—and never be good american citizen. I know here many persons, they live here 10 or moore years, and they are not citizens, they don't speak well english, they don't know geography and history of this country, they don't know constitution of America.—nothing. I don't like be like them I wanted they help me in english—they could not—because they knew nothing. I want go from them away. But where? Not in the country, because I want go in the city, free evening schools and lern. I'm looking for help. If somebody could give me another job between american people, help me live with them and lern english—and could tell me the best way how I can fast lern —it would be very, very good for me. Perhaps you have somebody, here he could help me?

If you can help me, I please you.

I wrote this letter by myself and I know no good—but I hope you will understand whate I mean.

Excuse me,
F.N.

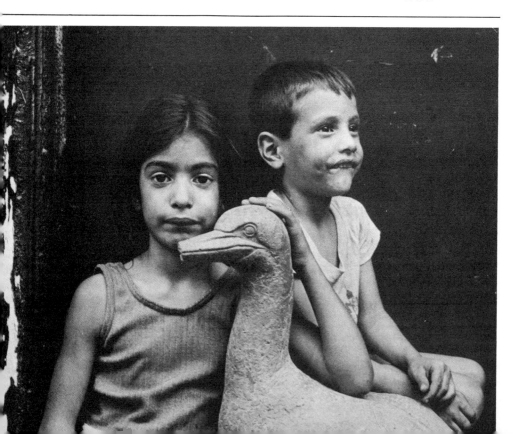

ADAM

Kurt Vonnegut, Jr.

It was midnight in a Chicago lying-in hospital.

"Mr. Sousa," said the nurse, "your wife had a girl. You can see the baby in about twenty minutes."

"I know, I know, I know," said Mr. Sousa, a sullen gorilla, plainly impatient with having a tiresome and familiar routine explained to him. He snapped his fingers. "Girl! Seven, now. Seven girls I got now. A houseful of women. I can beat the stuffings out of ten men my own size. But, what do I get? Girls."

"Mr. Knechtmann," said the nurse to the other man in the room. She pronounced the name, as almost all Americans did, a colorless Netman. "I'm sorry. Still no word on your wife. She is keeping us waiting, isn't she?" She grinned glassily and left.

Sousa turned on Knechtmann. "Some little son of a gun like you, Netman, you want a boy, bing! You got one. Want a football team, bing, bing, bing, eleven, you got it." He stomped out of the room.

The man he left behind, all alone now, was Heinz Knechtmann, a presser in a dry-cleaning plant, a small man with thin wrists and a bad spine that kept him slightly hunched, as though forever weary. His face was long and big-nosed and thin-lipped, but was so overcast with good-humored humility as to be beautiful. His eyes were large and brown, and deep-set and long-lashed. He was only twenty-two, but seemed and felt much older. He had died a little as each member of his family had been led away and killed by the Nazis, until only in him, at the age of ten, had life and the name of Knechtmann shared a soul. He and his wife, Avchen, had grown up behind barbed wire.

He had been staring at the walls of the waiting room for twelve hours now, since noon, when his wife's labor pains had become regular, the surges of slow rollers coming in from the sea a mile apart, from far, far away. This would be his second child. The last time he had waited, he had waited on a straw tick in a displaced-persons camp in Germany. The child, Karl Knechtmann, named after Heinz's father, had died, and with it, once more, had died the name of one of the finest cellists ever to have lived.

When the numbness of weary wishing lifted momentarily during this second vigil, Heinz's mind was a medley of proud family names, gone, all gone, that could be brought to life again in this new being—if it lived. Peter Knechtmann, the surgeon; Kroll Knechtmann, the botanist; Friederich Knechtmann, the playwright. Dimly recalled uncles. Or if it was a girl, and if it lived, it would be Helga Knechtmann, Heinz's mother, and she would learn to play the harp as Heinz's mother had, and for all Heinz's ugliness, she would be beautiful. The Knechtmann men were all ugly, the Knechtmann women were all lovely as angels, though not all angels. It had always been so—for hundreds and hundreds of years.

"Mr. Netman," said the nurse, "it's a boy, and your wife is fine. She's resting now. You can see her in the morning. You can see the baby in twenty minutes."

Heinz looked up dumbly.

"It weighs five pounds nine ounces." She was gone again, with the same prim smile and officious, squeaking footsteps.

"Knechtmann," murmured Heinz, standing and bowing slightly to the wall. "The name is Knechtmann." He bowed again and gave a smile that was courtly and triumphant. He spoke the name with an exaggerated Old World pronunciation, like a foppish footman announcing the arrival of nobility, a guttural drum roll, unsoftened for American ears. *"Khhhhhhhh-hhhhhhNECHT! mannnnnnnnnnnnn."*

"Mr. Netman?" A very young doctor with a pink face and close-cropped red hair stood in the waiting-room door. There were circles under his eyes, and he spoke through a yawn.

"Dr. Powers!" cried Heinz, clasping the man's right hand between both of his. "Thank God, thank God, thank God, and thank you."

"Um," said Dr. Powers, and he managed to smile wanly.

"There isn't anything wrong, is there?"

"Wrong?" said Powers. "No, no. Everything's fine. If I look down in the mouth, it's because I've been up for thirty-six hours straight." He closed his eyes, and leaned against the doorframe. "No, no trouble with your wife," he said in a faraway voice. "She's made for having babies. Regular pop-up toaster. Like rolling off a log. Schnipschnap."

"She is?" said Heinz incredulously.

Dr. Powers shook his head, bringing himself back to consciousness. "My mind—conked out completely. Sousa—I got your wife confused with Mrs. Sousa. They finished in a dead heat. Netman, you're Netman. Sorry. Your wife's the one with pelvis trouble."

"Malnutrition as a child," said Heinz.

"Yeah. Well, the baby came normally, but, if you're going to have another one, it'd better be a Caesarean. Just to be on the safe side."

"I can't thank you enough," said Heinz passionately.

Dr. Powers licked his lips, and fought to keep his eyes open. "Uh huh. 'S O.K.," he said thickly. " 'Night. Luck." He shambled out into the corridor.

The nurse stuck her head into the waiting room. "You can see your baby, Mr. Netman."

"Doctor—" said Heinz, hurrying out into the corridor, wanting to shake Powers' hand again so that Powers would know what a magnificient thing he'd done. "It's the most wonderful thing that ever happened." The elevator doors slithered shut between them before Dr. Powers could show a glimmer of response.

"This way," said the nurse. "Turn left at the end of the hall, and you'll find the nursery window there. Write your name on a piece of paper and hold it against the glass."

Heinz made the trip by himself, without seeing another human being until he reached the end. There, on the other side of a large glass panel, he saw a hundred of them cupped in shallow canvas buckets and arranged in a square block of straight ranks and files.

Heinz wrote his name on the back of a laundry slip and pressed it to the window. A fat and placid nurse looked at the paper, not at Heinz's face, and missed seeing his wide smile, missed an urgent invitation to share for a moment his ecstasy.

She grasped one of the buckets and wheeled it before the window. She turned away again, once more missing the smile.

"Hello, hello, hello, little Knechtmann," said Heinz to the red prune on the other side of the glass. His voice echoed down the hard, bare corridor, and came back to him with embarrassing loudness. He blushed and lowered his voice. "Little Peter, little Kroll," he said softly, "little Friederich—and there's Helga in you, too. Little spark of Knechtmann, you little treasure house. Everything is saved in you."

"I'm afraid you'll have to be more quiet," said a nurse, sticking her head out from one of the rooms.

"Sorry," said Heinz. "I'm very sorry." He fell silent, and contented himself with tapping lightly on the window with a fingernail, trying to get the child to look at him. Young Knechtmann would not look, wouldn't share the moment, and after a few minutes the nurse took him away again.

Heinz beamed as he rode on the elevator and as he crossed the hospital lobby, but no one gave him more than a cursory glance. He passed a row of telephone booths and there, in one of the booths with the door open, he saw a soldier with whom he'd shared the waiting room an hour before.

"Yeah, Ma—seven pounds six ounces. Got hair like Buffalo Bill. No, we haven't had time to make up a name for her yet . . . That you, Pa? Yup, mother and daughter doin' fine, just fine. Seven pounds six ounces. Nope, no name. . . . That you, Sis? Pretty late for you to be up, ain't it? Doesn't look like anybody yet. Let me talk to Ma again. . . . That you, Ma? Well, I guess that's all the news from Chicago. Now, Mom, Mom, take it easy—don't worry. It's a swell-looking baby, Mom. Just the hair looks like Buffalo Bill, and I said it as a joke, Mom. That's right, seven pounds six ounces. . . ."

There were five other booths, all empty, all open for calls to any-place on earth. Heinz longed to hurry into one of them breathlessly, and tell the marvelous news. But there was no one to call, no one waiting for the news.

But Heinz still beamed, and he strode across the street and into a quiet tavern there. In the dank twilight there were only two men, tête-à-tête, the bartender and Mr. Sousa.

"Yes sir, what'll it be?"

"I'd like to buy you and Mr. Sousa a drink," said Heinz with a heartiness strange to him. "I'd like the best brandy you've got. My wife just had a baby!"

"That so?" said the bartender with polite interest.

"Five pounds nine ounces," said Heinz.

"Huh," said the bartender. "What do you know."

"Netman," said Sousa, "wha'dja get?"

"Boy," said Heinz proudly.

"Never knew it to fail," said Sousa bitterly. "It's the little guys, all the time the little guys."

"Boy, girl," said Heinz, "it's all the same, just as long as it lives. Over there in the hospital, they're too close to it to see the wonder of it. A miracle over and over again—the world made new."

"Wait'll you've racked up seven, Netman," said Sousa. "*Then* you come back and tell me about the miracle."

"You got seven?" said the bartender. "I'm one up on you. I got eight." He poured three drinks.

"Far as I'm concerned," said Sousa, "you can have the champion-ship."

Heinz lifted his glass. "Here's long life and great skill and much happiness to—to Peter Karl Knechtmann." He breathed quickly, excited by the decision.

"*There's* a handle to take ahold of," said Sousa. "You'd think the kid weighed two hundred pounds."

"Peter is the name of a famous surgeon," said Heinz, "the boy's great-uncle, dead now. Karl was my father's name."

"Here's to Pete K. Netman," said Sousa, with a cursory salute.

"Pete," said the bartender, drinking.

"And here's to *your* little girl—the new one," said Heinz.

Sousa sighed and smiled wearily. "Here's to her. God bless her."

"And now, *I'll* propose a toast," said the bartender, hammering on the bar with his fist. "On your feet, gentlemen. Up, up, everybody up."

Heinz stood, and held his glass high, ready for the next step in camaraderie, a toast to the whole human race, of which the Knechtmanns were still a part.

"Here's to the White Sox!" roared the bartender.

"Minoso, Fox, Mele," said Sousa.

"Fain, Lollar, Rivera!" said the bartender. He turned to Heinz. "Drink up, boy! The White Sox! Don't tell me you're a Cub fan."

"No," said Heinz, disappointed. "No—I don't follow baseball, I'm afraid." The other two men seemed to be sinking away from him. "I haven't been able to think about much but the baby."

The bartender at once turned his full attention to Sousa. "Look," he said intensely, "they take Fain off of first, and put him at third, and give Pierce first. Then move Minoso in from left field to shortstop. See what I'm doing?"

"Yep, yep," said Sousa eagerly.

"And then we take that no-good Carrasquel and . . ."

Heinz was all alone again, with twenty feet of bar between him and the other two men. It might as well have been a continent.

He finished his drink without pleasure, and left quietly.

At the railroad station, where he waited for a local train to take him home to the South Side, Heinz's glow returned again as he saw a co-worker at the dry-cleaning plant walk in with a girl. They were laughing and had their arms around each other's waist.

"Harry," said Heinz, hurrying toward them. "Guess what, Harry. Guess what just happened." He grinned broadly.

Harry, a tall, dapper, snub-nosed young man, looked down at Heinz with mild surprise. "Oh—hello, Heinz. What's up, boy?"

The girl looked on in perplexity, as though asking why they should be accosted at such an odd hour by such an odd person. Heinz avoided her slightly derisive eyes.

"A baby, Harry. My wife just had a boy."

"Oh," said Harry. He extended his hand. "Well, congratulations." The hand was limp. "I think that's swell, Heinz, perfectly swell." He withdrew his hand and waited for Heinz to say something else.

"Yes, yes—just about an hour ago," said Heinz. "Five pounds nine ounces. I've never been happier in my life."

"Well, I think it's perfectly swell, Heinz. You should be happy."

"Yes, indeed," said the girl.

There was a long silence, with all three shifting from one foot to the other.

"Really good news," said Harry at last.

"Yes, well," said Heinz quickly, "well, that's all I had to tell you."

"Thanks," said Harry. "Glad to hear about it."

There was another uneasy silence.

"See you at work," said Heinz, and strode jauntily back to his bench, but with his reddened neck betraying how foolish he felt.

The girl giggled.

Back home in his small apartment, at two in the morning, Heinz talked to himself, to the empty bassinet, and to the bed. He talked in German, a language he had sworn never to use again.

"They don't care," said Heinz. "They're all too busy, busy, busy to notice life, to feel anything about it. A baby is born." He shrugged. "What could be duller? Who would be so stupid as to talk about it, to think there was anything important or interesting about it?"

He opened a window on the summer night, and looked out at the moonlit canyon of gray wooden porches and garbage cans. "There are too many of us, and we are all too far apart," said Heinz. "Another Knechtmann is born, another O'Leary, another Sousa. Who cares? Why should anyone care? What difference does it make? None."

He lay down in his clothes on the unmade bed, and, with a rattling sigh, went to sleep.

He awoke at six, as always. He drank a cup of coffee, and with a wry sense of anonymity, he jostled and was jostled aboard the downtown train. His face showed no emotion. It was like all the other faces, seemingly incapable of surprise or wonder, joy or anger.

He walked across town to the hospital with the same detachment, a gray, uninteresting man, a part of the city.

In the hospital, he was as purposeful and calm as the doctors and nurses bustling about him. When he was led into the ward where Avchen slept behind white screens, he felt only what he had always felt in her presence—love and aching awe and gratitude for her.

"You go ahead and wake her gently, Mr. Netman," said the nurse.

"Avchen—" He touched her on her white-gowned shoulder. "Avchen. Are you all right, Avchen?"

"Mmmmmmmmmmm?" murmured Avchen. Her eyes opened to narrow slits. "Heinz. Hello, Heinz."

"Sweetheart, are you all right?"

"Yes, yes," she whispered. "I'm fine. How is the baby, Heinz?"

"Perfect. Perfect, Avchen."

"They couldn't kill us, could they, Heinz?"

"No."

"And here we are, alive as we can be."

"Yes."

"The baby, Heinz—" She opened her dark eyes wide. "It's the most wonderful thing that ever happened, isn't it?"

"Yes," said Heinz.

THE ETHICS OF LIVING JIM CROW

AN AUTOBIOGRAPHICAL SKETCH

Richard Wright

I

My first lesson in how to live as a Negro came when I was quite small. We were living in Arkansas. Our house stood behind the railroad tracks. Its skimpy yard was paved with black cinders. Nothing green ever grew in that yard. The only touch of green we could see was far away, beyond the tracks, over where the white folks lived. But cinders were good enough for me and I never missed the green growing things. And anyhow cinders were fine weapons. You could always have a nice hot war with huge black cinders. All you had to do was crouch behind the brick pillars of a house with your hands full of gritty ammunition. And the first woolly black head you saw pop out from behind another row of pillars was your target. You tried your very best to knock it off. It was great fun.

I never fully realized the appalling disadvantages of a cinder environment till one day the gang to which I belonged found itself engaged in a war with the white boys who lived beyond the tracks. As usual we laid down our cinder barrage, thinking that this would wipe the white boys out. But they replied with a steady bombardment of broken bottles. We doubled our cinder barrage, but they hid behind trees, hedges, and the sloping embankments of their lawns. Having no such fortifications, we retreated to the brick pillars of our homes. During the retreat a broken milk bottle caught me behind the ear, opening a deep gash which bled profusely. The sight of blood pouring over my face completely demoralized our ranks. My fellow-combatants left me standing paralyzed in the center of the yard, and scurried for their homes. A kind neighbor saw me and rushed me to a doctor, who took three stitches in my neck.

I sat brooding on my front steps, nursing my wound and waiting for my mother to come from work. I felt that a grave injustice had been done me. It was all right to throw cinders. The greatest harm a cinder could do was leave a bruise. But broken bottles were dangerous; they left you cut, bleeding, and helpless.

When night fell, my mother came from the white folks' kitchen. I raced down the street to meet her. I could just feel in my bones that she would understand. I knew she would tell me exactly what to do next time. I grabbed her hand and babbled out the whole story. She examined my wound, then slapped me.

"How come yuh didn't hide?" she asked me. "How come yuh awways fightin'?"

I was outraged, and bawled. Between sobs I told her that I didn't have any trees or hedges to hide behind. There wasn't a thing I could have used as a trench. And you couldn't throw very far when you were hiding behind the brick pillars of a house. She grabbed a barrel stave, dragged me home, stripped me naked, and beat me till I had a fever of one hundred and two. She would smack my rump with the stave, and, while the skin was still smarting, impart to me gems of Jim Crow wisdom. I was never to throw cinders any more. I was never to fight any more wars. I was never, never, under any conditions, to fight *white* folks again. And they were absolutely right in clouting me with the broken milk bottle. Didn't I know she was working hard every day in the hot kitchens of the white folks to make money to take care of me? When was I ever going to learn to be a good boy? She couldn't be bothered with my fights. She finished by telling me that I ought to be thankful to God as long as I lived that they didn't kill me.

All that night I was delirious and could not sleep. Each time I closed my eyes I saw monstrous white faces suspended from the ceiling, leering at me.

From that time on, the charm of my cinder yard was gone. The green trees, the trimmed hedges, the cropped lawns grew very meaningful, became a symbol. Even today when I think of white folks, the hard, sharp outlines of white houses surrounded by trees, lawns, and hedges are present somewhere in the background of my mind. Through the years they grew into an overreaching symbol of fear.

It was a long time before I came in close contact with white folks again. We moved from Arkansas to Mississippi. Here we had the good fortune not to live behind the railroad tracks, or close to white neighborhoods. We lived in the very heart of the local Black Belt. There were black churches and black preachers; there were black schools and black teachers; black groceries and black clerks. In fact, everything was so solidly black that for a long time I did not even think of white folks, save in remote and vague terms. But this could not last forever. As one grows older one eats more. One's clothing costs more. When I finished grammar school I had to go to work. My mother could no longer feed and clothe me on her cooking job.

There is but one place where a black boy who knows no trade can get a job, and that's where the houses and faces are white, where the trees, lawns, and hedges are green. My first job was with an optical company in Jackson, Mississippi. The morning I applied I stood straight and neat before the boss, answering all his questions with sharp yessirs and nosirs. I was very careful to pronounce my *sirs* distinctly, in order that he might know that I was polite, that I knew where I was, and that I knew he was a *white* man. I wanted that job badly.

He looked me over as though he were examining a prize poodle. He questioned me closely about my schooling, being particularly insistent about how much mathematics I had had. He seemed very pleased when I told him I had had two years of algebra.

"Boy, how would you like to try to learn something around here?" he asked me.

"I'd like it fine, sir," I said, happy. I had visions of "working my way up." Even Negroes have those visions.

"All right," he said. "Come on."

I followed him to the small factory.

"Pease," he said to a white man of about thirty-five, "this is Richard. He's going to work for us."

Pease looked at me and nodded.

I was then taken to a white boy of about seventeen.

"Morrie, this is Richard, who's going to work for us."

"Whut yuh sayin' there, boy!" Morrie boomed at me.

"Fine!" I answered.

The boss instructed these two to help me, teach me, give me jobs to do, and let me learn what I could in my spare time.

My wages were five dollars a week.

I worked hard, trying to please. For the first month I got along O.K. Both Pease and Morrie seemed to like me. But one thing was missing. And I kept thinking about it. I was not learning anything and nobody was volunteering to help me. Thinking they had forgotten that I was to learn something about the mechanics of grinding lenses, I asked Morrie one day to tell me about the work. He grew red.

"Whut yuh tryin' t' do, nigger, get smart?" he asked.

"Naw; I ain' tryin' t' git smart," I said.

"Well, don't, if yuh know whut's good for yuh!"

I was puzzled. Maybe he just doesn't want to help me, I thought. I went to Pease.

"Say, are yuh crazy, you black bastard?" Pease asked me, his gray eyes growing hard.

I spoke out, reminding him that the boss had said I was to be given a chance to learn something.

"Nigger, you think you're *white*, don't you?"

"Naw, sir!"

"Well, you're acting mighty like it!"

"But, Mr. Pease, the boss said . . ."

Pease shook his fist in my face.

"This is a *white* man's work around here, and you better watch yourself!"

From then on they changed toward me. They said good-morning no more. When I was just a bit slow in performing some duty, I was called a lazy black son-of-a-bitch.

Once I thought of reporting all this to the boss. But the mere idea of what would happen to me if Pease and Morrie should learn that I had "snitched" stopped me. And after all the boss was a white man, too. What was the use?

The climax came at noon one summer day. Pease called me to his work-bench. To get to him I had to go between two narrow benches and stand with my back against a wall.

"Yes, sir," I said.

"Richard, I want to ask you something," Pease began pleasantly, not looking up from his work.

"Yes, sir," I said again.

Morrie came over, blocking the narrow passage between the benches. He folded his arms, staring at me solemnly.

I looked from one to the other, sensing that something was coming.

"Yes, sir," I said for the third time.

Pease looked up and spoke very slowly.

"Richard, *Mr.* Morrie here tells me you called me *Pease.*"

I stiffened. A void seemed to open up in me. I knew this was the show-down.

He meant that I had failed to call him Mr. Pease. I looked at Morrie. He was gripping a steel bar in his hands. I opened my mouth to speak, to protest, to assure Pease that I had never called him simply *Pease*, and that I had never had any intentions of doing so, when Morrie grabbed me by the collar, ramming my head against the wall.

"Now, be careful, nigger!" snarled Morrie, baring his teeth. "*I* heard yuh call 'im *Pease!* 'N' if yuh say yuh didn't, yuh're callin' me a *lie*, see?" He waved the steel bar threateningly.

If I had said: No, sir, Mr. Pease, I never called you *Pease*, I would have been automatically calling Morrie a liar. And if I had said: Yes, sir, Mr. Pease, I called you *Pease*, I would have been pleading guilty to having uttered the worst insult that a Negro can utter to a southern white man. I stood hesitating, trying to frame a neutral reply.

"Richard, I asked you a question!" said Pease. Anger was creeping into his voice.

"I don't remember calling you *Pease*, Mr. Pease," I said cautiously. "And if I did, I sure didn't mean . . ."

"You black son-of-a-bitch! You called me *Pease*, then!" he spat, slapping me till I bent sideways over a bench. Morrie was on top of me, demanding:

"Didn't yuh call 'im *Pease*? If yuh say yuh didn't, I'll rip yo' gut string loose with this bar, yuh black granny dodger! Yuh can't call a white man a lie 'n' git erway with it, you black son-of-a-bitch!"

I wilted. I begged them not to bother me. I knew what they wanted. They wanted me to leave.

"I'll leave," I promised. "I'll leave right *now.*"

They gave me a minute to get out of the factory. I was warned not to show up again, or tell the boss.

I went.

When I told the folks at home what had happened, they called me a fool. They told me that I must never again attempt to exceed my boundaries. When you are working for white folks, they said, you got to "stay in your place" if you want to keep working.

II

My Jim Crow education continued on my next job, which was portering in a clothing store. One morning, while polishing brass out front, the boss and his twenty-year-old son got out of their car and half dragged and half kicked a Negro woman into the store. A policeman standing at the corner looked on, twirling his night-stick. I watched out of the corner of my eye, never slackening the strokes of my chamois upon the brass. After a few minutes, I heard shrill screams coming from the rear of the store. Later the woman stumbled out, bleeding, crying, and holding her stomach. When she reached the end of the block, the policeman grabbed her and accused her of being drunk. Silently, I watched him throw her into a patrol wagon.

When I went to the rear of the store, the boss and his son were washing their hands at the sink. They were chuckling. The floor was bloody and strewn with wisps of hair and clothing. No doubt I must have appeared pretty shocked, for the boss slapped me reassuringly on the back.

"Boy, that's what we do to niggers when they don't want to pay their bills," he said, laughing.

His son looked at me and grinned.

"Here, hav' a cigarette," he said.

Not knowing what to do, I took it. He lit his and held the match for me. This was a gesture of kindness, indicating that even if they had beaten the poor old woman, they would not beat me if I knew enough to keep my mouth shut.

"Yes, sir," I said, and asked no questions.

After they had gone, I sat on the edge of a packing box and stared at the bloody floor till the cigarette went out.

That day at noon, while eating in a hamburger joint, I told my fellow Negro porters what had happened. No one seemed surprised. One fellow, after swallowing a huge bite, turned to me and asked:

"Huh! Is tha' all they did t' her?"

"Yeah. Wasn't tha' enough?" I asked.

"Shucks! Man, she's a lucky bitch!" he said, burying his lips deep into a juicy hamburger. "Hell, it's a wonder they didn't lay her when they got through."

III

I was learning fast, but not quite fast enough. One day, while I was delivering packages in the suburbs, my bicycle tire was punctured. I walked along the hot, dusty road, sweating and leading my bicycle by the handlebars.

A car slowed at my side.

"What's the matter, boy?" a white man called.

I told him my bicycle was broken and I was walking back to town.

"That's too bad," he said. "Hop on the running board."

He stopped the car. I clutched hard at my bicycle with one hand and clung to the side of the car with the other.

"All set?"

"Yes, sir," I answered. The car started.

It was full of young white men. They were drinking. I watched the flask pass from mouth to mouth.

"Wanna drink, boy?" one asked.

I laughed as the wind whipped my face. Instinctively obeying the freshly planted precepts of my mother, I said:

"Oh, no!"

The words were hardly out of my mouth before I felt something hard and cold smash me between the eyes. It was an empty whisky bottle. I saw stars, and fell backwards from the speeding car into the dust of the road, my feet becoming entangled in the steel spokes of my bicycle. The white men piled out and stood over me.

"Nigger, ain' yuh learned no better sense'n tha' yet?" asked the man who hit me. "Ain' yuh learned t' say *sir* t' a white man yet?"

Dazed, I pulled to my feet. My elbows and legs were bleeding. Fists doubled, the white man advanced, kicking my bicycle out of the way.

"Aw, leave the bastard alone. He's got enough," said one.

They stood looking at me. I rubbed my shins, trying to stop the flow of blood. No doubt they felt a sort of contemptuous pity, for one asked:

"Yuh wanna ride t' town now, nigger? Yuh reckon yuh know enough t' ride now?"

"I wanna walk," I said, simply.

Maybe it sounded funny. They laughed.

"Well, walk, yuh black son-of-a-bitch!"

When they left they comforted me with:

"Nigger, yuh sho better be damn glad it wuz us yuh talked t' tha' way. Yuh're a lucky bastard, 'cause if yuh'd said tha' t' somebody else, yuh might've been a dead nigger now."

IV

Negroes who have lived South know the dread of being caught alone upon the streets in white neighborhoods after the sun has set. In such a simple situation as this the plight of the Negro in America is graphically symbolized. While white strangers may be in these neighborhoods trying to get home, they can pass unmolested. But the color of a Negro's skin makes him easily recognizable, makes him suspect, converts him into a defenseless target.

Late one Saturday night I made some deliveries in a white neighborhood. I was pedaling my bicycle back to the store as fast as I could, when a police car, swerving toward me, jammed me into the curbing.

"Get down and put up your hands!" the policemen ordered.

I did. They climbed out of the car, guns drawn, faces set, and advanced slowly.

"Keep still!" they ordered.

I reached my hands higher. They searched my pockets and packages. They seemed dissatisfied when they could find nothing incriminating. Finally, one of them said:

"Boy, tell your boss not to send you out in white neighborhoods after sundown."

As usual, I said:

"Yes, sir."

V

My next job was a hall-boy in a hotel. Here my Jim Crow education broadened and deepened. When the bell-boys were busy, I was often called to assist them. As many of the rooms in the hotel were occupied by prostitutes, I was constantly called to carry them liquor and cigarettes. These women were nude most of the time. They did not bother about clothing, even for bell-boys. When you went into their rooms, you were supposed to take their nakedness for granted, as though it startled you no more than a blue vase or a red rug. Your presence awoke in them no sense of shame, for you were not regarded as human. If they were alone, you could steal side-long glimpses at them. But if they were receiving men, not a flicker of your eyelids could show. I remember one incident vividly. A new woman, a huge, snowy-skinned blonde, took a room on my floor. I was sent to wait upon her. She was in bed with a thick-set man; both were nude and uncovered. She said she wanted some liquor and slid out of bed and waddled across the floor to get her money from a dresser drawer. I watched her.

"Nigger, what in hell you looking at?" the white man asked me, raising himself upon his elbows.

"Nothing," I answered, looking miles deep into the blank wall of the room.

"Keep your eyes where they belong, if you want to be healthy!" he said.

"Yes, sir."

VI

One of the bell-boys I knew in this hotel was keeping steady company with one of the Negro maids. Out of a clear sky the police descended upon his home and arrested him, accusing him of bastardy. The poor boy swore he had had no intimate relations with the girl. Nevertheless, they forced him to marry her. When the child arrived, it was found to be much lighter in complexion than either of the two supposedly legal parents. The white men around the hotel made a great joke of it. They spread the rumor that some white cow must have scared the poor girl while she was carrying the baby. If you were in their presence when this explanation was offered, you were supposed to laugh.

VII

One of the bell-boys was caught in bed with a white prostitute. He was castrated and run out of town. Immediately after this all the bell-boys and hall-boys were called together and warned. We were given to understand that the boy who had been castrated was a "mighty, mighty lucky bastard." We were impressed with the fact that next time the management of the hotel would not be responsible for the lives of "trouble-makin' niggers." We were silent.

VIII

One night, just as I was about to go home, I met one of the Negro maids. She lived in my direction, and we fell in to walk part of the way home together. As we passed the white night-watchman, he slapped the maid on her buttock. I turned around, amazed. The watchman looked at me with a long hard fixed-under stare. Suddenly he pulled his gun and asked:

"Nigger, don't yuh like it?"

I hesitated.

"I asked yuh don't yuh like it?" he asked again, stepping forward.

"Yes, sir," I mumbled.

"Talk like it, then!"

"Oh, yes, sir!" I said with as much heartiness as I could muster.

Outside, I walked ahead of the girl, ashamed to face her. She caught up with me and said:

"Don't be a fool! Yuh couldn't help it!"

This watchman boasted of having killed two Negroes in self-defense.

Yet, in spite of all this, the life of the hotel ran with an amazing smoothness. It would have been impossible for a stranger to detect anything. The maids, the hall-boys, and the bell-boys were all smiles. They had to be.

IX

I had learned my Jim Crow lessons so thoroughly that I kept the hotel job till I left Jackson for Memphis. It so happened that while in Memphis I applied for a job at a branch of the optical company. I was hired. And for some reason, as long as I worked there, they never brought my past against me.

Here my Jim Crow education assumed quite a different form. It was no longer brutally cruel, but subtly cruel. Here I learned to lie, to steal, to dissemble. I learned to play that dual role which every Negro must play if he wants to eat and live.

For example, it was almost impossible to get a book to read. It was assumed that after a Negro had imbibed what scanty schooling the state furnished, he had no further need for books. I was always borrowing books from men on the job. One day I mustered enough courage to ask one of the men to let me get books from the library in his name. Surprisingly, he consented. I cannot help but think that he consented because he was a Roman Catholic and felt a vague sympathy for Negroes, being himself an object of hatred. Armed with a library card, I obtained books in the following manner: I would write a note to the librarian, saying: "Please let this nigger boy have the following books." I would then sign it with the white man's name.

When I went to the library, I would stand at the desk, hat in hand, looking as unbookish as possible. When I received the books desired I would take them home. If the books listed in the note happened to be out, I would sneak into the lobby and forge a new one. I never took any chances guessing with the white librarian about what the fictitious white man would want to read. No doubt if any of the white patrons had suspected that some of the volumes they enjoyed had been in the home of a Negro, they would not have tolerated it for an instant.

The factory force of the optical company in Memphis was much larger than that in Jackson, and more urbanized. At least they liked to talk, and would engage the Negro help in conversation whenever possible. By this means, I found that many subjects were taboo from the white man's point of view. Among the topics they did not like to discuss with Negroes were the following: American white women; the Ku Klux Klan; France, and how Negro soldiers fared while there; French women; Jack Johnson; the entire northern part of the United States; the Civil War; Abraham Lincoln; U.S. Grant; General Sherman; Catholics; the Pope; Jews; the Republican Party; slavery; social equality; Communism; Socialism; the 13th and 14th Amendments to the Constitution; or any topic calling for positive knowledge or manly self-assertion on the part of the Negro. The most accepted topics were sex and religion.

There were many times when I had to exercise a great deal of ingenuity to keep out of trouble. It is a southern custom that all men must take off their hats when they enter an elevator. And especially did this apply to us blacks with rigid force. One day I stepped into an elevator with my arms full of packages. I was forced to ride with my hat on. Two white men stared at me coldly. Then one of them very kindly lifted my hat and placed it upon my armful of packages. Now the most accepted response for a Negro to make under such circumstances is to look at the white man out of the corner of his eye and grin. To have said "Thank you!" would have made the white man *think* that you *thought* you were receiving from him a personal service. For such an act I have seen Negroes take a blow in the mouth. Finding the first alternative distasteful, and the second dangerous, I hit upon an acceptable course of action which fell safely between these two poles. I immediately—no sooner than my hat was lifted—pretended that my packages were about to spill, and appeared deeply distressed with keeping them in my arms. In this fashion I evaded having to acknowledge his service, and, in spite of adverse circumstances, salvaged a slender shred of personal pride.

How do Negroes feel about the way they have to live? How do they discuss it when alone among themselves? I think this question can be answered in a single sentence. A friend of mine who ran an elevator once told me:

"Lawd, man! Ef it wuzn't fer them police 'n' them ol' lynch-mobs, there wouldn't be nothin' but uproar down here!"

TAKE A CITY TO LUNCH

Art Hoppe

"We're making real progress," said my friend, George Washington X. "Nobody calls me 'Colored' any more.

"I attribute this to the National Association for the Advancement of Colored People, which got folks to stop calling me a 'Colored People' and start calling me a 'Negro.'

"There was a real advance. But then the Student Non-Violent Co-ordinating Committee got violent about Black Power and people began calling me 'Black.'

"I figured this was about as far as one man could struggle upward in one lifetime. But, much to my surprise, they've now come up with a brand new name for me."

What's that?

"Now they call me," said Mr. X with pardonable pride, "a 'City'."

A "City"? "That's right," said Mr. X. "You just listen to our leaders—Nixon, Humphrey, Spiro T. Whatshisname. Every one of them is going around saying, 'We must do something about the growing crisis of our Cities.'

"That's me they're talking about, man. And that's not the half of it. More often than not, they get specific and call me an 'Urban Core,' 'A Decaying Innercity' and an 'Impacted Area.'

"Now, I don't much mind being an Urban Core. I guess a man could stand an Urban Core moving in next door to him. But would you want your sister to marry an Impacted Area?

"Naturally, they got other names for me down South. To George Wallace I'm either a 'Bearded Pseudo-Intellectual,' which I kind of like, or, best of all, a 'Power-Mad Federal Bureaucracy.'

"How about that? Only in America could a little Colored boy aspire to grow up to be the whole Federal Government."

He must be terribly proud of an achievement like that.

"You bet," said Mr. X. "And it fills my heart to hear how every politician wants to do something for me. Either they want to revitalize us Urban Cores or make us Decaying Innercities thrive again.

"At first, I fiured I was going to get free vitamin pills. But it turns out they merely aim to kick me out of my house and cut off the welfare check."

That didn't sound too promising.

"Well," said Mr. X philosophically, "it sure beats Re-establishing Law & Order in Our Strife-torn Cities."

He was against Law & Order?

"Do you expect me," he said with surprise, "to be in favor of shooting us uppity Niggers?"

I thanked Mr. X for providing a clearer understanding of what on earth the candidates will be constantly talking about in the upcoming campaign. But I couldn't see where it would contribute much to Mr. X's progress toward full equality.

"Maybe not," he agreed. "But I sure am building one hell of a vocabulary."

DOWN THESE MEAN STREETS

PROLOGUE

Piri Thomas

Yee-ah!! Wanna know how many times I've stood
    on a rooftop and yelled out to anybody:
"Hey, World—here I am. Hallo, World—this is Piri.
    That's me.
"I wanna tell ya I'm here—you bunch of mother-jumpers—
    I'm here, and I want recognition, whatever that
    mudder-fuckin word means."

Man! How many times have I stood on the rooftop of
    my broken-down building at night and watched
    the bulb-lit world below.
Like somehow it's different at night, this my Harlem.
There ain't no bright sunlight to reveal the stark naked
    truth of garbage-lepered streets.
Gone is the drabness and hurt, covered by a friendly night.
It makes clean the dirty-faced kids.

This is a bright *mundo*, my streets, my *barrio de noche*.
With its thousands of lights, hundreds of millions of colors
Mingling with noises, swinging street sounds of cars
    and curses,
Sounds of joys and sobs that make music.
If anyone listens real close, he can hear its heart beat—

Yee-ah! I feel like part of the shadows that make
     company for me in this warm *amigo* darkness.
I am "My Majesty Piri Thomas," with a high on anything
     and like a stoned king, I gotta survey my kingdom.
I'm a skinny, dark-face, curly-haired, intense
     Porty-Ree-can—
Unsatisfied, hoping, and always reaching.

I got a feeling of aloneness and a bitterness that's growing
     and growing
Day by day into some kind of hate without *un nombre.*
Yet when I look down at the streets below, I can't help
     thinking
It's like a great big dirty Christmas tree with lights but no
     fuckin presents.
And man, my head starts growing bigger than my body
     as it gets crammed full of hate.
And I begin to listen to the sounds inside me.
Get angry, get hating angry, and you won't be scared.
What have you got now? Nothing.
What will you ever have? Nothing.
. . . Unless you cop for yourself!

EL PASO DEL NORTE

John Rechy

This is about El Paso (and Juarez: the Southwest), which so long was just
a hometown to me and which now is different from any other section in
America.

El Paso and Juarez are in the middle of the Texas, New Mexico, and
Mexico white, white desert surrounded by that range of mountains jutting
unevenly along the border. At sundown the fat sun squats on the horizon
like a Mexican lady grandly on her frontporch. Appropriately.

Because only geographically the Rio Grande, which in the Southwest
is a river only part of the time and usually just a strait of sand along
the banks of which spiders weave their webs, divides the United States
from Mexico. Only geographically. The Mexican people of El Paso, more
than half the population—and practically all of Smeltertown, Canutillo,

Ysleta—are all and always and completely Mexican, and will be. They speak only Spanish to each other and when they say the Capital they mean Mexico DF.

Oh, but, once it was not so. When the War came, Christ, the Mexicans were American as hell. The young men went to war wearing everything that was authorized, sometimes even more. Huge stars appeared on the southside tenements and government-project windows. OUR SON IS SERVING AMERICA. My mother wore my brother's Purple Heart to Mass and held it up when the Priest gave his blessing.

Outside El Paso City, giant machines dig into the mountains for ores (Smeltertown), and beyond that (where I used to climb poetic as hell) is a tall, beautiful mountain.

The Mountain of Cristo Rey.

Huge processions go up this holy mountain. The people of El Paso, Ysleta, Canutillo, of Smeltertown and of Juarez march up climbing for hours, chanting prayers. The procession starts downtown in El Paso, outside the churches, and the groups join each other in the streets, kneeling at intervals on inspiration, carrying placards of the Virgin, Saints in colors. Small bands jazz solemnly, crying dissonant sounds. The shawled ladies of the Order of Saint Something grip rosaries and mumble and feel—as rightly so as anyone in the world—Holy. The priests in bright drag lead them up. They carry sadfaced saints. The small bands stay behind at the foot of the mountain, the musicians wiping the sweat off their dark faces, and drinking cool *limonada* and mingling with the sellers of coca-cola, religious medals. The procession winds up the moutain slowly past the crude weatherbeaten stations of the cross along the path. And at the top, finally—where they say Mass, the people kneeling on the rocks in the blazing white sun— is The Statue.

It is primitive Christ.

Fifty-feet tall. And it looks like a Mexican peasant. Mr. Soler made it. I think he was a kind of semi-atheist who didn't believe in God but believed in the Virgin Mary.

But the poor Mexican Christ, what it has to look down on—the line of desperate ants, as the Magazine (I think it was *Time*, or if it wasn't, they would have) called it, of mustached, strawhatted men, *braceros* invading America.

Because the Rio Grande, no matter what you think, is usually dry, as I said, just sand and scrawny spiders and fingery indentations where water should be or was. Sometimes it is very full, though, and beautiful, and then the Rio Grande is like a dirty young black animal full of life rushing along the sand, swallowing the bushy dry banks. And I would walk along its bank, to the mountains. But usually it is so dry that the wetbacks can enter Sacred Country by merely walking across the River.

On their way to Georgia?

Well, Ive heard that from I dont know how many people. They say, for some strange reason, that Georgia is a kind of heaven where all good spiks go—some crossing into the country illegally, others standing at the Santa Fe Bridge lined up all rags and cloth bags and wooden and cardboard boxes and holy amulets, whiskers, waiting to be inspected by the Customs-gods. The Magazine also said, well, wasn't it natural, those wetbacks wanting to come into America?—Christ, they heard about sweet-tasting toothpaste. It really said that. And if sweet-tasting American toothpaste aint enough to make a man face the Border Patrol (as Bad as L.A. fuzz) and the excellent labor conditions in progressive Georgia, well, man, what is? The Magazine said it was sad, all those displaced wetbacks, but all that happened though was that they were sent back, but they tried to come across again and again and again.

(I remember a dead *bracero* near the bank of the Río Grande, face down drowned in the shallow water, the water around him red, red, red. Officially he had drowned and was found, of course, by the Border Patrol. And his wife will go on thinking forever he made it with a beautiful blonde Georgia woman—loaded with toothpaste—and so, therefore, never came back to her and the even-dozen kids.)

Which brings me to this—

The hatred in much of Texas for Mexicans. It's fierce. (They used to yell, Mexicangreaser, Mexicangreaser, when I went to Lamar Grammar School, and I thought, well, yes, my mother did do an awful lot of frying but we never put any grease on our hair, and so it bothered me—if God was Mexican, as my mother said, why did He allow this?) Many of them really hate us pathologically, like they hate the Negroes, say, in Arkansas. Here, it's the bragging, blustering bony-framed Texan rangers/farmers/ ranchers with the Cadillacs and the attitude of Me-and-god on My ranch. It has nothing to do with the Alamo any more. It's just the full-scale, really huge (consistent with everything Big in Texas—and Alaska won't change anything) Texan inferiority complex. Dig: the Texas rancher strutting across San Jacinto Plaza, all bones and legs, getting kicks from sitting, later, booted-feet propped, getting a shine from the barefoot spik kid, tipping him 50 cents—not just sitting like you and I would get a shine but sitting Grandly, and strutting across the Border owning the streets, I hope he gets rolled. They dont really dislike Mexicans in Texas if theyre maids and laborers.

So the Mexicans live concentrated on the Southside of El Paso largely, crowded into tenements, with the walls outside plastered with old

Vote-for signs from years back and advertisements of Mexican movies at the Colon—the torn clothes just laundered waving on rickety balconies along Paisano Drive held up God knows how. Or if not, in the Government projects, which are clean tenements—a section for the Mexicans, a section for the Negroes. Politely. Row after row of identical boxhouses speckled with dozens and dozens of children.

So this, the Southside, is of course the area of the Mean gangs. The ones on the other side are not as dangerous, of course, because they are mostly Blond and mostly normal Anglo-American kiddies growing up naturally and what can you expect? Like the ones from Kern Place—all pretty clean houses at the foot of Mount Franklin—and if those kiddies carry switchblade knives, at least they keep them clean, and when they wear boots, they are Cowboy Boots.

The southside gangs—that's a different thing. Theyre blackhaired. And tense. Mean and bad, with Conflict seething. El Paso's southside (the Second Ward) gave birth to the internationally famous Pachucos. (Paso-Pacho.) They used to call them boogies, marijuanos, the zootsuits—and the baggy pants with pegged ankles were boogiepants, and, man, those tigers walked cool, long graceful bad strides, rhythmic as hell, hands deep into pockets, shoulders hunched. Much heart. They really did wear and still sometimes do those hats that Al Capp draws—and the chains, too, from the belt to the pocket in a long loop.

And sitting talking Mexican jive, *mano*, under the El Paso streetlamps along Hill and Magoffin and Seventh, around Bowie High School and next to the Palace Theater digging Presley and Chuck Berry and Fats Domino, outside the dingy 40-watt-bulb-lighted Southside grocery stores, avoiding *la jura*, the neo-Pachucos with dreamy junk eyes and their chicks in tight skirts and giant pompadours and revealing 1940-style sweaters hang in the steamy El Paso nights, hunched, mean and bad, plotting protest, unconscious of, though they carry it, the burden of the world, and additionally, the burden of Big Texas.

Well, look. In East Texas. In Balmorhea, say. In Balmorhea, with its giant outdoor swimming pool (where that summer the two blond tigers and I went swimming, climbed over the wall and into the rancid-looking night water) there were signs in the two-bit restaurant, in Balmorhea-town then, that said WE DO NOT SERVE MEXICANS, NIGGERS OR DOGS. That night we went to the hick movie, and the man taking the tickets said, You boys be sure and sit on the right side, the left is for spiks. So I said I was on the wrong side and walked out. Later at Kit's aunt's ranch, the aunt waited until the Mexican servant walked out and then said, miserably, Ah jaist caint even eat when they are around. And because earlier had made me feel suddenly a Crusader and it was easy now, I walked out of the dining-

room and said well then I shouldnt be here to louse up your dinner, lady.
And you never know it—to look at that magnificent Texas sky.

And something quite something else. . . .

Once upon a time in El Paso there was a band of fairies—yes, really, in El Paso, Texas—and this city became a crossroads between the hot Eastcoast and the cool Westcoast (fuzzwise, vice-wise) or the hot West-coast and the cool Eastcoast, depending on where oh where the birls had got Caught Jay-Walking. And soon San Jacinto Plaza (or Alligator Plaza—sleepy crocodiles in a round pond, so tired and sleepy they dont even wake up when little kids grab them by their tails and flip them into the water) was a fairy paradise, rebel. The birls would camp there in that little park—the queens with pinched-in waists, lisps, painted eyes, digging the soldiers from Fort Bliss, proclaiming Too Much. Alas, they went the way of all fairies. The Inevitable Clean-Up came, and the fuzz swooped on them jealously and to jail they went, all fluttering eyelashes justifying gay mother love.

Now it is not the same passing through the park not seeing the queens, not hearing their delighted squeals of approbation floating into the clean summer Texas air. Not the same at all.

At Christmas is when Mexican El Paso is magnificent. I dont mean the jazz at San Jacinto Plaza (trees and lights and Christmas carols and Santa Claus). I mean the Southside Christmas. A lot of them—most of them, in fact—put up trees, of course, but many of them put up nacimientos. My father used to start putting ours up almost a month before Christmas when we lived on Wyoming Street. It's a large box-like thing—ours was, anyway—about six-feet wide, six-feet tall, eight-feet deep, like a room minus the front wall (the minus faces the windows, which are cleaned to sparkle), and inside is a Christmas scene. Ours had the manger and the Virgin of course and St. Joseph, and angels hanging from strings floating on angelhair clouds. To the sides of the manger were modern-looking California miniature houses, with real lights in them—some had swimming pools. And stone mountains. On one was the Devil, red, with a wired neck so that the slightest movement made it twitch, drinking out of a bottle. Christ was coming, and naturally the Devil would be feeling low. My father painted an elaborate Texas-like sky behind the manger, with clouds, giant moon, the works—lights all over, and he enclosed the box-like nacimiento with Christmas-tree branches, and then, one year, he had a real lake—that is, real water which we changed daily. The wisemen on their way. Christmas lights, bulbs, on top. He moved the wise men each night, closer to the manger. The Christchild wasnt there yet—he wasnt born. Then on Christmas Eve everyone came over. My mother led the rosary. We all knelt. Someone had been chosen to be the padrino—the godfather—of the Christchild to be born that night. He carried the Child in his hands, everyone kissed it ("adored" it), and then finally He was put into the manger, in the hay. We prayed some more. *Dios te salve, Maria; llena eres de Gracia. . . .* At the stroke of midnight, the Child was born. Then there was a party—tamales, buñuelos, liquor.

Most Mexicans are Catholic, of course. My friend Sherman is an intelligent Catholic from Evanston and he said it was bad when Catholics substitute, like the Mexican people he loves so much (Sherman in Chihuahua City that time, trying so hard to look like a Mexican peasant, with Indian sandals and muslin shirt—him, six-feet-two and Scandinavian curly blond!—and people staring at him thinking he came probably from the American moon), the image of the Virgin for that of Christ. He loves the Virgin himself, a lot, but still he says Christianity should mean Christ. (He says he would rather see the Mexicans worship the Sun, incidentally, like their Indian ancestors, than become Protestants, because for a while the Baptists especially had a full-scale campaign going, and pretty soon, on the doors of the broken-down southside houses they tried to invade with irresistible chocolate American candy and bright colors for the shoeless children living in cardboard houses along the Border appeared signs THIS IS A CHRISTIAN HOME PROTESTANT PROPAGANDA WILL NOT BE ALLOWED.)

But that's not what I started to say, which was this—

The Patron of Mexico is the Virgin of Guadalupe. The story says She appeared to Juan Diego, one day, and in order to make the incredulous know that he had indeed seen Her, She stamped Herself on his shawl, and that is the one you see in Mexican churches, all stars and blue robe. Oh, how tenderly they believe in the Virgin of Guadalupe (*even the Priests!*), and how they love Her, the Mother of all Mexico.

How they Respect mothers because of it. Mothers are a Grand Mexican thing. They belong sacredly in Mexico and the Mexican Southwest.

Dig: a serious Mexican movie. The favorite theme. The son goes away. The little Old Mexican Mother stands at the dingy door with her black shawl sheltering her from the drizzling rain. Christ. The son goes away, and forgets about her. He becomes a Great Matador, lured by women like María Bonita before the President's wife—and this is only gossip— chased her out. Wow! The little Mother in the Black Shawl wanders over Mexico, working for harsh people—like sewing in a factory where, she's so old, poor thing, she cant keep up with the heftier ladies. She comes at last into a very rich home in Mexico City. Of course. It's her son's home. But he doesnt recognize her, and she decides not to tell him who she is so hc wont bc ashamed of her. She'll just be satisfied to be near him. He is gruff. "Old woman, look how much dust has accumulated on this my favorite table." "Yes, sir." She wipes it. He is cruel, yells at her despite the pitiful black shawl. She takes it, and this is true. Mexican mothers and wives do take it—not Americans, and this is what grips a Mexican audience. Loyalty. One day the Big Corrida comes on. The wife is digging it on television (she cant bear to go it live). The matador is gored. The shawled Mother screams, MI HIJO!!!! The wife knows now, and being Mexican herself and on the way to becoming a Mexican Mother, she hugs the Old Lady. The run out, get a cab, go to the bullring. There he is. Unconscious. Dying. The beautifully dressed wife pulls the shawl off the little old Mother and proclaims to the dying matador, "Die if God wills it —but not without knowing that—This—Is—Your—Mother!!!!" Everyone is crying, the unnatural son repents (as he must), and all three live happily ever after.

This is real. Mexicans really love Mothers. Americans dont. I dont have a single American acquaintance whose mother faints everytime he comes home and again when he leaves. Mine does. The Mexican mother-love has nothing to do with sex, either. You can imagine an American wanting to make it with his mother. She is slick. She looks almost as young and bad as he does. But can you imagine making it with your mother if she wears a Black Shawl, and even if she doesnt, if she acts all the time like she is wearing One? . . .

Mexican religion is a very real thing, not lukewarm at all, nor forbidding and awesome. Mexican Catholics (and this, again, includes the Priests) believe in a God with two hands, two feet, eyes—the works. The Devil has horns, a tail, and he is most certainly red. Each church in the Mexican sections of the Southwest, and all of them in Juarez have Real patron saints, who guard them. On their days, they have kermesses—this is like a fair. On the really big days (for example, in May, the month of the Virgin Mary), the Indians (who are Catholics although their religion is still magnificently pagan, having room in it for Mayan, Aztec, other legends—witchcraft—right along with the story of Jesus) come into the City. The matachines (they used to scare me, like the beggars are Indians dressed in all kinds of feathers, painted all over, making dance marathons, dancing for hours. Some Indians—I think the Taranhumaras—run all the way from somewhere like Chihuahua City to Juarez, offering I suppose that amount of exerted energy to the Virgin. In religious frenzy, they burn an effigy of Satan—a kind of man-shaped catherine wheel. They light him up, and the bastard burns shooting fire straight from hell. The people yell up a storm, and the Politicians and Gangsters shoot real bullets into the air in this tribute to the Virgin Mary.

FOOD FOR ALL HIS DEAD

Frank Chin

"Jus 'forty-fie year' go, Doctah Sun Yat-sen Free China from da Manchus. Dats' why all us Chinee, alla ovah da woil are celebrate Octob' tan or da Doubloo Tan . . . !"

The shouted voice came through the open bathroom window. The shouting and music was still loud after rising through the night's dry air; white moths jumped on the air, danced through the window over the voice, and lighted quickly on the wet sink, newly reddened from his father's attack. Johnny's arms were around his father's belly, holding the man upright against the edge of the sink to keep the man's mouth high enough to spit lung blood into the drain. . . .

The man's belly shrank and filled against Johnny's arms as the man breathed and spat, breathed and spat, the belly shrinking and filling. The breaths and bodies against each other shook with horrible rhythms that could not be numbed out of Johnny's mind. "Pride," Johnny thought, "Pa's pride for his reputation for doing things . . . except dying. He's not proud of dying, so it's a secret between father and son. . . ." At the beginning of the man's death, when he had been Johnny's father, still commanding and large, saying, "Help me. I'm dying; don't tell," and removing his jacket and walking to the bathroom. Then came the grin—pressed lips twisted up into the cheeks—hiding the gathering blood and drool. Johnny had cried then, knowing his father would die. But now the man seemed to have been always dying and Johnny always waiting, waiting with what he felt was a coward's loyalty to the dying, for he helped the man hide his bleeding and was sick himself, knowing he was not waiting for the man to die but waiting for the time after death when he could relax.

". . . free from da yoke of Manchu slab'ry, in'epen'ence, no moah queue on da head! Da's wha'fo' dis big a parade! An' here, in San Francisco, alla us Chinee-'mellican 're pwowd! . . ."

"It's all gone . . . I can't spit any more. Get my shirt, boy. I'm going to make a speech tonight. . . ." The man slipped from the arms of the boy and sat on the toilet lid and closed his mouth. His bare chest shone as if washed with dirty cooking oil and looked as if he should have been chilled, not sweating, among the cold porcelain and tile of the bathroom.

To the sound of herded drums and cymbals, Johnny wiped the sweat from his father's soft body and dressed him without speaking. He was full of the heat of wanting to cry for his father but would not.

His father was heavier outside the house.

They staggered each other across the alleyway to the edge of Portsmouth Square. They stood together at the top of the slight hill, their feet just off the concrete onto the melted fishbone grass, and could see the brightly lit reviewing stand, and they saw over the heads of the crowd, the dark crowd of people standing in puddles of each other, moving like oily things and bugs floating on a tide; to their left, under trees, children played and shouted on swings and slides; some ran toward Johnny and his father and crouched behind their legs to hide from giggling girls. And they could see the street and the parade beyond the crowd. The man stood away from the boy but held tightly to Johnny's arm. The man swallowed a greasy sound and grinned. "I almost feel I'm not dying now. Parades are like that. I used to dance the Lion Dance in China, boy. I was always in the parades."

Johnny glanced at his father and saw the man's eyes staring wide with the skin around the eyes stretching for the eyes to open wider, and Johnny patted his father's shoulder and watched the shadows of children running across the white sand of the play area. He was afraid of watching his father die here; the man was no longer like his father or a man; perhaps it was the parade. But the waiting, the lies and waiting, waiting so long with a flesh going to death that the person was no longer real as a life but a parody of live things, grinning. The man was a fish drying and shrinking inside its skin on the sand, crazy, mimicking swimming, Johnny thought, but a fish could be lifted and slapped against a stone, thrown to cats; for his father, Johnny could only wait and help the man stay alive without helping him die. "That's probably where you got the disease," Johnny said.

"Where, boy?"

"Back in China."

"No, I got it here. I was never sick for one day in China." The man began walking down the hill toward the crowd. "Back in China. . . ."

They walked down the hill, the man's legs falling into steps with his body jerking after his falling legs; Johnny held his father, held the man back to keep him from falling over his own feet. The man's breath chanted dry and powdered out of his mouth and nostrils to the rhythm of the drums, and his eyes stared far ahead into the parade; his lips opened and showed brickcolored teeth in his grin. "Not so fast, *ah-bah*!" Johnny shouted and pulled at his father's arm. He was always frightened at the man's surges of nervous life.

"Don't run," Johnny said, feeling his father's muscles stretch as he pulled Johnny down the hill toward the crowd. "Stop running, pa!" And his father was running and breathing out fog into the hot night and sweating dirty oil, and trembling his fleshy rump inside his baggy trousers, dancing in stumbles with dead senses. "Pa, not so fast, dammit! You're going to have another attack! Slow down!"

"I can't stop, boy."

They were in the shadow of the crowd now, and children chased around them.

"Look! There they are!" the man said.

"Dere you're, ladies and genullmans! Eben da lion are bow in respack to us tonigh'!"

The crowd clapped and whistled, and boys shoved forward to see. Old women, roundbacked in their black overcoats, lifted their heads to smile; they stood together and nodded, looking like clumps of huge beetles with white faces.

"Closer to the platform, boy; that's where I belong," the man said. He leaned against Johnny's shoulder and coughed out of his nostrils. Johnny heard the man swallow and cringed. The man was grinning again, his eyes anxious, the small orbs jumping scared spiders all over the sockets. "Aren't you happy you came, boy? Look at all the people."

"Take time to catch your breath, *ah-bah*. Don't talk. It's wrong for you to be here anyhow."

"Nothing's wrong, boy, don't you see all your people happy tonight? As long as . . ." he swallowed and put his head against Johnny's cheek, then made a sound something like laughter, "As I've been here . . . do you understand my Chinese?" Then slowly in English, catching quick breaths between his words, "I be here, allabody say dere chilldren're gonna leab Chinatong and go way, but 'snot so, huh?" His voice was low, a guttural monotone. "Look a'em all; dey still be Chinee. I taught da feller dat teach dem to dance how to do dat dancer boy. Johnny? dis're you home, here, an' I know you gat tire, but alla you fran's here, an' dey likee you." His face was speaking close to Johnny and chilled the boy's face with hot breath.

The boy did not look at his father talking to him but stared stiffly out to the street, watching the glistening arms of boys jerking the bamboo skeletons of silk-hided lions over their heads. His father was trying to save him again, Johnny thought, trying to be close like he had been to him how long ago when his father was a hero from the war. The man spoke as if he had saved his life to talk to his son now, tonight, here among the eyes and sounds of Chinese.

"I'm sorry, *ah-bah*, I can't help it . . ." was all Johnny could answer sincerely. He knew it would be cruel to say, "Pa, I don't want to be a curiosity like the rest of the Chinese here. I want to be something by myself," so he did not, not only because of the old man, but because he was not certain he believed himself; it had been easy to believe his own shouted words when he was younger and safe with his parents; it had been easy not to like what he had then—when he knew he could stay; then, when the man was fat and not dying, they were separate and could argue, but not now; now he was favored with the man's secret; they were horribly bound together now. The old man was dying and still believing in the old ways, still sure—even brave, perhaps—and that meant something to Johnny.

"An' you see dam bow in respack now, an' da's good lucks to ev'ey-body!"

The lion dancers passed, followed by a red convertible with boys beating a huge drum on the back seat.

Johnny knew the parades; the lion dancers led the wait for the coming of the long dragon, and the end. The ends of the parades with the dragon were the most exciting, were the loudest moment before the chase down the streets to keep the dragon in sight. He was half aware of the air becoming brittle with the noise of the dances and the crowd, and, with his father now, was almost happy, almost anxious, dull, the way he felt when he was tired and staring in a mirror, slowly realizing that he was looking at his own personal reflection; he felt pleased and depressed, as if he had just prayed for something.

"You know," the man said, "I wan' you to be somebody here. Be doctor, mak' moneys and halp da Chinee, or lawyer, or edgenerer, make moneys and halp, and people're respack you." He patted the boy's chest "You tall me now you won' leab here when I die, hokay?"

"I don't know, pa." The boy looked down to the trampled grass between his feet and shrugged off what he did not want to say. They were hopeless to each other now. He looked over his shoulder to his father and could not answer the chilled face and they stared a close moment onto each other and were private, holding each other and waiting.

Policemen on motorcycles moved close to the feet of the crowd to move them back. The boys wearing black-and-red silk trousers and white sweatshirts, coaxing the clumsy dragon forward with bells and shafts could be seen now; they were dancing and shouting past the reviewing stand. The dragon's glowing head lurched side to side, rose and fell, its jaw dangling after the goading boys. As the dragon writhed and twisted about itself, boys jumped in and out from under its head and belly to keep the dragon fresh.

"Maybe I'm not Chinese, pa! Maybe I'm just a Chinese accident. You're the only one that seems to care that I'm Chinese." The man glared at the boy and did not listen. "Pa, most of the people I don't like are Chinese. They even *laugh* with accents, Christ!" He turned his head from the man, sorry for what he said. It was too late to apologize.

"You dare talk to your father like that?" the man shouted in Chinese. He stood back from the boy, raised himself and slapped him, whining through his teeth as his arm swung heavily toward the boy's cheek. "You're no son of mine! No son! I'm ashamed of you!"

The shape of the bamboo skeleton was a shadow within the thinly painted silk of the dragon, and boys were shouting inside.

"Pa, *ah-bah*, I'm sorry."

"Get me up to the platform, I gotta make a speech."

"Pa, you've got to go home."

"I'm not dead yet; you'll do as I say."

"All right, I'll help you up because you won't let me help you home. But I'll leave you up there, pa. I'll leave you for ma and sister to bring home."

"From da Pres'den, of da United State' 'mellica! 'To alla ob da Chinee-'mellican on da celebrate ob dere liberate from da Manchu. . . .'"

"I'm trying to make you go home for your own good."

"You're trying to kill me with disgrace. All right, leave me. Get out of my house, too."

"Pa, I'm trying to help you. You're dying!" The boy reached for his father, but the man stepped away. "You'll kill ma by not letting her take care of you."

"Your mother's up on the platform waiting for me."

"Because she doesn't know how bad you are. I do. I have a right to make you go home."

"It's my home, not yours. Leave me alone." The man walked the few steps to the edge of the platform and called his wife. She came down and helped him up. She glanced out but did not see Johnny in the crowd. Her cheeks were made up very pink and her lipstick was still fresh; she looked very young next to Johnny's father, but her hands were old, and seemed older because of the bright nail polish and jade bracelet.

Johnny knew what his father would tell his mother and knew he would have to trust them to be happy without him. Perhaps he meant he would have to trust himself to be happy without them . . . the feeling would pass; he would wait and apologize to them both, and he would not have to leave, perhaps. Everything seemed wrong, all wrong, yet everyone, in his own way, was right. He turned quickly and walked out of the crowd to the children's play area. He sat on a bench and stretched his legs straight out in front of him. The dark old women in black coats stood by on the edges of the play area watching the nightbleached faces of children flash in and out of the light as they ran through each other's shadows. Above him, Johnny could hear the sound of pigeons in the trees. Chinatown was the same and he hated it now. Before, when he was younger, and went shopping with his mother, he had enjoyed the smells of the shops and seeing colored toys between the legs of walking people; he had been proud to look up and see his mother staring at the numbers on the scales that weighed meat to see the shopkeepers smile and nod at her. And at night, he had played here, like the children chasing each other in front of him now.

"What'sa wrong, Johnny? Tire?" He had not seen the girl standing in front of him. He sat up straight and smiled. "You draw more pitchers on napkin for me tonigh'?"

"No, I was with pa." He shrugged. "You still got the napkins, huh?"

"I tole you I want dem. I'm keeping 'em." She wore a short white coat over her red *cheongsam* and her hair shook down over her face from the wind.

"I wanta walk," he said. "You wanta walk?"

"I gotta gat home before twelve."

"Me too."

"I'll walk for you dan, okay?" She smiled and reached a hand down for him.

"You'll walk *with* me, not *for* me. You're not a dog." He stood and took her hand. He enjoyed the girl; she listened to him; he did not care if she understood what he said or knew what he wanted to say. She listened to him, would listen with her eyes staring with a wide frog's stare until he stopped speaking, then her body would raise and she would sigh a curl of girl's voice and say, "You talk so nice. . . ."

The tail of an embroidered dragon showed under her white coat and seemed to sway as her thigh moved. "You didn't come take me to the parade, Johnny?"

"I was with pa." Johnny smiled. The girl's hand was dryfeeling, cold and dry like a skin of tissue-paper covered flesh. They walked slowly, rocking forward and back as they stepped up the hill. "I'm always with pa, huh?" he said bitterly, "I'm sorry."

" 'sall right. Is he still dying?"

"Everyone's dying here; it's called the American's common cold."

"Don't talk you colleger stuff to me! I don' unnerstan' it, Johnny."

"He's still dying . . . always. I mean, sometimes I think he won't die or is lying and isn't dying."

"Wou'n't that be good, if he weren't dying? And if it was all a joke? You could all laugh after."

"I don't know, Sharon!" He whined on the girl's name and loosened her hand, but she held.

"Johnny?"

"Yeah?"

"What'll you do if he dies?"

Johnny did not look at the girl as he answered, but lifted his head to glance at the street full of lights and people walking between moving cars. Grant Avenue. He could smell incense and caged squabs, the dank smell of damp fish heaped on tile from the shops now. "I think I'd leave. I know what that sounds like, like I'm waiting for him to die so I can leave; maybe it's so. Sometimes I think I'd kill him to stop all this waiting and lifting him to the sink and keeping it a secret. But I won't do that."

"You won' do that . . ." Sharon said.

"An' now, I like to presan' da Pres'den ob da Chinee Benabolen'. . . ."

"My father," Johnny said.

The girl clapped her hands over her ears to keep her hair from jumping in the wind. "You father?" she said.

"I don't think so," Johnny said. They walked close to the walls, stepped almost into doorways to allow crowding people to pass them going down the hill toward the voice. They smelled grease and urine of open hallways, and heard music like birds being strangled as they walked over iron gratings.

"You don't think so what?" Sharon asked, pulling him toward the crowd.

"I don't think so what you said you didn't think so. . . ." He giggled, "I'm sort of funny tonight. I was up all last night listening to my father practice his speech in the toilet and helping him bleed when he got mad. And this morning I started to go to classes and fell asleep on the bus; so I didn't go to classes, and I'm still awake. I'm not tired but kind of stupid with no sleep, dig, Sharon?"

The girl smiled and said, "I dig, Johnny. You the same way every time I see you almos'."

"And I hear myself talking all this stupid stuff, but it's sort of great, you know? Because I have to listen to what I'm saying or I'll miss it."

"My mother say you cute."

They were near the top of the street now, standing in front of a wall stand with a fold-down shelf covered with Chinese magazines, nickel comic books, postcards and Japanese souvenirs of Chinatown. Johnny, feeling ridiculous with air between his joints and his cheeks tingling with the anxious motion of the crowd, realized he was tired, then realized he was staring at the boy sitting at the wall stand and staring at the boy's leather cap.

"What are you loo' at, huh?" the boy said in a girl's voice. Sharon pulled at Johnny and giggled. Johnny giggled and relaxed to feeling drunk and said:

"Are you really Chinese?"

"What're you ting, I'm a Negro soy sauce chicken?"

"Don't you know there's no such thing as a real Chinaman in all of America? That all we are are American Indians cashing in on a fad?"

"Fad? Don' call me fad. You fad youselv."

"No, you're not Chinese, don't you understand? You see it all started when a bunch of Indians wanted to quit being Indians and fighting the cavalry and all, so they left the reservation, see?"

"In'ian?"

"And they saw that there was this big kick about Chinamen, so they braided their hair into queues and opened up laundries and restaurants and started reading Margaret Mead and Confucius and Pearl Buck and became respectable Chinamen and gained some self-respect."

"Chinamong! You battah not say Chinamong."

"But the reservation instinct stuck, years of tradition, you see? Something about needing more than one Indian to pull off a good rain dance or something, so they made Chinatown! And here we are!"

He glanced around him and grinned. Sharon was laughing, her shoulders hopping up and down. The boy blinked then pulled his cap lower over his eyes. "It's all right to come out now, you see?" Johnny said. "Indians are back in vogue and the Chinese kick is wearing out. . . ." He laughed until he saw the boy's confused face. "Aww nuts," he said, "this is no fun."

He walked after Sharon through the crowd, not feeling the shoulders and women's hips knocking against him. "I'd like to get outta here so quick, Sharon; I wish I had something to do! What do I do here? What does anybody do here? I'm bored! My mother's a respected woman because she can tell how much monosodium glutamate is in a dish by smelling it, and because she knows how to use a spittoon in a restaurant. Everybody's Chinese here, Sharon."

"Sure!" the girl laughed and hopped to kiss his cheek. "Didn' you like that?"

"Sure, I like it, but I'm explaining something. You know, nobody shoulda let me grow up and go to any school outside of Chinatown." They walked slowly, twisting to allow swaggering men to pass. "Then, maybe everything would be all right now, you see? I'm stupid, I don't know what I'm talking about. I shouldn't go to parades and see all those kids. I remember when I was a kid. Man, then I knew everything. I knew all my aunts were beautiful, and all my cousins were small, and all my uncles were heroes from the war and the strongest guys in the world that smoked cigars and swore, and my grandmother was a queen of women." He nodded to himself. "I really had it made then, really, and I knew more then than I do now."

"What'd'ya mean? You smart now! You didn't know how to coun' or spall, or nothin'; now you in colleger."

"I had something then, you know? I didn't have to ask about anything; it was all there; I didn't have questions, I knew who I was responsible to, who I should love, who I was afraid of, and all my dogs were smart."

"You lucky, you had a dog!" The girl smiled.

"And all the girls wanted to be nurses; it was fine! Now, I'm just what a kid should be—stupid, embarrassed. I don't know who can tell me anything.

"Here, in Chinatown, I'm undoubtedly the most enlightened, the smartest fortune cookie ever baked to a golden brown, but out there . . . God!" He pointed down to the end of Grant Avenue, past ornamented lamps of Chinatown to the tall buildings of San Francisco. "Here, I'm fine —and bored stiff. Out there—Oh, Hell, what'm I talking about. You don't know either; I try to tell my father, and he doesn't know, and he's smarter'n you."

"If you don't like stupids, why'd you talk to me so much?"

"Because I like you. You're the only thing I know that doesn't fight me. . . . You know I think I've scared myself into liking this place for awhile. See what you've done by walking with me? You've made me a good Chinese for my parents again. I think I'll sell firecrackers." He was dizzy now, overwhelmed by the sound of too many feet and clicking lights. "I even like you, Sharon!" He swung her arm and threw her ahead of him and heard her laugh. "Christ! my grandmother didn't read English until she watched television and read 'The End'; that's pretty funny, what a kick!" They laughed at each other and ran among the shoulders of the crowd, shouting "Congratulations!" in Chinese into the shops, "Congratulations!" to a bald man with long hair growing down the edges of his head.

"Johnny, stop! You hurt my wrist!"

It was an innocent kiss in her hallway, her eyes closed so tight the lashes shrank and twitched like insect legs, and her lips puckered long, a dry kiss with closed lips. "Goodnight, Johnny . . . John," she said. And he waved and watched her standing in the hallway, disappearing as he walked down the stairs; then, out of sight, he ran home.

He opened the door to the apartment and hoped that his father had forgotten. "Fine speech, pa!" he shouted.

His little sister came out of her room, walking on the toes of her long pajamas. "Brother? Brother, *ah-bah*, he's sick!" she said. She looked straight up to Johnny as she spoke and nodded. Johnny stepped past his sister and ran to the bathroom and opened the door. His mother was holding the man up to the sink with one hand and holding his head with the other. The man's mess spattered over her *cheongsam*. The room, the man, everything was uglier because of his mother's misery in her bright *cheongsam*. "*Ah-bah?*" Johnny said gently as if calling the man from sleep for dinner. They did not turn. He stepped up behind the woman. "I can do that, *ah-mah*, I'm a little stronger than you."

"Don't you touch him! You!" She spoke with her cheek against the man's back and her eyes closed. "He told me what you did, what you said, and you're killing him! If you want to leave, just go! Stop killing this man!"

"Not me, ma. He's been like this a long time. I've been helping him almost every night. He told me not to tell you."

"You think I don't know? I've seen you in here with him when I wanted to use the bathroom at night, and I've crept back to bed without saying anything because I know your father's pride. And you want to go and break it in a single night! First it's your telling everybody how good you are! Now go and murder your father. . . ."

"Ma, I'm sorry. He asked me, and I tried to make him understand. What do you want me to do, lie? I'll call a doctor."

"Get out, you said you're going to leave, so get out," the man said, lifting his head.

"I'll stay, ma, *ah-bah*, I'll stay."

"It's too late," his mother said, "I don't want you here." The time was wrong . . . nobody's fault that his father was dying; perhaps, if his father was not dying out of his mouth Johnny could have argued and left or stayed, but now, he could not stay without hate. "Ma, I said I'm calling a doctor. . . ."

After the doctor came, Johnny went to his room and cried loudly, pulling the sheets from his bed and kicking at the wall until his foot became numb. He shouted his hate for his father and ignorant mother into his pillow until his face was wet with tears. His sister stood next to his bed and watched him, patting his ankle and saying over and over, "Brother, don't cry, brother. . . ."

Johnny sat up and held the small girl against him. "Be a good girl," he said. "You're going to have my big room now. I'm moving across the bay to school." He spoke very quietly to his sister against the sound of their father's spitting.

Sharon held his sister's elbow and marched behind Johnny and his mother. A band played in front of the coffin, and over the coffin was a large photograph of the dead man. Johnny had a miniature of the photograph in his wallet and would always carry it there. Without being told, he had dressed and was marching now beside his mother behind the coffin and the smell of sweet flowers. It was a parade of black coats and hats, and they all wore sunglasses against the sun; the sky was green, seen through the glasses, and the boys playing in Portsmouth Square had green shadows about them. A few people stopped on the street and watched.

VIVE NOIR!

Mari Evans

i
am going to rise
en masse
from Inner City
        sick
          of newyork ghettos
        chicago tenements
    l a's slums
weary
        of exhausted lands
        sagging privies
        saying yessur yessah
        yesSIR
        in an assortment
        of geographical dialects i
have seen my last
broken down plantation
even from a
distance

                   i
will load all my goods
in '50 Chevy pickups '53
Fords fly United and '66
caddys I
            have packed in
            the old man and the old lady and
            wiped the children's noses
                    I'm tired
                        of hand me downs
                            shut me ups
                                pin me ins
                                    keep me outs
                                        messing me over have
                                    just had it
                                baby
                            from
                        you . . .
i'm
gonna spread out
over America
            intrude
my proud blackness
all
        over the place
                    i have wrested wheat fields
                    from the forests

                    turned rivers
                    from their courses

                    leveled mountains
                    at a word
                    festooned the land with
                    bridges
                                    gemlike
                                on filaments of steel
                                        moved
                    glistening towers of Babel in place

                    sweated a whole
                    civilization

now
i'm
gonna breathe fire
through flaming nostrils BURN
a place for

me
in the skyscrapers and the
schoolrooms on the green
lawns and the white
beaches

i'm
gonna wear the robes and
sit on the benches
make the rules and make
the arrests say
who can and who
can't
baby you don't stand
a
chance
i'm
gonna put black angels
in all the books and a black
Christchild in Mary's arms i'm
gonna make black bunnies black
fairies black santas black
nursery rhymes and
black
ice cream
i'm
gonna make it a
crime
to be anything BUT   black
pass the coppertone
gonna make white
a twentyfourhour
lifetime
J.O.B.
an' when all the coppertone's gone . . . ?

5

ECONOMICS
Big Money
for Whom?

A lot of money passes through a few big hands in the banks and businesses of America's financial centers. And a lot of little people, teased by television and in pursuit of dignity, are working for a fairer split of the profits.

Some say there's no money left under the mahogany conference tables in the velvet-carpeted city halls. It was all won in the forties and blown in suburbs or rice-paddies. The city lost wave after wave of middle-class taxpayers while the poor kept rolling in, requiring expensive services in welfare, education, police, and sanitation from municipal governments with a dwindling tax base. To some urban experts, therefore, the city is a loser, not worth dealing in on the big money games of the Federal government and private business. Insurance brokers, stock investors, construction companies, and mortgage lenders can't play free enterprise with a hopeless bankrupt.

But other observers, some of whom write in this section, have harder-hitting ideas about the hard-hit city. The money game may be broken up for good, they warn, unless corporations, Washington, unions, and state governments shell out some support from their own huge public fortunes to make room for the city's poor majorities at the big table. The first four selections here deal with specific problems of the urban poor and their cities, which are the major centers of both wealth and poverty.

Woodie Guthrie's song, "There Was a Rich Man Who Lived in Detroitium," records the early movements of the working class toward a just share in the profits of Ford's auto empire. On their Detroit picket lines, they set the pattern by which city workers across the country would force the bosses to deal them in. These methods are still available to the poor whites from Appalachia, the Indians from the reservations, and the blacks from the rural South described by Ben H. Bagdikian in "Coming to the City." Since Woody Guthrie's time, however, a new problem for the wageless and houseless city population is the corruption and insensitivity of the unions themselves.

"The Mafia: Conglomerate of Crime," an analysis of La Cosa Nostra's main forms of activity—the political fix, gambling, loan-sharking, narcotics traffic, labor racketeering, and business infiltration—shows in how many ways the poor are the victims of organized crime.

Next are two views of welfare, the institution at the other end of the economic table. "Barbara Dugan's Story," the personal narrative of a welfare mother, gives a voice to the faceless poverty statistics listed in almanacs. Her story is a chapter from Richard Elman's book, *The Poorhouse State*, a study of the lives of welfare clients, revealing, among other things, that the Welfare Department in New York City spends more money on maintaining itself—paying the salaries of welfare workers and the expenses of running an office—than it gives to the poor it was created to help. Ernest van den Haag considers the avenues of escape open to large welfare families in a conservative-liberal dialogue, "Ending the Welfare Mess." Whereas the liberal speaker advocates more Federal poverty programs, the conservative side suggests such cures as birth-control pills, jobs, education, day-care centers, and sterilization.

The last four selections concern different approaches, by no means exhaustive, to the economic plight of the poor, which invite evaluation in the light of the problems covered in the first half of the section. Lee Berton, in "Aiding the Poor," reports on the efforts of ghetto residents in Bedford-Stuyvesant, St. Louis, Washington, D.C., and Harlem to beat the various consumer rackets that flourish in the slums to cheat the poor out of the little money they have.

The Urban League, the Urban Coalition, and the National Alliance of Businessmen have urged the business community to hire more black employees as another step toward breaking the cycle of welfare dependency. "Quietus," a short story by Charlie Russell, reveals that often the black employee, like the story's main character "Randolph, Besso Oil's First Negro Salesman," becomes a token bought to build an image and used to raise the spiral of corporate profits, ruining another small businessman in the ascent. "Abolish Poverty Directly" by Martin Luther King, Jr., is an excerpt from his book, *Where Do We Go from Here: Chaos or Community?* His solution to the poverty of blacks and whites is to assure all a minimum yearly income.

In "Why We're against the Biggees," James S. Kunen explains why many young people blame urban and national problems on the corporate structure. Each of the preceding selections offered remedies for poverty that could be worked out within the existing capitalistic system. But Kunen argues that few problems, especially those caused by the greed of big business—pollution, ghettos, urban ugliness, exploitation of poor people—can be eliminated until the system itself is radically changed. The "Biggees" must either drop out or be expelled.

THERE WAS A RICH MAN AND
HE LIVED IN DETROITIUM

Woody Guthrie

There was a rich man and he lived in Detroitium,
Glory hallelujah, heirojarum.
And all the workers he did exploitium,
Glory hallelujah, heirojarum.

Chorus:
Heirojarum, heirojarum,
Skinnamalinkadoolium,
Skinnamalinkadoolium,
Glory hallelujah, heirojarum.
(Repeat after each verse)

204

The poor man worked til he was nearly deadium,
Glory hallelujah, heirojarum.
When he got home he fell right into bedium,
Glory hallelujah, heirojarum.

He asked for a raise but the boss only saidium,
Glory hallelujah, heirojarum.
"Get out of here, you lousy little redium,"
Glory hallelujah, heirojarum.

The poor man finally came to the conclusion,
Glory hallelujah, heirojarum.
To get his raise he'd better join the union,
Glory hallelujah, heirojarum.

He talked to the boss again but not alonium,
Glory hallelujah, heirojarum.
They said, "Don't forget what the union did to
    Sloanium,"
Glory hallelujah, heirojarum.

The boss wouldn't talk so they sat in the plantium,
Glory hallelujah, heirojarum.
All the boss could do was rave and rantium,
Glory hallelujah, heirojarum.

The moral of this story is that unions are no jokium,
Glory hallelujah, heirojarum.
A boss who gets smart with the union may go brokium,
Glory hallelujah, heirojarum.

COMING TO THE CITY

Ben H. Bagdikian

Into the cities they pour, refugees from a silent revolution.

In Chicago the white folk from the countryside come mostly by Trailway bus, carrying all they own: a suitcase tied with rope, an old trunk, three shopping bags, a folded baby buggy, a bag of grits, clutching a letter from a relative come earlier with an address and a warning, "Don't take the cabs, they'll cheat you."

If they are colored they come mostly by that great iron artery in Southern Negro life, the Illinois Central Railroad, getting off in awe under the largest building they ever saw, carrying their old suitcases and trunks, cardboard boxes with clothes and pans, and they, too, have a carefully written address, an address that may no longer exist because newcomers go to the slums and massive redevelopment is turning many slums into vacant lots or luxury apartments.

If they are American Indians they may come in rickety old cars from the Dakotas and Utah and Arizona, fleeing the hunger of the reservations, making Chicago the fourth largest concentration of aborigines in the United States.

They all gravitate toward the city, entering Chicago at the rate of fifty a day.

In a city as big as Chicago the newcomers face a strange new world. Old courage is not enough, previous skills meaningless, and what may have been minor disadvantages in education or family cohesion suddenly become catastrophic. It is possible, walking among the newcomers in their tenements, to hear these stories and these voices, and to see these signs:

"Why, this contract you signed says you have to pay carrying charges for the furniture that are more than the furniture itself! Didn't you read this before you signed it?"

"Well, Sister, the man said it would be a small charge and I couldn't find my glasses that day."

"You mean you can't read, don't you?"

"Well, not very well, Sister."

The twenty-four-year-old white girl, infant in arms, herding two other small children before her, has hitchhiked continuously for two days and two nights from West Virginia and found her husband in the middle of Chicago during a blizzard, but when a social worker gives her applications to fill out and bus tokens to get to the agency for help, the girl who has braved four hundred miles of the unknown, telephones five times in panic because the buses, the city, and the forms in triplicate are frightening.

"Mr. Donovan, my husband's back from jail so the welfare cut out my ADC because I got a unreported male in the house. Does that mean my kids can't eat because their Daddy's home?"

At Stewart Elementary School in Chicago about one thousand students enter in the fall and about one thousand students leave before June because their parents have been evicted, have departed the district for another house, or have gone back South. A teacher said, "It's hard to teach a child much of anything in a school with a 100 per cent turnover every year."

"Joe, you got to stay and help me. I need help."
"Ma, I'm going. I'm leaving for good. I don't know what I'll do but I can't stand it no more. I'm seventeen and I'll get along somehow. It's not my fault Pa's a drunk and you got eleven kids. Now you'll only have ten."

The heavy black pencilled letters, written large and painfully, are on grey cardboard tacked to the plaster in the damp corridor of 4860 North Winthrop: "Absolutely Do Not Throw Trash Out Bathroom Windows. Children Are Not to Run, Shout, or Play in Halls."

But it is not just Chicago. It is the same in New York, Los Angeles, Philadelphia, Detroit, Cleveland, Washington, St. Louis—all the great cities. In the last four decades a vast migration of 27,000,000 men, women, and children have flocked to metropolis. It is greater than the international migration which at its fullest flow from 1880 to 1920 brought 24,000,000 foreigners to America's cities. This time it is native Americans.

Almost all of them are poor. An alarming number of them remain poor for a long time.

The poverty of the newcomers is familiar and at the same time different. Prolonged lack of money can arise from a number of causes but whatever its cause it can have serious side effects that deepen the disease.

There are enormous differences in each person's response to adversity and because some people have been celebrated for personal triumph over poverty this has led to the assumption—usually by the well-fed—that to be poor makes one more noble. This was never true for most of the poor and it is not true now. Yet the belief persists that the poor compared with the affluent ought to be more honest, more resourceful, more puritanical, more disciplined, more resilient against despair, more emotionally stable, and simultaneously more aggressive and more submissive. They are not. Poverty is the pressure of living at the bottom of the social sea and this pressure finds the weakness in every personality. Poverty is dirty, vermin-infested, cold in winter, broiling in summer, and worst of all it is lonely and self-reproaching.

Ironically, the native American poor of the 1960's are worse off in some ways than the foreign immigrants of two generations ago. Both came practically penniless, went into the worst housing, got the worst jobs, and suffered the isolation and discrimination that comes to the impoverished stranger.

But the foreigners had their own culture and countrymen and history to give them assurance while they were being shunned by the new culture. In the old days if a man was disdained as a "wop" or a "mick" or a "kike," he or his parents knew that there were a time and a place in which the Italians ruled the world and created a great culture, or the Irish wrenched freedom from the world's greatest power and defended their Roman Catholic faith, or the Jews shared the making of modern civilization and survived the suffering millennia with learning and art. The lash of prejudice made its scars, as it always does, but there was some psychological solace in one's own history and bitter satisfaction that the tormentor was so ignorant he didn't even know this history. But the Negro called "nigger" or turned away with a crocodilian "Sir," and the Alabama white sneeringly called "hillbilly" hear this from their own countrymen. From the viper within the nest there is little room for retreat.

The foreign immigrant had his small solace but he also had a spur to drive him on. His was a total commitment to the new land: he had no way to leave. He could not hitchhike back to the farm, or take a bus to the home village, or go back again to the stream of migrant agricultural workers. Most had barely managed the ocean voyage here. There was no turning back.

They came from abroad at an opportune time. The New World was abuilding—railroads, canals, factories—and this was still done mainly by human hands. Pick and shovel required no diploma; there was work for the unskilled and the illiterate. It was a simple time of no application forms or Social Security cards or suitability tests or pension plans, the lack of which the workingman would feel bitterly one day, but which made the entry to casual work quicker. It was also a time for the small entrepreneur, the pushcart operator, the door-to-door peddler, the sidewalk salesman.

The foreign immigrants, too, were crowded into the worst housing. But cities were still growing in a more or less haphazard way, still mixtures of rich and poor, old and new, all living within sight and sound of each other. In the tightest immigrant slum it was possible to see or hear the ways of older settlements with all the clues these offered to successful living in a metropolis. The foreigner was highly conscious that he was in a new land and needed to learn new ways. He may have come from a city abroad. But his greatest advantage over his native contemporary was the presence of older inhabitants from whom he could learn. The friendly neighbor—or even an unfriendly one—was a powerful figure in the making of new Americans. In the city of fifty years ago, the established Americans could hardly avoid knowing the immigrants were there. People walked. The center of business and industry was downtown. All parts of the city were close at hand and brushing against each other.

The young foreigners went to schools populated by the native-born. From the American children and their teachers the immigrants not only learned the habits and idioms of city living, but they also absorbed the ambitions and standards of normal hope. This was not always a pleasant process and integration often came with bitterness and cruelty. But the country recognized that it had masses of newcomers. In the great cities of the East and Midwest no one doubted that the new element in the American population required some reaction from native society. Hundreds of organizations, some from within the immigrant groups and some from outside, turned to the job of integrating the newcomers with public schools, adult education, community houses, and systematic visitations by religious groups, private charities, and the local political chieftains.

The modern American immigrant comes to the city at a bad time. The Negro and, to a lesser extent, the white rural migrant encounter discrimination harsher for coming from their own countrymen. From this the white man and the American Indian can usually retreat. There is a constant shuttling between farm and city, or reservation and city, in one direction when conditions at home get too grim, in the other when jobs in the city are too scarce. But the periodic retreats increase family instability, disrupt education, and prevent serious commitment to making a decent, permanent home. For the Negro there is no such easy return, since he escapes not only hunger but repression. But other conditions delay his setting down roots: an even lower level of education than the rural white, more discrimination against him with jobs and the almost impermeable barrier that keeps the Negro out of the housing market.

The chief disadvantage for the native migrant is the erosion of the traditional foothold for the novice in the metropolis: the unskilled job. The ditchdigger, the factory hand, the street peddler—these were typical roles for the newcomer starting upward from 1880 to 1920. But these are the jobs that are now shrinking. . . .

The city itself has changed, almost entirely to the disadvantage of the impoverished newcomer. The transition from rural poverty to urban poverty is bewildering under any circumstances. The newcomer probably came from dilapidated farmhouses or shacks in the field without running water or electricity. In 1960 there were still 7,000,000 dwellings, 12 percent of the total, that lacked running water or a toilet. In the city a gas stove, plaster on the walls, electric wiring, plumbing, rigid rules of trash and garbage disposal may be unfamiliar and seem unimportant. Life in the city is almost always overwhelming. The life-time face-to-face personal relations of the village are replaced by fast-moving, fast-talking, impatient people in business suits sitting in remote high offices requesting forms in triplicate. Mass transit—subways, multiple bus lines, transfers, endless blocks of huge buildings—can be dizzying. The punctuality and impersonality of city jobs can be depressing. The new legal and social demands for proper clothing and medical care for school children and the competition on the basis of writing on school applications and job forms and welfare reports, all may seem mysteries comparable to the language barrier of the earlier foreigners and, in one way, worse. Most bureaucrats assume that any native-born American can write the mother tongue, can fill out forms, understand rapidly-uttered directions in business protocol, and can get around unaided in his own city. It is not a valid assumption. But few native migrants are willing to admit it. There is a glossary for the semi-literate—"I don't have my glasses with me," or "My hands are dirty, would you please fill it out?" or, "Oh, was I supposed to bring that paper with me?"—phrases used not only to avoid admission of difficulty with writing or reading, but also to avoid the painful moment when a parent has to admit to his own child that he is illiterate.

The new city deepens all the traditional problems. Since World War II the experienced city-dwellers have moved to the suburbs or to new housing developments away from downtown. With them have gone the big stores, the supermarkets, many of the factories and office buildings. The private car squeezed mass transit offstage and prosperous American life accommodated itself to the victor. Homes, stores, working places, even entertainment (Philadelphia has five downtown theaters but thirty summer suburban ones) all built themselves for the convenience of the automobile rather than for the railroad or bus or subway or pedestrian. This left the central cores of cities decayed and abandoned and this is where the newcomers settle. Instead of living interspersed among older residents, they crowd into whole blocks and entire neighborhoods that have emptied out their original residents en masse, sometimes in a matter of a few months. This process has broken an important chain of inheritance by which the accumulated experience of civilized urban living was normally passed on to the newcomer. Conformity, a curse to those who have learned the crucial mechanics of living, serves its purpose in the struggle to master a new environment.

THE MAFIA:
CONGLOMERATE OF CRIME

Time

Nobody will listen. Nobody will believe. You know
what I mean? This Cosa Nostra, it's like a second
government. It's too big.   JOE VALACHI

At the beginning of the decade, even J. Edgar Hoover denied its existence. Its structure was a mystery, and if it had a name, no one on the outside was sure of what it was. Yet, almost unnoticed, it exerted a profound impact on American life. It still does. Small wonder that Valachi, the thug-turned-informer, doubted that anybody would believe or care when he talked about an organization called La Cosa Nostra.

Today people do care. Organized crime is suddenly a high-priority item in Congress. The Nixon Administration and several key states are striving to improve law-enforcement efforts. The Justice Department is sending special anti-Mob "strike forces" into major cities, more money is being spent by police forces, and more men are being thrown into the battle. Hollywood makes movies about it *(The Brotherhood)*, and readers have put it on the top of the bestseller list (Mario Puzo's novel *The Godfather* and Peter Maas's *The Valachi Papers*). Organized crime is no longer quite the mystery that it was. It is a vast, sprawling underground domain impossible to trace fully; but there is no longer any doubt that its most important part, its very nucleus, is La Cosa Nostra (LCN), otherwise known as the Mafia.[1] . . .

THE MULTIPLIER EFFECT

. . . La Cosa Nostra and the many satellite elements that constitute organized crime are big and powerful enough to affect the quality of American life. LCN generates corruption on a frightening scale. It touches small firms as well as large, reaches into city halls and statehouses, taints facets of show business and labor relations, and periodically sheds blood. It has a multiplier effect on crime; narcotics, a mob monopoly, drives the addicted to burglaries and other felonies to finance the habit. Cosa Nostra's ability to flout the law makes preachment of law and order a joke to those who see organized crime in action most often: the urban poor and the black. Says Milton Rector, director of the National Council on Crime and Delinquency: "Almost every bit of crime we study has some link to organized crime."

Yet La Cosa Nostra itself, the Italian core of organized crime, consists of only 3,000 to 5,000 individuals scattered around the nation in 24 "families," or regional gangs, each headed by a boss and organized loosely along military lines. There is no national dictator or omnipotent unit giving precise direction on all operations. Rather, the families constitute a relatively loose confederation under a board of directors called the Commission.

1"Mafia," literally, means swank, or dolled up, but it probably derives from a Sicilian term meaning beauty or pride. In the context of crime, Mafia applies to the older, strictly Sicilian element of the Mob. "La Cosa Nostra," or Our Thing, is a broader term that means the modern American-born organization.

From this soft center the mob's web spreads to many thousands of allies and vassals representing most ethnic groups. "We got Jews, we got Polacks, we got Greeks, we got all kinds," Jackie Cerone, a member of the Chicago gang, once observed with both accuracy and pride.

"In many respects," says Ralph Salerno, who was the New York City police department's chief Mafia expert until his retirement in 1967, "the leadership has always been a 'happy marriage of Italians and Jews.'" Salerno adds: "It's the three Ms—moxie, muscle and money. The Jews provide the moxie, the Italians provide the muscle, and they both provide the money." In the public mind, however, Cosa Nostra is identified with the Italians, and about 22 million Italian-Americans are being hurt in reputation by the depredations of a very few.

In money terms, the organization is the world's largest business. The best estimate of its revenue, a rough projection based on admittedly inexact information of federal agencies, is well over $30 billion a year. Even using a conservative figure, its annual profits are at least in the $7 billion-to-$10 billion range. Though he meant it as a boast, Meyer Lansky, the gang's leading financial wizard, was actually being overly modest when he chortled in 1966: "We're bigger than U.S. Steel." Measured in terms of profits, Cosa Nostra and affiliates are as big as U.S. Steel, the American Telephone and Telegraph Co., General Motors, Standard Oil of New Jersey, General Electric, Ford Motor Co., IBM, Chrysler and RCA put together.

HOW IT WORKS

Two years ago, the President's Commission on Law Enforcement and Administration of Justice simply threw up its hands at the prospect of estimating the crime conglomerate's full penetration. "The cumulative effect of the infiltration of legitimate business in America cannot be measured," it said. Robert Kennedy, who began the first big push against the Mafia when he became Attorney General, warned that "if we do not on a national-scale attack organized criminals with weapons and techniques as effective as their own, they will destroy us." No one now disputes its potential for destruction.

Despite its continuing evolution, organized crime follows certain basic patterns that vary little. It must buy or force freedom from the law and from accepted rules of commerce. It must milk gambling, the narcotics trade, industrial relations and usury. It must find outlets for its accumulated profits. These are its main forms of activity:

The political fix takes many forms, but the most important, from LCN's view, is obtaining the cooperation of the policeman and the politicians. East of the Mississippi, particularly, it is the rare big-city government that is completely free of the fix. In Newark, corruption is rampant. One gangster recently confided to another that $12,000 a month flows to police superiors for protection—which sometimes goes beyond a shield for illicit activities. When he vacationed on the West Coast last spring, for example, Thomas Pecora, a boss of Teamsters Local 97 as well as a Mafia man, took along a Newark city detective as a bodyguard.

Newark Police Director Dominick Spina was recently indicted for failing to enforce gambling laws. He was acquitted. Mayor Hugh Addonizzio has refused to give his personal financial records to a grand jury that asked for them. So pervasive is the aura of corruption, a governor's committee reported, that it contributed heavily to the Newark riot of 1967, in which black resentment of police was a major factor.

In Illinois, La Cosa Nostra exerts major influence in a dozen Chicago wards and dictates the votes of as many as 15 state legislators. Known as the West Side Bloc, a newspaper euphemism to avoid libel suits, the Mob opposes anticrime bills in the state legislature, forces gangsters onto the payroll of Mayor Richard Daley's Chicago machine, and corrupts the city police department. Salvatore ("Momo") Giancana may be hiding in Mexico, but his stand-ins, Tony ("Big Tuna") Accardo and Paul ("The Waiter") DeLucia still pack influence. Example: When a Justice Department report charged 29 Chicago policemen with being grafters, Daley poohpoohed the allegations, took no action. Some of the 29 were subsequently promoted.

Protection can also mean death for informers. Richard Cain, once chief investigator for the Cook County, Ill., sheriff's office, gave lie-detector tests to a quintet of bank robbery suspects. Cain, now in prison, was not after the guilty man but in search of the FBI informant among the five. The tipster, Guy Mendolia, Jr., was subsequently murdered.

Three federal men arrived in Columbus last year to investigate gambling. They were soon arrested by local police, accused of being drunk in public. The G-men were acquitted and eight Columbus cops were indicted for taking $8,000 a month in bribes.

Ralph Salerno, co-author of an upcoming book on the Mob, *The Crime Confederation*, estimates that the votes of about 25 members of Congress can be delivered by mob pressure. New Jersey Congressman Cornelius Gallagher was an associate of Joe Zicarelli, a Cosa Nostra power in New Jersey. Zicarelli's command over Gallagher was strong enough, in fact, to bring Gallagher, whom Zicarelli calls "my friend the Congressman," off the floor of the House of Representatives to accept Zicarelli's telephone calls. Although Gallagher has denied the allegation with varying degrees of indignation, he has never bothered to sue *Life* for its disclosures about him. He has since been reelected, and remains a member of the House Government Operations Committee, which watches the federal agencies that watch the Mob.

Even the judiciary is not beyond reach, and the Mob has a special set of instructions for judges on the payroll. An FBI "bug" placed in the First Ward Democratic organization on La Salle Street, a favorite gathering place for Chicago gangsters, overheard the following conversation between Illinois Circuit Court Judge Pasqual Sorrentino and Pat Marcy, a friend of the Chicago LCN family. What should he do, Sorrentino asked, if federal agents questioned him about his associations with gangsters? Marcy's answer: "Stand on your dignity. Don't answer those questions. Tell them they're trying to embarrass you. Stay on the offensive. Remember, you're a judge." The trouble is, of course, that Sorrentino and some of his colleagues, on federal as well as state benches, have forgotten just that fact.

Nowhere has organized crime subverted more than a tiny minority of public officials. But a minority can be enough both to undermine law enforcement and to bend regulations, purchasing procedures and legislation to a shape pleasing to the mob.

Gambling is far and away the Mob's biggest illicit income producer, more than taking the place that bootleg liquor held during Prohibition. No one can more than guess how much money is bet illegally in the U.S. each year, but a conservative estimate is that about $20 billion is put down on horse racing, lotteries and sports events. Perhaps a third is pure profit for LCN and its affiliates.

In the slums, the bets are usually on "the numbers." The gambler picks the number that he thinks will come up in some agreed-upon tabulation—the total dollars bet at a race track, for example—and puts down as little as 25¢ or as much as $1. In some places $10 bets are allowed. The bet taker himself, called the policy writer, is too small—and too vulnerable —to be a formal member of La Cosa Nostra. He works instead under contract as a "sharecropper."

Bookmaking is next up the ladder from the numbers, and the bookmaker, who usually employs several solicitors, is a man of substance. When FBI agents seized Gil Beckley, the king of layoff men (a banker to smaller bookies), in Miami in January, 1966, his records showed that on that day alone he had handled $250,000 in bets, for a profit, by his own reckoning, of $129,000. He is now appealing a ten-year prison sentence in the case.

An operator like Beckley is not necessarily a full member of LCN.

Beckley has a kind of associate status, in which favors and profits flow back and forth. As in certain other areas, LCN is content to get a cut while leaving active management to a relative outsider. Another big layoff man, Sam DiPiazzo, once told of an attempt by Giancana's Chicago family to extort 50% of his six-figure take. As DiPiazzo related the story, he was forced to go before a committee in Chicago, where he haggled the bite down to a mere $35 a day. His big bargaining point was that he co-operated with "the Little Man," Louisiana Family Boss Carlos Marcello.

General affluence and increasing public interest in sports such as football and basketball hike the stakes and make the potential for corrupting athletes great. Even if he does not succeed in fixing a game, the Cosa Nostra agent finds information about a team's morale or physical condition priceless in helping him to set odds. On just such an information hunt, a scout for Chicago Handicapper Burton Wolcoff wangled his way into the clubhouse of the Los Angeles Dodgers a few years back. Learning that Sandy Koufax, who was scheduled to pitch that day, was having even more arm trouble than usual, the agent flashed the news to Wolcoff, who put down $30,000 against the Dodgers. Koufax gave up five runs in early innings and the Dodgers lost.

The National Football League has gone to considerable lengths to detect the fix, relying, ironically, on Gil Beckley. Apparently the league operated on the theory that it takes one to know one. "I want the games square," Beckley told league officials when he announced his proposition. "If I know that something's wrong, I'll give you the name of the club. But I won't give you names of the players." Tips from Beckley have touched off a number of secret investigations by the league.

Until the mid-'60s, one of Cosa Nostra's most profitable gambling operations was at one of the few places in the U.S. where most kinds of gambling are legal: Las Vegas. The Mob's technique there, known as "skimming," was as simple as larceny and as easy as shaking the money tree: a part of the cash profits from six LCN-controlled casinos was simply diverted before the figures were placed in the ledger books. How much cash was spirited away in this manner, eluding both state and federal taxes, no one can say precisely. After the Government became aware of mob influence and forced the gangsters out of most of the casinos in 1966 and 1967—LCN still has interests in two big casinos—revenue reported for tax purposes jumped by more than $50 million a year.

Loan-sharking or usury nets several billions—it is impossible to say how many—in revenue for the Mob. Dollar for dollar, usury is LCN's best investment; though the gross is lower than it is in gambling, profit is higher.

Interest rates commonly run at 20% per week, or, in the Mob's words, "six for five"—borrow $5 on Monday and pay back $6 by Saturday noon, the normal deadline. Borrowers are frequently gamblers who have lost heavily or hope to make a big strike, but they also include factory workers, businessmen on the verge of bankruptcy, or anyone else who needs cash but cannot meet a bank's credit check.

Many of the Cosa Nostra's legitimate business fronts were acquired when the owner could not pay his debt. Some public officials were acquired in the same manner. Over his head in various business deals, James Marcus, the former Water Commissioner of New York City, took a loan at 104% annual interest. When he was unable to pay, the gangsters found him a willing victim for other schemes, including graft on city projects. In the case of Marcus, as with many other public officials, the loan was almost certainly a come-on for what the Mob really wanted: a good friend in a high place. Marcus, Mobster Anthony ("Tony Ducks") Corallo, and Contractor Henry Fried were convicted in the kickback scheme.

Narcotics traffic, chiefly in heroin, is less lucrative than gambling, but still profitable enough, bringing in more than $350 million in revenue and $25 million in profits. Because of the risks involved in peddling drugs directly, Cosa Nostra once again contracts the retail trade to its sharecroppers, saving for itself the less dangerous and infinitely more profitable role of importer and wholesaler. The sums involved are substantial. By the time opium from Turkey, the chief supplier for the U.S., is processed into heroin and shipped to New York, it is worth about $225,000 per kilogram. The price to society is beyond measure.

So far, there is no evidence that the Mafia has tried to penetrate the marijuana market. The source of supply in Mexico is too close, and the competition from travelers passing over the border too intense. One unforeseen by-product of the Federal Government's crackdown on the marijuana trade, however, may be to create an LCN monopoly. If the "independents" are driven out, the mobsters might find pot as profitable as heroin. Just that happened in book-making, when police put many freelance operators out of business.

Labor racketeering has no price tag, but obviously nets the Mob many millions. It takes several forms. One of the simplest is extortion. The gangsters might thus inform a small businessman, who has perhaps only a dozen employees, that from that minute on his enterprise is unionized. Though the employees may never know that they belong to a "union"— and never receive any of the benefits of being in a union—the employer nevertheless pays the "union organizers" the workers' initiation fees and monthly dues. In another variation, the bogus union settles for "sweetheart" contracts that are grossly unfair to the workers it is supposed to represent. The difference between what a legitimate union might win for the workers and what the Mob union actually obtains is split between the mobsters and the company owners. In one such contract, writes Donald Cressey in his definitive work, *Theft of the Nation*, the president of a paper local won his union only one paid holiday a year: Passover. His membership was exclusively Puerto Rican.

In other ways as well, union racketeering can be as profitable to a company as it is to the Mob. Once the gangsters have taken over a union —they find their easiest prey is unskilled and semi-skilled occupations— they can guarantee both labor peace and a competitive edge over other companies in wages and benefits. There is, of course, a fee, but that is often lower for the businessman than the real costs of strikes or higher wages.

Business infiltration is the organization's fastest-growing source of revenue. Its interests extend to an estimated 5,000 business concerns. Indeed, Cosa Nostra's penetration of the above-ground world of finance and commerce is probably the greatest threat that it poses to the nation today. A business can be acquired in any number of ways, from foreclosure on a usurious loan to outright purchase. LCN, after all, has more venture capital than any other nongovernmental organization in the world. New York's Carlo Gambino and his adopted family own large chunks of real estate in the New York area valued at $300 million. Until recently, they also ran a labor consulting service. Marcello of New Orleans, another real estate millionaire, has been buying up land in the path of the Dixie Freeway and hopes to make a bundle in federal highway funds.

Once brought under the Mob's umbrella, a business almost always ceases to operate legitimately. If it is a restaurant—favorite targets—or a nightclub, it buys coal or oil from one LCN affiliate, rents linen from another, ships garbage out through still another. Its entertainers, parking-lot attendants and even its hat check girls must always be approved by the Mob—and sometimes they must kick back part of what they take in. When the gangsters were big in Las Vegas, they sometimes used skimmed cash to supplement the fees paid to featured performers. The under-the-table funds went untaxed and left the compliant performer with an obligation. This was repaid by appearances elsewhere at the Mob's request.

Unfortunately, the gangs' business methods do not stop with such relatively innocuous, if illegal, tactics. The giant Atlantic & Pacific grocery can testify to that. Taking control of a company that manufactured detergent, the powerful New York-New Jersey gangster brothers, Gerardo and the late Gene Catena, tried to put the product on A&P shelves. When the A&P officials rejected the inferior Brand X, marketed by the Catenas' Best Sales Company, the brothers tried traditional means of persuasion. Four A&P employees died violently. Six stores were fire-bombed. Finally, two union locals threatened to strike, rejecting out of hand a contract that seemed more than generous.

Dumfounded by tactics not taught at the Harvard Business School, A&P officials seemingly never connected Catena detergent with strikes and terror. The government did, however, and impaneled a grand jury to investigate the Catena brothers' marketing procedures. Brand X was apparently not worth the bother of federal heat. The Catenas got out of detergents, the unions signed their contracts, and the A&P was left at peace.

Generally, the Mob favors businesses in the service and retail fields, particularly things like coin-operated machines, liquor stores and laundries. These offer, among other advantages, cash turnovers susceptible to skimming. With these companies the mobsters can rake off funds without anyone, particularly anyone in the Internal Revenue Service, being the wiser. When FBI agents searched the house belonging to the son of Buffalo Boss Stefano Magaddino last December, they found in a suitcase $521,020 in skimmed cash, most of it from Magaddino's 15 companies in the Buffalo area. It may not have been worth all of Magaddino's trouble. Not only has the Government confiscated his money, but the other mobsters are infuriated because Magaddino had told them that he had no funds to help them meet common expenses. This month, in fact, LCN's top hierarchy took the highly unusual step of sending a team to investigate Magaddino's finances. Mrs. Magaddino, who had never looked into the suitcase, was also upset. "Son of a bitch!" she muttered when the FBI carted the money away. "He said we have no money for Florida this year. $500,000!"

Jukeboxes, funeral parlors, small garment firms and other marginal enterprises that have long attracted gangsters have little effect on the general economy. Big-time construction is another matter, and by playing both the union and management sides, LCN begins to exercise major impact. The Crime and Delinquency Council's Milton Rector says air-freight trucking operations have been so deeply penetrated that gangsters could bring New York's Kennedy Airport "to its knees at any time."

As the boodle piles up, repositories bigger than Magaddino's suitcase must be found. Many millions go to foreign banks. Switzerland, with its numbered bank accounts, is the favorite. Funds from these reservoirs often come back in the form of "loans" for investment purposes. Asked to produce collateral for a jukebox import deal, Philadelphia Boss Angelo ("Mr. A.") Bruno quickly came up with a certified check backed by a Swiss account. The amount: $50 million. . . .

THE LAW'S DELAY

Where is the law? Why, despite some troubles, does Cosa Nostra survive and thrive? Beyond its own inherent strength and tradition is its ability to corrupt civil officials. Probably no other group in history has made such a fine art of corruption. Without the fix, Cosa Nostra would not last out the year. Nor are local cops the only ones who yield to temptation. Three days after a report on skimming in Las Vegas was sent to the U.S. Attorney General's office in 1963, a complete copy was in the hands of the criminals cited in the report. The conduit for the leak has never been found.

Even in the absence of official dishonesty, law enforcement has often proved inept. Most city and state police agencies are still not equipped to deal effectively with clever, well-financed conspiracies that extend across city and state lines. The FBI is better trained, of course, but its special agents hardly constitute a national police force, and were never intended to do so. Until the beginning of the decade, federal authorities merely nodded while the mobsters nibbled away at the country. Besides, coordination among law-enforcement agencies at all levels is frequently weak or totally absent. Even when pressure is applied vigorously, resulting in arrests and convictions, LCN can quickly fill personnel gaps.

Not that prosecution is easy under the best of circumstances. The gangsters' well-paid legal corps takes full advantage of the Bill of Rights. The Mob's muscle often takes care of potential witnesses. It takes a brave citizen to call the police. Also, most of the evidence gathered by the FBI, until recently, was not admissible in court.

Much is changing. Though more vigilant observation might have detected it long before, a major revelation occurred in 1957, when New York state police happened upon a meeting of the Commission and its lieutenants at the estate of Joseph Barbara in upstate Apalachin. The authorities were able to find out who the mobsters were and, more important, that they were together. In 1962, Joe Valachi, the Cosa Nostra soldier-turned-informer, confirmed and explained what the FBI had been hearing from its bugs for months. Though he looked at the Mob from the bottom up, Valachi's remarkable memory nonetheless provided invaluable insights into its organization. From January 1961 to December 1968, the Government indicated 290 members of Cosa Nostra and obtained 147 convictions, with many cases still pending. Some of the bosses themselves have been jailed, while many have found their activities severely curtailed because of continuous scrutiny.

STRENGTHENING HAND

Most of the surveillance has come from electronic bugs and telephone taps, which have supplied something like 80% of the information the Government has on the Mob. While bugging is still the subject of considerable controversy—and can be a serious danger to civil liberties if misused—a law passed by Congress last year at least clarifies the Government's powers and gives the Justice Department broader jurisdiction. For the time being, electronic snooping seems to be a necessary, if risky weapon.

Federal funds are now available in increasing amounts to help city and state agencies prepare for the challenge. Two major bills now pending in Congress could have significant results. One would strengthen the hand of prosecutors and grand juries in mounting investigations and make involvement in organized crime generally—regardless of the specific violation—a federal offense. The second measure would invoke civil procedures, such as antitrust action, to attack organized crime behind its screen of bogus legitimacy.

Beyond new statutes and energetic reinforcement, the nation needs another, stronger weapon: public indignation. There is not nearly enough of that in the U.S. No other Western, industrial country in modern times has suffered criminal abuses on such a scale. America's porous, pluralistic and permissive society offers extraordinary opportunities, chances to hide and to advance, for the enterprising and imaginative criminal. But, most fundamentally, U.S. society helps the criminal by toleration (occasionally even admiration) and by providing a ready market for his services. Illicit gambling thrives because of the popular demand for it. Politicians of questionable integrity remain in office because the electorate allows it. Entrepreneurs who half-knowingly accept dirty money with the rationale that business is business are as corrupt as grafting politicians.

TOLERATING THE MOB

In large measure, the modern Mob lacks the traditional justification for crime—the bitter spur of poverty. It also lacks the occasional, near-heroic dimension of defying law and the established order for the sake of rebellion. It is by and large a middle-class sort of Mob, more or less tolerated by the affluent. Among the public there is often a certain psychological hypocrisy. Rage is great over conspicuous criminal acts, but there is less anger over the far more harmful depredations that are the specialty of organized crime. Until there is a popular revolt, La Cosa Nostra will probably endure.

TWO VIEWS OF WELFARE

BARBARA DUGAN'S STORY

Richard M. Elman

"I wish I could remember when I got this sickle-cell anemia. A lot of us here have got it. They say we got it down South, but when you got it you just don't feel like doing too much. It makes your blood slow. Hard not to do too much when you are on the Welfare. They give you the pills and the special diets, and they send you to homemaking classes if they think it will help you, but they don't help you otherwise, so you still have a lot to do. They is picking up the kids after school because you don't want them walking home alone in a neighborhood like this . . . and they's cooking and shopping and laundry and housecleaning, and then well-baby clinic and sick-baby clinic and the clinic for yourself and that sickle-cell anemia. It's a full day.

"What I mean by a neighborhood like this is they's a lot of junkies and queers around here. Well, you just don't want to take a chance on them. So you carry your kids to school in the morning, and you carry them home after school. My kids live ten blocks away from the school. Ain't no buses down here . . .

"Ain't no lazy people on Welfare. Oh, maybe they is a few, but they ain't many. Seems like you got to pull your lazy butt from one place to the next, and you got to pull your kids with you wherever you go because they ain't no place you can leave them where they be safe . . . And sometimes you just don't feel like doing too much, but you still got to do it if you don't want them to take your kids away from you. *They find you lying in bed with nothing to do that's just what they going to do— sickle-cell anemia and all.* I got two sick kids like me and another in the Kennedy Home in the Bronx . . . I don't know about him . . . and some times you get pretty tired, but you just got to do certain things. After all, they say, if you don't take care of these kids, who will? They got a point.

Ain't nobody else around here . . . and, after all, they's givin' you a special diet . . .

"But every time you want something extra from them, it's a whole nuisance. Like carfare. Sometimes I got to spend ninety cents for carfare for me and the kids to go off to Bellevue, because, as I told you, you can't leave them alone if you got to go there for some reason. And when I come back from Bellevue clinic, I got to rush over here to 28th Street for that carfare money or else I'm going to run short on food. Well, even so, they don't just give you your money like that. Sometimes they want proof. Sometimes they say they will owe it to you. You got to be careful about the ones who say that. I learned you got to insist right then and there you want that carfare or else you don't get it. So you just got to sit there and wait for the man until he gives it to you. You think they care? Sometimes I think I spend half my life waiting somewhere for ninety cents.

"And what I mean is, if I send my boy to get the money for me, how do I know if the man is going to listen to him? They don't like kids there. You know what they tell my boy when he goes? 'You make sure that gets to your mother. Don't you go spending on yourself.' Shit!

"And if they think they can get away with it, they liable to ask your boy all kinds of questions which they just know they got no business asking. They ask. Nothing private with them . . . Except when you want some money. Then you got a case against them.

"Shit! I could put up with anything if it weren't for the going this place and that. It's just about enough to make me give up everything sometimes, especially when I wake up feeling like I just can't do too much. But you know as well as I do that if you stay that way you are going to end up in a lot of trouble. So it's off to well-baby clinic and sick-baby clinic and now they even got my big girl seeing this psychiatrist. You think I let her go there alone? She goes there with me. Otherwise they say, 'Look at Barbara Dugan. She don't give a good goddamn,' and they try to take my kids away from me.

"Barbara Ann goes to the psychiatrist because they said so at school but if you ask me, it's because we've been pushed down for so long even the kids know it. She cries a lot. I used to be that way. You mustn't believe them when they say we get something for nothing. You may not have to work when you are on the Welfare, but you don't get anything for nothing. They make it hard as dirt. If you want something, you got to go and get it. And you can't ask the man to help because how should he know. He don't even know you're alive half the time, and the other half it's always so much this and that. Takes a genius to know what anybody is talking about.

"Worse thing of all is when they decide you haven't done right. Then they get awful mean. They'll threaten you. Some of these women get sulky after one of those visits. They get sunk down real low. Every time they's a visit they get that way . . . real low . . . I don't get that way anymore Any time they get after my tail, I take my kids and march right over here and I just start scuffling. They see me barging in like that, hollering for the man, and they just know I know my rights. You think they would treat me like those others?

"Well, you can't do that every day of the week when you got sickle-cell anemia. Sometimes you just wake up too tired. Sometimes you just don't want to go out looking for bargains. So, when night comes, you send your kids out for some of the *cuchifritos* or maybe delicatessen or a pizza pie and cokes and you just sitting around having an early supper when he comes by.

"He says, 'I just wanted to see how things are coming along.' Or he says, 'I thought I would like to find out how you are getting on.'

"And then he looks at all that food and he gets real mean. Gives you a big lecture about how you got sickle-cell anemia and should eat the proper food or what is the use of the special diet anyway. And sure enough, next time you get a check they have taken away that special diet and you got to start all over again at Bellevue with a letter from the doctor.

"Seems like you're always doing the same things over and over again. You get an apartment. You start furnishing it. Then you got to move because of the relocation and it starts all over again. The man won't give you security. The man don't want you to live in that building. You go to look for an apartment and the man say, 'Who's looking after the children?' Seems like they always got to make remarks.

"That's why I don't want my boy to come home from that school. I know Welfare would give me more money. You think I want them snooping around? Kids grow up too fast here. That little Puerto Rican girl next door—she's fifteen and Welfare just give her money for the layette.

"Well, you just can't expect any different from people like us. It is the way people live, I guess. I think they ought to take all the kids away from some of these women. The way they bring up kids. You wouldn't want it to happen to your kid. They just don't know any better, and they afraid to ask without getting into trouble. It's a hard life. Every time you want something they's somebody there to make it hard for you. You say, 'I don't want to cause any trouble. I'll do just as they say.' Then you get a new investigator, and he's changed his mind about everything . . .

"I guess the Seventh Day Adventists do best on Welfare. They just like Jews. Strict about everything, even food. If I was going to stay on

Welfare, I would become a Seventh Day Adventist. But it is hard. You got to keep kosher. I think the Welfare likes these people better than us because you never see one of them getting into any trouble. They know how to live on the Welfare better than anybody else. Don't kid yourself. It must be hard, living like one of them. You can get money for the special diets, but they make you live just like a Jew . . .

"Some of the Puerto Ricans also do good because rice and beans and bananas are cheap, but they don't speak good English many of them, and some of them can't read or write. They can get all fouled up sometimes. I've seen it happen. Seems they will never understand why you don't ever get the same check twice. Well, I don't understand it either. I once asked the man and he said if you got a complaint to make . . . I ain't complaining, I told him. I was just wondering why. You think he ever told me? Probably he don't know himself. Like that time I caught that girl making a mistake in my arithmetic. I told her, 'You know you cheating me for fifty cents?' Well, she give me the money, but she turned red in the face and screamed, 'Keep a civil tongue in your mouth, Barbara!'

"Worst of all, though, are the special men who come at night. Like this one man asked me, 'If you got no man in the house what you got those pills?'[1] Well, I told him they give me them over at the Planned Parenthood two years ago and I ain't used any of them, as he can plainly see. Then he says, 'You make sure you stay that way,' as if there was a law against going to bed with a man—I mean if he is not your husband . . .

"Speaking of husbands, they used to come around to some of these women. Early in the morning you could hear them running down the stairs. You think they'd ask these women when they suspected something? No. They come around asking you. Well, I ain't going to tell on any of these girls when I know I'm likely to get my head split in.

"And what's so wrong if the men do drop by? Most of them got no place else to go. You know it's hard on women too not having their enjoyment once in a while. I don't do any of that stuff any more and I'm used to it. I don't even miss it. Maybe it's this damned anemia. But if I had a man I would want to have a separate room. It's not so nice when you sleep in the same room with your kids. Once I lived in a place. They was plaster falling on us every time. You go tell that to the Welfare. I have three rooms here, but one of them got no heat so we all sleep here in the living room as a practical matter. When I asked the Welfare for a bigger apartment, they said you got enough for just the three of you, and the man told me not to apply.

1 Welfare agencies commonly attempt to ascertain the presence of a man in the house, capable of providing support, as a way of avoiding or terminating their obligations to women with dependent children.

"And that's the way it goes. You're always asking and being told and going from this place to that place. You're always waiting on lines. And all you ever think about is your Welfare. You're right. The way they got it fixed, it's just like being a junkie. You get your checks twice a month, but you got to keep going over there every few days for that extra little fix, and sometimes when you need it worst of all the man ain't nowhere to be seen.

"Worst of all, though, is when you got kids. They need gym shoes. You got to go to Welfare. They need a doctor's examination for camp, and again you got to arrange it for the Welfare. If you spend the money for food to buy your girl shoes (because she needs them for school and you figure you can save yourself a trip), the next thing you know the man wants to know why you ain't got no money. Kids just don't understand budgets, and when they want something, they really want it. I'd like to see the mother who thinks differently. But it don't work that way on Welfare. I get maybe $4.00 a week for their clothes and for me, but I am always using it to do other things. So then, when I need something, I got to go down and get the money from the Welfare, and they likely to want to know why. When you got kids, it's not a good thing to be on the Welfare.

"Well, nobody wants to get rid of their kids. Least I don't see how they could. So you are always buying now and asking questions later, and then they get angry with you and you catch hell. It's the goddamnedest life. If you buy at the store, they overcharge. If you go to the supermarket, you got to carry all that stuff back—and who's taking care of your kids meanwhile? I tell you it isn't easy when you got sickle-cell anemia . . . And some of these women got worse things than that. My neighbor's daughter is an epileptic . . . so when I asked the doctor for a housekeeper because they give her one, this man say, 'You got anybody with brain damage?' Seems it's different if you got brain damage because this man said if he gives me a housekeeper what am I going to do?

"Yes, seems like they always going to make remarks. I don't care if they white or colored. They make remarks. The colored's the worst sometimes. The young ones are a little better, but the way some of them come sniffing around, you think maybe they looking for the wrong thing. Worst of all is that you got to put up with this every day of the week. Except Sunday. They can't do much to you on Sunday. Last Sunday I took my kids in the subway up to the Bronx because this social worker said I should go to visit that other boy. I made a picnic lunch because it was supposed to be a nice day. Then it rained, and then we had to eat in the classrooms. Anyway, when we got back I only had 50¢, so I made my kids hot cereal with raisins for supper, and early next morning I sent my boy with a note to the Welfare center to get us back some of that money.

"Well, my boy say the man had this white stuff all over his face. He had a bad sunburn. It was the week before school was supposed to close, but he say, 'What are you doing out of school?' So he called the guidance counselor and told him he had my boy in his office, and then I had to come to school the next morning with my boy and explain or else they said they would suspend him. Well, I told that man at the school that we just didn't have any money so I had to send my boy over to the Welfare to get reimbursed because I had all this laundry to do else there wouldn't be clean clothes for anybody. You know what that man say then? He say, 'Next time that happens you just telephone.' Can you imagine? He wants me to telephone. Don't he know they don't give us any money to do that?

"It's like when I first started on the Welfare, and they said I was 'mismanaging.' This nice girl—she was a social worker—heard about me and she said she would take my case. So every time I would get a check from the Welfare, I cashed it and brought the money to her and she would put it in this little metal box in her desk. Then I could come over there every day, and she would give me a few dollars for the shopping because she said it was better to shop every day on what I was earning. She was a good, sweet girl and she liked me, I think. It was better leaving the money with her than leaving it at home where I could get robbed. So every day I would come to her and get some of that money. Then one day toward the end of the month I come to her and she says, 'I'm sorry, Barbara, I just haven't got any more money for you,' and she opens up that box and shows me that it is empty. Sure enough, we sit down then and do some figuring, and I've taken out more than there was, but she says it isn't my fault. There just wasn't enough to begin with. And she says, 'Let me give you something from my pocketbook until the end of the month.' But when she opens her purse, she's only got about three or four dollars and some change.

" 'I don't know what we are going to do now,' I say. I look over at this girl. She's crying.

" 'Barbara, she says, 'I'm sorry. I'm really sorry. If I give you this I just won't have anything.'

"So I had to go out then and buy at the Spanish grocer, and I've been paying him back ever since. You know, because I was short. Well, after that I figured I'll hold onto my money myself because if they ain't enough, they ain't much sense to budgeting. You know what I mean? I mean it's a little silly. 'Course, things can change. I get this special diet now, and I get a little more money. I don't wish to sound ungrateful. I just wish it wasn't always so hard. You know what I mean. And those remarks all the time. You know what I mean, don't you?"

ENDING THE WELFARE MESS

A CONSERVATIVE-LIBERAL DIALOGUE

Ernest van den Haag

Liberal: It is a shame that a country as wealthy as ours—the wealthiest country in the world—allows so many people to live in misery.

Conservative: Allows?

L: No, I don't mean the poor volunteer for poverty. They don't want to be poor. And we can and should help them to live better. We must solve the problem of poverty.

C: Don't we spend immense amounts of money doing just that—more than was ever spent before by any country?

L: Not enough; and we spend humiliatingly and bureaucratically. The poor are still there—worse off than ever in the midst of plenty. Nothing we do seems to help.

C: Well, then why do you think spending more would?

L: What else? We must spend more and in new ways.

C: One reason for our failure may be that we have done just what you urge: whenever the old programs did not prove effective enough we added some new ones and spent some additional money. Though there is plenty of fancy rhetoric— "wars" against poverty, etc.—no one has even outlined what *specifically* and quantitatively is to be achieved!

The result is a wasteful, ineffective hodgepodge of overlapping local, state and federal welfare programs. They support a resentful yet steadily increasing welfare population and a bureaucracy increasing even faster. Actually the poor population is *decreasing* rapidly; paradoxically, the welfare population is *increasing* even more rapidly.

L: Surely the poor population is not decreasing? Or is the war on poverty that effective? It was started because the poor population was not decreasing.

C: I doubt that: the size of the group classified as poor has rapidly declined since the turn of the century.

L: Perhaps we were worse off in the nineteenth century. But our problem is now. We have too many poor in the twentieth century.

C: "Too many" implies a comparison to some standard—either the past, or some ideal. Let me consider both. If we follow the present definition of the Social Security Administration, and classify as poor all those families (defined as four persons, in urban areas) receiving (in dollars of 1964 purchasing power) less than $3,130 a year (or in dollars of 1967 purchasing power, less than $3,300), we find that at the turn of the century nearly 90 percent of all families were "poor"; in 1920 about 50 per cent, in 1962 about 20 per cent, in 1966 about 15–16 per cent. In 1967, about 11 per cent —5.3 million families out of 49.8 million (less than $\frac{1}{9}$ of all American families) were poor. This is a performance never equalled anywhere, at any time. It is ignored by our intellectuals—perhaps because it was done, in the main, by the free market and not by the government.

L: But what about the remaining 11 per cent of our families who do not live on a decent scale? . . .

C: We can reduce the size of the "poor" group; and the degree of poverty the poor suffer—the gap between them and the lower middle class.

Which is what we have done. I already pointed out the amazing reduction of the proportion of poor people in the population. It is difficult to measure the gap between poor and non-poor at various times. Perhaps it is enough to know that the poorest 11 per cent of our population—"the poor"—live much better—command much more purchasing power—than 60 per cent of the families in the Soviet Union. Our poorest Negroes command about ten times as much purchasing power as their African contempories. (The average Negro commands as much as the average French or Italian worker.)

L: Why then are poor Negroes so unhappy if they are not that poor?

C: They don't identify themselves with Africans—despite all the fantasy talk—or Europeans. They compare themselves with white Americans. And they have less; which, understandably, they resent. Indeed, if there are fewer poor, they resent their poverty more.

L: Can we reduce the number of poor, and their poverty, more than we have?

C: We can. But we cannot hope to make progress as fast as in the past. For one thing the "war against poverty" has created agencies and bureaucrats with a vested interest in the poor—they make their living and derive their power and status from the existence of the poor. They will not let their clientele disappear. Some present poor have a symbiotic interest: it pays more for them to be "poor" than to work. I do not know how important this antagonistic symbiosis is. But in the past no one had an interest in being poor and very few people could gain status, or make a living, by being poverty experts, or bureaucrats. Whereupon poverty rapidly diminished. . . .

L: In your view, what should we do instead?

C: Let me first give you an idea of who the poor are.

According to government data and standards, there are (1967) about 5.3 million poor families (about 25.9 million poor persons); 25 per cent of these have family heads who are over 65 years old; 22 per cent are headed by women. The remaining (about) 50 per cent of all poor families have employed family heads, who do not earn enough to get the family above the poverty line. One-third of all poor families are black (a much higher percentage of the black than of the white population).

One other point: 15 per cent of all poor families have five or more children; 40 per cent of all poor persons are under eighteen years of age.

In the light of these data, a satisfactory welfare system must attempt three things which are not always easy to reconcile.

(1) We must provide in the simplest way—with the least administrative cost—for those who cannot provide for themselves and are unlikely ever to be able to, while yet trying to encourage them to do what they can to earn money. Above all, we must try to reduce the number of people in this permanently dependent class.

(2) We must persuade poor families not to have more children than rich families do, a) by making contraception easier for them, b) by making it more rewarding to have fewer children and less rewarding to have more.

(3) We must help those who work but earn less than they need to go above the poverty level—to earn more by a) up-grading their skills and giving them better opportunities; b) subsidizing them meanwhile in such a way as to encourage them to continue to earn and to increase their earnings. At present, higher earnings—often any

earnings—are penalized by deduction of these earnings from the welfare subsidy, sometimes by deductions greater than the earnings. This means that people who can work, but cannot earn much, do better not working. They are helped more if they give up than if they keep trying.

L: The principles are fine. But what do you propose concretely? What will you do about slums, low wages, no jobs, no skills, too many children, too little education, destitute old age? Do you propose a guaranteed annual income? A negative income tax? The government as employer of last resort? Subsidies for businesses to employ "unemployables"? . . .

L: Let's go on to female family heads, many with five or more children.

C: Such families are usually poor because the father has deserted and does not support them and the mother has to take care of the children and, therefore, can earn only very little money if any. We need answers to two questions: a) what can be done to improve the lot of these families; b) what can be done to discourage other men from deserting and women from being left with their children.

L: Well, do you intend to punish them for bringing children into the world whom they cannot support?

C: If conception were deliberate, or even merely inadvertent, a case for punishment could be made; but it would be hard to inflict any punishment without also punishing the children, which would be unjust.

Most of the women in question do not have their children deliberately. Some don't know how to avoid conception; some don't have the means to do so; some, finally, neglect precautions. Very few are deliberate.

The first thing to do, therefore, is to inform them. All non-objecting nubile female welfare clients should be given complete contraceptive information. Secondly, contraceptives should be available for a nominal charge to all welfare clients. Thirdly, they should be impressed with the disadvantages—for all concerned—of having children without having established a stable union with the father. I think these measures would greatly reduce the number of families headed by females and the number of children per family. The remaining families without male breadwinners and with many children would be either families in which the breadwinner disappeared for unforeseeable reasons, such as death or illness; or families created by a mother who deliberately had them, counting on the community to support her and her children. There is not much we can do about the first case except try to take care of the bereft family. As for those who deliberately bring children into the world for whom they cannot provide, I think ways can be found to discourage this—without harming the children.

L: Really? Why isn't it done?

C: There is little point worrying about this until we know how much of the problem will disappear once we make information and contraceptive devices easily and fully available.

L: Wouldn't that involve costly medical examinations?

C: They certainly would be less costly than children. Contraceptive loops indeed have to be inserted by physicians.

And only physicians can sterilize. But there is no medical reason for classifying contraceptive pills as prescription drugs except to increase the income of physicians.

L: Aren't there possible dangers and contra-indications?

C: There are. And they might be mentioned on the label. But the dangers are few and less acute than those threatening if a person who should not, eats sugar. Yet we have not made sugar a prescription drug, nor do we even label it "dangerous for diabetics."

L: What would you do with those families who already have many children and no father?

C: Often the father is absent because he could not earn enough to offset the welfare payments that stop with his presence. When there are many children these welfare payments may exceed what he can earn. Such payments should not depend on the absence of a breadwinner. They should supplement the income he can earn.[1]

As for families actually without a male breadwinner, we must give mothers an incentive, and the opportunity, to work. At present, work would reduce their income—they might earn less than they lose on welfare payments. The incentive can be provided by reducing welfare payments much less than the income earned, so as to leave a considerable net increase of income, if the mother works.

L: But how can the mother leave her children? To hire someone to take care of them would cost as much as she can earn.

C: Once the youngest child has reached the age of three, even before, babysitters may set mothers free for part of the day. Some mothers could be provided with a little instruction—very little is needed—and with rented space. They could be hired then, to take care of the children of other mothers who thus would be freed to work. This may be combined with some elementary instruction of the children.

[1] I should also favor an economic incentive for families to stay together—the opposite of what is now done. But this cannot be elaborated here.

L: This seems simple and feasible. Why isn't it done?

C: I'm tempted to say *because* it is simple and feasible. In effect, our welfare bureaucracy likes the old ways. And things like "Headstart," useless as far as the evidence goes, but more pretentious and costly, are therefore preferred.

L: What can you do about that?

C: A lot. One could require that employable mothers accept jobs and classify them as employable unless there are special circumstances which prevent them from working. However, given incentives, encouragement and opportunities, most women in that situation would prefer to work—if their children are taken care of, and if their net income is increased thereby. Certainly a program to hire welfare mothers to take care of the children of others who are out working or to baby-sit, would easily pay for itself (if it is done informally, locally and without bureaucratic frills). . . .

L: Certainly this would be better than the present system. Yet I feel it does not go to the root of the matter. Why do these people earn so little? Why are so many of them unemployed?

C: I do not believe that there is an over-all cause, or solution. Some have low skills; some have big families; some are unproductive; some are not allowed to work where they could (or to acquire skills) by unions and by employers who do their bidding.

L: Why could we not have a system that makes sure that everybody has a minimum decent income? Why do you insist on the piecemeal measures you have outlined, and which—regardless of their merits —do not solve the problem of poverty, of slums, of unemployment, of inferior education?

C: Because there is "*a* problem of

poverty" only in the sense that there are poor people. As soon as you ask: why? you find *many* problems. The symptoms, but not the causes, can be eliminated by spending money. The causes have far more to do with the way the money is spent and with legislation creating poverty.

L: Laws create poverty? Are you serious?

C: Consider unemployment. It also illustrates the singularity of each, and the relationship among the problems of poverty. Unemployed people can't find jobs—or refuse to take those available (legally they are obliged to take them; but not in practice).

L: You don't mean that the 30 per cent of Negro adolescents at present unemployed—a rate more than double that of whites—simply don't want to work?

C: They do. But not at the jobs available to them—or at the pay available. Yet these are the only jobs for which they have sufficient skills.

L: Well, shouldn't we do something about these skills then?

C: Many are not capable, others are not willing to acquire skills. This attitude will persist as long as they are made to feel that they have a "right" to better jobs than they have the skill for.

L: But don't you think they are kept out of better jobs by racial discrimination?

C: Certainly some capable people are discriminated against—though not necessarily for racial reasons. And discriminatory practices doubtless played a role in placing American Negroes into their present situation —and in making them the people they are. Our problem is what to do with the presently unemployed adolescents. I think they would gain if they were employed according to their present capacities.

This, more than anything, will help them, and make them want to acquire skills.

L: What would you do to employ them?

C: I would not make the government "the employer of last resort." Nobody acquires decent work habits by working for the government.

There are private jobs that are not being filled. And many refuse to do unskilled work for the pay offered—which cannot be raised because they do not produce enough to permit higher pay. Have you ever looked for a handyman? Or a Skycap at the airport? The work does not demand much skill. Nor does cleaning, or working as a bellboy, or busboy, or elevator man, or parking lot attendant, or delivery boy; yet applicants are scarce—despite unemployment.

L: So what would you do?

C: Again, I would—along the lines of the negative income tax—subsidize such persons—*on condition that they accept jobs at market pay*. If they show aptitude and inclination, it would help them to acquire skills at the same time.

L: It has been proposed that employers be subsidized to pay these unskilled and "undermotivated" (i.e. unreliable) employees "normal" wages.

C: That seems a complicated and unsatisfactory thing. They should get the wages the marketplace is willing to pay. If that keeps them poor, *they*, not the *employer*, should be subsidized—on condition that they accept the available jobs. At the same time, we ought to make available every opportunity to improve or acquire skills. But this will work only as people acquire work habits and get interested in better jobs. . . .

L: Can I get you to summarize the proposals emerging from our meandering conversation? . . .

C: OK. My proposals are:

(1) to make it easier for people a) to have fewer children (make contraceptives available), b) not to desert them (give subsidies not to dependent children but to families), c) to encourage and enable mothers to work (by incentive subsidies and arrangements for their children);

(2) to give old or incapacitated people a block subsidy upon their declaration of (insufficient) income, and reduce the subsidy in proportion to their income from other sources, in such a way that they retain an incentive to earn that income;

(3) to give a block subsidy in similar ways to employed people who earn too little;

(4) to give such a subsidy to idle but employable people who would earn too little on condition that they accept jobs at market wages;

(5) to introduce legislation to exempt categories of workers from contractual or legal minimum pay.

I would modify the "negative income tax" by adding to the income declaration the condition that employment at market wages must be sought and accepted by people not employed or incapacitated.

(6) I would eliminate most of the present multitude of poverty programs and change the emphasis from helping the poor to become a pressure group that extorts money from those who work, to helping them to work themselves.

My proposals will not solve all problems. But they will improve the situation for all concerned—the poor, the welfare clients, the unemployed, the taxpayers and the children.

AIDING THE POOR

Lee Berton

Mrs. Louise Barrett, a 42-year-old Negro mother of three, recently discovered that the poor *do* pay more. She learned the hard way.

A "pushy" door-to-door salesman quoted her a "reduced" price of $60 on a Bible and dictionary he said usually went for a total of $80 she relates. But when her bill arrived, it read $77.23—for books she could have bought elsewhere for a total of no more than $45, according to their publisher. She couldn't meet the "small monthly payment," and her modest salary as a supermarket clerk was garnisheed.

She bought an off-brand TV set from another door-to-door operative, only to have it break down quickly. Fees and interest on her monthly installment contract for the set added up to a rate exceeding 20% a year, well above normal. Also, she had trouble with her back and went to a chiropractor who gave her dozens of treatments. Her back still hurts and she owes the chiropractor $395. He is under Federal indictment for fraud.

Mrs. Barrett, the sole support of her family, admits she has been gullible—though no more so than those Negro and Puerto Rican families in an Upstate New York city who paid $500 each for a set of ordinary cookware because the salesmen said its use would prevent cancer. She confesses she knows little about budget-keeping, installment interest rates and the like. She concedes she has spent too much on luxuries in her eagerness to give her family the things middle-class families have, a yearning sociologists say is common in the ghetto. Still, she wistfully wonders why "every crook picks on the poor."

Of course, unethical salesmen don't confine their activities to poor neighborhoods. Many a comfortable suburb has proved fertile ground for the slick seller of "special deals" on aluminum siding or magazine subscriptions.

Nevertheless, consumer rackets flourish most profusely in the slums, according to anti-fraud experts. Until recently, however, comparatively little was being done about it. Now, however, there are clear signs that Federal, state and local authorities will be cracking down harder on price discrimination, exorbitant credit rates, sales fraud and other shoddy commercial practices that plague the poor. And ghetto residents themselves are banding together to fight their own battles against those who victimize them.

One of the principal targets is price discrimination. A special House inquiry into consumer-government relations has heard considerable testimony indicating that many items cost more in the ghetto than elsewhere. A consumer group from the Bedford-Stuyvesant section of Brooklyn, for example, said it paid 6.6% more for 20 grocery items at a chain store in the ghetto than it did for the same items at another outlet of the same chain in a middle-class neighborhood. The price difference climbed to 8.5% the day after welfare checks were distributed, the group reported.

A St. Louis consumer group did some comparison shopping at Kroger Co. supermarkets. It told the House group it found a price differential of 13.6% between a ghetto store and one in a higher-income neighborhood. Walter W. White, manager of Kroger's St. Louis division, denies the chain has deliberately pegged prices higher in the ghetto but adds: "The speed and frequency and volume of price changes create conditions under which inadvertent errors can occur. Certainly we can improve."

. . . Some chain store operators on occasion have conceded that some prices were higher in ghetto stores. In defense, however, they assert that stores in such neighborhoods are plagued by excessive pilferage, high insurance premiums and other abnormal costs that tend to push prices up.

Wherever the truth lies in the pricing argument, ghetto dwellers are acting on their own to get lower prices. Last September six neighborhood clubs in Washington, D.C., formed a consumers' association that has been getting food direct from wholesalers and marketing it to between 100 and 150 families. Mrs. Janie Boyd, association chairman, claims her own food bill has plummeted 50%. She says the association hopes to expand the program to include up to 1,000 families, most of them poor.

In St. Louis, a Catholic church in a Negro area has been busing 25 to 30 neighborhood residents to an open-air market four miles away in a white, middle-class area. "The savings on vegetables alone range from 10% to 15%," says Father Robert A. Marshall, associate pastor of the church, St. Bridget's of Erin.

In Harlem, a new cooperative is being formed to operate a supermarket scheduled to open in April; the project is being financed through the sale of $5 shares and $50 debentures which pay 6% and through loans. Cora T. Walker, attorney for the group, the Harlem River Consumers Cooperative Inc., says initial prices at the store will run 5% to 10% lower than those at most other Harlem food stores; co-op members (those who have purchased an interest) will get an annual rebate from any profits, she adds.

Fraud and deceptive lending practices also are under heavier attack now from every government level and from the poor themselves. The poor are particularly affected by shady dealings, according to sociologists and others. For one thing, the poor's lack of sophistication as consumers (many can't comprehend the terms of a sales contract—a handicap shared by some of the more affluent and better educated), coupled with their intense yearning for the material things most other people enjoy, makes them easy marks for glib salesmen. Also, since they lack ready cash to buy items outright, they are heavy users of installment credit.

Often they don't realize how much extra they may be paying in the form of interest, insurance and other added-on fees. Champions of "truth-in-lending" legislation claim that if they have their way, much of this uncertainty would be removed.

Presently, many installment sellers don't disclose the cost of insurance and other extras to the buyer. They also quote interest rates that don't really tell the buyer exactly how much a year he will have to pay in interest. The 1.5% monthly "revolving credit" offered by some stores doesn't sound like much, for example, but it adds up to an annual interest rate of 18%, more if compounded. Basically, truth-in-lending legislation would force many retailers and other credit sellers to cite the annual cost and to tell prospective borrowers how much would be added to their payments by insurance and other fees. Many retailers have argued that conforming with the requirements of truth-in-lending would be an immensely complex and costly task for them. . . .

Regent Discount regrets Mrs. Barrett's plight but sees little remedy for it. "This state of affairs has existed in Harlem for years, and unless these people (the customers) become more educated as consumers, there's nothing we can do about it," says Irving Fineman, secretary.

Many Federal officials are convinced that giving the low-income consumer more purchasing savvy is necessary, too. An aide to Betty Furness, the President's special assistant for consumer affairs, says her office may add an education director who would be responsible for combating the problem. One possible approach: to raise a warier breed of ghetto consumers of the future by blending buying know-how into school curricula. English students might evaluate ad claims as part of their work, and math students might be taught how to figure credit charges.

Other tactics are being devised by the ghetto groups seeking to aid poor consumers. The recently formed Harlem Consumer Education Council, for example, says it already has helped 10 ghetto residents hopelessly burdened with debt go into bankruptcy, thus eliminating their debts, and indicates it hopes to steer at least three or four people a week in the same direction from now on. The Legal Aid Society is assisting the council. Mrs. Barrett, who has been in contact with the council, has been advised to seek bankruptcy.

The NAACP Legal Defense and Educational Fund Inc. has just filed suit against L.B. Spears Furniture Co., a Harlem store, accusing it of overcharging and fraud in the sale of a food freezer to a Negro mail clerk for $1,087. The price included $247.93 in service and insurance charges, says a fund attorney, who puts the maximum value of the freezer at $450. "It was sold to the plaintiff by a door-to-door salesman who used the ruse of bringing lollipops to the buyer's daughter to get him to sign an unconscionable contract," the attorney says.

Godfrey Daum, president of L. B. Spears, says the freezer was sold by someone from a leased department within the store and denies any wrongdoing on his company's part. "We're strictly a one-price house, and these people must prove they've overpaid," he declares. "We will contest the suit." The plaintiff is asking $10,000 in punitive damages. The fund says it plans to file "dozens" more such suits "to protect minority and poor people from unscrupulous selling practices."

QUIETUS

Charlie Russell

No two ways about it. Randolph, Besso Oil's first Negro salesman, knew better. Now, he can offer himself no excuse, really. You simply don't go around acting on impulses, even good ones, not if you want to keep your job. Twenty-seven. He is tall, dark and thin: gray Brooks Brothers; with a thick moustache of which he is excessively proud. Randolph sits down and slaps a fist into his open palm: I blew, baby, I blew! If I don't ever blow another one, I blew that one. Though a college man, he still thinks in the language of the streets. In a less turbulent time he would tell you he is bilingual.

"I blew, I blew!" Though released unconsciously, the expression feels good as it leaves the rim of his mouth. But, this only paves the way for an added agitation: Has Evelyn heard? He fingers his heavy moustache, turns, and brings into focus Evelyn Manning. Boss receptionist. Headquarters, Eastern Division. Her head is bent. Engrossed in typing, apparently she has not heard. Yet he stares. Thin face. Natural blond hair. While he is looking at her the hair on the left side of her face unfurls itself mischievously. In one motion there is a toss of her head and a flick of her hand, as she artfully pushes the renegade hair back into place.

Class. Randolph decides that Evelyn has almost as much class as his wife. He likes that, women with class. And he likes being the company's first and only Negro salesman, too. He has just finished a four months' training course, in which he finished first in a class of twenty, and until a few minutes ago he looked forward to a long and profitable career with Besso Oil.

"Damn," he curses himself. What had he been thinking about? He has an urge to break something. Like that night when he was fifteen, and had broken all the windows in the front of the school with rocks. Afterwards he had spent an hour ducking and dodging around corners, setting up a false trail, just in case he was hunted. But no one had followed and later in bed he was overcome with a tingling sensation that had given him a feeling of inner peace, engulfing him entirely. He had had that feeling only a few times since: once or twice hearing Charlie Parker, and when he had first entered his virginal wife, Stacey.

For one moment he almost loses control by giving way to the anger, as it swells then sweeps swiftly through his body.

"Be cool. Nerves! Be cool." Prayer-like, he repeats the phrase several times and soon he is calm. Randolph lights a cigarette, then quickly loses interest in it. Would you believe it, just ten minutes ago my world was neat as a six-pack, and now it is all gone because of some jive nigger I don't even know.

"Tch," Randolph's tongue feels heavy as it makes the sound against the roof of his mouth. Suddenly he stands and walks towards the far wall where there are pictures hanging. The room is elongated. Black wall-to-wall carpeting. The furniture, done in dull orange leather, has a contemporary motif. Heavy copper ashtrays shaped like boomerangs. The pictures are abstract originals, too. He stares.

He and Teddy discovered Charlie Parker at a party one Friday night. Hip sixteen. The party was in a dimly lit basement and they were drinking wine from paper cups, when somebody put on "Birds of Paradise." Their heads were light from the tokay, and Teddy demanded that the record be played again and again. The music was so good that even he had danced. Finally Teddy had stolen the record, and they spent the rest of the summer listening to "the Bird" weaving in and out of notes.

Stacey. Randolph has a sudden desire to talk to his wife. He walks over towards Evelyn's desk. Evelyn, the receptionist for both J. B. Nash and Larry Weeks, looks up as he approaches. "Say, look!" he hesitates. "I'm going down the hall to my office to make a phone call. If Larry should call for me, tell him I've gone to make a phone call. Tell him I'm just down the hall in my office, and I'll be right back." Now that he is finished he feels drained.

"OK," Evelyn says, returning to her typing.

Her simple dismissal adds to his anxiety. Why is she so busy all of a sudden? Most of the time, every time I look up there she is in my face. Had he missed a signal between her and Larry, and was she typing up his final papers? He almost asks her, but then decides his name is Sam, and he doesn't give a damn. He turns and walks towards the door. Where however:

It is not "Sam" but Randolph Williams V he sees reflected in the glass door. Old Randy of the drooping shoulders, scared witless, going to call his wife to tell her she must return to work because he has just made his last stand.

Randolph stands over his desk, dials his number; and wonders what Stacey will say. Beautiful Stacey who is so proper and knows what fork to use when; who comes, whispering hot obscenities into his ear. It seems only natural that he dials the wrong number. He dials again. Five. Six. Seven. He throws the phone on the cradle, and thinks: She is either out shopping, or playing bridge, or at the beauty parlor; but wherever she is, she is doing what she does best—spending my money. He has a second thought: Maybe it is best after all, give the girl a few hours before she gets the news.

Randolph returns to the waiting room. Evelyn looks up from the typewriter, thin lips stretched into a smile, and before he can ask, she glances furtively at Larry's door, then at him and shakes her head, "No."

Randolph answers by making a silent, "Oh," with his mouth. He turns away. It seems forever he's been waiting. There is movement behind him, but even knowing it is Evelyn he jumps, anyway.

He turns. Watches her approach. Evelyn is tall, willowy and promiscuous. Head tilted slightly upwards. Simply attired: black one-piece dress. Just a dab of rouge. Nothing flashy. She is willing to try anything, but she will remain all her life below pain or joy.

Sweetly: "How is it going, Randy?"

It takes some effort, but he shrugs his shoulders. Smiles. "Fine, just fine." Such control gives him joy. He asks, "Why so busy?" indicating the typewriter.

"Oh, that," Evelyn answers matter-of-factly, "my monthly letter to the folks."

Randolph sighs deeply; he should have known. He looks into her eyes and finds in them something mysterious and hard. How could you explain a girl like her? Comes from big money, went to Wellesley, but works as a receptionist? In a real way he feels sorry for her; if he had money, he would do all his work on the French Riviera!

"You were simply wonderful in there," she says, holding his arm. A week ago she had asked him if he was weird and exotic. He had laughed and said no. She has a thing for him, he knows, but since taking this job he has been faithful and has decided that playing the role of the noble savage, or the big black buck for empty white women is no longer an adventure.

He pulls away. Gently. The smile does not leave Evelyn's lips. She is game. Discovering this about her makes him love her a second. However, when Evelyn says, "But I hadn't realized you cared so deeply about things," Randolph regrets even that second.

"Well, sometimes you have to make a stand," he explains. Softly. "You can only let them push you so far." He sees her smile broaden.

"What would you have done?" Randolph asks.

Evelyn turns from his gaze. "Frankly, I would have taken it. What does it matter, really? They can always find someone to do their dirt; but I am rather proud that you didn't." There are tears. Evelyn turns her head quickly and returns to her desk.

Randolph, resuming his pacing, returns to the picture and remembers. It had all begun two months ago and had happened because every Wednesday night he ate 'soul' food at the Red Rooster, a bar/restaurant in Harlem. Larry, after taking him on a tour of the company's service stations in Harlem, had offered to drop him off at the Rooster. Passing through his old neighborhood, he had noticed an independent station run by an elderly

Negro, and observed to Larry that this man had no competitors. And did a large volume of business. "Why don't we open a station across the street?" he had suggested playfully.

This afternoon they had suddenly sprung it on him. Anyway you looked at it, it had been a tough lay and a jive scene. It had taken J. B. just twenty minutes to turn years' worth of hustling into cinders.

At lunch, Larry had casually mentioned to him that J. B., the first vice-president, wanted to see him. Routine business. Just to congratulate him for completing his training course. But Randolph had not finished top man by sleeping. From the nuance in Larry's voice he could tell there was more to it than that.

"Well, here he is," bright-eyed Larry, everybody's fat man, had bellowed. Larry, the fourth vice-president, a handshaker and a backslapper, always won at poker. He presented Randolph to J. B. as if he was a prize.

J. B., a short, slight, graying man, had shaken his hand firmly. Randolph decided that the mantle of inherited power rested easily upon J. B.'s shoulders. J. B. made a slight motion, and they had sat down.

"Well, how are things?" J. B. had begun.

Small talk.

God, these guys are cool. Power with a capital P. Sometimes he hardly remembered that they were the rulers of the world. But he knew their game. "Wonderful, sir. I envision unlimited opportunities with Besso." J. B. supposed that now that he was part of the team he and his wife would be thinking about raising a family soon. "Oh, yes sir, we were just talking about that very subject last week. Children are so wonderful." Oh, yes, he had been hip to their game.

Then, just like that it was over and J. B. had buzzed Evelyn, inviting her in for a drink.

More small talk.

And while Randolph was plotting a graceful exit, J. B. had said confidentially, "Larry here tells me you have suggested a location for a new station. Good idea. I see why Larry speaks so highly of you. How would you like to be the manager?" Before J. B. finished, the others had stopped talking.

Larry had a conspiratorial expression.

"Ah . . . , sir . . . ," Randolph had faltered, as J. B. continued.

"Twelve pumps, twenty by thirty garage. The whole works. Leave it open twenty-four hours a day. But I'm sure you and Larry can work out the details."

By this time Randolph's wits had returned: So that was their game. He was not only to be their Negro on display, they also meant to use him to put other Negroes out of business. Why, with him running the place, and by staying open twenty-four hours a day, the poor guy across the street wouldn't last two months. The mive mothers!

"But, why me, what about all my training?" he had asked calmly.

"Be good for you, really. Learn the business inside and out." J. B. had turned to Larry. "How long you think it'll take to set it up?"

Without giving Larry time to answer, without realizing that he was going to do it, Randolph had said:

"If I have a choice, I'd just as soon not." Though he had not meant it, his voice sounded stringent. Evelyn lifted an eyebrow, smiled; Larry, shocked, trembled; only J. B. had remained unperturbed.

"Ah, yes," J. B. seemed tired. "You take that up with Larry."

Randolph, who had not meant to venture so far, was relieved to feel Larry tugging at his sleeve.

"I think you've taken our young friend here by surprise, J. B. Let me talk to him. Ha, ha," Larry had interrupted nervously. "Ha, you didn't mention the extra thousand dollars in it for him."

"Yes, yes," J. B.'s voice sounded distant. Randolph had suddenly realized that the old man was almost asleep on his feet. He had heeded the tug and followed Larry out of the office. When they entered the waiting room, Larry had said curtly: "I'll talk to you in a minute," and had slammed his door, leaving Randolph standing alone in the waiting room. Terror had momentarily set in Randolph's eyes, leaving him with a sense of dread.

Randolph, still deep in thought turns from the picture, walks to the window and looks down into the streets below: mid-February. Cold. Dark, dull, dank. Too cold even for love.

Randolph stands stroking his moustache thoughtfully. There is in his eyes a trace of sadness. He feels alone. No more Teddy. No more "Bird." Nothing. Teddy, over ten years ago, died in Korea in a riot with "cracker" soldiers. And in the circle in which he now travels, Charlie Parker was never in style. Once he and Stacey had some friends over, and he had put on a "Bird" record. For some reason it had been no good, and he finally made everyone happy by putting on Dave Brubeck.

"Stacey!" Unconsciously. He wants to talk to her in the worst sort of way. Why not try the number again? No. Wait. He decides to think further about his situation:

So. They want to use me to keep other Negroes down, you hip to that? Do they think I'm some kinda nut? I can get another job. I don't have to stand for this mess. Ha, ha, his laughter is profane and deep. Randolph knows the game. Why, he can even predict the line Larry will take with him:

Larry will talk to me like we're all green, as if they are not using me against another colored man. White people are good at that, boy can they talk. Always trying to hide the real issues behind some abstract or unrelated principle. And when old Larry starts talking about free enterprise, I'll tell him to shove it!

Randolph again feels the urge to smash something. To run amuck. His heart cries out that it is so unfair. You spend most of your life just fighting to get on their side. You give up Charlie Parker for them, you even cut down on chasing women and all for what? Only to be used. What right did they have to decide things among themselves and then tell him he must make a choice? Some choice! Either him, or another black man.

The yen for his wife's voice returns and Randolph finds himself standing in front of Evelyn's desk. "Look, I'm going to . . . ," he begins, but the buzz of the intercom interrupts him. Evelyn, her smile erased, speaks:

"Yes, Larry." Pause. Then, tiredly: "Yes, he's standing right here, I'll send him right in." She hangs up the phone, and Randolph has no time to protest that he must call his wife. In a way he is relieved.

"Randy . . . ," Evelyn begins earnestly, "you were sweet in there before. But don't do or say anything you'll be sorry for afterwards."

Gee thanks. Her attitude bugs him. Next she'd be telling him she knew just how he felt. . . . She. They had some nerve. Telling him how to fight his battle. A battle that they themselves had once been involved in, but had never completed. But out loud, Randolph says, not unkindly, "Thanks, Evelyn, I really want to thank you for that little bit of advice."

She is a sweet kid, really, and he does not resent her always. And because he feels guilty, he asks: "How do elephants make love in tall grass?" She does not know. "Successfully," he calls over his shoulder and knocks on Larry's door.

Randolph enters, and silently closes the door behind him. Larry is busy with papers. Randolph approaches his desk. Larry, he notices, is wearing his "con-artist" expression. It is a mixture of smugness and cunning; which he tries to hide behind an inoffensive smile. Randolph hesitates, then sits down. He feels giddy and tries several matches before finally lighting his cigarette.

If only I'd had time to call Stacey.

"Randy, baby, relax, relax," Larry urges in a jovial manner. "I know how you're feeling, Randy. You're probably thinking it's all some kind of conspiracy between me and J. B. But let me assure you, I was just as surprised at J. B. as you were." Larry pauses as if weighing his words, and Randolph notices a certain detachment about his manner as he adds, "I guess old J. B. caught you by surprise, eh, fellow?"

I got your "eh, fellow" hanging, baby. Randolph checks this impulsive response; he had had enough of that today. Out loud he says: "Yes, he did sort of catch me off guard. I know what J. B. said, but still the idea of putting an old man out of business. . . ."

"Come on, Randy," Larry urges. "You're a bright fellow. You know what way the wind is blowing. Everything is big now, from the government on up. Somebody has to do it. If we didn't, Standard would do it," he snaps a finger, "just like that. Free Enterprise! It's the law of supply and demand, fellow, the law that our system is based on," Larry finishes, obviously pleased with himself.

Now, he knows, is the time to tell Larry to go to hell. That the real issue is his being used. That he does not mind being the "quota-Negro," but does mind very much indeed being used against other Negroes. However, Randolph finds himself unable to speak. Stacey, Stacey! Suddenly he realizes that he has known all along what Stacey would say; just as he knows that he will follow the voice that even now cries out inside him:

They got you in a cross, baby. And they can beat you in so many ways. From your first breath the odds are against you. And they get to you early, they start you out with Mickey Mouse, and you are hooked by the time you are three. Yea, baby, everybody's got a number, and you have to play the game whether you want to or not. When you think about it you don't really have a choice. You just got to go for yourself.

Randolph stirs uncomfortably in his chair.

"Randy, baby, why the long face?" Larry asks, lightly, yet firmly, "I know that this is all sort of sudden. You want some time to think it over? Maybe J. B. wouldn't mind. He probably likes a man who takes his time. You wanna talk it over with your wife?"

"No, no, that's all right," Randolph raises his head with a jerk. "Ha, my wife goes along with anything I say. Yeah. It just doesn't seem right, that's all." He sounds unreasonable he knows.

But Larry cries out in genuine surprise, "Why, Randy, you old slickster, you amaze me, really. Holding out for more money. Amazing. All right, you got yourself a deal. I'll tell J. B. to make it fifteen hundred. Randy, fellow, I can see you are going far with Besso, you're gonna make a lot of money."

"Yes, I'll make a lot of money," Randolph agrees, not caring whether Larry has deliberately misunderstood him or not. But even as he agrees with Larry, even as he thinks of the two cars and the split-level, he feels something in him die: that part of him that had always been free. He feels the loss already. It was vital. As long as he had it, he felt somehow better and different from them.

"So, what you say, kid?" There is a certain urgency in Larry's voice.

"Yea, sure. OK, Larry, we'll get started on it right away," Randolph says and Larry relaxes, transformed before his eyes.

Then Larry is on his feet, congratulating him warmly, and proudly. Patting his shoulders and repeating that he will go far and make tons of money. He knows this. Yet, he feels unclean, and there is a grimy taste in his mouth.

After several minutes the ritual of the backslapping and handshaking is done. Then Randolph's hand is on the doorknob. He can hardly believe it is over. But as his hand turns the shining knob he hears Larry call, in a friendly manner:

"There is one thing, though, that J. B. did notice, Randy, fellow, you're the only one in the outfit who has a moustache."

ABOLISH POVERTY DIRECTLY

Martin Luther King, Jr.

I am now convinced that the simplest approach to solving the problem of poverty will prove to be the most effective. The solution is to abolish it directly by the guaranteed income.

Two conditions are indispensable if we are to insure that the guaranteed income operates as a consistently progressive measure. First, it must be pegged to the median income of society, not at the lowest levels of income. To guarantee an income at the floor would simply perpetuate welfare standards and freeze into the society poverty conditions.

Second, it must automatically increase as the total social income grows. Were it permitted to remain static under growth conditions, the recipients would suffer a relative decline. Without these safeguards a creeping retrogression would occur nullifying the gains of security and stability.

This is not a "civil rights" program in the sense that that term is currently used. The program would benefit all the poor, including the two-thirds of them who are white. I hope that both Negro and white will act in coalition to effect this change, because their combined strength will be necessary to overcome the fierce opposition we must realistically anticipate.

Our nation's adjustment to a new mode of thinking will be facilitated if we realize that for nearly 40 years two groups in our society have already been enjoying a guaranteed income: the wealthy who own securities have always had an assured income; and their polar opposite, the relief clients, have been guaranteed an income, however minuscule, through welfare benefits.

The curse of poverty has no justification in our age. It is socially as cruel and blind as the practice of cannibalism at the dawn of civilization, when men ate each other because they had not yet learned to take food from the soil or to consume the abundant animal life around them. The time has come for us to civilize ourselves by the total, direct and immediate abolition of poverty.

WHY WE'RE AGAINST THE BIGGEES

James S. Kunen

I have surveyed the opinions of the well-intentioned American middle class regarding Columbia. That is, I have spoken to my mother about it. She's been reading the *New Republic*, and is currently fond of saying that the Columbia rebellion was set up in advance by people who are not students at Columbia, and who do not have its interests at heart. This is entirely true.

The Columbia rebellion was set in motion by a nebulous group of outsiders who are variously known as the corporate power elite, the military-industrial complex, the Establishment. A friend of mine refers to them as the Biggees.

The Biggees are a small group of men. Little else about them is known. They are probably old. They possess wealth surpassing the bounds of imagination. They have no real needs or desires, but cultivate avarice as a sort of obsessive hobby. They sit in smoke-filled rooms, so it may be presumed that they smoke cigars. In the councils of the Biggees, one might hear decisions that one thought no one could make. Buy Uruguay. Sell Bolivia. Hold India. Pollute New York. The decisions are of incomprehensible variety, but they have in common the fact that they are swiftly implemented and invariably soak the Little Man.

Sometimes the Biggees slug it out with each other, as in the gold market, where they get down to the nitty-gritty of buying and selling *money* (a commerce that no one else can understand, let alone participate in), but more often they are after *our* coin.

The Biggees lie. They shout up and down that Vitalis has V_7, but they don't say what V_7 *is*. They say that Arrid stops wetness, but they don't explain why wetness should be stopped. (I can think of a lot of things that qualify for stoppage way ahead of wetness.) They lie about little things like that, and big things like Vietnam, the ghetto, Democracy. It's all the same—truth in lending, truth in labeling, truth in government; none of them exist.

The Biggees *control*. I read a six-grader's history paper about the Spanish-American War. The young boy, having put away his Mattel M-16 automatic rifle for the evening to do his homework, wrote that the 1898 war was fought by America to set the poor Cubans free from tyranny. He added that America traditionally fights on the side of right for justice and freedom and therefore always wins, "like in Vietnam today." The Biggees have that kid right where they want him. They've got his mind; when he's eighteen, they'll take his body.

Look around you. The Biggees are everywhere. Look in your driveway. They build cars that dissociate in three years, and they make everybody buy them, and they're in on the gas biz too, so you can forget about mileage. And no one can make them change. You get organized and ask them to please just put all bumpers at a standard level so maybe a little less than 50,000 of us will die on the roads next year, but no, they can't do it. They can't do it because it will *cost* to do it, and anyway, if all bumpers were at the same height, then there wouldn't be any choice, and that's what democracy's all about. If you didn't know that that's what democracy's all about, there are frequent ads to remind you. It seems, for instance, that in socialist countries there are only three colors of lipstick, whereas capitalism provides forty.

And with these forty shades of lipstick the Biggees turn our women into nauga-babes (vinyl girls) who in pre-fab sexiness sit tracing cheap pictures in the air with cigarettes they never made up their minds to start smoking. And, arguing about what to-do to do next, one of these naugas might be heard to say, "It's a free country."

But it isn't a free country. You can't drop out of school because you'd be drafted, and you have to study certain things to get a degree, and you have to have a degree to make it, and you have to make it to get what you want, and you can't even decide what you want, because it's all programmed into you beforehand. You can *say* whatever you want, but you won't be heard because the media control that, but if you do manage to be heard, the People won't like it, because the people have been told what to like. And if they don't like you, they might even kill you, because the government endorses killing by exemplification.

All of which brings us to Columbia, because at Columbia we're all together and we teach each other and feel strong. The Biggees are killing people in Vietnam and keeping the blacks down at home, because they have to keep some people at the bottom for their system to work, or so they thought. Now they're finding out that the downs can really screw them up bad, so they'd like to raise them just a bit, but that would certainly cost, so for the moment they'll try to keep them down by promising them rewards if they behave.

So here we all are at Columbia not comprehending this great money motivation because we didn't grow up in a depression and have always had coin and therefore don't value it as highly as we might. We're right at Harlem, so we see how it is. And we've got the draft right on us, so we know how that is. And we don't like it. We don't like it at all, because we've got a lot of life ahead of us and we're for it. Killing and dying just don't make it with us.

And lo and behold, right here at Columbia where all we young angries are seething, who should be president but Grayson Kirk, a Biggee if ever there was one. Consolidated Edison, IBM, Socony Mobil, Asia Foundation, IDA—he's got an iron in every fire that's consuming us. And it turns out that Military Intelligence has offices at the university, and Electronic Research Laboratories is raking in about $5 million per annum on radar, and we're in the Institute for Defense Analysis in a big way, and the School of International Affairs is hitting it off really well with the CIA. All the while the university is systematically desiccating the integrated community of Morningside Heights, and has its eyes on land all the way over to Seventh Avenue, so that some fine day there'll be a nice white suburban buffer zone in the middle of Manhattan, which people will know, by the inevitable iron gates around it, to be Columbia.

Seeing all this, we decided to change it. Of course, if you don't like it you can leave, but if you leave you're going to run into something else you don't like, and you can't go on leaving forever because you'll run out of places to go. So we decided to change it. We petitioned, we demonstrated, we wrote letters, and we got nowhere. We weren't refused; we were ignored. So one day we went into the buildings, and one day somewhat later we were pulled out and arrested, and many people were beaten. In the intervening days we were widely accused of having ourselves a good time in the buildings. We did have a good time. We had a good time because for six days we regulated our own lives and were free.

But Dr. Kirk and his associates saw that we were free and they knew of course that that sort of thing must not be permitted. They knew also that they could not deal with our demands, because that would mean a breakdown of their law and a violation of their order. So they called in the police. And they expressed regret that the police injured 150 people, and they really did regret it, because the brutal bust showed everybody how far the powerful will go to retain their power, how far they will go rather than answer a single question, rather than admit that questions can be asked.

As I write this, and as you read it, people are dying. So you see it isn't really a topic for suburban conversation or magazine articles. It's something that must be dealt with. That's what's happening at Columbia, not a revolution but a counterattack. We are fighting to recapture a school from business and war and rededicate it to learning and life. Right now nobody controls Columbia, but if we get it, we will never give it back. And there are 5 million college students in the country watching us. And a lot of them have just about had it with the Biggees.

6

POLITICS
AND
POWER STRUGGLES

According to the traditional concept of American democracy, politicians are responsible for dealing with the problems of environment, housing, race, and finance exposed in the four preceding sections. Because of its tone of determination to build the future rather than sink beneath the problems of the past and present, the Inaugural Address of Richard Hatcher, Mayor of Gary, Indiana, opens this section. It also reflects that some men are still willing to try to save the cities by working within the traditional political framework. But in "The Flight from City Hall . . . One Mayor Who Isn't Running Again," Fred Powledge interviews retiring mayor Naftalin of Minneapolis, (one among many) whose anger and pessimism contrast sharply with Hatcher's optimism. Naftalin says a mayor's job is doomed to failure without the help of the President and Congress. Since 1969 the Republican Administration in Washington has had more important priorities than saving the cities.

In the essay "Journey to Atlanta," James Baldwin explains the cynicism with which black people regard all politicians, regardless of party. He describes what happened in 1948 when his younger brother was working on the campaign of Henry Wallace, the Progressive Party's candidate for President. Baldwin shows that the exploitation of black voters by the now defunct Progressive Party is the prototype of the behavior of all political parties toward the powerless. As his younger brother says, "They're all the same. . . . Ain't none of 'em gonna do a thing for *me*."

The next three selections show what middle-class workers, student organizers, and Black Panthers are doing about the problems of the urban poor in the face of the paralysis of regular political processes.

"Tactics for the Seventies" is an interview with Chicago-born Saul Alinsky, known today as this country's foremost organizer of community action groups. Here he talks about the role of the white middle-class in the fight for justice.

In "Rent Strike in Newark," Jesse Allen describes the concrete details of one successful community action project. As a worker in a movement which organized the neighborhoods against a "Negro removal" plan of urban renewal, he found out first hand about the indifference of urban landlords, mayors, and judges toward the grievances of the poor.

The "Black Panther Party Platform and Program: What We Want, What We Believe" states the ten goals of an organization created to help the black people of the urban ghettos achieve a human existence. Because its objectives are so comprehensive, it is possible to discuss many controversial issues within the context of this one selection: community control, guaranteed income, capitalism, school reform, Black studies, the draft, police brutality, genocide, amnesty for all prisoners, and judicial reform.

The revolutionary mood in the urban ghettos alarms the official guardians of society, the police. In "Undercover Cops," David Brand reports on the city of Houston's response to the political militancy growing on that city's campuses. Its police department is raising an army of spies to combat an enemy seen as a threat to law and order.

The final selection, "Confronting the Urban Wilderness," a speech by Robert F. Kennedy, reiterates the plea of Richard Hatcher's speech of the beginning of this section. For both men, "the long march through the existing institutions," in the words of the young German activist Rudi Dutschke, is the only way to humanize the quality of urban life and to fulfill the promises in the Constitution.

Mayor Kenneth Gibson of Newark campaigning with Harry Belafonte, right.

INAUGURAL ADDRESS, GARY, INDIANA

Richard Hatcher

My fellow Americans, today we are witnessing a rebirth of Gary's determination to take its rightful place among the great cities of our nation. With a resolute mind we embark upon a four-year journey, to change the face of our city and unite the hearts of our citizens; to tear down slums and build healthy bodies; to destroy crime and create beauty; to expand industry and restrict pollution.

Gary, Indiana, is a warm city—it has welcomed in large numbers into its midst emigrants from southern Europe, black people from the deep South, and those who come from south of the border. In diversity, we have found strength; however, today is a new day. Let it be known that as of this moment, there are some who are no longer welcome in Gary, Indiana. Those who have made a profession of violating our laws are no longer welcome. Those who would stick up our businessmen and rape our women are no longer welcome. Those who would bribe our policemen and other public officials and those public officials who accept bribes are no longer welcome, and those who would sow the seeds of discord and peddle the poison of racism, let it be clearly understood, are no longer welcome in Gary, Indiana.

A special word to my brothers and sisters who because of circumstances beyond your control find yourselves locked into miserable slums, without enough food to eat, inadequate clothing for your children and no hope for tomorrow. It is a primary goal of this administration to make your life better. To give you a decent place to live. To help create job opportunities for you and to assist you in every way in breaking the vicious chain of poverty. To give you your rightful share of the good life.

To our business community, including United States Steel Corporation and other large corporations, I say that Gary has been good to you, but it can be better. We assure you that this administration stands ready to support you in your efforts to rejuvenate our downtown, that it will work closely with you in attempting to attract new industry and enterprise in developing a healthy economic climate. In return, we shall ask you to roll up your sleeves and stand with us as we attempt to rebuild this city. Share with us your technical expertise, and your know-how and your money. Help us save our city. Each of you has a moral commitment to this community, and to your fellow man. And if you think so, now's the time to say so. There is nothing sacred in silence, nothing Christian in cowardice, nothing temperate in timidity.

To organized labor, we make a special plea that in the great tradition of your movement and out of your deep concern for the little man, the average man, you join us in this effort. Join us as we attempt to put into practice the great principle espoused by Samuel Gompers long ago and Joseph Germano more recently . . . "To every man his due."

To those who will be employees of this city, I say that the highest standards of integrity will be expected of you, and anyone who fails to meet that requirement will be summarily discharged. Graft and corruption shall end and efficiency shall begin.

Today we have sworn in a new city council. Represented there are men and women of integrity and great ability. I look forward to working closely with them for I am honored to call them all friend. Their responsibility is clear cut—to give you, the citizens of Gary, four years of the finest most progressive government in this city's history. To engage in constructive criticism and opposition to this administration when conscience so dictates, but never to oppose simply for opposition's sake. Our city is suffering. And unless the right medicine is administered, it may die. We have long since passed the point where either this administration or this council can afford the luxury of playing politics with the lives of our people.

To the press, we ask your understanding, patience, and help—all of our judgments shall not be correct, but they shall be honestly made. You have a responsibility not only to report the news accurately but to interpret it with restraint.

Let me for a moment speak to our young people. Your city needs you. We shall seek ways to capture your spirit, imagination, and creativity in order that they may be true assets in our city's fight to improve itself. Our future depends upon the dedication of our young people today.

And finally, to all of our citizens, whether you live in Glen Park, in midtown, or in Miller, I make a special appeal. We cannot solve our problems, we cannot save our city if we all are divided.

The great promise of our city will not be realized until we treat each other as equals without respect to race or religion. To quote our President, "Until justice is blind to color, until education is unaware of race, until opportunity is unconcerned with the color of men's skins, emancipation will be a proclamation and not a fact. The Negro today asks justice. We do not answer him when we reply by asking patience." We have talked long enough in this city about equality. The time is here to live it. If we really want good government, peace, and unity, now's the time to practice what we preach. Good government comes in assorted colors and nationalities.

Together, we shall walk through our valleys of hope; together we shall climb the steep mountains of opportunity, for we seek a high and beautiful new plateau—a new plateau of economy and efficiency in government, a new plateau of progress in government; a new plateau where every man, Democrat and Republican, rich or poor, Jew and gentile, black and white, shall live in peace and dignity.

And so my fellow Americans, as we go from this place, let us understand clearly our role and our responsibility. This is a God-given opportunity to become builders of the future instead of guardians of a barren past, and we must not waste it. Let us pray for this wisdom and guidance. Let us dare to make a new beginning. Let us shatter the walls of the ghetto for all time. Let us build a new city and a new man to inhabit it. Let each and every one of us have the courage to do what we all know must be done. For we here in Gary, Indiana, have much to say about what will happen in urban America.

Our problems are many. But our determination is great, and we feel as Tennyson must have felt when he said:

Oh yet we trust that somehow good will be the final goal of ill. . . .
That nothing walks with aimless feet
That not one life shall be destroyed
Or cast as rubbish to the void
When God hath made the pile complete.

Behold, we know not anything
I can but trust that good shall fall at last—far off—at last to all
And every winter change to spring.

And every winter change to spring. In Gary, together, we seek to change all winters to spring. We know the way is difficult, but that does not discourage us. One of America's outstanding black poets, a scholar and wise man, Professor Arna Bontemps, once wrote the following:

We are not come to make a strife
With words upon this hill;
It is not wise to waste the life
Against a subborn will
Yet we would die as some have done,
Beating a way for the rising sun.

Gary is a rising sun. Together, we shall beat a way; together we shall turn darkness into light, despair into hope and promise into progress. For God's sake, for Gary's sake—let's get ourselves together.

THE FLIGHT FROM CITY HALL:
ONE MAYOR WHO ISN'T RUNNING AGAIN

Fred Powledge

It used to be in this country that a mayor was a kind of genial town fool. He presided at some committee meetings: the city councilmen were invariably out to get him, and usually succeeded without too much difficulty. He managed a hardware store or a movie house. He was competent enough to cut ribbons withouts hurting himself and pleasant enough to welcome foreign visitors without insulting them, but he was about as imaginative as the tax collector. He was relatively harmless. Occasionally he would come out with a statement about fluoridation or higher pay for firemen, and the citizens would read about it and wonder what he was up to now. Or, in the larger cities, he would manifest himself just before reelection by doing a little paving, planting, and dedicating. There were notable exceptions, of course—the La Guardias, the Humphreys, the Mavericks—but this was the general rule. Mayors of both large and small cities would spend a good part of their time begging before the state legislators, who were their intellectual inferiors but owned the checkbook. It was a humdrum existence, and a thankless one, but not too great a strain on a man.

Then something happened. It started about the time John Kennedy gave his inaugural. The cities became more important. Someone discovered that the votes were in the cities. In the early 1960s, a number of mayors of the new style took office. Most of them were liberal Democrats; many of them had no previous experience in elective politics. Some bypassed the machinery and the machines that had dominated city politics before, and they got elected anyway, and then reelected. . . .

It is unlikely that many of the new-style mayors are quitting because of money. They cite various reasons for retiring, from bad health to assertions that they have accomplished what they set out to accomplish. Privately, some of them say that they suspect some of the *others* are quitting because their polls show they couldn't win again; they all say their own polls show them capable of winning handily.

The more fundamental reasons probably have something to do with the end of an era. The new-style mayors started out, many of them, in a time dominated by John Kennedy, by his concern with the cities and the people who lived in them. And then came Lyndon Johnson, who put millions of dollars behind the ideas the Kennedy Administration had started to formulate. The cities were in their heyday. Now the prospects are not so great. As one mayor, who did not want his name used, put it, "If you think anybody with any integrity or any executive ability in the field of public administration is going to hang around for four years and watch this guy screw up, then you're crazy."

NAFTALIN OF MINNEAPOLIS

How would you describe the problems that confront the cities now?

There's a long, long list. Everybody knows them. On the physical side, you name it: transportation, sewage disposal, airports, housing. In some respects the *social* problems aren't more obvious, but they are more ominous. Discrimination and poverty, insecurity, alienation. Modern life is in many ways contradictory and oppressive. From my experience, black people—not all of them, but *so* many black people—feel oppressed in our society. And they *are* oppressed. Many of our young people feel oppressed. *Black* young people feel doubly oppressed. Bright and sensitive people feel oppressed by the growing congestion, the noise, the emptiness, the materialism—so many things that only bewilder us. And old people often feel oppressed, feel that they've been used and are being discarded. The manifestation of this whole sense of oppression takes pathological forms: divorce, alcoholism, drugs, insecurity, sadism.

We live in a time of profound revolution. We don't understand very clearly what these pressures are generating, and they worry us; they frighten us; they're obviously creating magnificent new opportunities that we don't quite know how to utilize. We're tied by our myths and prejudices and our biases out of the past. We're terrified by the destructive potential and by the *actual* destruction that's taking place. Only against this background can one talk about racial disturbances, law and order, the rebellion of youth, the problems of cities. I regard much of what I see as obscene. I regard the Congress as in *retreat*. I don't think Congress and President Nixon have an awareness of the real depth of the disturbance that is going on in this country and in the world.

They may reflect the retreat of the public. But my criticism of the President is very severe, because I don't think anybody ought to aspire to be President unless he has an awareness of the character of this enormous transition and is prepared to mobilize the full resources of the nation. What we have instead is business as usual: wait until the war in Vietnam is over; wait until we've gone to the moon, to Mars, to where not; wait until we've given a tax reduction to the middle class and the upper class. Wait, wait, wait, wait, wait. And then this myth of trying to use the state —this new federalism—is just *junk*, really. There's no other way to describe it.

This inaction is all because it's supposed to be politically hep to do what the American people want. There's *never* been a time when leadership should be challenged the way it ought to be now. Nixon ought to be talking like I'm talking, saying to the American people that we've got to massively produce the resources we need for a public school system, for higher education, for distributing income so we *really* destroy poverty. We don't have to take ten years to destroy poverty; we can do it in a year or two. There'd be some waste in it; maybe some boondoggling. Maybe some scoundrels would get away with a little more than they should. So what? American businessmen have been doing that for two hundred years.

The cities are immobilized. That's the key: the city. You can't escape in the city. But the city can't *act*, either.

We have to do two things. We've got to have a reassumption on the part of the national government of its responsibility. We have to have national programs, and we have to have massive national commitments. Second, we've got to do something about the fragmentation at the local level. The default there has got to be ended by reconstituting local governments in a naturally organic way. That means, to begin with, that we should take the 212 Standard Metropolitan Statistical Areas in this country, the SMSAs, and reconstitute them into viable governments. We don't need four hundred units of government in this metropolitan area of 1.8 million people. We ought to reduce them to one effective government and permit it to use proper computers, all the modern instruments of technology. . . .

Would the voters approve it [metropolitan government]?

It might be one of the worst donnybrooks you ever saw. But it would be a donnybrook worth having. All we have now is paralysis. Some people in the suburban communities think they've got an advantage. They think they don't have any poor people, which is true in some cases. They figure they've got their petty little operation and that they can have their own restrictive zoning patterns; they figure they know the cop on the corner and if they get drunk they don't have to be worried about being clapped into jail in downtown Minneapolis. They figure they're going to *hide* from the rest of the city. I think it would liberate all our communities if we had one metropolitan government. . . .

What will happen to the cities if none of this is done?

What I see happening is the continued deterioration of our physical environment. I don't see anything reversing it. We *could* reverse it pretty easily. It's a matter of having the public will to do it. But our problems are going to get worse and worse, and more and more wealthy people will retreat from the urban centers. It's going to become more and more expensive to build the island in the city, the luxury skyscraper. It almost looks like a garrison already—uniformed men outside, patrolling with guns, padlocks on every door. The inner city is going to become more riddled with difficulties. The suburban rings are going to become more defensive and protective. Industry is going to become more decentralized, creating complications in transportation. And we'll see further fragmentation. And I suppose, then, by and by, when we seem to be almost at the breaking point, maybe we'll undertake some massive programs.

Socially, the situation is even more ominous. The lower one-fifth of the population is going to continue from bad to worse. And the rest of us are going to rationalize that this problem isn't as bad as everybody makes it out to be. But I see nothing that's even answering the problem of *starvation*, much less the other problems.

Is the public at this point ready to do anything massive?

There's no *leadership* asking them to do it. We're blinded; we're so caught up, the 70, 80 percent, the affluent, in enjoying all the wonders of this great wonderland that we really don't see the poor. Black people are still invisible for most Americans. It's so very difficult for most people to really understand what it's like to be black. Just as it's difficult for a well person to understand what it's like to be handicapped. And just as it's so hard for the happily married mother of five who's made it the hard way to understand why that woman who's on welfare should have an illegitimate child and have a lover who's run out by a night-rider; *offended* by this.

There are disjunctions in this society, and we're hung up; all kinds of people are just hung up. We're going to remain hung up until there begins to be channeled into the national dialogue, from the White House, and permeating the country, ideas such as those we've been talking about.

JOURNEY TO ATLANTA

James Baldwin

The Progressive Party [1947–48] has not, so far as I can gather, made any very great impression in Harlem, and this is not so much despite as because of its campaign promises, promises rather too extravagant to be believed. It is considered a rather cheerful axiom that all Americans distrust politicians. (No one takes the further and less cheerful step of considering just what effect this mutual contempt has on either the public or the politicians, who have, indeed, very little to do with one another.) Of all Americans, Negroes distrust politicians most, or more accurately, they have been best trained to expect nothing from them; more than other

Americans, they are always aware of the enormous gap between election promises and their daily lives. It is true that the promises excite them, but this is not because they are taken as proof of good intentions. They are the proof of something more concrete than intentions: that the Negro situation is not static, that changes have occurred, and are occurring and will occur—this, in spite of the daily, dead-end monotony. It is this daily, dead-end monotony, though, as well as the wise desire not to be betrayed by too much hoping, which causes them to look on politicians with such an extraordinarily disenchanted eye.

This fatalistic indifference is something that drives the optimistic American liberal quite mad; he is prone, in his more exasperated moments, to refer to Negroes as political children, an appellation not entirely just. Negro liberals, being consulted, assure us that this is something that will disappear with "education," a vast, all-purpose term, conjuring up visions of sunlit housing projects, stacks of copybooks and a race of well-soaped, dark-skinned people who never slur their R's. Actually, this is not so much political irresponsibility as the product of experience, experience which no amount of education can quite efface. It is, as much as anything else, the reason the Negro vote is so easily bought and sold, the reason for that exclamation heard so frequently on Sugar Hill: "Our people never get anywhere."

"Our people" have functioned in this country for nearly a century as political weapons, the trump card up the enemies' sleeve; anything promised Negroes at election time is also a threat levelled at the opposition; in the struggle for mastery the Negro is the pawn. It is inescapable that this is only possible because of his position in this country and it has very frequently seemed at least equally apparent that this is a position which no one, least of all the politician, seriously intended to change.

Since Negroes have been in this country their one major, devastating gain was their Emancipation, an emancipation no one regards any more as having been dictated by humanitarian impulses. All that has followed from that brings to mind the rather unfortunate image of bones thrown to a pack of dogs sufficiently hungry to be dangerous. If all this sounds rather deliberately grim, it is not through any wish to make the picture darker than it is; I would merely like to complete the picture usually presented by pointing out that no matter how many instances there have been of genuine concern and good-will, nor how many hard, honest struggles have been carried on to improve the position of the Negro people, their position has not, in fact, changed so far as most of them are concerned.

Sociologists and historians, having the historical perspective in mind, may conclude that we are moving toward ever-greater democracy; but this is beyond the ken of a Negro growing up in any one of this country's ghettos. As regards Negro politicians, they are considered with pride as *politicians*, a pride much akin to that felt concerning Marian Anderson or Joe Louis: they have proven the worth of the Negro people and in terms, American terms, which no one can negate. But as no housewife expects Marian Anderson's genius to be of any practical aid in her dealings with the landlord, so nothing is expected of Negro representatives. The terrible thing, and here we have an American phenomenon in relief, is the fact that the Negro representative, by virtue of his position, is ever more removed from the people he ostensibly serves. Moreover, irrespective of personal integrity, his position—neatly and often painfully paradoxical— is utterly dependent on the continuing debasement of fourteen million Negroes; should the national ideals be put into practice tomorrow, countless prominent Negroes would lose their *raison d'être*.

Finally, we are confronted with the psychology and tradition of the country; if the Negro vote is so easily bought and sold, it is because it has been treated with so little respect; since no Negro dares seriously assume that any politician is concerned with the fate of Negroes, or would do much about it if he had the power, the vote must be bartered for what it will get, for whatever short-term goals can be managed. These goals are mainly economic and frequently personal, sometimes pathetic: bread or a new roof or five dollars, or, continuing up the scale, schools, houses or more Negroes in hitherto Caucasian jobs. The American commonwealth chooses to overlook what Negroes are never able to forget: they are not *really* considered a part of it. Like Aziz in *A Passage to India* or Topsy in *Uncle Tom's Cabin*, they know that white people, whatever their love for justice, have no love for them.

This is the crux of the matter; and the Progressive Party, with its extravagant claims, has, therefore, imposed on itself the considerable burden of proof. The only party within recent memory which made equally strident claims of fellowship were the Communists, who failed to survive this test; and the only politician of similar claims was, of course, [Henry A.] Wallace's erstwhile master, Roosevelt, who did not after all, now that the magic of his voice is gone, succeed in raising the darker brother to the status of a citizen. This is the ancestry of the Wallace party, and it does not work wholly in its favor. It operates to give pause to even the most desperate and the most gullible.

It is, however, considered on one level, the level of short-term goals, with approval, since it does afford temporary work for Negroes, particularly those associated in any manner with the arts. The rather flippant question on 125th Street now is: "So? You working for Mr. Wallace these days?" For at least there is that: entertainers, personalities are in demand. To forestall lawsuits, I must explain that I am not discussing "names"—who are in rather a different position, too touchy and complex to analyze here —but the unknown, the struggling, endless armies of Negro boys and girls bent on, and as yet very far from, recognition. A segment of this army, a quartet called *The Melodeers*, made a trip to Atlanta under the auspices of the Progressive Party in August, a trip which lasted about eighteen days and which left them with no love for Mr. Wallace. Since this quartet included two of my brothers, I was given the details of the trip; indeed, David, the younger, kept a sort of journal for me—literally a blow-by-blow account.

Harlem is filled with churches and on Sundays it gives the impression of being filled with music. Quartets such as my brothers' travel from church to church in the fashion of circuit preachers, singing as much for the love of singing and the need for practice as for the rather indifferent sums collected for them which are then divided. These quartets have "battles of song," the winning team adding, of course, immensely to its prestige, the most consistent winners being the giants in this field. The aim of all these quartets, of course, is to branch out, to hit the big time and sing for a livelihood. The Golden Gate Quartet, judging at least from its music, had its roots here, and out of such a background came Sister Rosetta Tharpe, whom I heard, not quite ten years ago, plunking a guitar in a store-front church on Fifth Avenue. *The Melodeers* have not been singing very long and are very far from well-known, and the invitation to sing on tour with the Wallace party in the South seemed, whatever their misgivings about the Mason-Dixon line, too good an opportunity to pass up.

This invitation, by the way, seems to have been the brainstorm of a Clarence Warde, a Negro merchant seaman once employed as a cottage father in a corrective institution up-state; it was he in New York who acted as a go-between, arranging, since *The Melodeers* are minors, to be their legal guardian and manager on the road. An extended tour, such as was planned, met with some opposition from the parents, an opposition countered by the possible long-term benefits of the tour in so far as the boys' careers were concerned and, even more urgently, by the assurance that, at the very least, the boys would come home with a considerably larger sum of money than any of them were making on their jobs. (The political implications do not seem to have carried much weight.) A series of churches had been lined up for them presumably throughout the South. "The understanding," writes David, "was that we were supposed to sing"; after which the party was to take over to make speeches and circulate petitions. "The arrangement," David notes laconically, "sounded very promising, so we decided to go."

And, indeed, they traveled South in splendor, in a Pullman, to be exact, in which, since what David describes as a "Southern gentleman and wife" took exception to their presence, they traveled alone.

At the Wallace headquarters in Atlanta they were introduced to a Mrs. Branson Price, a grey-haired white woman of incurably aristocratic leanings who seems to have been the directress of the Party in that region.

The graciousness of her reception was only slightly marred by the fact that she was not expecting singers and thought they were a new group of canvassers. She arranged for them to take rooms on Butler Street at the YMCA. Here the first gap between promise and performance was made manifest, a gap, they felt, which was perhaps too trifling to make a fuss about. In New York they had been promised comparative privacy, two to a room; but now, it developed, they were to sleep in a dormitory. This gap, in fact, it was the province of Mr. Warde to close, but whether he was simply weary from the trip or overwhelmed by the aristocratic Mrs. Price, he kept his mouth shut and, indeed, did not open it again for quite some time.

When they returned to headquarters, somewhat irritated at having had to wait three hours for the arrival of Louis Burner, who had the money for their rooms, Mrs. Price suggested that they go out canvassing. This was wholly unexpected, since no one had mentioned canvassing in New York and, since, moreover, canvassers are voluntary workers who are not paid. Further, the oldest of them was twenty, which was not voting age, and none of them knew anything about the Progressive Party, nor did they care much. On the other hand, it is somewhat difficult to refuse a grey-haired, aristocratic lady who is toiling day and night for the benefit of your people; and Mr. Warde, who should have been their spokesman, had not yet recovered his voice; so they took the petitions, which were meant to put the Wallace party on the ballot, and began knocking on doors in the Negro section of Atlanta. They were sent out in pairs, white and black, a political device which operates not only as the living proof of brotherhood, but which has the additional virtue in intimidating into passive silence the more susceptible beholder, who cannot, after all, unleash the impatient scorn he may feel with a strange, benevolent white man sitting in his parlor.

They canvassed for three days, during which time their expenses— $2.25 per man per day—were paid, but during which time they were doing no singing and making no money. On the third day they pointed out that this was not quite what they had been promised in New York, to be met with another suggestion from the invincible Mrs. Price: how would they like to sing on the soundtruck? They had not the faintest desire to sing on a soundtruck, especially when they had been promised a string of churches; however, the churches, along with Mr. Warde's vigor, seemed unavailable at the moment; they could hardly sit around Atlanta doing nothing; and so long as they worked with the party they were certain, at least, to be fed. "The purpose of our singing," David writes, "was to draw a crowd so the party could make speeches." Near the end of the singing and during the speeches, leaflets and petitions were circulated through the crowd.

David had not found Negroes in the South different in any important respect from Negroes in the North; except that many of them were distrustful and "they are always talking about the North; they have to let you know they know somebody in New York or Chicago or Detroit." Of the crowds that gathered—and, apparently, *The Melodeers* attracted great numbers—"many of these people couldn't read or write their names" and not many of them knew anything at all about the Progressive Party. But they did divine, as American Negroes must, what was expected of them; and they listened to the speeches and signed the petitions.

Becoming both desperate and impatient, *The Melodeers* began making engagements and singing on their own, stealing time from canvassing to rehearse. They made more appointments than they were able to keep; partly because the lack of money limited their mobility but also because the Party, discovering these clandestine appointments, moved in, demanding to be heard. Those churches which refused to make room for the Party were not allowed to hear the quartet, which thus lost its last hope of making any money. The quartet wondered what had happened to Mr. Warde. David's account all but ignores him until nearly the end of the trip, when his position during all this is perhaps given some illumination.

Things now began to go steadily worse. They got into an argument with the manager of the Y, who objected to their rehearsing, and moved to a private home, for which the Party paid 75¢ per man per day; and the Party, which was, one gathers, furiously retrenching, arranged for them to eat at Fraziers' Café, a Negro establishment on Hunter Street, for $1.25 per man per day. My correspondent notes that they had no choice of meals —"they served us what they liked"—which seems to have been mainly limp vegetables—and "we were as hungry when we walked out as we were when we walked in." On the other hand, they were allowed to choose their beverage: tea or coffee or soda pop.

Heaven only knows what prompted Mrs. Branson Price to give a party at this point. Perhaps the campaign was going extraordinarily well; perhaps Fraziers' Café, where the party was held, was in need of a little extra revenue as well as the knowledge that its adoption of the Party would help to bring about a better world; perhaps Mrs. Price merely longed to be a gracious hostess once again. In any case, on a Sunday night she gave a party to which everyone was invited. My brother, who at this point was much concerned with food, observed glumly, "We had ice-cream."

The quartet sat at a table by itself, robbed, however, of the presence of Mr. Warde, who was invited to sit at Mrs. Price's table: "she said it would be an honor," my correspondent notes, failing, however, to say for whom. "There was a man there called a *folk*-singer," says David with venom, "and, naturally, everybody had to hear some *folk* songs." Eventually, the folksy aspect of the evening was exhausted and the quartet was invited to sing. They sang four selections, apparently to everyone's delight for they had to be quite adamant about not singing a fifth. The strain of continual singing in the open air had done their voices no good and it had made one of them extremely hoarse. So they refused, over loud protests, and apologized. "This displeased Mrs. Price."

Indeed, it had. She was not in the least accustomed to having her suggestions, to say nothing of her requests, refused. Early Monday morning she called Mr. Warde to her office to inquire who those black boys thought they were? and determined to ship them all back that same day in a car. Mr. Warde, who, considering the honors of the evening before, must have been rather astounded, protested such treatment, to be warned that she might very well ship them off without a car; the six of them might very well be forced to take to the road. This is not a pleasant mode of traveling for a Negro in the North and no Negro in Atlanta, particularly no Northern Negro, is likely to get very far. Mr. Warde temporized: they could not leave on such short notice; for one thing, the boys had clothes at the cleaners which would not be ready for a while and which they could hardly afford to lose. Mrs. Price, every aristocratic vein pounding, did not wish to be concerned with such plebeian matters and, finally, losing all patience, commanded Mr. Warde to leave her office: Had he forgotten that he was in Georgia? Didn't he know better than to sit in a white woman's office?

Mr. Warde, in whose bowels last night's bread of fellowship must have acquired the weight of rock, left the office. Then the quartet attempted to secure an audience; to be met with implacable refusal and the threat of the police. There were, incidentally, according to my brother, five Negro policemen in Atlanta at this time, who, though they were not allowed to arrest whites, would, of course, be willing, indeed, in their position, anxious, to arrest any Negro who seemed to need it. In Harlem, Negro policemen are feared even more than whites, for they have more to prove and fewer ways to prove it. The prospect of being arrested in Atlanta made them a little dizzy with terror: what might mean a beating in Harlem might quite possibly mean death here. "And at the same time," David says, "it was funny"; by which he means that the five policemen were faint prophecies of that equality which is the Progressive Party's goal.

They did not see Mrs. Price again; this was their severance from the Party, which now refused to pay any expenses; it was only the fact that their rent had been paid in advance which kept them off the streets. Food, however, remained a problem. Mr. Warde brought them a "couple of loaves of bread" and some jam; they sang one engagement. During this week Mrs. Price relented enough to get their clothes from the cleaners and send Mr. Warde, in custody of a white man who had been at the party, to the bus station for tickets. This man, whose resemblance to the Southern Gentleman of the Pullman is in no way diminished by his allegiance to Mr. Wallace, bought the tickets and threw them on the ground at Mr. Warde's feet, advising him not to show his black face in Georgia again.

The quartet, meanwhile, had gotten together six dollars doing odd jobs, which was enough, perhaps, for three of them to eat on the road. They split up, three leaving that Friday and the other two staying on about ten days longer, working for a construction company. Mr. Warde stopped off to visit his family, promising to see *The Melodeers* in New York, but he had not arrived as this was being written. *The Melodeers* laugh about their trip now, that good-natured, hearty laughter which is, according to white men, the peculiar heritage of Negroes, Negroes who were born with the fortunate ability to laugh all their troubles away. Somewhat surprisingly, they are not particularly bitter toward the Progressive Party, though they can scarcely be numbered among its supporters. "They're all the same," David tells me, "ain't none of 'em gonna do you no good; if you gonna be foolish enough to believe what they say, then it serves you good and right. Ain't none of 'em gonna do a thing for *me*."

TACTICS FOR THE SEVENTIES

Saul Alinsky

. . . Well, I suppose these are rough times and anyone in a fight who is really doing something becomes a target. I've had my sticky scenes, a couple really up-tight, but you don't worry about it because if you do you've got no business being in the arena to begin with, and after all, none of us are going to come out of life alive anyway. I get these threats all the time—from the Klan, the Minutemen, the Young Republican Clubs of California, the Birchers, any time I land in what I call my kooky country.

Maybe with luck I still have ten good productive years ahead of me. So I keep thinking—what's the best use I can make of them? I've come to see very clearly that this country is predominantly middle-class economically. Almost four-fifths of our people are in that bracket, so that's where the power is. Hell, we would have to be blind not to see that this is where organization has to go. This became plenty clear when we were fighting Eastman Kodak and went into the proxy deal. We had to go to the churches and the middle-class groups that owned stocks and had proxies they could turn over to us. That's where we found the strength to carry on the fight for the organization of the poor in Rochester. We saw the same thing when Cesar Chavez staged the grape boycott—a middle-class consumer boycott. So that's the job we've got to take on and train organizers to do.

One thing I've learned in spades—though I didn't want to accept it for a long time—is this: organization doesn't come out of an immaculate conception. It takes a highly trained, politically sophisticated, creative organizer to do the job. And it can't be done just on a local basis because the problems today are regional and national so you need a national power organization. But to build it you've got to have pieces to put together, local pieces. And to build them you've got to have trained organizers. That's why I'm doing what I'm doing now—training the organizers.

Another thing that matters is that this is a corporate economy. That's where the power—the political and economic power—is. Now where are you going to find the strength to make the corporations use that power for the things that need to be done? Suppose you could get all the blacks in the country, all the Mexican-Americans, all the poor whites, all the Puerto Ricans organized. And suppose some genius formed them into a coalition. That would be maybe 55 million people by the end of the 1970s. But the population will be around 225 million by then. So the poor will still be a minority who need allies and they'll have to find supporters among the three-quarters of our people who are middle-class.

I'm including here the lower-lower middle-class, making up to about $7,500—the employed poor, the "have a little, want more" group. Then you have the lower middle class at around nine, ten, or eleven thousand a year. Like the working poor they're in hock up to their ears with time payments. So are the middle middle class, making $15,000 a year or so. In some ways the middle-class groups are more alienated, more out of the scene even than the poor. There aren't any special funding programs for them. They don't have special admissions to universities. They don't have a special anything except getting constantly clobbered by taxes and inflation.

These people are just thrashing around in their own frustrations. They couldn't be effective allies for anyone because they're overcome, completely confused by their own problems. So they fall back on two common clichés. One is: "I don't care to be involved." Or maybe someone else will call himself a "concerned citizen." This is really saying the rest of the citizens are not concerned, so they're not citizens at all. When masses of people disengage in this way it's a perfect setup for the extreme Right, for the dictators whose pitch is, "Just follow me and all will be well."

How do you organize these frustrated middle-class people? You find out what they care about, what they are worried about, and you organize them around these issues. . . .

. . . The average policeman is typical of the lower middle class. He's married, he and his wife go to church, he has a small house, a car, and a library full of installment-payment books. His job and a fireman's are a little more romantic than a garbage collector's. Still he knows it's the kind of job most people look down on. He has some opportunity for advancement. But he sees that in the last fifteen or twenty years anyone who really went upstairs in the department was a college graduate or a professional of some sort. So the fact he never went to college is very important to him. He hopes his kids will go.

Then his whole world goes smash. The kids who are rampaging on campus don't seem to know the value of anything. They never had to work. They go around yelling slogans about Che Guevara—and he doesn't know who Che was, except some damn Red—or some Chinaman named Mao. He thinks these kids should get their goddam asses beaten.

He finds he isn't respected anymore. In the old days he could walk any place, go into a dark alley, and except in rare instances no one would dare assault him. If you were a cop-killer, then God help you. The department would go out and get you. In Chicago, if a cop was killed the mobs would send the word back, "We didn't have anything to do with it." Or, "We already took care of the guy who did it." Because when a cop's been killed the heat's on. Well, the policeman doesn't have that kind of protection anymore. And he has no status, no rationale for being. The way he looks at it, why are his hands tied when nutty kids occupy buildings and take out confidential files? From his point of view they're defecating on his most precious values. It's not just the police who feel this way.

One day when I was lecturing at a big university, there was some kind of uproar. A Marine recruiter was driven off campus. I didn't see it happen, in fact I didn't hear about it till dinner that evening. I got back to my hotel around one o'clock and went into the bar for a nightcap. The place was empty except for the bartender and a Marine master sergeant in dress uniform, with a chestful of campaign ribbons and hash marks up to his elbows. He was sitting way down at the end of the bar, putting away one drink after another and crying audibly. It was very upsetting—a middle-aged man, very masculine, totally demoralized and crying.

I asked the bartender, "What's up?" He shrugged his shoulders and said, "He's been that way for the last three hours." I took my drink and sat down next to the sergeant and said, "Come on, buddy, things can't be that tough." Pretty soon he started talking. It turned out he was the recruiting sergeant who had been driven off campus. His eyes were filled with complete confusion—it wasn't just that he was pretty well stoned. He kept saying, "I don't get it. I don't know what's happening. I was at Iwo Jima. I was at Tarawa. I've seen my buddies alongside me getting their guts blown out; they died for these punks. And now I go on a college campus and you'd think I was a goddam Nazi, the way they treat me. I just don't understand what's happening to the world."

This is how the policeman feels. So what does he do to have some rationale for living? Well, the super-duper patriots in the community who are screaming for law and order seem to be about the only people who have any respect for him. So he gets active in the American Legion, in the John Birch Society maybe. This gives him some status.

We've been contacted by a small group of policemen about going into our training program, men we think can become organizers in their communities and at the same time get some real status for themselves.

We've been talking with some black policemen also. In a lot of ways the black policeman is having the same trouble as the black intellectual. On the surface the black intellectual has never had it so good. If he has a master's degree he'll be offered a job that a white Ph.D. couldn't get. But at the same time he's trapped. He's joined the other side, moved away from his own people. So he may work out his guilt by militant rhetoric, by becoming what I call an Uncle Tough-Talk or the black in the gray flannel dashiki.

The black policeman is in an even worse spot. He's assigned to the ghetto, where he's not only a pig but a black pig. The hate expressed toward black cops in many ghettos is much worse than the feeling toward white cops. One black officer we had in training said to me, "We're in a real bind, a real box. Which comes first, our job or our people? Well, we have to be with our people. We couldn't stand it otherwise and after a while our lives wouldn't be worth a nickel in the neighborhood." In other words, if they don't express some hostility to whites their own people will denounce them.

The answer isn't just to organize black police unions which would give them better opportunities for promotion. Our idea is to train them to become leaders among their own people, to help them develop mass power organizations that will fight for better housing, schools, and so forth. Our program with this group has been suspended at this point. Maybe this is the wrong time to start.

One of the biggest problems we face on the whole race issue is a complete collapse of communications. This goes both ways and all kinds of walls are up now which in some ways are as bad as the old segregationist walls. This is very important because it doesn't make any difference what ideas come up on the white side or on the black side; so long as we can't communicate with each other except in what I would call a crippled communication, then we're in for real trouble. You get a combination of screwed-up white and black neurotics whose vocabulary is all crapped up with masochism and sadism, and it's a goddam mess.

Right now you have the blacks saying, "Whitey, get lost, stay away from us, do your own thing with your own people." So I accept the fact that today, in spite of my record, my white skin disqualifies me from the kind of direct organizing work I've done in Chicago and Rochester and other ghettos.

In this climate, I'm convinced that all whites should get out of the black ghettos. It's a stage we have to go through. I'd like to see legislation enacted making it mandatory for all white businessmen and slum landlords in the ghettos to sell their stuff to blacks within an eighteen-month period. If they haven't done it by that time, then let the government come in—just like Urban Renewal—appraise their properties and businesses, condemn them, and then turn around and help blacks buy them with special funding or low-interest-rate loans. This is what they say they want. And until the blacks have the experience of being exploited by their own people as they were by the whites, this will be a constant thorn, a constant source of anti-Semitism because so many of the businessmen are Jews who stayed on after they moved their homes out of the ghetto. . . .

There's been a complete loss of communication between blacks and whites. If a white guy says something really far out, your reaction is, "You ought to go to Bellevue and get a spinal test." But if it's a black man, you listen politely and say, "That's a very interesting approach." You're so scared of being tarred with the label of racist or bigot. Actually, what you're doing is even worse. You're treating him like a problem child. It's paternalism, condescension.

After one of my campus lectures, a really militant black got up, just oozing hostility. "Mr. Alinsky," he said, "I want to ask you a question. But first I want to know, will you be speaking for all the rest of the honkies?" "Okay," I said, "I'll answer your question. But first I want to know are you speaking for all the rest of the niggers?" Then I walked to the end of the platform and looked at all the blacks who were sitting together. "Look, get this straight," I said, "all of you blacks. One: I am your *equal*. Two: I am not one of those guilt-ridden, screwed-up, neurotic liberals you characters have been dealing with. Like the ones in the San Francisco Bay area who went around wearing big buttons saying HONKIES FOR HUEY during the Huey Newton trial. If I were in a jam I wouldn't expect you to wear big buttons saying NIGGERS FOR SAUL. And you know damn well you wouldn't do it. So don't give me any of that crap."

There was a moment's silence. Then the fellow who had asked the question said, "Well what I meant was—is your answer going to be typical of the white position?" I answered, "Is your question going to be typical of the black position? Now let's talk." We had quite a good discussion and the white students all of a sudden began sitting up like people. . . .

RENT STRIKE IN NEWARK

Jesse Allen

Some of the people from the neighborhood council came around to visit me and they saw the condition of the building I was living in, such as peeling paint, broken plaster, bad plumbing, bad wiring, broken stair steps, rats and roaches, and they began to visit more houses on the blocks and found most of the houses in the same condition. We complained to City Hall. We got no cooperation from the Board of Health. We did not get any cooperation from our mayor, and the landlords just wouldn't fix up. So some of us got together and started talking, and we decided to set up a block committee and talk to people. Once you start talking to people and bring them together you can start moving to do something for your neighborhood. We organized eight blocks in our neighborhood in about six weeks. We called a meeting with the people and discussed our problems. We found that most all of us had the same problems. We decided to go on a rent strike. We were not going to pay the landlord any more money until he did something. When the landlords came around for the rent we told them we're not paying any more rent to them. We had their money, but we were putting it into the bank until they fixed the houses. Some of the landlords started to repair right away, such as Lee Bernstein, our South Ward City Councilman. Others did not do anything.

We started picketing the houses we were renting in our neighborhood. First we picketed at Ray Shustak's building, one that the Mayor himself had come down and looked at and found 125 violations (after a delegation of people had complained to him about it). The Mayor made us all sorts of promises but failed to carry out any of them. Our City Councilman Lee Bernstein told us we should have come to him before and he would have done something about it. At the time he had apartment houses in the neighborhood with lots of violations and he wasn't doing anything about fixing them up. But he was collecting $110 dollars a month rent from each of his apartments. He tried to get us not to picket, but we picketed anyway. Bernstein called it a disgrace.

The landlords took us into court, and the judge took the money into the court and told Robert Inlander, a landlord, that he would take the money every time our rent was due. The landlord and the city called us troublemakers. About two months later the landlord took us back into court again. This time he did not want any rent money. He wanted us out of his buildings. We told the judge that we were still paying our money to the court. The judge said to us that the landlord didn't want the money, that we had to move out of the buildings. Our lawyer, Felix Neals, argued the case, but the judge would not give out any justice. He was all the way on the landlords' side.

We found out that Inlander lived in the richest part of Maplewood, his house valued at $90,000. So we decided to put a picket line around it. Three days later he asked us if we were going to continue to picket if we moved. We told him yes. He said why would you keep on picketing when the judge says that you must move anyway. We told him that we wanted a decent place to live for the next tenants that moved in. So he said that if we wanted to stay on in the building, we could. He had stated in the newspaper after we picketed his home that he was not the owner of the property in question, but merely the overseer. By doing research, we found that he did own the property, so we told him that if he didn't own the property how could he tell us that we could stay on after all. He said don't worry about that, I can fix it up. We told him that we were sorry that we had spent his money, and he said some of you are good people, so we told him that when we were willing to pay the money to the court, that he wouldn't accept the money, and after the judge had given us a week to move out, we told the judge and the landlord that if we found decent apartments to live in within a week, we would move out. But if we didn't we would stay on and be thrown out. Some of us found apartments, but did not move into them at the time. We wanted to see if the city would continue to let absentee landlords have their way when they knew the conditions of the buildings we were living in. So we stayed on a couple of weeks longer, but no one ever came to throw us out. . . .

BLACK PANTHER PARTY
PLATFORM AND PROGRAM:
WHAT WE WANT WHAT WE BELIEVE

The Black Panther Party

1. WE WANT FREEDOM. WE WANT POWER TO DETERMINE THE DESTINY OF OUR BLACK COMMUNITY.

We believe that black people will not be free until we are able to determine our destiny.

2. WE WANT FULL EMPLOYMENT FOR OUR PEOPLE.

We believe that the federal government is responsible and obligated to give every man employment or a guaranteed income. We believe that if the white American businessmen will not give full employment then the means of production should be taken from the businessmen and placed in the community so that the people of the community can organize and employ all of its people and give a high standard of living.

3. WE WANT AN END TO THE ROBBERY BY THE CAPITALIST OF OUR BLACK COMMUNITY.

We believe that this racist government has robbed us and now we are demanding the overdue debt of 40 acres and two mules. Forty acres and two mules was promised 100 years ago as restitution for slave labor and mass murder of black people. We will accept the payment in currency which will be distributed to our many communities. The Germans are now aiding the Jews in Israel for the genocide of the Jewish people. The Germans murdered 6 million Jews. The American racist has taken part in the slaughter of over 50 million black people; therefore, we feel that this is a modest demand that we make.

4. WE WANT DECENT HOUSING, FIT FOR SHELTER OF HUMAN BEINGS.

We believe that if the white landlords will not give decent housing to our black community, then the housing and the land should be made into cooperatives, so that our community, with government aid, can build and make decent housing for its people.

5. WE WANT EDUCATION FOR OUR PEOPLE THAT EXPOSES THE TRUE NATURE OF THIS DECADENT AMERICAN SOCIETY. WE WANT EDUCATION THAT TEACHES US OUR TRUE HISTORY AND OUR ROLE IN THE PRESENT-DAY SOCIETY.

We believe in an educational system that will give to our people a knowledge of self. If a man does not have knowledge of himself and his position in society and the world, then he has little chance to relate to anything else.

6. WE WANT ALL BLACK MEN TO BE EXEMPT FROM MILITARY SERVICE.

We believe that black people should not be forced to fight in the military service to defend a racist government that does not protect us. We will not fight and kill other people of color in the world who, like black people, are being victimized by the white racist government of America. We will protect ourselves from the force and violence of the racist police and the racist military, by whatever means necessary.

7. WE WANT AN IMMEDIATE END TO POLICE BRUTALITY AND MURDER OF BLACK PEOPLE.

We believe we can end police brutality in our black community by organizing black self-defense groups that are dedicated to defending our black community from racist police oppression and brutality. The Second Amendment to the Constitution of the United States gives a right to bear arms. We therefore believe that all black people should arm themselves for self-defense.

8. WE WANT FREEDOM FOR ALL BLACK MEN HELD IN FEDERAL, STATE, COUNTY AND CITY PRISONS AND JAILS.

We believe that all black people should be released from the many jails and prisons because they have not received a fair and impartial trial.

9. WE WANT ALL BLACK PEOPLE WHEN BROUGHT TO TRIAL TO BE TRIED IN COURT BY A JURY OF THEIR PEER GROUP OR PEOPLE FROM THEIR BLACK COMMUNITIES, AS DEFINED BY THE CONSTITUTION OF THE UNITED STATES.

We believe that the courts should follow the United States Constitution, so that black people will receive fair trials. The 14th Amendment of the U.S. Constitution gives a man a right to be tried by his peer group. A peer is a person from a similar economic, social, religious, geographical, environmental, historical and racial background. To do this the court will be forced to select a jury from the black community from which the black defendant came. We have been, and are being tried by all-white juries that have no understanding of the "average reasoning man" of the black community.

10. We Want Land, Bread, Housing, Education, Clothing, Justice and Peace. And as Our Major Political Objective, a United Nations-Supervised Plebiscite to be Held Throughout the Black Colony in Which Only Black Colonial Subjects Will be Allowed to Participate, for the Purpose of Determining the Will of Black People as to Their National Destiny.

When, in the course of human events, it becomes necessary for one people to dissolve the political bands which have connected them with another, and to assume, among the powers of the earth, the separate and equal station to which the laws of nature and nature's God entitle them, a decent respect to the opinions of mankind requires that they should declare the causes which impel them to the separation.

We hold these truths to be self-evident, that all men are created equal; that they are endowed by their Creator with certain unalienable rights; that among these are life, liberty, and the pursuit of happiness. *That, to secure these rights, governments are instituted among men, deriving their just powers from the consent of the governed, that, whenever any form of government becomes destructive of these ends, it is the right of the people to alter or to abolish it, and to institute a new government, laying its foundation on such principles, and organizing its powers in such form, as to them shall seem most likely to effect their safety and happiness.* Prudence, indeed, will dictate that government long established should not be changed for light and transient cause; and, accordingly, all experience hath shown, that mankind are more disposed to suffer, while evils are sufferable, than to right themselves by abolishing the forms to which they are accustomed. *But, when a long train of abuses and usurpations, pursuing invariably the same object, evinces a design to reduce them under absolute despotism, it is their right, it is their duty, to throw off such government, and to provide new guards for their future security.*

UNDERCOVER COPS

David Brand

Charlie Smith, a Negro veteran of Vietnam and now a student at Texas Southern University, has an odd sort of extracurricular job: He's a spy.

Mr. Smith (that's not his real name) isn't concerned with such traditional college administration headaches as campus sex or pot parties or even library book thieves. He's an informer for the Houston police department—and he infiltrates Negro organizations.

Dangerous work? "Man, oh man, you must be kidding," says Mr. Smith. "Sure, it's risky, but I've faced the Vietcong and I'm not afraid of black power."

Mr. Smith joins a growing army of informers recruited by police intelligence agents throughout the country. Police obviously aren't too explicit about how many infiltrators are out spying for them, but intelligence activities are expanding. Detroit's intelligence division increased from zero to 70 officers in seven years, Boston now has 40 agents and even Houston's smaller police force has a 14-man intelligence unit.

Police are concentrating intelligence activities heavily on racial matters these days. Detroit's former police commissioner, Ray Girardin, says that Negro extremists are "becoming increasingly active and a threat to tranquility." As a result, "we are devoting an increasing amount of time and effort just to keep track of what's going on among extremist groups."

Houston police are similarly occupied. "Since 1965, we haven't put as much effort into criminal investigation because of this racial thing," says Lt. M.L. Singleton, who heads the intelligence unit. "Around here, we're known as the men from the CIA."

The analogy isn't as farfetched as it might seem, for on a smaller scale Houston's police intelligence unit engages in activities as clandestine —and at times as controversial—as those of the Central Intelligence Agency.

Civil rights activities are trailed, observed from parked cars, photographed by policemen posing as news photographers, tape-recorded by informers and cultivated by undercover agents acting as businessmen or ex-convicts.

And, as with the CIA, Houston police are sometimes accused of overstepping their bounds. A number of prominent Negroes, for instance, are convinced their phones are tapped. "Every time I pick up my phone," says the Rev. Bill Lawson, a Baptist minister, "a red light goes on somewhere." Police deny the charge.

Many policemen say that the undercover work is essential. Houston Police Chief Herman Short, in fact, says that the intelligence unit is largely responsible for preventing any racial unrest in Houston from blossoming into a full-scale riot. "We've been very effective in combating criminal unrest," he says.

Few arrests have been made as a result of intelligence activity; however, members of the Houston intelligence unit say they provide an important source of information for other police units.

Many informers "are in danger of their lives," says Mr. Short. His department goes to great lengths to protect infiltrators. Before Charlie Smith can discuss his work with a reporter, a meeting has to be set up in a nondescript building on Houston's outskirts. Mr. Smith, a patrolman and a police intelligence agent separately enter a small room. Finally, the reporter is permitted to join the group, and the door is locked.

Although informers are paid from $5 to $400 for a single item of information, Charlie Smith says he's not in this for money.

"I just don't want to see this country burn," he says.

Mr. Smith enrolled in Texas Southern last year, shortly after returning from Army service in Vietnam. University security police with whom he became friendly passed his name on to Patrolmen Charles Howard and Thomas Blair, two Negro intelligence unit members.

He belongs to civil rights groups and reports plans for demonstrations, movements of leaders and "anything that is said at meetings that sounds militant."

Police consider the predominantly Negro college as the city's racial cauldron. They say that Houston's only racial riot occurred there in May, 1967, when a rookie policeman was killed in a fierce gun battle and hundreds of students were arrested. Since then, police have kept close watch over campus affairs.

Charlie's constant fear is that, if fellow students don't discover his spy role, the faculty will. "You see, even the professors here are involved in the black power movement," he says. "And if they ever found out, they'd flunk me for sure."

One civil rights activist who scoffs at Mr. Smith's spying is Lee Otis Johnson, 28, head of Houston's Student Nonviolent Coordinating Committee. "Man, we know who those cats (informers) are," he says. "We hold our strategy meeting on Sunday and a public meeting on Monday, and those cats don't know nothing about the strategy meeting. We know more about the police than they know about us."

Houston police have their own views of Mr. Johnson. In interviews, they describe him as "a hate peddler," "Communist" and "anarchist." An undercover agent arrested him last April for the possession and sale of marijuana. He was convicted a few days ago and sentenced to 30 years in prison. He is now in the Houston city jail pending an appeal.

Even civil rights leaders who haven't been arrested—such as the Reverend Mr. Lawson and other activist ministers—are scathingly attacked by Houston undercover police. Black demonstrators are "professional agitators," says Lt. Singleton. "They're arrogant bastards looking for an issue."

The Rev. Earl Allen, a 34-year-old Negro Methodist minister who runs an antipoverty program, is described by one policeman as "definitely Communist-influenced." He bases this conclusion on the assertion that Mr. Allen has "been seen with known Communists."

These charges are rejected by the Negro leaders, and Mr. Allen describes them as "subtle bigotry" and "psychological brutality." Moderate civil rights leaders and black militants doubt there is any Communist influence in the city's civil rights movement.

One member of Houston's undercover unit, Patrolman Lin Fowler, went underground for 18 months in an investigation of the Houston Committee to End the War in Vietnam. Mr. Fowler posed as a real estate man—he kept For Rent signs on his car seat—but his cover was destroyed when a committee member saw him walking out of police headquarters.

Since then, Mr. Fowler has turned to "uncovering Socialists, pacifists and do-gooders in the civil rights movement." Mr. Fowler, who mingles with newsmen to take photos of demonstrators, also keeps careful note of which civil rights leaders read such "radical publications" as The Nation and The New Republic. He says the "tip-off" that Communist influence is involved comes when someone "talks about social change."

Intelligence unit members say they have been successful—but decline to elaborate on just what evidence of conspiracy they have discovered. "One reason we're so effective is we've kept our actions quiet," says a Houston police captain sitting beneath a citation proclaiming him an honorary member of George Wallace's staff. "We haven't let people know what we're doing."

But all undercover work isn't fruitful. Recently a reporter accompanied two agents as they drove through Houston for two hours, apparently following another car. Suddenly the agents stopped their car in a parking lot, and the officers stared at a small white house for another hour.

No one entered or left the house, and one of the agents eventually started the engine. "I guess he wasn't there," he said mysteriously.

CONFRONTING THE URBAN WILDERNESS

Robert F. Kennedy

To speak of the urban condition is to speak of the condition of American life. . . .

The city is not just housing and stores. It is not just education and employment, parks and theaters, banks and shops. It is a place where men should be able to live in dignity and security and harmony, where the great achievements of modern civilization and the ageless pleasures afforded by natural beauty should be available to all.

If this is what we want—and this is what we must want if men are to be free for that 'pursuit of happiness' which was the earliest promise of the American nation—we will need more than poverty programs, housing programs, and employment programs. . . .

We will need an outpouring of imagination, ingenuity, discipline, and hard work, unmatched since the first adventurers set out to conquer the wilderness.

For the problem is the largest we have ever known; and we confront an urban wilderness more formidable and resistant and, in some ways, more frightening than the wilderness faced by the pilgrims or the pioneers. . . .

Long ago, de Tocqueville foresaw the fate of people without community: 'Each of them living apart is a stranger to the fate of all the rest . . . he may be said . . . to have lost his country.' To the extent this is happening it is the gravest ill of all. For loneliness breeds futility and separation—and thus it cripples the life of each man and menaces the life of all his fellows.

7

EDUCATION
Up Against
the Classroom Wall

Though the topics of urban environment, housing, minorities, economics, and politics are each considered separately in this book, they all overlap—perhaps most strikingly in the area of education. The burden of all that's wrong in each of these areas falls hardest on the cities' school systems.

Some critics blame the failure of the public school system on the chaotic street and home environment of urban children. Some, most notably Dr. Arthur Jensen, on the genetic makeup of the black students who are in the majority in the inner-city schools. It is lack of money—again, the bankrupt city—that causes boredom and illiteracy according to the Federal budget watchers. Less spent in Indochina would make more available for teaching machines, film strips, and remedial readers.

But the bitterest analysts see the ineffective urban school as the result of a conscious plot to keep the urban poor stupid and therefore politically powerless. This, so the theory goes, is important to the people in power who shudder over the lessons of history: Revolutionary politics has always begun in the cities with the descendants of dispossessed peasants making up the body of the revolution and the intellectuals, writers, and artists forming the head. The proponents of this view adopt political strategies to win community control of the schools, another movement manifesting the politics of "Power of the People" represented in Section 6. Here the people are reacting, not to an impotent city hall, but to fire-trap schools, tired teachers, and dull courses, demanding changes which frighten many and exhilarate others. All the diagnoses and prescriptions are summarized in the first article of this section, "What's Gone Wrong with Our Big City Schools?"

The next three selections focus on the actual and ideal commitment of the urban teacher. In his essay, "Teaching Life at an Early Age in the Slums," Jonathan Kozol calls on teachers in slum schools to become revolutionaries. Risking their job security is a small price to pay, he thinks, for the rewards of working for social change along with the people of the communities in which the schools are located.

In the short story, "Uncle Tom's Cabin: An Alternate Ending," LeRoi Jones implies that white teachers can't do anything for black students because white teachers are incurably racist. (The effect of the teacher's prejudice on the child's ability is examined for the enlightenment of inner-city teachers in *Pygmalion in the Classroom: Teacher Expectation and the Pupil's Intellectual Ability* by Robert Rosenthal and Lenore Jacobson, who argue that what teacher expects teacher gets—be it excellence or "culturally disadvantaged" behavior.)

In "Wanted: Teaching Job in City School," a pair of letters written by a new elementary school teacher in Chicago, Toni Hall explains her decision not to quit and run away to a "free" school in the mountains, but instead to work for change within the system. After one year of teaching, she is convinced that "We have to take our stand in the cities. . . ."

The next six authors discuss what taking a creative stand on behalf of urban students could mean. In an autobiographical essay, "On the Rim of Belonging" Alma Bagu, a Puerto Rican mother of four children, describes the suffering of Spanish-speaking children in all English-speaking schools. She makes a strong case for bilingual education. In the poem "The San Francisco Weather Report", Richard Brautigan's vision of a transformed high school curriculum corresponds with the mood and ideas of all who find standard subject matter completely out of touch with their personal experience and curiosities.

After probing the reasons for the failures of the public school system, Kenneth Clark prescribes six specific remedies in "Alternatives to Urban

Public Schools," originally a speech given at Stanford University. Paul Goodman, too, calls for the end of the present system and a new approach to the education of urban elementary students in "Mini-Schools: A Prescription for the Reading Problem." This article not only presents an exciting blueprint of how a system of tiny neighborhood schools would work; it also shows how important the city itself is as a stimulus and source of learning.

The last two articles tell what is happening and what could happen to education and the cities when students get involved in solving real community problems instead of doing workbook exercises. In "First Year at Federal City," David Swanston reports on problems and progress at Federal City College in Washington, D.C. In "Once Upon a Time—A Fable of Student Power," Neil Postman uses the powers of his imagination to show that if the energy and talents of students were used as a resource, the cities could be saved from the filth, pollution, schools, and crime that very well may, but need not, destroy them.

WHAT'S GONE WRONG
IN OUR BIG-CITY SCHOOLS?

Changing Times

Angry parents . . . picketing teachers . . . broken school windows . . . dropouts . . . embattled school boards . . . violence in the classroom. Day by day, newspapers tell the grim story of turmoil in our city schools.

A dozen years ago, all the talk about education seemed to focus on the suburbs. Parents complained that local schools weren't doing enough to prepare their kids for getting into college. Magazines and newspapers ran story after story about "new math," foreign languages in elementary school, new teaching techniques, modern science courses. Hardly anyone, it appeared, was much concerned about education in the cities, particularly the "inner cities" where the poor were concentrated. Yet, it was there— because they got so little national attention—that some of the country's most explosive educational problems were brewing. Now almost every major city faces the consequences: a massive school crisis.

THE TRANSFORMATION OF THE CITIES

Look at the dramatic change in city populations and you begin to understand the core of the problem. For years hundreds of thousands of poor people, especially Negroes, poured from rural areas, mostly in the South, into the large cities. At the same time, white families (and recently black middle-class families) have been leaving the central cities. Result: Though a majority of Americans now live in metropolitan areas, the inner cities are gradually becoming inhabited mostly by the black poor. As a consequence, black enrollment in the public schools is rapidly rising, too. Some examples [1969 figures]:

Baltimore	*64%*	*St. Louis*	*63%*
Philadelphia	*58%*	*Indianapolis*	*33%*
New York (+ about	*30%*	*Boston*	*26%*
22% Puerto Rican)		*Cincinnati*	*42%*
Detroit	*58%*	*Newark*	*71%*
Chicago	*52%*	*Pittsburgh*	*38%*
Cleveland	*56%*	*Buffalo*	*35%*
Dist. of Columbia	*92%*	*Rochester*	*27%*

What these children inherit as they take over city schools are conditions that seem designed to throttle education:

Almost total segregation.   A survey of 75 cities revealed that three out of four black elementary pupils attends schools that are 90% or more Negro. This means that they spend most of their time with disadvantaged children who, like themselves, are poorly prepared for school.

Severe overcrowding.   Example: In the District of Columbia a couple of years ago the one predominantly white school operated at lower than top capacity while Negro high schools were running at well over full capacity.

Old buildings and obsolete equipment.   "Inner-city schools," said the National Advisory Commission on Civil Disorders (Kerner Commission) last year, "are not only overcrowded; they also tend to be the oldest and most poorly equipped." According to another study of a typical big-city school system, 30% of the children in the lower economic half of the city go to schools that are at least 50 years old. None in the upper income half attend schools that old.

Lack of money.   With the middle class in their exodus to the suburbs went the tax dollar. Taxable property valuation, the most common basis for school financing, failed to keep pace with city needs. Besides, new highways, bridges, federal and state buildings, and slum clearance programs, all non tax - paying, have been eating up city space that might have yielded revenues for the schools. "Our society," said the Commission on Civil Disorders, "spends less money educating ghetto children than children of suburban families." The need, as many educators see it, is exactly the reverse.

Inexperienced teachers.   Qualified teachers shy away from the rough conditions of the inner city. A survey in Chicago a few years ago revealed that in the ten schools at the lowest economic level only slightly over 60% of the teachers were fully certified. In the ten schools at the highest economic level, 90% were. The Kerner report noted that many teachers, with no special training for work with disadvantaged students, often begin with negative attitudes toward the students, and become more and more dissatisfied with their jobs. Teachers who don't expect much from their students, as the report says, don't get much out of them.

Scanty materials, irrelevant courses.   City kids aren't given the wide variety of classroom materials—magazines, paperback books, filmstrips, recordings—that many suburban youngsters are accustomed to. The materials and courses they do get are aimed at middle-class students and don't have much connection with their own experiences. To the poor Negro child, school, like the white world ouside his ghetto, seems alien.

The effects of these conditions are obvious: "For the children of the racial ghetto," says the commission, "the schools have failed to provide the educational experience which could help overcome the effects of discrimination and deprivation." And the report adds, "The bleak record of public education for ghetto children is getting worse."

In the essential skills—verbal and reading ability—inner-city children fall steadily behind. The average Negro first-grader in a northeastern city gets somewhat lower test scores on standard achievement tests than a white pupil. By the sixth grade he is 1.6 grades behind; by the twelfth, he's 3.3 grades behind the white student. But by then thousands have quit.

Smoldering resentment is the end product. "The typical riot participant," said the Commission on Civil Disorders, "was a high school dropout." Ghetto adults as well as ghetto youth are aflame with anger against the schools. And it's this feeling that is now at the core of the school crisis in the cities.

WHAT'S TO BE DONE?

As the facts about city schools emerged in report after report, certain remedies seemed obvious, and many cities, supported by the federal government, moved to put them into effect. Yet the crisis grew worse and is now more acute than ever. What happened? What *is* the answer?

Desegregation. One of the first things that had to be done, it seemed clear, was to desegregate the schools. Back in 1954, the Supreme Court had ruled that segregated education was unequal education. Many studies subsequently showed that minority children do lag when they are educated in segregated schools. Most educators believe the reason is not race but poverty—poor children perform better in schools with more affluent children than they do in schools where most kids are poor. That's because achievement is affected more by the background and aspirations of other students than by the quality of the school's facilities or even of its teachers. And most Negroes are poor. Only 25% are middle class, that is, have a white-collar occupation, a high school education or a middle-class income, compared with 60% of whites.

The problem, then, was how to achieve a mix. Many experiments have been tried, with varied success. New Haven "paired" some elementary schools and redistricted a couple of junior high schools to change racial balance. Pasadena redistricted its high schools and adopted an open enrollment plan. Evanston began to reduce racial imbalance substantially in its elementary schools. In Berkeley, where the school population is about 41% black, elementary schools have been mixed to reflect this percentage. This required moving 2,000 white and 2,000 black children. According to one report, predictions that teachers would resign and white families move away did not come true. Right now, intensive teacher training and community relations programs are under way to make the plan work.

One of the most controversial methods being used to mix children of different races is "busing." Nearly a thousand students from Boston's black ghetto are bused to schools in 20 surrounding areas. Rochester transports some 10% of its black children to outer communities. New Haven, Waterbury, and Hartford move Negro and Puerto Rican students to a couple of dozen suburbs.

The Nixon administration has said that it will enforce the provisions of the Civil Rights Act of 1964 that help schools desegregate and cut off funds from those that should but don't. Some states—New York, California, Massachusetts, Washington—have gone further than the federal government in outlawing racial imbalance in schools.

Still, desegregation has been extremely slow. One reason is bitter white resistance. Lawsuits by individuals against busing are under way in several communities. The heavy concentration of black families in large cities also makes racial balance difficult to achieve. As a result, schools are now more segregated than ever.

The push toward racial balance will continue, but it certainly offers no immediate solution. Black families are resentful about its failure; many say they don't want to depend on the tolerance of whites to make it work; and most now demand that more be done to improve inner-city schools.

Compensatory education.   Most cities, using federal aid, are trying to give special attention to poor children to help them catch up with the rest of the population. At least 20,000 programs around the country offer remedial help in reading, arithmetic, speaking, vocabulary development and so on. In Milwaukee, poor children who showed a lack of speaking ability received intensive training by speech therapists. In Detroit, remedial reading centers were established. Flint has a program involving parents directed at raising the level of underachieving Negro pupils. One of the best-known projects is the More Effective Schools Program in New York City. It provides about 20,000 disadvantaged children with small classes, specialists and a variety of extra services and materials.

There's much argument about the effectiveness of compensatory programs. The New York City effort appears to help youngsters who are continuously exposed to it. Many of the other programs around the country, according to the Office of Education, have shown positive results. But there's not much evidence that improvement has been substantial or lasting, and certainly it hasn't been great enough to wipe out the gap between poor and nonpoor students. Compensatory education, says one influential critic, is a "Band-aid approach" to the problem, not a cure.

Many other approaches are being tried—"adoption" of ghetto schools by colleges for experimental projects, student-to-student tutoring, home visits by specialists, concentration of multiple services—educational, health, job training—on small groups of young people. The greatest gains occur when everything that seems to block achievement is taken into account—hunger, a broken home, lack of motivation, poor health.

A crucial problem in the ghetto is the lack of specially trained teachers, particularly young men who can understand and identify with poor children. The Teacher Corps tries to deal with this but is too small. That's the trouble with most approaches so far. Well-intentioned as they may be, they barely scratch the surface of the problem.

THE LOCAL-CONTROL RUCKUS

Everyone who looks into ghetto problems agrees on at least one thing: If there is to be any real improvement in the schools, local citizens, especially parents, must become involved in the education of their kids. Now ghetto parents *are* getting involved and the result is violent controversy over local control of schools.

Bitter at white resistance to desegregation and the failure of the city to educate their children, Negro parents declare: Now we'll tell the schools what we want for our kids just as middle-class white people do in the suburbs and small towns all over America.

"Many of you now accuse us of . . . 'separating ourselves' from the mainstream of the nation," says Dr. Norman Johnson, a Negro professor at the University of Pittsburgh. "The hard bitter truth . . . is that we have never . . . , regardless of personal success, been in the mainstream of American life. . . . We feel our responsibility now is to *our* community alone. . . . We have determined that *we* will take over the direction and control of our children's schools.

"We may make some mistakes. However, these mistakes can hardly be more serious than the ones being made at present. They certainly will not be as long-standing. Because we, holding the welfare of the children as our only criterion, will effect change as soon as we . . . deem it to be necessary. . . . When people have an opportunity to be really involved . . . , when they know that they can be part of making decisions that have meaning, we will not have to worry about parental apathy or student disinterest. When members of the school board know that they are *accountable* to all the people whose children they serve, and *to the students themselves,* they will [respond] . . . to the needs and desires of these groups."

Opponents argue that decentralization plays into the hands of local pressure groups. Teachers say it undercuts tenure and the criteria for teacher selection. We've spent years, they argue, taking education out of city politics in order to improve professional standards; decentralization throws it right back into politics.

Local boards, goes another objection, cannot provide a wide enough range of programs or sufficient financial support. What's needed is the opposite of decentralization—a broader base of support, more metropolitan, more state, more federal commitment. All that local control will do is turn anger away from the city board, says the president of the New York City teachers union. "It gives people the trappings of power and local control without really giving them the ability to do anything." And he predicts increased conflict.

Last year's upheaval in New York City revealed the depth of the bitterness behind the controversy. The clash between the teachers union and a local school board in Brooklyn produced strikes that paralyzed the city schools, affecting over a million children. Other clashes occurred this year and more may be ahead.

Despite the controversy, many cities are talking about local control; some are trying it. Washington, D.C.'s Morgan community school has a locally elected board that decides how funds will be spent, what kind of staff and what curriculum changes are needed. In Los Angeles, 13 schools have "critical authority" over their own budgets. St. Louis involves local citizens in planning through "Parent Congresses." Chicago is trying out a four-school subdistrict. In Boston several schools are run by a local board supported by state funds.

Though evidence is scanty, the effects of decentralization for the moment look promising. A *Wall Street Journal* report on Brooklyn's Ocean Hill-Brownsville district, scene of last year's trouble, says that under local control student interest is high, discipline has improved, suspensions and vandalism have declined. A new individualized reading program has "turned on" children who once resisted reading. Chief reasons for progress: involvement of residents as "community liaison workers" and classroom aides; imaginative teaching; determined young teachers (most of whom happen to be white) who believe in local control.

There's no longer any real argument about whether inner-city residents ought to have a voice in the operation of their schools. The only question is how much actual control they should have. "The day has passed," said President Nixon's task force on education, "when external agencies . . . can tell the black man, the Puerto Rican . . . in the ghetto what is good for him. His ideas and his resources must form the basis of any new approaches."

Actually, much of the argument about control is semantic. Not many parents, according to a 13-city study for the Urban Coalition, really want to operate their schools. What they're after is "accountability," the right to see that the schools do their job. "What we are talking about is not parents . . . becoming teachers and principals," says one of the most militant local-control supporters. ". . . We are not telling [professionals] to get out. . . . We *are* saying that we want to be in there to see that [they] do the job of educating our children."

IT ALL COMES DOWN TO MONEY

The arguments about local control will spread. The push toward desegregation will continue. New compensatory education experiments will be tried. However, most experts now agree that nothing will really make a dent in the problem until ghetto schools get a much bigger chunk of the education dollar. But the outlook for more money is bleak.

Cities are going broke. As pointed out earlier, middle-class families moving to the suburbs take their taxes with them. In Baltimore the tax dollar behind each pupil dropped 19% in five years; at the same time it rose by over 10% in Maryland's rural and suburban areas. Cleveland suffered a 10% erosion of the tax base while noncity areas of the state gained almost 5%.

Another pressure on cities: They have to spend more on nonschool services—health, welfare, safety. On the average they can allocate only about a third of local taxes to education. Suburbs can give two-thirds of their income. In many places the difference is much greater.

State aid is off balance. State legislatures have traditionally favored rural areas over the cities. In the past noncity schools needed the help more; now the situation is reversed. Today city kids often get proportionately less aid from state funds than rural and suburban kids. In New York the discrepancy is over $100 per child. In some cities—Chicago, Detroit, Los Angeles, San Antonio—court suits have been filed to try to change unfair state allocations.

Even if some cities and states do manage to raise additional dollars, they can hardly produce enough to close the gap between the suburbs and the cities. A study of the 37 largest cities showed that $449 is spent per student compared with $573 in their suburbs, and the difference is widening.

Will the federal government produce the needed funds? The National School Boards Association, which not long ago opposed federal aid, says it should. The new Commissioner of Education, Dr. James E. Allen Jr., has said that he favors a program of "massive" federal aid to city schools.

He plans to develop and present to Congress an "urban education act" that would focus on big-city problems.

Meantime, nothing big enough is in the works right now. According to the National School Boards Association, as many as 30 of the largest cities may not have enough money to open their schools on time next autumn. Those that do open face continual crisis and turbulence. Time is running short.

TEACHING LIFE AT AN EARLY AGE IN THE SLUMS

Jonathan Kozol

In future years many of us will be asked by our children and grandchildren what we were doing when the students in the schools of the Negro slums of America were dying in their classrooms. I hope that some of us—above all, some of our teachers—will be able to give better answers than the ones that we have been giving up to now.

So much of the behavior of our teachers is bound in and delimited by a terrible acquiescence to an outworn code of "professional" reservation, "professional" withdrawal, "professional" restraint. Many teachers, like the rest of the people who know what is happening in the slums, are torn with shame and overwhelmed with their perceptions of the daily desiccation of the hopes of a million Negro children.

The teachers know well what is going on within their classrooms, but time and the timeworn habit of automatic self-denial have silenced their recognitions and compelled them to suppress their knowledge in the effort to fulfill the specific and clearly delineated obligation of an obedient teacher.

There is a higher obligation, however, than getting across the reading lesson. There is also the obligation to be an honest human being. The bewildered teacher, terrified to the very fibers of her spirit and shaken to the very center of her soul, smiles out at her black pupils, turns with them to the soiled flag above the doorway, and parrots a daily recitation of required fealty to a government which still claims, despite all evidence, to be "one nation, indivisible, with liberty and justice for all."

At times the irony is overwhelming. The books are junk, the paint peels, the rooms are so overcrowded that pupils can scarcely hear each other talking. In the midst of it all stands the kindly, well-intending white school-lady and she tells her Negro pupils to be thankful that they do not live in a nation like Russia or on a continent like Africa.

There is a great deal of talk now about technological innovations in the public classroom—new kinds of science, new forms of social studies, new language laboratories, new gadgets and new gimmickry. But what is the use of all this clever and expensive hardware if the same old goals are still sought after and the same old sad deceits still sold to children?

There is also, as we know, a great cry now being voiced to involve the ghetto communities in more meaningful participation in their public schools. But, again, what is the use of involving a black parent in the life of a ghetto classroom if she arrives there only to hear a teacher lying to her child?

I do not like to speak in terms that are needlessly apocalyptic, and I would not wish to be in the position of heightening the dangers that are ahead of us by making dire predictions. On the other hand, it is apparent to me daily—as I leave my apartment in a black Boston slum, as I talk to many of the kids and listen to their parents in the evenings—that "rebellion" and "revolution" are no longer inappropriate terms with which to describe the kind of mood that is developing.

What I am trying to say, without rancor but in the most serious and absolutely urgent tone that I can muster, is that the American teacher, no matter at what level, is somehow going to have to figure out a way to *join* this revolution and to become a part of living history. If she can, she may not only command—she may also for the first time be able to deserve— her pupils' loyalty.

There are thousands of young, bright, brave and revolutionary pupils in the liberal colleges of this country. It is up to our government to find a way to get the best of these young people directly into urban classrooms, to make it worth their while, to spare them from repressive educators and to enable them to achieve a strong and swift liaison with the black communities: a liaison based upon their mutual recognition of the need for immediate and overwhelming social change.

If we can do it for the poor and wretched of several dozen other nations, surely we can do it for the city-bound black people of our own society.

UNCLE TOM'S CABIN: ALTERNATE ENDING

LeRoi Jones

"6½" *was* the answer. But it seemed to irritate Miss Orbach. Maybe not the answer—the figure itself, but the fact it should be there, and in such loose possession.

"OH who is he to know such a thing? That's really improper to set up such liberations. And moreso."

What came into her head next she could hardly understand. A breath of cold. She did shudder, and her fingers clawed at the tiny watch she wore hidden in the lace of the blouse her grandmother had given her when she graduated teacher's college.

Ellen, Eileen, Evelyn . . . Orbach. She could be any of them. Her personality was one of theirs. As specific and as vague. The kindly menace of leading a life in whose balance evil was a constant intrigue but grew uglier and more remote as it grew stronger. She would have loved to do something really dirty. But nothing she had ever heard of was dirty enough. So she contented herself with good, i.e., purity, as a refuge from mediocrity. But being unconscious, or largely remote from her own source, she would only admit to the possibility of grace. Not God. She would not be trapped into *wanting* even God.

So remorse took her easily. For any reason. A reflection in a shop window, of a man looking in vain for her ankles. (Which she covered with heavy colorless woolen.) A sudden gust of warm damp air around her legs or face. Long dull rains that turned her from her books. Or, as was the case this morning, some completely uncalled-for shaking of her silent doctrinaire routines.

"6½" had wrenched her unwillingly to exactly where she was. Teaching the 5th grade, in a grim industrial complex of northeastern America; about 1942. And how the social doth pain the anchorite.

Nothing made much sense in such a context. People moved around, and disliked each other for no reason. Also, and worse, they said they loved each other, and usually for less reason, Miss Orbach thought. Or would have if she did.

And in this class sat 30 dreary sons and daughters of such circumstance. Specifically, the thriving children of the thriving urban lower middle classes. Postmen's sons and factory-worker debutantes. Making a great run for America; now prosperity and the war had silenced for a time the intelligent cackle of tradition. Like a huge, grey, bubbling vat, the country, in its apocalyptic version of history and the future, sought now, in its equally apocalyptic profile of itself as it had urged swiftly its own death since the Civil War. To promise. Promise. And that to be that all who had ever dared to live here would die when the people and interests who had been its rulers died. The intelligent poor now were being admitted. And with them a great many Negroes . . . who would die when the rest of the dream died, not even understanding that they, like Ishmael, should have been the sole survivors. But now they were being tricked. "6½" the boy said. After the fidgeting and awkward silence. One little black boy, raised his hand, and looking at the tip of Miss Orbach's nose said 6½. And then he smiled, very embarrassed and very sure of being wrong.

I would have said, "No, boy, shut up and sit down. You are wrong. You don't know anything. Get out of here and be very quick. Have you no idea what you're getting involved in? My God . . . you nigger, get out of here and save yourself, while there's time. Now beat it." But those people had already been convinced. Read Booker T. Washington one day, when there's time. What that led to. The 6½'s moved for power . . . and there seemed no other way.

So three elegant Negroes in light grey suits grin and throw me through the window. They are happy and I am sad. It is an ample test of an idea. And besides "6½" is the right answer to the woman's question.

[The psychological and the social. The spiritual and the practical. Keep them together and you profit, maybe, someday, come out on top. Separate them, and you go along the road to the commonest of Hells. The one we westerners love to try to make art out of.]

The woman looked at the little brown boy. He blinked at her, trying again not to smile. She tightened her eyes, but her lips flew open. She tightened her lips, and her eyes blinked like the boy's. She said, "How do you get that answer?" The boy told her. "Well, it's right," she said, and the boy fell limp, straining even harder to look sorry. The negro in back of the answerer pinched him, and the boy shuddered. A little white girl next to him touched his hand, and he tried to pull his own hand away with his brain.

"Well, that's right, class. That's exactly right. You may sit down now Mr. McGhee."

Later on in the day, after it had started exaggeratedly to rain very hard and very stupidly against the windows and soul of her 5th-grade class, Miss Orbach became convinced that the little boy's eyes were too large. And in fact they did bulge almost grotesquely white and huge against his bony heavy-veined skull. Also, his head was much too large for the rest of the scrawny body. And he talked too much, and caused too many disturbances. He also stared out the window when Miss Orbach herself would drift off into her sanctuary of light and hygiene even though her voice carried the inanities of arithmetic seemingly without delay. When she came back to the petty social demands of 20th-century humanism the boy would be watching something walk across the playground. OH, it just would not work.

She wrote a note to Miss Janone, the school nurse, and gave it to the boy, McGhee, to take to her. The note read: "Are the large eyes a sign of ———?"

Little McGhee, of course, could read, and read the note. But he didn't of course understand the last large word which was misspelled anyway. But he tried to memorize the note, repeating to himself over and over again its contents . . . sounding the last long word out in his head, as best he could.

Miss Janone wiped her big nose and sat the boy down, reading the note. She looked at him when she finished, then read the note again, crumpling it on her desk.

She looked in her medical book and found out what Miss Orbach meant. Then she said to the little Negro, "Dr. Robard will be here in 5 minutes. He'll look at you." Then she began doing something to her eyes and fingernails.

When the doctor arrived he looked closely at McGhee and said to Miss Janone, "Miss Orbach is confused."

McGhee's mother thought that too. Though by the time little McGhee had gotten home he had forgotten the "long word" at the end of the note.

"Is Miss Orbach the woman who told you to say sangwich instead of sammich," Louise McGhee giggled.

"No, that was Miss Columbe."

"Sangwich, my christ. That's worse than sammich. Though you better not let me hear you saying sammich either . . . like those Davises."

"I don't say sammich, mamma."

"What's the word then?"

"Sandwich."

"That's right. And don't let anyone tell you anything else. Teacher or otherwise. Now I wonder what that word could've been?"

"I donno. It was very long. I forgot it."

Eddie McGhee Sr. didn't have much of an idea what the word could be either. But he had never been to college like his wife. It was one of the most conspicuously dealt with factors of their marriage.

So the next morning Louise McGhee, after calling her office, the Child Welfare Bureau, and telling them she would be a little late, took a trip to the school, which was on the same block as the house where the McGhees lived, to speak to Miss Orbach about the long word which she suspected might be injurious to her son and maybe to Negroes In General. This suspicion had been bolstered a great deal by what Eddie Jr. had told her about Miss Orbach, and also equally by what Eddie Sr. had long maintained about the nature of White People In General. "Oh well," Louise McGhee sighed. "I guess I better straighten this sister out." And that is exactly what she intended.

When the two McGhees reached the Center Street school the next morning Mrs. McGhee took Eddie along with her to the principal's office, where she would request that she be allowed to see Eddie's teacher.

Miss Day, the old, lady principal, would then send Eddie to his class with a note for his teacher, and talk to Louise McGhee, while she was waiting, on general problems of the neighborhood. Miss Day was a very old woman who had despised Calvin Coolidge. She was also, in one sense, exotically liberal. One time she had forbidden old man Seidman to wear his pince-nez anymore, as they looked too snooty. Center Street sold more war stamps than any other grammar school in the area, and had a fairly good track team.

Miss Orbach was going to say something about Eddie McGhee's being late, but he immediately produced Miss Day's note. Then Miss Orbach looked at Eddie again, as she had when she had written her own note the day before.

She made Mary Ann Fantano the monitor and stalked off down the dim halls. The class had a merry time of it when she left, and Eddie won an extra 2 Nabisco graham crackers by kissing Mary Ann while she sat at Miss Orbach's desk.

When Miss Orbach got to the principal's office and pushed open the door she looked directly into Louis McGhee's large brown eyes, and fell deeply and hopelessly in love.

WANTED: TEACHING JOB IN CITY SCHOOL

Toni Hall

January 31, 1970

New Schools Exchange Newsletter
2840 Hidden Valley Lane
Santa Barbara, California 93103

Dear Friends,

Please put me in your "positions wanted" column: I'm presently teaching (no certificate; have a B.S.; this is my first year teaching) at an inner city elementary school in Chicago. The kids are beautiful but the adults (teachers) are impossible. I'd like to work together, starting next fall, with people who believe we need to change our society and who think that education can be one of the ways we can do this. I'm thinking of a free school, a community school, where people are free to experiment, and where teachers and students desire to grow together in the living and learning experience. The school could be away in the mountains or in the middle of a city. I'm teaching younger kids now, but I'd like to try older ones, anywhere from 8 to 18. . . . I just need enough money to live on. . . .

Thanks for your help. I think what you're doing is beautiful and also desperately needed to bring people together.

Sincerely,
Toni Hall

February 4, 1970

New Schools Exchange Newsletter
2840 Hidden Valley Lane
Santa Barbara, California 93103

Dear Friends,

Just having read in your Newsletter about people and schools has clarified in my mind the kind of place I'd like to be at next year, so if it's not too late, I'd appreciate your using the following instead of what I sent you previously (about Jan. 31):

When I heard about the concept and existence of free schools, my first impulse was to want to get as far away as possible from the cities and the present system which dehumanizes and deadens children, to a beautiful place that was for them, where they could really learn and grow. I'm teaching this year at an elementary school in Chicago's inner city. Some of the new, young teachers at the school have gotten together in trying to change things at the school. It's been slow going but we've had some success, particularly in getting together with the community to start solving mutual problems (an activity which the public schools distrust—they should!). The main problems for me are job insecurity (I'm not a certified teacher and I've just been reassigned to another school, putting an end to my participation in the things we've gotten going) and the "disunity" of our group—almost all the active teachers live outside the community. But in thinking about all this, I realized that I still feel that this is the place, if not quite the way, to work: that teaching kids who could afford to leave the city was not going to be changing any of the things I've lived with this year but just perpetuating the present system. The city's children are stuck with her schools; I can leave, but they can't. I think we have to fight for the creation of schools, street schools, community schools, that are free schools too; we have to take our stand in the cities in united, if small, groups of people committed to changing the educational system and to freeing the children in it for a creative life. I'd like to hear from people and schools that are doing this now or believe it can be done and want to try. Any city will do.

Thanks again.

Toni Hall

ON THE RIM OF BELONGING

Alma Bagu

Sitting in a classroom with about 33 English-speaking kids and staring at words on a blackboard that to me were as foreign as Egyptian hieroglyphics is one of my early recollections of school. The teacher had come up to my desk and bent over, putting her face close to mine.

"My name is Mrs. Newman," she said, as if the exaggerated mouthing of her words would make me understand their meaning. I nodded "yes" because I felt that was what she wanted me to do. But she just threw up her hands in a gesture of despair, and touched her fingers to her head to signify to the class I was dense, whereupon all 33 classmates fell into gales of laughter. From that day on, school became an ordeal I was forced to endure.

In the early grades I attended a special class for Spanish-speaking children who spoke no English. I did well in this class and learned the simple phrases I was taught, but when I was in my regular class, I would not participate in oral discussions nor answer questions because I was painfully self-conscious of my heavy Spanish accent.

Most of the time the Puerto Rican children stuck together because we felt more at ease with each other. "Spic" was a word with which I was very familiar. The other children at school rarely called us by our names. They just said, "hey, spic," and clucked like hens, making fun of our language.

People in school seemed annoyed when we spoke Spanish among ourselves. It was as if our teachers had taken upon themselves the task of straining out every drop of Puerto Rican culture we possessed to mold us into what they thought we should be. Some teachers would lecture us on how rude we were to speak a "strange" language in the presence of those who could not understand it. (This concern for propriety never made much sense to me, since the white English-speaking children didn't associate with us anyway. But I have to admit, I got a kick out of making the English-speaking children feel as uncomfortable around me as they made me feel around them.) Some teachers handed out punishments to those who spoke Spanish in school ("I must speak English in school" written five hundred times). Some Puerto Rican kids who found difficulty with English were considered retarded and placed in C.R.M.D. classes.

Literature was constantly being given us to bring home to our parents. Some of the literature insisted that our parents speak English in the home. Other pamphlets contained menus that the boards of health and education felt we should have. They warned of the perils of all-starch diets. For some reason they believed we ate nothing but rice and beans for breakfast, lunch, and dinner.

My mother read all the pamphlets, for they were printed in Spanish as well as English, and then tore them up and threw them away with the trash. "I feed my children well," she would say, and go right on speaking Spanish at home. Now, as an adult, I am grateful to her for not conforming and keeping our culture alive, at least in our home. But as a child I felt ashamed; I wanted my mother to be like the English-speaking mothers, who went to P.T.A. meetings and accompanied our class on trips.

I never tried to achieve scholastic success for fear of being laughed at for even trying. By the time I went to high school, I was completely fed up with education. I was part of a Puerto Rican clique. The only others treated worse than us, I felt, were the Negroes, a feeling that gave us a sense of superiority over them. We did our best to aggravate our teachers and white classmates, and there was among us an unspoken pact to speak English only when necessary.

I dropped out of school at 16, and later, when I had my own children, I wanted them to speak only English in order to avoid the same problems I had. For the sake of making things easier for my children when they went to school, I abandoned so many of the beautiful customs of my culture. I made little *Americanos* of them so they would not feel like aliens in the classroom. I finished the job on my children that my teachers started on me. I denied my offsprings some of my most beautiful memories. As a child I would ask for my mother's blessing as I left the house. *"Benedicion,"* I would say. *"Dios te bendiga,"* she would always answer. God bless you. The candles of appeasement to the saints and friendly spirits, which belonged to the religion my mother brought with her from Puerto Rico, no longer burn. The rebelliousness and desire to be known as a Puerto Rican—whether out of pride or a feeling that I couldn't make it in a white American society—was gone. Because I wanted my children to be accepted by the *Americanos*, I closed the door on my own heritage.

The irony of the whole thing was that my children weren't accepted anyway. One day my daughter came home from school, her hazel eyes brimming over with tears that spilled onto her tan cheeks. "I'm not a dirty spic," she cried. And my son reported to me that he was the second dirtiest kid in his class. "The dirtiest one is a colored boy. I'm darkest after him." His classmates, he said, were always asking what he was. I had taught him to say he was an American. But even his teacher, he said, wouldn't accept that answer. His olive complexion had made him different, and being Puerto Rican had set him apart.

Faced with the fear that the school system would make drop-outs of my children too, I moved from a fairly good neighborhood to one that was well populated with Puerto Ricans—in other words a "ghetto"—where my children would be—and were—accepted for what they are.

THE SAN FRANCISCO WEATHER REPORT

Richard Brautigan

Gee, You're so Beautiful That It's Starting to Rain

Oh, Marcia,
I Want your long blonde beauty
to be taught in high school,
so kids will learn that God
lives like music in the skin
and sounds like a sunshine harpsichord.
I want high school report cards
    to look like this:

Playing with Gentle Glass Things
    A

Computer Magic
    A

Writing Letters to Those You Love
    A

Finding out about Fish
    A

Marcia's Long Blonde Beauty
    A+!

ALTERNATIVES TO URBAN PUBLIC SCHOOLS

Kenneth B. Clark

The evidence of a massive breakdown in the efficiency of the public schools in American cities has now become a matter of public discussion. It is no secret that our urban public schools are no longer maintaining high standards of educational quality. To put it bluntly, these schools are inferior, and, so far, no one has found the formula for stemming this rising tide of educational inefficiency.

How do we explain these facts? Our urban schools are spawning hundreds of thousands of functional illiterates who are incapable of playing a constructive role in our society and who cannot be integrated into the economy without costly remedial education, even in such basics as reading and arithmetic. Many of these human beings are doomed to lives of random aggressiveness and self-destruction. Yet, as the negative symptoms in our schools grow more and more conspicuous, the ability to act positively is blocked by the rationalizations and self-serving explanations of many educators.

The problems are explained in terms of the changing racial composition of the schools. The basic racist implications of this explanation are obscured by a variety of euphemisms. The cumulative educational retardation of these young people is explained in terms of persistent racial discrimination, the high percentage of broken homes, and the whole pattern of "cultural deprivation," which allegedly interfere with the ability of these children to learn to read and to understand the language and logic of mathematics.

The common factor in all these explanations, however, is the assumption that the breakdown in efficiency in the public schools is not to be understood in terms of any deficiencies in the schools themselves, in their personnel, methods, or administration, but rather in terms of deficiencies on the part of the present crop of students and their parents. To borrow an analogy from industry: The raw materials are defective, so the product must be defective, in spite of efficient plant management.

Sometimes educators argue that if they were to receive more funds for public education, our city public schools could be made more efficient in spite of the societal, community, and human deficiencies. With more funds, they say, we could have small class size, team teaching, language laboratories, teaching machines, more audio-visual aids, and more impressive windowless schools blocking out the degradations of the ghetto. It is claimed that these educational "innovations" will eventually raise the academic achievement of children in our ghetto schools.

The evidence against this is quietly ignored. It is further obscured by the suggestion that increased compensatory educational programs will somehow provide the answer to the present crisis. Without getting into the current argument about whether these compensatory programs actually do or do not work in the long run, it seems to this observer that we are ignoring the chief problem posed by these programs. In spite of the positive fact that they help some of these children to fulfill their academic potentials, the uncritical proliferation of compensatory educational programs confuses the primary issue—that is, the continued inefficiency of the urban public school system.

The success or failure of these programs—the time, effort, money, good will, and good intentions invested in them—tend to let the regular public school systems off the hook. The administrators of our public schools can point with pride to these programs and deflect attention from the fact that the inefficiency of their schools makes these programs necessary.

Before the influx of minority-group youngsters into urban public schools, the American public school system was justifiably credited with being the chief instrument for making the American dream of upward social, economic, and political mobility a reality. Depressed immigrants from Southern and Eastern Europe could use American public schools as the ladder toward the goals of assimilation and success.

These past successes of American public education seem undebatable. Yet, the fact that American public schools were effective mobility vehicles for white American immigrants makes even more stark and intolerable their present ineffectiveness for minority-group children. Today it appears that the present system of urban public schools is a primary obstacle to the mobility of masses of Negro and other lower status minority-group children.

There remains the disturbing question—a question too painful for many educators themselves to ask—whether the selective process involved in training and promoting educators and administrators for our public schools emphasizes qualities of passivity, conformity, caution, smoothness, and superficial affability, rather than the boldness, creativity, and ability to demand and obtain those things that are essential for solid and effective public education for all children. If this is true—if our system of training and promotion rewards the wrong characteristics—then our hopes for reform are minimal, if not totally futile. In short, we are in bad shape if reform is dependent upon the present educational establishment.

To save our urban schools, we must first demonstrate to the public that the present level of public school inefficiency has reached a stage of public calamity. It must be demonstrated that minority-group children are not the only victims of the monopolistic inefficiency of the present system, but that white children—privileged white children, whose parents understandably seek to protect them by moving to suburbs and enrolling them in private and parochial schools—also suffer, both potentially and immediately.

It must further be demonstrated that business and industry suffer intolerable financial and tax burdens in seeking to maintain a stable economy in the face of the inefficiency of the public schools.

It must be demonstrated that the costs of correctional, welfare, and health services are intolerably high in seeking to cope with the consequences of educational inefficiency—that it would be more economical, even for an affluent society, to pay the price and meet the demands of efficient public education.

It must be demonstrated that a nation that presents itself to the world as the guardian of democracy cannot itself make a mockery of these significant ethical principles by dooming one-tenth of its own population to a lifetime of inhumane misery because of remediable educational deficiencies in its public schools. These things must be understood by the average American if our public schools and our cities are to be effective.

It seems most unlikely, however, that the changes necessary for increased efficiency of our urban public schools will come about simply because they should. Our urban public school systems represent the most rigid forms of bureaucracy. Paradoxically, they are most resilient and innovative in finding ways to resist rational or irrational demands for change.

Why are the public schools so effective in resisting change and so ineffective at educating children? The answer to this question lies in the fact that public school systems are protected public monopolies with only minimal competition from private and parochial schools. Few critics— even severe ones such as myself—dare to question the givens of the present organization of public education in terms of local control of public schools; in terms of existing municipal or political boundaries; or in terms of the rights and prerogatives of boards of education to establish policy and select professional staff, at least nominally or ritualistically if not actually. Few dare to question the relevance of the criteria for the selection of superintendents, principals, and teachers, or the relevance of the entire system to the objectives of public education.

A monopoly need not genuinely concern itself with these matters. So long as local school systems can be assured of stable aid and increasing federal aid, without the accountability that inevitably comes with aggressive competition, it is sentimental to expect any significant increase in the efficiency of our public schools. If there are no alternatives to the current

system—short of present private and parochial schools which are, themselves, approaching the limit of expansion—then the possibilities for improvement in public education are limited.

Alternatives—realistic, aggressive, and viable competitors—to the
present public school systems must be found. The development of competitive school systems will be attacked by the defenders of the present
system as attempts to weaken, if not destroy, public education. This
predictable, self-serving argument can be briefly and accurately disposed
of by demonstrating that truly effective competition strengthens, rather
than weakens, that which deserves to survive.

I would argue further that public education need not be identified
with the present system of organization of public schools. Public education can be more broadly and pragmatically defined in terms of that form
of educational system that functions in the public interest. Given this
definition, it becomes clear that:

> An inefficient system of public schools is not in the public interest.
>
> A system of public schools that destroys rather than develops positive
> human potentialities is not in the public interest.
>
> A system that consumes funds without demonstrating effective returns
> is not in the public interest.
>
> A system that insists that its standards of performance should not,
> or cannot, be judged by those who must pay the cost is not in the
> public interest.
>
> A system that blames its human resources and its society, while
> quietly acquiescing to the very injustices that supposedly limit its
> efficiency, is not in the public interest.

Given these assumptions, therefore, it follows that alternative forms
of public education must be developed if the children of our cities are to
be educated and made constructive members of our society.

In considering alternatives, all attempts must, at the same time, be
made to strengthen our present urban public schools. Such attempts
involve re-examination, revision, and strengthening of curricula, methods,
and personnel selection and evaluation; the development of more rigorous
procedures of supervision; reward for superior performance, along with
the institution of a realistic and tough system of accountability; and the
provision of meaningful ways of involving the parents and the community
in the activities of the school.

In spite of the above, I nonetheless suggest the following as possible
realistic and practical competitors to the present form of urban public
school systems:

1. *Regional state schools*: These schools would be financed by the states and would cut across present urban-suburban boundaries.

2. *Federal regional schools*: These schools would be financed by the federal government out of present state-aid funds or with additional federal funds. These schools would be able to cut through state boundaries and could make provisions for residential students.

3. *College- and university-related open schools*: These schools would be financed by colleges and universities as part of their laboratories in education. They would be open to the public and not restricted to children of faculty and students. Obviously, public students would be selected in terms of constitutional criteria, and their percentage determined by realistic considerations.

4. *Industrial demonstration schools*: These schools would be financed by industrial, business, and commercial firms for their employees and selected members of the public. These would not be vocational schools but elementary and comprehensive high schools of high quality. They would be sponsored by combinations of business and industrial firms in much the same way as various churches and denominations now sponsor and support parochial or sectarian schools.

5. *Labor union-sponsored schools*: These schools would be financed and sponsored by labor unions largely, but not exclusively, for the children of their members.

6. *Army schools*: The Defense Department has been quietly effective in educating some of the casualities of our present public schools. It is hereby suggested that the Department now go into the business of repairing hundreds of thousands of these human casualties with affirmation rather than apology. Schools for adolescent dropouts or educational rejects could be set up by the Defense Department adjacent to camps—though not necessarily as an integral part of the military. If it is necessary that such operations become an integral part of the military, so be it. The goal is to rescue as many of these young people as possible. They are not expendable on the altar of antimilitarist rhetoric.

In my enthusiasm to suggest specific alternatives or competitors to the present public school system, I was even going to suggest that schools be set up by social agencies and foundations. But I thought better of it. I now suggest that the foundations play their most meaningful and traditional role of supporting some of the alternatives suggested above—giving them the initial push.

With a strong, efficient, and demonstrably excellent parallel system of public schools, organized and operating on a quasi-private level, it would be possible to bring back into public education a vitality and dynamism that is now clearly missing. Even the public discussion of these possibilities might clear away some of the dank stagnation that pervades urban education today. American industrial and material wealth was made possible through industrial competition. American educational health may be made possible through educational competition.

If we succeed, we will have returned to the dynamic, affirmative goal of education—namely, to free man of irrational fears, superstitions, and hatreds. Specifically, in America, the goal of democratic education must be to free Americans of the blinding and atrophying shackles of racism. A fearful, passive, apologetic, and inefficient education system cannot help in the attainment of these goals.

If we succeed in finding and developing these, and better, alternatives to the present educational inefficiency, we will not only save countless Negro children from lives of despair and hopelessness; thousands and thousands of white children will also be rescued from cynicism, moral emptiness, and social ineptitude. We will also demonstrate the validity of our democratic system. We will have saved our civilization through saving our cities.

MINI-SCHOOLS:
A PRESCRIPTION FOR THE READING PROBLEM

Paul Goodman

A chief obstacle to children's learning to read is the present school setting in which they have to pick it up. For any learning to be skillful and lasting, it must be or become self-motivated, second nature; for this, the schooling is too impersonal, standardized, and academic. If we tried to teach children to speak, by academic methods in a school-like environment, many would fail and most would stammer.

Although the analogy between learning to speak and learning to read is not exact, it is instructive to pursue it, since speaking is much harder. Learning to speak is a stupendous intellectual achievement. It involves learning to use signs, acquiring a vocabulary, and also mastering an extraordinary kind of algebra—syntax—with almost infinite variables in a large number of sentence forms. We do not know scientifically how infants learn to speak, but almost all succeed equally well, no matter what their class or culture. Every child picks up a dialect, whether "correct" or "incorrect," that is adequate to express the thoughts and needs of his milieu.

We can describe some of the indispensable conditions for learning to speak.

1. The child is constantly exposed to speech related to interesting behavior in which he often shares. ("Now where's your coat? Now we're going to the supermarket, etc.")
2. The speakers are persons important to the child, who often single him out to speak to him or about him.
3. The child plays with the sounds, freely imitates what he hears, and tries to approximate it without interference or correction. He is rewarded by attention and other useful results when he succeeds.
4. Later, the child consolidates by his own act what he has learned. From age three to five he acquires style, accent, and fluency by speaking with his peers, adopting their uniform but also asserting his own tone, rhythm, and mannerisms. He speaks peer speech but is uniquely recognizable as speaking in his own way.

Suppose, by contrast, that we tried to teach speaking academically in a school-like setting:

1. Speaking would be a curricular subject abstracted from the web of activity and reserved for special hours punctuated by bells.
2. It would be a tool subject rather than a way of being in the world.
3. It would not spring from his needs in immediate situations but would be taught according to the teacher's idea of his future advantage, importantly aiming at his getting a job sixteen years later.
4. Therefore, the child would have to be "motivated," the exercises would have to be "fun," etc.
5. The lessons would be arranged in a graded series from simple to complex, for instance on a false theory that monosyllables precede polysyllables, or words precede sentences, or sentences precede words.
6. The teacher's relation to the infant would be further depersonalized by the need to speak or listen to only what fits two dozen other children as well.

7. Being continually called on, corrected, tested, and evaluated to meet a standard in a group, some children would become stutterers; others would devise a phony system of apparently speaking in order to get by, although the speech meant nothing: others would balk at being processed and would purposely become "stupid."

8. Since there is a predetermined range of what can be spoken and how it must be spoken, everybody's speech would be pedantic and standard, without truth to the child's own experience or feeling.

Turn now to teaching reading. These eight disastrous defects are not an unfair caricature of what we do. Reading is treated as abstract, irrelevant to actual needs, instrumental, extrinsically motivated, impersonal, pedantic, not expressive of truth or art. The teaching often produces awkwardness, faking, or balking. Let me also make four further points specific to learning reading:

1. Most people who have learned to read and write fluently have done so on their own, with their own material, whether library books, newspapers, comic books, or street signs. They may have picked up the ABCs in school, but they acquired skill, preserved what they had learned, on their own. This self-learning is an important point, since it is not at the mechanical level of the ABCs that reading retardation drastically occurs, but in the subsequent years when the good readers are going it alone.

2. On neurological grounds, an emotionally normal child in middle-class urban and suburban surroundings, constantly exposed to written code, should spontaneously learn to read by age nine just as he learned to speak by age two or three. (This is the conclusion of Walla Nauta of the National Institute of Mental Health.) It is impossible for such a child *not* to pick up the code unless he is systematically interrupted and discouraged, for instance by trying to teach him.

   But of course our problem has to do with children in the culture of poverty, which does not have the ordinary middle-class need for literacy and the premium put on it. Such children are not exposed to reading and writing in important relations with their parents and peers; the code does not constantly occur in every kind of sequence of behavior. Thus there is an essential need for the right kind of schooling, to point to the written words and read them aloud, in use.

3. Historically, in all modern countries, school methods of lessons, copying, and textbooks, have been used, apparently successfully, to teach children to read. But this evidence is deceptive. A high level and continuing competence were required of very few— e.g., in 1900 in the United States only 6 percent graduated from high school. Little effort was made with children of the working class, and none at all with those in the culture of poverty. It is inherently unlikely that the same institutional procedures could apply with such a change of scale and population. Where a dramatic effort has been made to teach adults to read, as in Cuba, the method has been "each one teach one," informally.

4. Also, with the present expansion of higher education, teachers of freshman English uniformly complain that the majority of middle-class students cannot really read and write, though they have put on a performance that got them through high school. As John Holt has carefully described, their real life need was not reading or writing but getting by. (This is analogous to the large group among Puerto Rican children in New York who apparently speak English well, but who in fact cannot say anything that they need or mean, that is not really simply parroted.)

I trust that the aim of the present concern is how to learn reading as truth and art and not just to fake and get by. Further, since poor children do not have the continual incentives and subtle pressures of middle-class life, it is much harder for them to learn even just to fake and get by. And even if they do get by, it will not pay off for them in the end, since they do not have money and connections. To make good, they must really be competent.

The question is, is it possible and feasible to teach reading somewhat in the way children learn to speak, by intrinsic interest, with personal attention, and relating to the whole environment of activity? Pedagogically it is possible and feasible. There are known methods and available teachers, and I will suggest an appropriate school setting. Economically it is feasible, since methods, staff, and setting do not cost more than the $850 per child that we now spend in the public schools. (This was demonstrated for two years by the First Street School on the Lower East Side, and it is in line with the budget of Erik Mann's new school for Negro children in Newark, which uses similar principles.) Politically, however, my present proposal is impossible and unfeasible, since it threatens both vested interests and popular prejudices, as will be evident.

For ages six to eleven, I propose a system of tiny schools, radically decentralized. As one who for twenty years has urged democratic decentralization in many fields, including the schools, I am of course interested in the Bundy recommendation to cut up the New York system into sixty fairly autonomous districts. This would restore some relevance of the culture (and the staff) of the school to the culture of the community. But however valuable politically, it is an administrative arrangement; it does not get down to the actual pedagogical operation. And it certainly is not child-centered; both poor and middle-class communities have their own ways of not paying attention to children according to their own prejudices and distant expectations. By "tiny school," therefore, I here mean twenty-eight children . . . with four teachers (one grownup to seven children), and each tiny school to be largely administered by its own staff and parents, with considerable say also for the children, as in Summerhill. The four teachers are:

> A teacher regularly licensed and salaried. Since the present average class size is twenty-eight, these are available.
>
> A graduate from the senior class of a New York college, perhaps just embarking on graduate study. Salary $2,000. There is no lack of candidates to do something interesting and useful in a free setting.
>
> A literate housewife and mother, who can also prepare lunch. Salary $4,000. No lack of candidates.
>
> A literate, willing, and intelligent high-school graduate. Salary $2,000. No lack of candidates.

Such a staff can easily be racially and ethnically mixed. And it is also the case, as demonstrated by the First Street School, that in such a small setting, with individual attention paid to the children, it is easy to get racially and ethnically mixed classes; there is less middle-class withdrawal when the parents do not fear that their children will be swamped and retarded. (We have failed to achieve "integration" by trying to impose it from above, but it can be achieved from below, in schools entirely locally controlled, if we can show parents that it is for their children's best future.) For setting, the tiny school would occupy two, three, or four rooms in existing school buildings, church basements, settlement houses otherwise empty during school hours, rooms set aside in housing projects, store-fronts. The setting is especially indifferent since a major part of activity occurs outside the school place. The setting should be able to be transformed into a clubhouse, decorated and equipped according to the group's own decision. There might be one school on every street, but it is also advisable to locate many in racial and ethnic border areas, to increase intermixture. For purposes of assembly, health services, and some games, ten tiny schools could use the present public school facilities.

The cost saving in such a setup is the almost total elimination of top-down administration and the kind of special services that are required precisely because of excessive size and rigidity. The chief uses of central administration would be licensing, funding, choosing sites, and some inspection. There would be no principals and assistants, secretaries and assistants. Curriculum, texts, equipment would be determined as needed—and despite the present putative economies of scale, they would be cheaper; much less would be pointless or wasted. Record-keeping would be at a minimum. There is no need for truant officers when the teacher-and-seven can call at the absentee's home and inquire. There is little need for remedial personnel since the staff and parents are always in contact, and the whole enterprise can be regarded as remedial. Organizational studies of large top-down directed enterprises show that the total cost is invariably at least 300 percent above the cost of the immediate function, in this case the interaction of teachers and children. I would put this 300 percent into increasing the number of adults and diversifying the possibilities of instruction. Further, in the conditions of New York real esate, there is great advantage in ceasing to build four-million-dollar school buildings, and rather fitting tiny schools into available niches.

Pedagogically, this model is appropriate for natural learning of reading:

1. It allows exposure to the activities of the city. A teacher-and-seven can spend half the time on the streets, visiting a business office, in a playground, at a museum, watching television, chatting with the corner druggist, riding the buses and subways, visiting rich and poor neighborhoods and, if possible, homes. All these experiences can be saturated with speaking, reading, and writing. For instance, a group might choose to spend several weeks at the Museum of Natural History, and the problem would be to re-label the exhibits for their own level of comprehension.

2. It allows flexibility to approach each child according to his own style and interests, for instance in choice of reading matter. Given so many contexts, the teacher can easily strike when the iron is hot, whether reading the destination of a bus or the label on a can of soup. When some children catch on quickly and forge ahead on their own, the teacher need not waste their time and can concentrate on those who are more confused. The setting does not prejudge as to formal or informal techniques, phonics, Montessori, rote drill, Moore's typewriter, labeling the furniture, Herbert Kohl's creative writing, or any other method.

3. For instance, as a writer I like Sylvia Ashton-Warner's way of teaching little Maoris. Each day she tries to catch the most passionate concern of each child and to give him a card with that key word: usually these are words of fear, anger, hunger, loneliness, or sexual desire. Soon a child has a large ineradicable but very peculiar reading list, not at all like Dick and Jane. He then easily progresses to read and write anything. From the beginning, in this method, reading and writing are gut-meaningful, they convey truth and feeling. This method could be used in our tiny school.

4. The ragged administration by children, staff, and parents is pedagogically a virtue, since this too which is real can be saturated with reading and writing, writing down the arguments, the rules, the penalties. Socially and politically, of course, it has the advantage of engaging the parents and giving them power.

I am assuming that for the first five school years, there is no merit in the standard curriculum. For a small child everything in the environment is educative, if he attends to it with guidance. Normal children can learn the first eight years' curriculum in four months anyway, at age twelve.

Further, I see little merit, for teaching this age, in the usual teacher-training. Any literate and well-intentioned grown-up or late teen-ager knows enough to teach a small child a lot. Teaching small children is a difficult art, but we do not know how to train the improvisational genius it requires, and the untrained seem to have it equally: compare one mother with another, or one big sister or brother with another. Since at this age one teaches the child, not the subject, the relevant art is psychotherapy, and the most useful course for a teachers' college is probably group therapy. The chief criterion for selection is the one I have mentioned: liking to be attentive to children. Given this setting, many young people would be introduced to teaching and would continue with it as a profession; whereas in the New York system the annual turnover approaches 20 percent, after years of wasted training.

As I have said, however, there are fatal political and administrative objections to this proposal. First, the Public School administration does not intend to go largely out of business. Given its mentality, it must see any radical decentralization as impossible to administer and dangerous, for everything cannot be controlled. Some child is bound to break a leg and the insurance companies will not cover; some teen-ager is bound to be indiscreet and the *Daily News* will explode in headlines.

The United Federation of Teachers will find the proposal to be anathema because it devalues professional perquisites and floods the schools with the unlicensed. Being mainly broken to the public school harness, most experienced teachers consider free and inventive teaching to be impossible.

Most fatally, poor parents, who aspire for their children, tend to regard unrigidly structured education as down-grading, not taking the children seriously, and also as vaguely immoral. In the present Black Power temper of Harlem, also, the possible easy intermixing is itself not desired. (Incidentally, I am rather sympathetic to black separatism as a means of consolidating the power of black communities. But children, as Kant said, must be educated for the future better society which cannot be separated.)

In spite of these fatal objections, I recommend that, instead of building the next new school building, we try out this scheme with 1200 children.

FIRST YEAR AT FEDERAL CITY

David Swanston

Washington, D.C.

Taped to the fuchsia-colored classroom wall is a sign: READING IS HIP! CAN YOU DIG IT?

That is hardly a typical message to encourage freshmen to use the library, but Federal City College is hardly a typical school. The nation's newest land-grant college, Federal City occupies a brightly painted cluster of cast-off government buildings four blocks from the Capitol. It is, depending on whom you listen to, a hotbed of black revolution; an important key to District of Columbia self-rule; a super-imaginative new concept in urban involvement; a long-overdue opportunity for low-cost public higher education for Washington's 850,000 residents.

To some extent, Federal City College, now groping through its first academic year, is all these things. It is also an important prototype of the nearly all-black, publicly funded college of America's inner cities. Congress created it in November 1966 after three years of studies and hearings. Except for a teachers' college, the District had been for more than a century without public higher education, and Congressional bipartisan support for the college was considerable.

THE BLACKBOARD
Cliff Joseph
Courtesy of the artist

Sen. Robert F. Kennedy tagged the lack of a public college in the District a "national disgrace." And Texas Sen. Ralph Yarborough added, "Congress rules the District, and it shouldn't be the most backward place educationally in the country." And Maine Republican Margaret Chase Smith said Washington students "merit opportunities for higher education comparable to those now available to young Americans in all our states, and in the Commonwealth of Puerto Rico."

District private schools were difficult to get into, and expensive. Tuition at American, Georgetown, Catholic and George Washington Universities is more than $1,500 a year—out of the question for the great majority of the District's families. Tuition at Howard University is considerably less—$400 a year—but limited space and stiff entrance requirements have been major obstacles.

Federal City is supposed to solve both tuition and admission problems. Tuition is low—$75 a year for District residents—and all local high school graduates are eligible for admission. Frank Farner, 40-year-old Dean of Graduate Studies at the University of Oregon, was hired as Federal City's first president, and the college began preparing for its first classes.

With a budget of $4.3 million and classrooms in remodeled World War II temporary buildings that had once housed the Securities and Exchange Commission, the college planned on an initial class of 1,800 students. More than 6,000 residents applied. The administration solved this problem with a lottery, admitting 2,400 full-time students for the classes that began last September. About 95 percent of the students are black; their average age is 21; more than 20 percent of them are over 30. Nearly all are attending college for the first time. The majority, college officials say, are interested in programs that will lead to employment in specific jobs.

"For better or worse, the students are interested in what they call a 'regular course,' " Provost David W. Dickson explained just before classes began. "The students' taste is more conservative than the faculty's."

The faculty—approximately half black, half white—was recruited from across the country, drawn by relatively high salaries ($7,125 to $21,000-plus a year) and the chance to "get in on the ground floor of a new college program." Some, like Kenneth Lynn, former chairman of the department of American Civilization at Harvard, were well-known scholars. Others, like James Garrett, the 26-year-old one-time leader of San Francisco State's Black Student Union, had done little or no college teaching. During the months of program planning, the faculty was often seriously divided between traditional education theories and radical ideas.

The radicals argued that the students would need a distinctly black faculty and a curriculum that drew little from the academic processes and standards of white America. "Black studies will take the position that the total liberation of people necessarily means that those people separate themselves in attitudes, social structures and technology from the forces which oppress them," Garrett said.

"Concurrent, then, with the liberation of African people must be the construction of a durable, productive and self-sufficient nation. The building of a lasting and meaningful African nation must be the end product of the Black Studies Program." Moderates countered that this heavy emphasis on blackness would topple academic standards and destroy the school.

Somewhere in between stood the students. "We recognize a need for educational opportunity and for the employment and life opportunities that success in college affords," the Student Government Association explained in a position statement. "However, we insist that the education given at FCC be relevant to the needs of the students, their families, their communities and the total District population."

For several months this argument—one of many about curricula and the direction of the college—boiled in offices, faculty meetings and planning sessions. Finally, in November, Provost Dickson violated a tacit agreement that internal faculty disagreements would not be publicized and leveled a stinging attack at the radicals, and the debate broke into the open.

"Racial tension, racial suspension, and racial polarization have almost blasted our lovely spring buds," Dickson, who is responsible for academic affairs, told a meeting of the National Association of State Universities and Land Grant Colleges. The 48-year-old educator described a "well-disciplined and intense cadre of black separatists" who "neglect academic principles for revolutionary ends," and charged that white radicals "are mainly intent on using students as cannon fodder for their own wars on the Establishment."

The next day President Farner said that Dickson's description of the college "overstates the conflict," adding, "I think most of the faculty would agree" that the disagreement wasn't as bad as Dickson had made out. A college-wide advisory board did agree. The Interim College Commission reported that the fuss was "healthy ferment" and should not be considered a "sign of chaos and racial factionalism." ˅

The tempest steamed for a few weeks, cooled and then heated up again when Lynn announced plans to leave Federal City. "The militants have won," he grumbled. "I just don't see that people with academic interests have much of a chance here."

Lynn's resignation and the public airing of the debate have had their effect on the college. For one thing, recruiting the new faculty of 180 has been made a little more difficult by the hassle. For another, any public flap makes Federal City administrators look anxiously toward Capitol Hill for signs of Congressional displeasure.

So far, Congress has ignored the trouble, and, Farner says, recruiting is "going along all right." Indeed, the college as a whole seems to be getting on with its business—encouraging the belief that the rhetoric of the debate and the disagreement in general were blown out of proportion. In addition, one college official observed, many faculty members have developed a real respect for the college and are willing to compromise to protect the school and insure that program proposals will be generally acceptable.

For example, a reasoned, detailed black studies program has been developed and its approval by the college's nine-member Board of Higher Education is expected. (As of now, Federal City teaches a range of lower-division classes and does not yet offer department majors.) The proposal, which calls for four years of black-oriented study, is innovative and radical in many ways, but contains none of the separatist rhetoric heard in the fall. According to Garrett, its director, it "focuses upon the realities and prospects of those of African origin where they exist on the continent of Africa, in the West Indies and in the Americas. In essence, the program is at once a cultural and educational vehicle for creative awareness, confidence and determination of black people."

According to the proposal, the first two years of the program will "focus primarily on channeling the student to a spirit of dedication and community work, and development of inter-operative skills"; the last two years will focus on one of three "curriculum cores"—technical, political or cultural. Included in the fourth year will be "extensive travel."

Curiously enough, at a time when students are demanding more and more say in what and how and under whom they study, the black studies proposal explains that "the Program will take total responsibility for the academic pursuits of students enrolled." A few students will allow their studies to be completely prescribed, others will ask for—and probably get —a larger number of choices for themselves, and the largest group, for a number of reasons, will major in something else and take black studies classes as electives.

Farner has from the start supported the concept of a significant black studies program: "One of the ways to address the problems of the inner city is to do it through a relevant black studies program." He notes with more than a touch of pride, "we have the largest black studies department in the country"; but adds, "not everyone has to be interested in black studies."

About 20 percent of Federal City's students are enrolled in at least one of the black studies classes, which comprise about 20 percent of the school's courses.

However, black studies are only one aspect of Federal City's attempt to be relevant to the community it was created to serve. Another—and in many ways more revolutionary—is its growing direct involvement in attempts to find solutions for Washington's problems. For example, the college conducts classes in proposal evaluation and community organization for the citizens board of a Washington Model Cities program. It created a program to train "para-professional nutritionists" to advise neighborhood women about cooking, shopping and homemaking, when a survey revealed the desperate need for better meals in ghetto homes. It conducts classes at the District's Lorton Reformatory so that inmates will be eligible for college when released. It is designing classes to prepare unemployed men and women for job openings that eight college investigators discovered in an employment survey of Washington. It conducts a year-long night class for suburbanites entitled "The Dilemma of White Americans," that will teach the thirty-five whites who take part to "deal with racism on an intellectual level."

The community involvement programs, the scope of the black studies, the overall direction of the college involve many new concepts and will probably continue to stir debate in the college community. So far, only the faculty and a few members of the administration have shown much propensity for serious wrangling. As important—and potentially more dangerous—are the two interested parties that thus far have stayed pretty well out of the controversies—the students and Congress.

Federal City's student population has shown itself to be interested primarily in studies and not at all interested in left-of-Center politics that are not connected with race. For example, when college officials agreed that the National Mobilization to End the War in Vietnam could use the campus buildings for a conference last January 18 and 19, the student government said no, and permission was withdrawn.

"Suppose the peaceful meeting here was to be followed by violence on the streets afterward?" student president Cornelius Williams explained. "Then nation-wide attention would include the report that it all started here. And we don't want that.

"We know what the Peace and Freedom Party and the Students for a Democratic Society are after, and their goals are not the same as ours."

When black people are directly involved, Federal City students are a little more demonstrative. The school closed to observe Malcolm X's birthday and John Carols, the runner expelled from the Olympics at Mexico City, was given a hero's welcome by several thousand students at a campus rally.

The college administration has taken care to involve students in decision making and to avoid causing confrontations—such as the strike that kept neighboring Howard in turmoil most of the winter. The students have responded with nine months of campus peace. However, a militant Black People's Liberation Movement has formed on campus and has vowed to work for "black control of the school." Exactly what the movement has in mind and what tactics it will use are not known, but there is some worry among college administrators that it will attempt disruption. (However, several of the officials say privately that the student population at Federal City won't tolerate disruption.)

Student demonstrations are a double problem for Federal City, since the school's funds come from Congress and Congress has indicated it is in no mood to fool around with young radicals. And even if the campus remains calm, Federal City could have tough sledding getting further funds out of the legislators.

As of today, though, Federal City's future seems relatively bright, if not completely assured. The District's Advisory Council on Higher Education predicts that the college will have 20,000 students by 1975. Plans for a new permanent campus are under way. Farner has weathered the first year and seems like a good bet to stay on for a while longer.

Eventually, the District will get self-government. The people will then have some control of their institutions, including the college, and one large worry will be eliminated.

If it does survive, Federal City College may well become a significant educational institution and an important factor in solving the problems of the nation's capital and sixteenth largest city. "The first graduating class from the college will be the best prepared to deal with [Washington's] problems of any graduating class in the country," student president Williams predicts. "Federal City College graduates will run this city and play a large part in running this country." If Federal City is given half a chance, Williams is probably right.

ONCE UPON A TIME:
A FABLE OF STUDENT POWER

Neil Postman

Once upon a time in the City civilized life very nearly came to an end. The streets were covered with dirt, and there was no one to tidy them. The air and rivers were polluted, and no one could cleanse them. The schools were rundown, and no one believed in them. Each day brought a new strike, and each strike brought new hardships. Crime and strife and disorder and rudeness were to be found everywhere. The young fought the old. The workers fought the students. The whites fought the blacks. The city was bankrupt.

When things came to their most desperate moment, the City Fathers met to consider the problem. But they could suggest no cures, for their morale was very low and their imagination dulled by hatred and confusion. There was nothing for the Mayor to do but to declare a state of emergency. He had done this before during snowstorms and power failures, but now he felt even more justified. "Our city," he said, "is under siege, like the ancient cities of Jericho and Troy. But *our* enemies are sloth and poverty and indifference and hatred." As you can see, he was a very wise Mayor, but not so wise as to say exactly how these enemies could be dispersed. Thus, though a state of emergency officially existed, neither the Mayor nor anyone else could think of anything to do that would make their situation better rather than worse. And then an extraordinary thing happened.

One of the Mayor's aides, knowing full well what the future held for the city, had decided to flee with his family to the country. In order to prepare himself for his exodus to a strange environment, he began to read Henry David Thoreau's "Walden," which he had been told was a useful handbook on how to survive in the country. While reading the book, he came upon the following passage:

"Students should not play life, or study it merely, while the community supports them at this expensive game, but earnestly live it from the beginning to end. How could youth better learn to live than by at once trying the experiment of living?"

The aide sensed immediately that he was in the presence of an exceedingly good idea. And he sought an audience with the Mayor. He showed the passage to the Mayor, who was extremely depressed and in no mood to read from books, since he had already scoured books of lore and wisdom in search of help but had found nothing. "What does it mean?" said the Mayor angrily. The aide replied: "Nothing less than a way to our salvation."

He then explained to the Mayor that the students in the public schools had heretofore been part of the general problem whereas, with some slight imagination and a change of perspective, they might easily become part of the general solution. He pointed out that from junior high school on up to senior high school, there were approximately 400,000 able-bodied, energetic young men and women who could be used as a resource to make the city livable again. "But how can we use them?" asked the Mayor. "And what would happen to their education if we did?"

To this the aide replied, "They will find their education in the process of saving their city. And as for their lessons in school, we have ample evidence that the young do not exactly appreciate them and are even now turning against their teachers and their schools." The aide, who had come armed with statistics (as aides are wont to do), pointed out that the city was spending $5-million a year merely replacing broken school windows and that almost one-third of all the students enrolled in the schools did not even show up on any given day. "Yes, I know," said the Mayor sadly. "Woe unto us." "Wrong," said the aide brashly. "The boredom and destructiveness and pent-up energy that are now an affliction to us can be turned to our advantage."

The Mayor was not quite convinced, but having no better idea of his own he appointed his aide Chairman of the Emergency Education Committee, and the aide at once made plans to remove almost 400,000 students from their dreary classrooms and their even drearier lessons, so that their energy and talents might be used to repair the desecrated environment.

When these plans became known, there was a great hue and cry against them, for people in distress will sometimes prefer a problem that is familiar to a solution that is not. For instance, the teachers complained that their contract contained no provision for such unusual procedures. To this the aide replied that the *spirit* of their contract compelled them to help educate our youth, and that education can take many forms and be conducted in many places. "It is not written in any holy book," he observed, "that an education must occur in a small room with chairs in it."

Some parents complained that the plan was un-American and that its compulsory nature was hateful to them. To this the aide replied that the plan was based on the practices of earlier Americans who required their young to assist in controlling the environment in order to insure the survival of the group. "Our schools," he added, "have never hesitated to compel. The question is not, nor has it ever been, to compel or not to compel, but rather, which things ought to be compelled."

And even some children complained, although not many. They said that their God-given right to spend 12 years of their lives, at public expense, sitting in a classroom was being trampled. To this complaint the aide replied that they were confusing a luxury with a right, and that, in any case, the community could no longer afford either. "Besides," he added, "of all the God-given rights man has identified, none takes precedence over his right to survive."

And so, the curriculum of the public schools of the City became known as Operation Survival, and all the children from 7th grade through 12th grade became part of it. Here are some of the things that they were obliged to do:

On Monday morning of every week, 400,000 children had to help clean up their own neighborhoods. They swept the streets, canned the garbage, removed the litter from empty lots, and hosed the dust and graffiti from the pavements and walls. Wednesday mornings were reserved for beautifying the city. Students planted trees and flowers, tended the grass and shrubs, painted subway stations and other eyesores, and even repaired broken-down public buildings, starting with their own schools.

Each day, 5,000 students (mostly juniors and seniors in high school) were given responsibility to direct traffic on the city streets, so that all the policemen who previously had done this were freed to keep a sharp eye out for criminals. Each day, 5,000 students were asked to help deliver the mail, so that it soon became possible to have mail delivered twice a day—as it had been done in days of yore.

Several thousand students were also used to establish and maintain day-care centers, so that young mothers, many on welfare, were free to find gainful employment. Each student was also assigned to meet with two elementary-school students on Tuesday and Thursday afternoons to teach them to read, to write, and to do arithmetic. Twenty thousand students were asked to substitute, on one afternoon a week, for certain adults whose jobs the students could perform without injury or loss of efficiency. These adults were then free to attend school or, if they preferred, to assist the students in their efforts to save their city.

The students were also assigned to publish a newspaper in every neighborhood of the city, in which they were able to include much information that good citizens need to have. Students organized science fairs, block parties and rock festivals, and they formed, in every neighborhood, both an orchestra and a theater company. Some students assisted in hospitals, helped to register voters, and produced radio and television programs which were aired on city stations. There was still time to hold a year-round City Olympics in which every child competed in some sport or other.

It came to pass, as you might expect, that the college students in the city yearned to participate in the general plan, and thus another 100,000 young people became available to serve the community. The college students ran a "jitney" service from the residential boroughs to The Central City and back. Using their own cars and partly subsidized by the city, the students quickly established a kind of auxiliary, semipublic transportation system, which reduced the number of cars coming into The Central City took some of the load off the subways, and diminished air pollution— in one stroke.

College students were empowered to give parking and litter tickets, thus freeing policemen more than ever for real detective work. They were permitted to organize seminars, film festivals, and arrange lectures for junior and senior high school students; and on a U.H.F. television channel, set aside for the purpose, they gave advanced courses in a variety of subjects every day from 3 P.M. to 10 P.M. They also helped to organize and run drug-addiction rehabilitation centers, and they launched campaigns to inform people of their legal rights, their nutritional needs, and of available medical facilities.

Because this is a fable and not a fairy tale, it cannot be said that all the problems of the city were solved. But several extraordinary things did happen. The city began to come alive and its citizens found new reason to hope that they could save themselves. Young people who had been alienated from their environment assumed a proprietary interest in it. Older people who had regarded the young as unruly and parasitic came to respect them. There followed from this a revival of courtesy and a diminution of crime, for there was less reason than before to be angry at one's neighbors and to wish to assault them.

Amazingly, most of the students found that while they did not "receive" an education, they were able to create a quite adequate one. They lived, each day, their social studies and geography and communication and biology and many other things that decent and proper people know about, including the belief that everyone must share equally in creating a livable city, no matter what he or she becomes later on. It even came to pass that the older people, being guided by the example of the young, took a renewed interest in restoring their environment and, at the very least, refused to participate in its destruction.

Now, it would be foolish to deny that there were not certain problems attending this whole adventure. For instance, there were thousands of children who would otherwise have known the principal rivers of Uruguay who had to live out their lives in ignorance of these facts. There were hundreds of teachers who felt their training had been wasted because they could not educate children unless it were done in a classroom. As you can imagine, it was also exceedingly difficult to grade students on their activities, and after a while, almost all tests ceased. This made many people unhappy, for many reasons, but most of all because no one could tell the dumb children from the smart children anymore.

But the Mayor, who was, after all, a very shrewd politician, promised that as soon as the emergency was over everything would be restored to normal. Meanwhile, everybody lived happily ever after—in a state of emergency, but quite able to cope with it.

THE SUBWAY
George Segal
Courtesy Sidney Janis Gallery, New York
Collection: Mr. and Mrs. Robert Mayer, Winnetka, Ill.

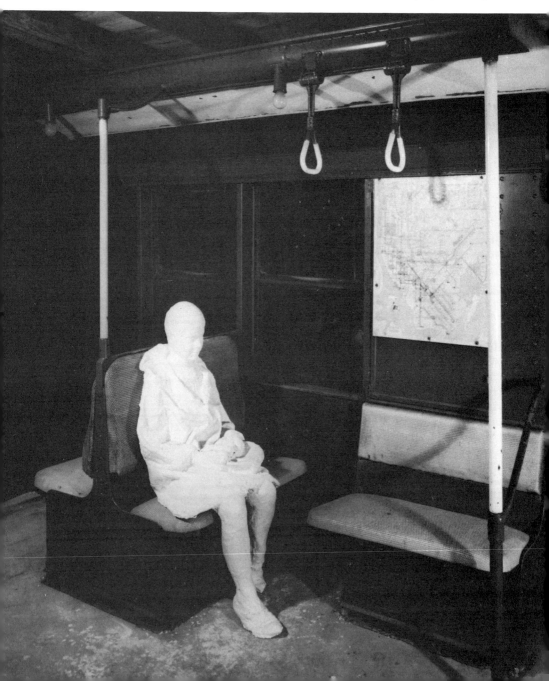

8

THE ARTISTS
AT WORK

Besides country enclaves, cities have always been the cultural capitals of America and most other countries of the world. The art produced there is one of the greatest fruits of urban life, one of the greatest affirmations of creativity, beauty, and human spirit. In the cities, the artists in all fields come together to live, work, and find their audience in one place. Apparently it is the stimulation from the people, the bustle, the art worlds, and the exchange of ideas that invites them in such numbers to work and develop their arts side by side. And although they work alone in most cases, their contribution to the urban environment is tremendous in terms of the vitality, beauty, romance, and meaning they offer. Every selection here was inspired in some way by the city as a place of life, so that artist and city seem to be working upon each other very poignantly.

The entire collection in this section on the artist is coherent in a special way, because *all the works here deal with the city in their own forms.* We emphasize this because some of the forms are not the familiar ones, like realistic paintings, stories, and songs. Take the Mondrian painting, for example, whose rhythm and composition are the city itself in a real sense. Or the bold shape and metal of the Tobias sculpture. Or the action in Martin's play and Ferlinghetti's San Francisco poem. Some of the works are realistic, some are not, but each is a positive artistic expression that invites reflection.

Here, then, is a presentation of the artist's work in the three fields of art, literature, and music, in that order. Examples are given as much as possible on the printed page: For art, there is painting, drawing, and sculpture; for literature, poetry, a short story, and drama; for music, blues, folk, and folkrock lyrics.

MUSIC

The song lyrics here and elsewhere in the book appear virtually as poems without the music or the sound of voices and instruments. They vary greatly, and should be heard on recordings. The tremendous boom in popular music that is partly rock and partly a rebirth of the blues is an urban phenomenon. The greatest according to many are city-centered and city-concerned.

The first two selections are blues lyrics. Leadbelly (Huddie Ledbetter) composed "Bourgeois Blues," which is literally about housing and other racial discrimination in Washington, D.C. W. C. Handy's famous "St. Louis Blues" are the cried-out longings of a woman who lost her man to a dazzling rival. The humorous folk ballad by Fred Hellerman of the Weavers tells of a completely different city problem; the lyrics to "There Once Was a Young Man Who Went to the City" sing about a country boy who meets his ruination in the big city with a single glass of beer and his fast new college friends.

On the theme of isolation, Melanie observes the masses of alienated city people around her who ride the same subway together but who have no connections. To her they are "Beautiful People" who should care for each other humanly. "The Sound of Silence" by Paul Simon of Simon and Garfunkel is the last song. It tells of a dreamy vision the character has at night when he is struck by the flash of a neon sign and he perceives, like Melanie, the thousands of noncommunicating people. He warns them against their cancerous silence. "The Sound of Silence" seems a likely conclusion to this section, for although the selections in art, literature, and music speak loudly, they are bound here to the silent process of reading that is in the nature of books.

ART

All the works of art in this exhibition deal in some visual or conceptual way with the urban environment in which they were created. The artists represented are a vigorous and varied group. Though all the work is twentieth-century American, some of the artists are living, some are now dead, some are natives, some immigrants, some are white, some black.

George Segal is the sculptor of "The Subway," which appears at the beginning of this section. He sculpts life-sized plaster of paris figures and sets them ghostly white into real environments to make his statement. A sample of Saul Steinberg's work is found at the beginning of the art section. Steinberg, a master of drawing and visual cartooning, superimposed this drawing on a city photograph. (Another example of Steinberg's work can be found at the opening of the economics section.)

Next is "An Exhibition of Urban Art." The first is Robert Rauschenberg's "Estate," which unites the techniques of painting and collage with contemporary subject matter. Photographic images are joined with areas of painted colors to create a conglomerate painting of the city. Another contemporary, Cliff Joseph, created "The Window," a painting whose warm colors and soft lines reflect an artistic response to a familiar urban sight. The painting by Stuart Davis, a Philadelphian by birth (1894–1964), is an abstracted and personal view of a city street somewhat earlier in this century, but the many shapes and signs and objects reflect the modern active and filled landscape in an especially rhythmic way. Before many others, Davis used the shapes of letters and words as part of his composition. The final painting in the exhibition is the famous "Broadway Boogie Woogie" by Piet Mondrian (1872–1944), a native of Holland before coming to America. Only the title suggests the connection of the painting to place and tempo; the geometric forms (squares and rectangles) are assembled and colored in such a way that the rhythm of the city, set in something of a grid street pattern, seems alive and vibrant.

The works of two sculptors follow. Lovett Thompson is a Boston artist whose sculpture "The Junkie" was shown in the exhibit "Afro-American Artists: New York and Boston." Julius Tobias' abstract sculpture "Circular Movement, No. 2" is a 16-inch-high aluminum model for a great sculpture made of the same material, to be 8 feet 3 inches high.

Next are two paintings reproduced in black and white. Don Merrick's "Listeners" is 1 foot square and captures the living presence of the factory/office building in the geometric cityscape. Mark Tobey, in the painting "San Francisco Street," *writes* the city in white lines, a technique he explains in the interview following the art in this section.

Following the exhibition of urban art are selections from *The Artist's Voice*, a collection of interviews with major American artists. There is part of a letter written by Mark Tobey and two fragments of interviews with Stuart Davis and Morris Graves. Each artist talks about the city as an influence on his work and as a source of creative stimulation and subject matter.

LITERATURE

The authors collected in this section are as varied a group as the artists, although in this section we have classified their work according to genre or type of literature. There are five poems for poetry, a short story for fiction, and a play and a dramatic happening for drama. Examples of each genre can be found elsewhere throughout *The Urban Reader*.

Poetry

The first poem, "I Am Thinking of Chicago and of What Survives" by Lou Lipsitz, is a set of four specific poetic images of the city that are almost photographic. The second is by the modern experimentalist e.e. cummings. The poem "the hours rise up putting off stars and it is" (the first line) concerns what the poet sees in a city from dawn till nighttime.

The poem "Last Night in Newark" by Ted Joans appears in his book *Black Pow-Wow: Jazz Poems.* Instead of a city-wide vista over the course of a day, Joans focuses on the events of one racial confrontation. Lawrence Ferlinghetti's poem also deals with one occurrence, in San Francisco this time: the raising of a statue and what occurs around this ceremony. The final poem by Robert Creeley, "The City," is shaped like a building. In it the poet discusses how things in nature are only used by man and aren't enjoyed.

Fiction

"Only the Dead Know Brooklyn" by Thomas Wolfe is the only short story in this section, though others (by Williams, Vonnegut, Russell, Jones, Chin, and Bradbury) can be found in the table of contents. This one, written in slightly overdone Brooklynese, is a yarn told by a native Brooklynite about the time he met a weird traveler in the subway who was entranced with his map and by fantasies about drowning. Both men are protagonists or central characters as they reveal their personalities in the dialogue.

Drama

A play and a dramatic happening are offered here. The play, "Dialogue," was written by poet Herbert Woodward Martin and is about a confrontation between a black man and a suspecting white policeman whose ambition causes the final crisis. The dramatic happening is "The Nose of Sisyphus" by Lawrence Ferlinghetti. Here the Greek Sisyphus, who was doomed to push a rock up a mountain only to watch it roll down again and again, is placed in a city playground, pushing a globe up a slide with the same result. A crowd of typically varied urbanites gather and shout phrases together until a whistle stops everything and the character called Big Baboon enters to take over the spotlight in his own symbolic drama.

Scene from Street Theatre production of Society Hill Playhouse,
South Eighth Street, Philadelphia.

MUSIC

BOURGEOIS BLUES

Leadbelly

Tell all the colored folks to listen
    to me,
Don't try to buy no home in
    Washington, D.C.

Chorus:

> (Lord) It's a bourgeois town, it's
>   a bourgeois town,
> Got the bourgeois blues, gonna
>   spread the news all around.

Me an' my wife run all over town,
Everywhere we'd go, the people
   turn us down.

Me an' Marthy, we was standing
   upstair,
I heard the white man say, "I don't
   want no niggers up there."

Chorus:

> He was a bourgeois man living
>   in a bourgeois town,
> Got the bourgeois blues, gonna
>   spread the blues all around.

The white folks in Washington,
   they know how
Chuck a colored man a nickel just
   to see him bow.

The D.A.R. wouldn't let Marion
   Anderson in,
But Mrs. Roosevelt was her best
   friend.

In the home of the brave, land of
   the free,
I don't want to be mistreated by no
   bourgeoisie.

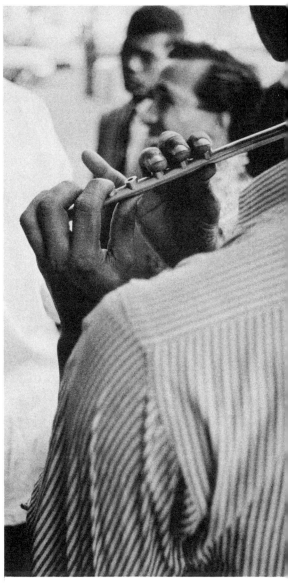

SAINT LOUIS BLUES

W. C. Handy

I hate to see de ev'nin' sun go down,
Hate to see de ev'nin' sun go down,
Cause my baby, he done lef' dis town.

Feelin' tomorrow lak Ah feel today,
Feel tomorrow lak Ah feel today,
I'll pack my trunk make my get away.

Saint Louis woman wid her diamon' rings
Pull dat man roun' by her apron strings.
'Twant for powder an' for store bought hair,
De man I love would not gone no where.

Chorus

Got de Saint Louis Blues jes as blue as Ah can be.
Dat man got a heart lak a rock cast in the sea.
Or else he wouldn't have gone so far from me.

THERE ONCE WAS A YOUNG MAN WHO WENT TO THE CITY

Fred Hellerman

THE WEAVERS

1. Well, there was a poor young man
   Who left his country home,
   And came to the city—to seek employment.
   He promised his dear mother
   That he'd lead the simple life,
   And always shun the fatal curse of drink.

2. Well he came to the city
   And found employment in a quarry,
   And while there he made the acquaintance of some
       college men.
   He little knew that they were demons
   For they wore the best of clothes,
   But clothes do not always make the gentleman.

3. So one night he went out
   With his new-found friends to dine,
   And while there they tried to persuade him to take a drink.
   They tempted him and tempted him
   But he refused and he refused
   'Til finally he took a glass of beer.

4. When he saw what he had done
   He dashed the liquor to the floor
   And staggered out the door with delirium tremens.
   And while in the grip of liquor
   He met a Salvation Army lassie
   And cruelly he broke her tambourine.

5. All she said was "Heaven bless you,"
   And laid a mark upon his brow
   With a kick that she had learned from before she was saved.
   So kind friends take my advice,
   And shun the fatal curse of drink,
   And don't go around breaking people's tambourines.

BEAUTIFUL PEOPLE

Melanie

BEAUTIFUL PEOPLE
You live in the same world as I do
But somehow I never noticed
You before today
I'm ashamed to say
BEAUTIFUL PEOPLE
We share the same back door
And it isn't right
We never met before
But then
We may never meet again
If I weren't afraid You'd laugh at me
I would run and take all your hands
And I'd gather everyone together for a day
And when we're gather'd

I'd pass buttons out that say
BEAUTIFUL PEOPLE
Then you'll never be alone
'Cause there'll always be someone
With the same button on as you
Include him in everything you do.

BEAUTIFUL PEOPLE
You ride the same subway
As I do ev'ry morning
That's got to tell you something
We have so much in common
I go the same direction that you do
So if you take care of me
Maybe I'll take care of you

BEAUTIFUL PEOPLE
You look like friends of mine
And it's about time
That someone said it here and now
I make a vow that some time, somehow
I'll have a meeting
Invite ev'ryone you know
I'd pass out buttons to
The ones who come to show
BEAUTIFUL PEOPLE
Never have to be alone
'Cause there'll always be someone
With the same button on as you
Include him in ev'rything you do
He may be sitting right next to you
He may be a BEAUTIFUL PEOPLE too
And if you take care of him
Maybe he'll take care of you
And if you take care of him
Maybe he'll take care of you . . .

THE SOUND OF SILENCE

Paul Simon

SIMON AND GARFUNKEL

Hello darkness my old friend,
I've come to talk with you again,
Because a vision softly creeping,
Left its seeds while I was sleeping
And the vision that was planted in my brain
Still remains within the sound of silence.

In restless dreams I walked alone,
Narrow streets of cobble stone
'Neath the halo of a street lamp,
I turned my collar to the cold and damp
When my eyes were stabbed by the flash of a neon light
That split the night, and touched the sound of silence.

And in the naked light I saw
Ten thousand people maybe more,
People talking without speaking,
People hearing without listening,
People writing songs that voices never share
And no one dares disturb the sound of silence.

"Fools!" said I, "You do not know
Silence like a cancer grows.
Hear my words that I might teach you
Take my arms that I might reach you."
But my words like silent raindrops fell
And echoed, in the wells of silence.

And the people bowed and prayed
To the neon God they made,

And the sign flashed out its warning
In the words that it was forming.
And the sign said:
> "The words of the prophets are written
> on the subway walls and tenement halls"
And whispered in the sounds of silence.

ART

an exhibition of urban art

ESTATE, 1963
Robert Rauschenberg
Collection of The Philadelphia Museum of Art

THE WINDOW
Cliff Joseph
Courtesy of the artist

NEW YORK UNDER GASLIGHT, 1941
Stuart Davis
Collection of The Israel Museum

BROADWAY BOOGIE WOOGIE, 1942–43
Piet Mondrian
Oil on canvas, 50 x 50"
Collection, The Museum of Modern Art, New York

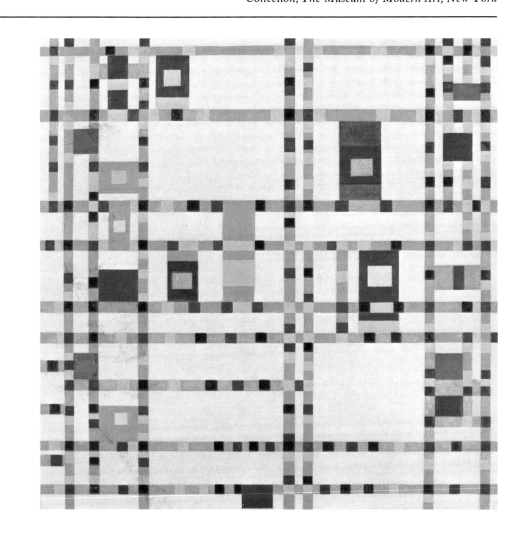

THE JUNKIE
Lovett Thompson
Wood Carving 1970.
Courtesy of the artist and The Boston Museum of Fine Arts.

CIRCULAR MOVEMENT, NO. 2
Julius Tobias
Courtesy of the artist

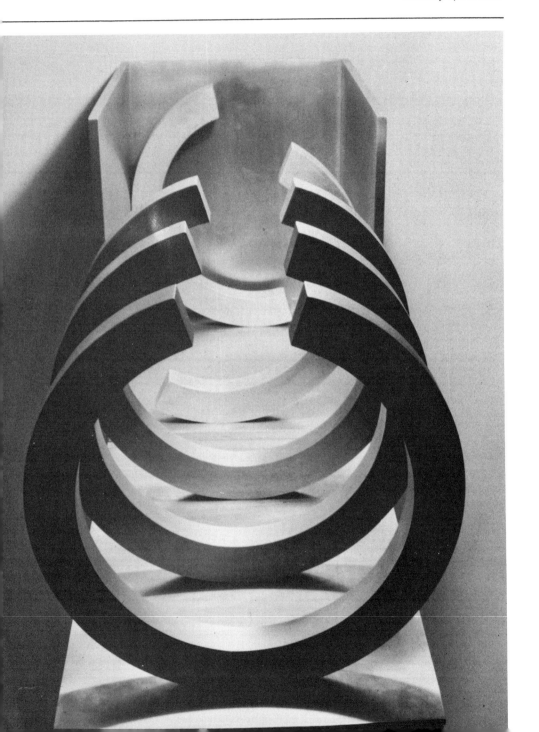

THE LISTENERS
Don Merrick
Courtesy of the artist

SAN FRANCISCO STREET
Mark Tobey
From the collection of The Detroit Institute of Arts Purchase, General Membership Fund

THE ARTIST'S VOICE

Mark Tobey

Earlier I got the idea of 'writing' cities and city life. At last I had found a technical approach which enabled me to capture what specially interested me in the city—its lights—threading traffic—the river of humanity chartered and flowing through and around its self-imposed limitations, not unlike chlorophyll flowing through the canals of a leaf. Naturally I didn't consciously know what I was doing. The fact that I had to express things in this way often resulted in denying the way even while or after doing it, as there were no existing standards to give me support. I couldn't use much color, any more, I suppose, than the cubists could in the first years of cubism, for the problems were already complicated enough. Naturally color came back. During the forties and fifties my work varied from the use of a direct dynamic brush to the use of white dynamic flashes of line married to a geometry of space.

I have never wished to continue in any particular style. The path has been a zigzag—in and out of old cultures, seeking new horizons— meditating and reviewing for a better position to see. Subject matter has changed from the Middle West to the most microscopic worlds. On pavements and the bark of trees I have found whole worlds.

FROM A LETTER TO KATHARINE KUH , OCTOBER 28, 1954, PARIS

THE ARTIST'S VOICE

Stuart Davis

Question: Do you feel your work is basically American?

Davis: I've never lived anywhere else for an extended length of time— only once in Cuba for a few months and in Paris for a year and a half. Otherwise I've always lived here. Of course my work is American—it couldn't be anything else, but America is increasingly part of the world. It's the big cities here, I suppose, that have impressed me the most. I've accepted the noise, the cacophony (to use a big word) of present-day life as subject matter. I'm a thorough urbanite—one hundred per cent. New York City and my warm affection for Philadelphia have played a strong part in my paintings. One reason I liked Paris was because it reminded me of Philadelphia in the 1890's. You know I was born in Philadelphia. But all this isn't too conscious. You're born with a genetic tape that has a coded prescription for your behavior throughout your entire life—and never forget that it's in code.

FROM AN INTERVIEW WITH KATHARINE KUH

THE ARTIST'S VOICE

Morris Graves

Question: Do you think that where you live influences your work? For instance, Ireland or Seattle?

Graves: This was true in the past, but no longer. In the past, what receptivity I had was, of course, responsive to what was available in my immediate environment. It sustained my thoughts as a painter. Now, I could be in Moscow, Tokyo, Rome, Seattle or New York, and the demands of scientific culture would have their impact regardless of where I was. You see, years ago in Seattle I lived quite remotely in the country. It would have taken a long time for me to hear of, let's say, the space shots. Now, were I living in that same place, they would come into my experience immediately. You simply can't keep that world out any longer. Even Ireland is not a haven for a nature-romantic now. The result is I can no longer be a solitary romantic. Some friends regret it. They want me to remain a solitary—as a respite for themselves. They want to feel that everyone is not caught in the mad race, though I don't believe that what we've been caught in could really be called the mad race. Like everyone else I've been caught in our scientific culture. I thought when I went to Ireland in 1954 that it would be a haven for me; I was then reacting violently against the machine age. The machine age is now universal, and that's what affected my state of mind. My earlier impulse was to recede, withdraw into nature and nature's quietude. It's no longer possible.

Question: Do you think you could stand living in New York or one of our large cities?

Graves: I don't know, but more and more I feel that I don't want to turn my back on our times. The city is a concentrated dose of it. A city is physically superenergized. Air travel is creating a city of our earth.

FROM AN INTERVIEW WITH KATHARINE KUH

LITERATURE

I AM THINKING OF CHICAGO
AND OF WHAT SURVIVES

Lou Lipsitz

In the shadows of old buildings, human bodies are opened
and fingered perfunctorily, like prayer books.

Near the mills, there are cash registers shining in the dimness
of bars, stolid as the helmets of soldiers at a crucifixion.

Along the railroad tracks I see poor men's windows
opening into a vacant eternity like the dusty mouths of the dead.

Yet, hidden in alleys the children practice their strange devotions
before the small churches of garbage and snow.

THE HOURS RISE UP PUTTING OFF STARS
AND IT IS

e. e. cummings

the hours rise up putting off stars and it is
dawn
into the street of the sky light walks scattering poems

on earth a candle is
extinguished   the city
wakes
with a song upon her
mouth having death in her eyes

and it is dawn
the world
goes forth to murder dreams . . . .

i see in the street where strong
men are digging bread
and i see the brutal faces of
people contented hideous hopeless cruel happy

and it is day,

in the mirror
i see a frail
man
dreaming

dreams
dreams in the mirror

and it
is dusk   on earth

a candle is lighted
and it is dark.
the people are in their houses
the frail man is in his bed
the city

sleeps with death upon her mouth having a
        song in her eyes
the hours descend,
putting on stars . . . .

in the street of the sky night walks scattering poems

LAST NIGHT IN NEWARK

Ted Joans

Last night   in Newark   summer Newark
We black men three and sister soul in back
rode Volkswagen bus cutting our way through hot
humid Newark summer Newark   a city of vacant lust
Then out of nowhere   white they came
rude/ crude/ oatmeal pale & lame
following our bus   with their sneers & frowns
muttering their Italian accented cuss at us
We black three with sister soul in back
They pull up beside to provoke in Newark summer Newark
but before they could say 'boy'
they were greeted with a barrage of black poetry
from LeRoi
        in Newark   summer Newark
with three/LeRoi/ a blood/ sister soul
                         & me
the wop cops had to flee
                in Newark   summer Newark
it was the wrong bus for them to cuss
                    in Newark summer Newark

A CONEY ISLAND OF THE MIND #6

Lawrence Ferlinghetti

They were putting up the statue
     of Saint Francis
   in front of the church
     of Saint Francis
        in the city of San Francisco
 in a little side street
         just off the Avenue
                where no birds sang
    and the sun was coming upon time
             in its usual fashion

and just beginning to shine
                         on the statue of Saint Francis
          where no birds sang

     And a lot of old Italians
                         were standing all around
               in the little side street
                         just off the Avenue
          watching the wily workers
                         who were hoisting up the statue
     with a chain and a crane
                         and other implements
And a lot of young reporters
                         in button-down clothes
     were taking down the words
                         of one young priest
          who was propping up the statue
                         with all his arguments

          And all the while
                         while no birds sang
                         any Saint Francis Passion
and while the lookers kept looking
                         up at Saint Francis
     with his arms outstretched
                         to the birds which weren't there
          a very tall and very purely naked
                         young virgin
          with very long and very straight
                         straw hair
          and wearing only a very small
                         bird's nest
               in a very existential place
                         kept passing thru the crowd
                                   all the while
               and up and down the steps
                         in front of Saint Francis
          her eyes downcast all the while
                         and singing to herself

THE CITY

Robert Creeley

Not from that
could you get it,
nor can things
comprise a form

just to be made.
Again, let
each be this or
that, they, together,

are many whereas,
one by one,
each is a wooden
or metal or even

water, or vegetable,
flower, a crazy orange
sun, a windy
dirt, and here is

a place to sit
shaded by tall buildings
and a bed that
grows leaves on

all its branches
which are
boards I know
soon enough.

fiction

ONLY THE DEAD KNOW BROOKLYN

Thomas Wolfe

Dere's no guy livin' dat knows Brooklyn t'roo an' t'roo, because it'd take a guy a lifetime just to find his way aroun' duh f—— town.

So like I say, I'm waitin' for my train t' come when I sees dis big guy standin' deh—dis is duh foist I eveh see of him. Well, he's lookin' wild, y'know, an' I can see dat he's had plenty, but still he's holdin' it; he talks good an' is walkin' straight enough. So den, dis big guy steps up to a little guy dat's standin' deh, an' says, "How d'yuh get t' Eighteent' Avenoo an' Sixty-sevent' Street?" he says.

"Jesus! Yuh got me, chief," duh little guy says to him. "I ain't been heah long myself. Where is duh place?" he says. "Out in duh Flatbush section somewhere?"

"Nah," duh big guy says. "It's out in Bensonhoist. But I was neveh deh befoeh. How d'yuh get deh?"

"Jesus," duh little guy says, scratchin' his head, y'know—yuh could see duh little guy didn't know his way about—"yuh got me, chief. I neveh hoid of it. Do any of youse guys know where it is?" he says to me.

"Sure," I says. "It's out in Bensonhoist. Yuh take duh Fourt' Avenoo express, get off at Fifty-nint' Street, change to a Sea Beach local deh, get off at Eighteent' Avenoo an' Sixty-toid, an' den walk down foeh blocks. Dat's all yuh got to do," I says.

"Gwan!" some wise guy dat I neveh seen befoeh pipes up. "Whatcha talkin' about?" he says—oh, he was wise, y'know. "Duh guy is crazy! I tell yuh what yuh do," he says to duh big guy. "Yuh change to duh West End line at Toity-sixt'," he tell him. "Get off at Noo Utrecht an' Six-teent' Avenoo," he says. "Walk two blocks oveh, foeh blocks up," he says, "an' you'll be right deh." Oh, a wise guy, y'know.

"Oh, yeah?" I says. "Who told you so much?" He got me sore because he was so wise about it. "How long you been livin' heah?" I says.

"All my life," he says. "I was bawn in Williamsboig," he says. "An' I can tell you t'ings about dis town you neveh hoid of," he says.

"Yeah?" I says.

"Yeah," he says.

"Well, den, you can tell me t'ings about dis town dat nobody else has eveh hoid of, either. Maybe you make it all up yoehself at night," I says, "befoeh you go to sleep—like cuttin' out papeh dolls, or somp'n."

"Oh, yeah?" he says. "You're pretty wise, ain't yuh?"

"Oh, I don't know," I says. "Duh boids ain't usin' my head for Lincoln's statue yet," I says. "But I'm wise enough to know a phony when I see one."

"Yeah?" he says. "A wise guy, huh? Well, you're so wise dat some-one's goin' t'bust yuh one right on duh snoot some day," he says. "Dat's how wise *you* are."

Well, my train was comin', or I'da smacked him den and dere, but when I seen duh train was comin', all I said was, "All right, mugg! I'm sorry I can't stay to take keh of you, but I'll be seein' yuh sometime, I hope, out in duh cemetery." So den I says to duh big guy, who'd been standin' deh all duh time, "You come wit me," I says. So when we gets onto duh train I says to him, "Where yuh goin' out in Bensonhoist?" I says. "What numbeh are yuh lookin' for?" I says. *You* know—I t'ought if he told me duh address I might be able to help him out.

"Oh," he says. "I'm not lookin' for no one. I don't know no one out deh."

"Then whatcha goin' out deh for?" I says.

"Oh," duh guy says, "I'm just goin' out to see duh place," he says. "I like duh sound of duh name—Bensonhoist, y'know—so I t'ought I'd go out an' have a look at it."

"Whatcha tryin t'hand me?" I says. "Watcha tryin t'do—kid me?" *You* know, I t'ought duh guy was bein' wise wit me.

"No," he says, "I'm tellin' yuh duh troot. I like to go out an' take a look at places wit nice names like dat. I like to go out an' look at all kinds of places," he says.

"How'd yuh know deh was such a place," I says, "if yuh neveh been deh befoeh?"

"Oh," he says, "I got a map."

"A *map*?" I says.

"Sure," he says, "I got a map dat tells me about all dese places. I take it wit me every time I come out heah," he says.

And Jesus! Wit dat, he pulls it out of his pocket, an' so help me, but he's *got* it—he's tellin' duh troot—a big map of duh whole f—— place with all duh different pahts mahked out. You know—Canarsie an' East Noo Yawk an' Flatbush, Bensonhoist, Sout' Brooklyn, duh Heights, Bay Ridge, Greenpernt—duh whole goddam layout, he's got it right deh on duh map.

"You been to any of dose places?" I says.

"Sure," he says, "I been to most of 'em. I was down in Red Hook just last night," he says.

"Jesus! Red Hook!" I says. "Whatcha do down deh?"

"Oh," he says, "nuttin' much. I just walked aroun'. I went into a coupla places an' had a drink," he says, "but most of the time I just walked aroun'."

"Just walked aroun'?" I says.

"Sure," he says, "just lookin' at t'ings, y'know."

"Where'd yuh go?" I asts him.

"Oh," he says, "I don't know duh name of duh place, but I could find it on my map," he says. "One time I was walkin' across some big fields where deh ain't no houses," he says, "but I could see ships oveh deh all lighted up. Dey was loadin'. So I walks across duh fields," he says, "to where duh ships are."

"Sure," I says, "I know where you was. You was down to duh Erie Basin."

"Yeah," he says, "I gues dat was it. Dey had some of dose big elevators an' cranes an' dey was loadin' ships, an' I could see some ships in drydock all lighted up, so I walks across duh fields to where dey are," he says.

"Den what did yuh do?" I says.

"Oh," he says, "nuttin' much. I came on back across duh fields after a while an' went into a coupla places an' had a drink."

"Didn't nuttin' happen while yuh was in dere?" I says.

"No," he says. "Nuttin' much. A coupla guys was drunk in one of duh places an' started a fight, but dey bounced 'em out," he says, "an' den one of duh guys stahted to come back again, but duh bartender gets his baseball bat out from under duh counteh, so duh guy goes on."

"Jesus!" I said. "Red Hook!"

"Sure," he says. "Dat's where it was, all right."

"Well, you keep outa deh," I says. "You stay away from deh."

"Why?" he says. "What's wrong wit it?"

"Oh," I says, "It's a good place to stay away from, dat's all. It's a good place to keep out of."

"Why?" he says. "Why is it?"

Jesus! Whatcha gonna do wit a guy as dumb as dat? I saw it wasn't no use to try to tell him nuttin', he wouldn't know what I was talkin' about, so I just says to him, "Oh, nuttin'. Yuh might get lost down deh, dat's all."

"Lost?" he says. "No, I wouldn't get lost. I got a map," he says.

A map! Red Hook! Jesus.

So den duh guy begins to ast me all kinds of nutty questions: how big was Brooklyn an' could I find my way aroun' in it, an' how long would it take a guy to know duh place.

"Listen!" I says. "You get dat idea outa yoeh head right now," I says. "You ain't neveh gonna get to know Brooklyn," I says. "Not in a hundred yeahs. I been livin' heah all my life," I says, "an' I don't even know all deh is to know about it, so how do you expect to know duh town," I says, "when you don't even live heah?"

"Yes," he says, "but I got a map to help me find my way about."

"Map or no map," I says, "yuh ain't gonna get to know Brooklyn wit no map," I says.

"Can you swim?" he says, just like dat. Jesus! By dat time, y'know, I begun to see dat duh guy was some kind of nut. He'd had plenty to drink, of course, but he had dat crazy look in his eye I didn't like. "Can you swim?" he says.

"Sure," I says. "Can't you?"

"No," he says. "Not more'n a stroke or two. I neveh loined good."

"Well, it's easy," I says. "All yuh need is a little confidence. Duh way I loined, me older bruddeh pitched me off duh dock one day when I was eight yeahs old, cloes an' all. 'You'll swim,' he says. 'You'll swim all right—or drown.' An' believe me, I *swam*! When yuh know yuh got to, you'll do it. Duh only t'ing yuh need is confidence. An' once you've loined," I says, "you've got nuttin' else to worry about. You'll neveh forget it. It's somp'n dat stays with yuh as long as yuh live."

"Can yuh swim good?" he says.

"Like a fish," I tells him. "I'm a regulah fish in duh wateh," I says. "I loined to swim right off duh docks wit all duh oddeh kids," I says.

"What would you do if yuh saw a man drownin'?" duh guy says.

"Do? Why, I'd jump in an' pull him out," I says. "Dat's what I'd do."

"Did yuh eveh see a man drown?" he says.

"Sure," "I see two guys—bot' times at Coney Island. Dey got out too far, an' neider one could swim. Dey drowned befoeh anyone could get to 'em."

"What becomes of people after dey've drowned out heah?" he says.

"Drowned out where?" I says.

"Out heah in Brooklyn."

"I don't know whatcha mean," I says. "Neveh hoid of no one drownin' heah in Brooklyn, unless you mean a swimmin' pool. Yuh can't drown in Brooklyn," I says. "Yuh gotta drown somewhere else—in duh ocean, where dere's wateh."

"Drownin'," duh guy says, lookin' at his map. "Drownin'." Jesus! I could see by den he was some kind of nut, he had dat crazy expression in his eyes when he looked at you, an' I didn't know what he might do. So we was comin' to a station, an' it wasn't my stop, but I got off anyway, an' waited for duh next train.

"Well, so long, chief," I says. "Take it easy, now."

"Drownin'," duh guy says, lookin' at his map. "Drownin'."

Jesus! I've t'ought about dat guy a t'ousand times since den an' wondered what eveh happened to 'm goin' out to look at Bensonhoist because he liked duh name! Walkin' aroun' t'roo Red Hook by himself at night an' lookin' at his map! How many people did I see get drowned out heah in Brooklyn! How long would it take a guy wit a good map to know all deh was to know about Brooklyn!

Jesus! What a nut *he* was! I wondeh what eveh happened to 'im, anyway! I wondeh if someone knocked him on duh head, or if he's still wanderin' aroun' in duh subway in duh middle of duh night wit his little map! Duh poor guy! Say, I've got to laugh, at dat, when I t'ink about him! Maybe he's found out by now dat he'll neveh live long enough to know duh whole of Brooklyn. It'd take a guy a lifetime to know Brooklyn t'roo an' t'roo. An' even den, yuh wouldn't know it all.

drama

DIALOGUE

Herbert Woodward Martin

Characters

The Policeman . . . is, I would say, American, white,
aged thirty-five years, somewhat angry and primarily overly
ambitious for having remained a foot patrolman since
he joined the city's police force.

The Pedestrian . . . is an American Negro, personifying
a conceit. He is youthful, handsome, dressed casually, and
is aged twenty-five or six.

The Scene . . . is a West Side street. In particular it is
95th street and Columbus aveune. It has suddenly begun to rain,
and just as suddenly, there are no people to be seen, except
the two who are hurrying towards this not intended meeting.

Policeman: Hey . . . you there, come over here!! *(The young man does not stop.)* I mean, you, there, STOP! Come Over Here!!

Pedestrian: Yes?

Policeman: Where are you going?

Pedestrian: I'm not going; I'm coming.

Policeman: Where are you coming to?

Pedestrian: No, I think I'm going.

Policeman: Don't make things difficult for me; either you're going or you're coming; you're doing one or the other. Everybody knows you can't do but one thing at a time.

Pedestrian: Oh, but there I beg to disagree with you, officer. A person can do two specific things at once. One can walk and talk, dance and sing, write and think. . . . *(a slight pause)*

Pedestrian: Don't you think about your family when you're off duty?

Policeman: Why should I? There's a patrolman who guards my wife and kids, same as I do this neighborhood.

Pedestrian: I suppose he has your wife and kids at heart?

Policeman: Sure.

Pedestrian: How do you know?

Policeman: I talked to him.

Pedestrian: And he told you that?

Policeman: Yes.

Pedestrian: So that leaves you with extra time to apply to this beat.

Policeman: Yes, that's it. That's the way it should be. Every man protecting his own.

Pedestrian: Well I would think you could find some other time to protect your own like on a bright sunny day or on a cool afternoon, but certainly not in a rain storm. That's a hell-of-a-way to protect something you love. Stopping a person in this downpour, really officer, one would think you had better sense.

Policeman: I stopped you because I want to know what you're carrying in that box?

Pedestrian: Whaaaat?

Policeman: I want to know what you have in that box?

Pedestrian: *(Indignantly.)* A bomb.

Policeman: *(Aside, to himself.)* He's more of a fool than I took him for.

Pedestrian: What did you say?

Policeman: I want to see what you have in that box.

Pedestrian: Now wait, just, a, minute.

Policeman: Come on, give it to me!

Pedestrian: I will not! I DON'T HAVE TO!! You don't have a search warrant, so I don't have to give you anything.

Policeman: You're forgetting something.

Pedestrian: Like what??

Policeman: I am the LAW!!!

Pedestrian: You won't be anything, if you cause me trouble. I have friends I'll have you know.

Policeman: Oh, sure, all of us have friends.

Pedestrian: I have *(emphasized)* important friends.

Policeman: Come on, *(pointing to the box)* Give me the box.

Pedestrian: *(A little bit shaken by the officer's insistence.* Look officer, let's forget the whole thing? How about it, huh?

Policeman: *(Forcefully)* Hand it over!

Pedestrian: There's nothing in here, *(points to the box)* I swear to you.

Policeman: Swearing to the law.

Pedestrian: There isn't a law against swearing.

Policeman: There is now.

Pedestrian: Aw, come off it officer, I'm getting wet clear through.

Policeman: Look Buddy, I get wet every time it rains, and I really get wet. If it isn't rain, it's snow, and if it isn't snow it's sweat, and if I'm not sweating the-hell-out-of-my-self, it's too goddam cold and I'm freezing to death. So don't cry to me about being stopped one night in the rain.

Pedestrian: Things are against you all around.

Policeman: Things are against all of us. From the looks of it, they ain't going to get any better. I ain't going to get to a sitting position until I prove I've been out here thinking about the people on this beat. I want you to know that I've been thinking about you personally. I want all of you people to know you're my constant worry, and that's day in, day out, night in, night out.

Pedestrian: You know it's good to know someone has your interests at heart.

Policeman: You're damn right, it's a good thing to know.

Pedestrian: Well I'll rest a lot easier now that I know you're around, because in this neighborhood, with all the Puerto Ricans moving in on every side, well. . . . It's just good to know you're out here protecting the Americans in this community. I don't want to seem like a bigot. You probably have an idea about what I'm saying.

Policeman: Say whatever you want, say it, don't be afraid, I may be the Law, but I have to admit I don't know everything, that's why I'm out here, watching, loving, pro-

tecting, *(He gets carried away as he begins to believe himself)* rain or shine, sleet or snow, sick or well, I'm out here because I love the people on this beat. Every, last, one, of, them.

Pedestrian: I hope that doesn't include the P.Rs. You know they're . . . infiltrating our country, . . . *(very slowly)* INFILTRATING *(sudden realization)* You understand? I bet their coming here is Communist inspired.

Policeman: Say, you just might have something there, I never would have thought about them, in that way.

Pedestrian: I bet your superiors would be interested in what you might find out. They should be investigated!! It is getting worse and worse—even TV commercials are in Spanish. I tell you we're being undermined by the Communists, and there ought to be something done before we find ourselves under their thumb. And something ought to be done about the P.Rs. they're taking over everything, and on top of that, forcing the working people to take care of them when they don't feel like working. God damn they're so street-corner-lazy . . . but you have to give it to them—they do stick together, always talking in Spanish. Why I bet you it's all a plot to take over the whole country.

Policeman: Say, you've got a good idea, there.

Pedestrian: Officer, I'm not so smart; anyone with a little bit of sense can see what's happening around here.

Policeman: Yes, but I'd say you were pretty smart though . . . By the way, what's your name?

Pedestrian: Washington.

Policeman: Washington what?

Pedestrian: Mr. George Washington.

Policeman: Look, I like you, you don't have to kid around with me.

Pedestrian: That's my name.

Policeman: Your old lady sure must have been patriotic.

Pedestrian: Yes, you might say that. She was always telling me to love my country. It's too bad she isn't here to see my equality. Say . . . Now that you know my name, what's your number?

Policeman: Huh?

Pedestrian: Your identification number.

Policeman: Oh, one-one, three-three, five, but the people who know me call me Abe.

Pedestrian: Same here, George.

Policeman: (*They shake hands; and the Policeman in a very calm and friendly voice.*) Now George, if you don't have any objections, I'd like to have a look at your bomb.

Pedestrian: (*Unaware at first.*) What bomb? I don't have a bomb.

Policeman: (*Pointing to the box.*) You said you had a bomb in that box.

Pedestrian: Oh, that, I was just kidding.

Policeman: Do you think the Law is something to kid around with, George?

Pedestrian: No, you may not kid around, but you sure as hell have been screwing around with my health in this downpour.

Policeman: Alright, Mr. George Washington, Let's Go.

Pedestrian: Go? Go where?

Policeman: I'm running you in.

Pedestrian: And what, might I ask is the charge?

Policeman: I'll think of something by the time we get to the station.

Pedestrian: Look, you don't have a right to run me anywhere!

Policeman: You'd better remember while you're talking so smart that I'm still the Law.

Pedestrian: *You* are just a plain and simple foot-cop, and *you* had better remember that, because (*pause*) *I have important friends* who can fix you. You'd better watch out you don't make too many mistakes or you'll be out here for life.

Policeman: Look you don't scare me. I've always said the minute one of you guys gets ahead you show your ass. *You* think you're pretty damn important because you're smart and know somebody?

Pedestrian: I'd say both of them were important, and anyone who didn't have them would be foolish. I know my rights.

Policeman: You don't have any rights! You have what I tell you you got, and right now I'd say you don't have anything. Now either you turn over that box or . . .

Pedestrian: There's nothing in this box that concerns you!

Policeman: Let me decide that, George.

Pedestrian: Now Looooook. There's nothing in here but my *laundry*.

Policeman: A pretty unorthodox way to be carrying laundry, I'd say.

Pedestrian: (*With arrogance*) I carry my laundry any way I damn please.

Policeman: For the last time, are you going to tell me what's in the box?

Pedestrian: Wet clothes. Why? What are you, some kind of a wet clothes inspector? (*The policeman forcibly takes hold of the box.*) Now look here officer.

Policeman: Goddamn, they are wet, and now my hands are all wet too.

Pedestrian: Nobody invited you to go poking your hands in my laundry box. *(He then gives the policeman a dirty look as if he were a fucking nut.)*

Policeman: Don't look at me as if I were some kind of a fucking nut.

Pedestrian: LOOK, 1 2 3 4 5

Policeman: One-one, three-three, five. Got it?

Pedestrian: Well whatever the hell it is, you are a fucking nut, you were born that way, and there are some things a person can't help, and that you can't help. Not even time can help you. It's too bad about you. For the rest of your life you can look forward to being nothing more than a flunky of a foot-cop. But that's the way the breaks fall. *(The Pedestrian jerks his box, turns and begins to walk away. The Policeman immediately draws his pistol, fires several shots, and the Pedestrian falls dead.)*

Policeman: I'm the law. You *made* me this way!!! And that's that. You gave me the Law, you smart bas-

tard . . . Maybe you think you gave it to me for a little while, but that was your mistake. You were right—time will never change me, but there's a chance *I* may change *it. (He goes to his Police-car and begins a radio report)* X one-one, three-three, five calling headquarters, come in.

An Answering Voice: Headquarters, go ahead X one-one, three-three, five.

Policeman: Area problem . . . suspicious characters . . . two Negroes, One got away . . . Send morgue wagon . . . 95th and Columbus. X one-one, three-three, five out. *(He gets out of the car, looks about, the rain has stopped. He goes over to the body, visibly plants a plastic bag under the clothes in the box, stands up, heaves a sigh and folds his arms, looks down at the dead body and says)* I'm going to sit behind that desk yet, colored boy, I'LL SIT BEHIND THAT DESK, YET.

Curtain

THE NOSE OF SISYPHUS

Lawrence Ferlinghetti

A grey day on a city playground. A very large child's slide, its high end just off stage, right. Left, a huge iron jungle gym. In the background, a fence with pennants flying from the tops of its posts, and a flagpole with a national flag.

Prostrate on the child's side, trying to climb up it and at the same time trying to push a globe of the world up the slide with his huge nose, *Sisyphus* himself, in sweatshirt, track pants & gym shoes. Each time he gets the globe up a foot or two, he slides back down the slide, the globe with him.

A high wind is blowing through this playground, pennants & flags streaming in it. A *crowd of citizens* is just starting to climb onto the left side of the jungle gym. This *crowd* consists of as many of the following as there is room for: fashionable ladies in floppy hats carrying umbrellas, gypsy fortune-tellers in feather boas carrying crystal balls, striptease artists with inflatable bras carrying bicycle pumps with which they now and then re-inflate their breasts, subway riders in snapbrim hats carrying briefcases and newspapers they attempt to read as they climb and hang as on subway straps, Indians in feather headdresses with feather lances, railroad switch-men with little red flags, ski champions wearing skis, fishermen with casting rods & feather hooks, sandwich men, vacuum cleaner salesmen with vacuums, toy balloon vendors, firemen with hoses, all climbing into the wind, over or through the jungle gym, with all their problems & equipment, the wind growing stronger and stronger as *Sisyphus* turns and beckons furiously for the *crowd* to follow him, resumes his climbing, turns & beckons again, resumes his climbing, turns & beckons again, resumes his climbing as the citizens redouble their efforts to advance over or through the jungle gym against the wind, some laughing, some crying, some applauding each other, as

Sisyphus begins to shout and sing spontaneous combinations of the following phrases: "Hard Hilltop! Soft Shoe! Nailed Foot! Broken Hoboken! Gringo Hat Check! Bent Banana! Blue Baboon! Drunk Boat! Beat Battlements! Brainpan Plumbing! Dream Crapper! Cricket & Violin! Sweet Sin! Stone Tattoo! O Seasons! O Chateaux! Sylph Skin! Lost Lips! Light! Light! Kiss Kiss! In Photo Finish! In Hook of Time!" And the citizens begin to chant after him improvised combinations of the same liturgy, all still straining forward into the wind which grows still stronger & stronger, as

A whistle is blown loudly offstage right and the great wind all at once ceases completely, flags and citizens fall limp, and bright sun bursts out, as *Big Baboon* in baseball cap with whistle on cord around neck slides down slide from offstage right and lands on top of *Sisyphus* who tumbles off onto ground. *Big Baboon* grabs globe and throws it over slide & out of sight, furiously blowing his whistle as citizens frantically disentangle themselves from jungle gym & each other and straggle off, left, as *Big Baboon* still blowing his whistle pulls off *Sisyphus'* fake nose and puts it on himself, mugs, scratches, runs & leaps & swings on top of jungle gym, still blowing his whistle, as *Sisyphus* jumps up holding his face in both hands and runs off after last citizen calling "Light! Light!" "Kiss! Kiss!" as

Big Baboon swings down from jungle gym, somersaults to edge of stage, glares at audience, takes off false nose & throws it into audience, blows whistle furiously at audience, and roars.

IN MEMORY OF
OUR DEAD MOTHER
ELLEN HEFFERN
WIFE OF
WILLIAM HEFFERN
DIED
AGED

9

THE FUTURE
A Bad Trip?

How are we going to live in the cities of the year 2000? John Dewey once wrote that "to the being fully alive, the future is not ominous but a promise; it surrounds the present as a halo." But several writers in this book have predicted an inhuman future for the cities unless radical changes revive each of the seven systems discussed in the various sections. The following selections, then, present both promising and frightening visions of the future city—its architecture, its economic, political, and educatonal systems, and its physical and psychological environments.

"Plans for Future Cities" are imaginative visual examples of what man as architect and engineer could contribute to the cities of tomorrow. Because architects and designers like Soleri, Fuller, Pelli, and Chambless are working on such structures now, these photographs show exciting promises which could be fulfilled.

In "Drop City: A Total Living Environment," Albin Wagner describes life in some of the communes beginning to appear in the western and southwestern United States. Made up of people who reject life within a technologically polluted urban society, Drop City exemplifies one kind of future human community. The Cuando Community described in the next selection is worlds apart from Drop City. In his letter to the editor headlined "The Cuando Community: Beacon in a Dark City," George Dennison describes the social revolution being waged by a communal "family" in present-day New York City, and proposes it as a model of hope for all cities, present and future.

"The Pedestrian," a short story by Ray Bradbury, and "Last Gasps," a one-act TV play by Terrence McNally, project not models of liberation or hope but images of disaster for the future. Based on the present facts of indifference and alienation among city dwellers (seen in Section 1) and the poisoning of the air (seen in Section 2), their predictions must be taken seriously, although other selections in this book show that human beings can change such facts of urban life. The final printed selection in this book is an essay by the modern philosopher J. Krishnamurti called "The Individual and Society," which encourages the reader to see the city as the creation of the men who live there, as "the outward expression of man." To see the connection between the quality of a given society and the quality of the men who make it up is to realize the blindness of the theories which insist that the city has an evil, incurable identity separate from the men who live in it. City dwellers themselves must ultimately choose whether to save or destroy their settlements.

The Urban Reader has presented throughout signs and prophecies of doom and promise. It follows them with a photographic essay of city people. To look into their faces and our own, to see their troubles and their celebrations, is to imagine our way into the human city. And that trip is the first step on the journey toward a future worth creating.

PLANS FOR FUTURE CITIES

HEXAHEDRON

Paolo Soleri

In Hexahedron, for 170,000 people, Soleri superimposed two pyramids. The sides of the pyramids function as membranes, one living/working unit that is thick, for a hollowed out interior almost twice the height of the Empire State Building. Like a prism, it fractures light by day and reflects light at night. Hexahedron more than confirms the notion that high-density living does not result in a loss of environmental richness. Man can, in fact, achieve an artificial landscape which competes successfully with the natural. The model was conceived and built in the period 1967–1969. D. Wall, Curator, Paolo Soleri Exhibition, Corcoran Gallery of Art. Photograph by Jon Eaton.

TETRAHEDRAL CITY

R. Buckminster Fuller

Buckminster Fuller's design for a floating tetrahedronal city (shown superimposed on San Francisco Bay)—In sizes up to two-and-a-half miles high, it
could make possible habitation of the earth's water surfaces. Courtesy
R. Buckminster Fuller.

THE MEGASTRUCTURE

Cesar Pelli

One possible solution to the problem of space and time in our cities is the megastructure. Essentially a city in one vast, continuous building, the megastructure would encompass dwellings, stores, service facilities, offices and recreation centers within one concentrated urban structure. Everything would be within walking or easy driving distance—including the countryside, which would surround the city, not be broken into fragments within it. This concentration would provide a richer, more diverse life than that of suburbia, while preserving the countryside from suburban sprawl. In addition, it would reduce the size of today's metropolis to the more workable, cohesive political unit of under 50,000 population that environmental planners suggest. The plan for one such megastructure is shown here, a "contour-rise" urban core designed for the Santa Monica mountains of southern California by Cesar Pelli and A. J. Lumsden, Director of Design, Daniel, Mann, Johnson and Mendenhall.

PROJECT FOR ROADTOWN

Edgar Chambless

Chambless assumed that buildings grouped along a route of travel ought logically to incorporate the means of transportation itself, and so he planned a continuous concrete house of indefinite length, with trains in the basement and a pedestrian street on the roof. The designer observed that commuting time to and from a major city would be reduced; there would be great economies in the construction of utility systems; and such a compact linear city would protect cultivated land from the blight of suburban sprawl. The drawing was executed in 1910. Reprinted by permission of The Museum of Modern Art.

DROP CITY: A TOTAL LIVING ENVIRONMENT

Albin Wagner

It is impossible to define Drop City. It fell out a window in Kansas three years ago with a mattress and a balloon full of water and landed in a goat pasture near Trinidad, Colorado. At first Droppers lived in tents and tarpaper shacks. And then others began to see the same vision and began making things. Geodesic domes. Now there are sixteen to twenty Droppers living in ten domes and as many different ideas of what Drop City is as there are Droppers.

We have attempted to create in Drop City a total living environment, outside the structure of society, where the artist can remain in touch with himself, with other creative human beings.

We live in geodesic domes and domes of other crystalline forms because the dome shape is easier to construct. We live on a subsistence level and almost entirely scrounge the materials for our own buildings. All materials are used. Car tops, cement, wood, plastic. The cheapest and least structural of building materials are structurally sound when used in a true tension system.

We can buy car-tops in Albuquerque, N.M., for 20¢ each. We jump on top of a car with an ax and chop them out, stomp out the back glass, strip off the mirrors, and pull out the insulation. All of it can be used to cover a large dome for the small cost of about $30.

We have discovered a new art form: creative scrounging. We dismantle abandoned bridges by moonlight. We are sort of advanced junkmen taking advantage of advanced obsolescence. Drop City was begun without money, built on practically nothing. None of us is employed or has a steady income. Somehow we have not gone hungry, or done without materials. Things come to us.

America, the affluent waste society. There is enough waste here to feed and house ten thousand artists. Enough junk to work into a thousand thousand works of art. To the townspeople in Trinidad, five miles away, we are scroungers, bums, garbage pickers. They are right. Perhaps the most beautiful creation in all Drop City is our junk pile. The garbage of the garbage pickers.

Drop City is a tribal unit. It has no formal structure, no written laws, yet the intuitive structure is amazingly complex and functional. Not a single schedule has been made, and less than three things have come to a vote. Even though Droppers rarely, if ever, agree on anything, everything works itself out with the help of the cosmic forces. We are conscious of ourselves and others as human beings.

Each Dropper is free. Each does what he wants. No rules, no duties, no obligations. Anarchy. But as anarchistic as the growth of an organism which has its own internal needs and fulfills them in a natural, simple way, without compulsion.

Droppers are not asked to do anything. They work out of the need to work. Out of guilt or emptiness the desire to work, hopefully, arises. It is no longer work, but pleasure. Doing nothing is real work. We play at working. It is as gratifying as eating or loving. We are based on the pleasure principle. Our main concern is to be alive.

Droppers come in all sizes, shapes, colors: painters, writers, architects, panhandlers, film-makers, unclassifiables. Each has his own individual endeavors and achievements. These perhaps tell what we are doing more than anything else. But they cannot be enumerated. They have to be seen, read, touched, heard. They speak for themselves. But we do all have this in common—whatever art we produce is not separated from our lives.

Droppers have painted the Ultimate Painting. A rotating infinite sphere, a circular geodesic structure loaded with spatial paradox, complete with strobatac. A painting to walk up the stairs into and lose your mind by. The Ultimate Painting was done by five Droppers, to make it five times better. The Ultimate Painting is for sale for $60,000.

The Droppers have printed a comic book called The Being Bag. We welcome the feds and postal inspectors who come to harangue us about its content. Our poet looks forward to the inspectors and their reading of his work.

Droppers make movies, black-and-white wind poems, flickering TV beauties with all the subliminal delights of pulsating Coke ads, the crystal-molecular good sense of a dome going into time-lapse, and the grunting goodness of sex. We have two movies on Drop City for distribution.

The second weekend in June we held a Joy Festival. The First Annual Drop City Festival and Bacchanal Post Walpurgis and Pre-Equinox Overflow and Dropping. Over 300 people attended. It was a freakout in all media, 96 hours of continuous mind-blow.

We want to use everything, new, junk, good, bad, we want to be able to make limitless things. We want TV videotape recorders and cameras. We want computers and miles of color film and elaborate cine cameras and tape decks and amps and echo-chambers and everywhere. We want millionaire patrons. We need the most up-to-date equipment in the world to make our things. We want an automatic reactor.

Drop City is the first attempt to use domes for housing a community. Buckminster Fuller gave us his 1966 Dymaxion Award for "poetically economic structural achievements." We hope to buy more land, build more Drop Cities all over the world, the universe. Free and open way stations for every and anyone. Living space and heat can be made available to all at a fraction of the present cost through application of advanced building techniques such as solarheated domes. Already Drop South is firmly established near Albuquerque, N.M.

Drop City is Home. It is a strange place. An incredible webbing of circumstance and chance, planning and accidents, smashed thumbs and car-tops. We are not responsible for what and where we are, we have only taken our place in space and light and time. We are only people who want love, food, warmth. We have no integrity. We borrow, copy, steal any and all ideas and things. We use everything. We take things, we make things, we give things.

Drop City pivots on a sublime paradox, opposing forces exist side by side in joy and harmony. A psychedelic community? Chemically, no. We consider drugs unnecessary. But etymologically, perhaps. We are alive. We dance the Joy-dance. We listen to the eternal rhythm. Our feet move to unity, a balanced step of beauty and strength. Creation is joy. Joy is love. Life, love, joy, energy are one. We are all one. Can you hear the music? Come dance with us.

THE CUANDO COMMUNITY: BEACON IN A DARK CITY

George Dennison

Dear Sir:

I'm sending this letter to friends and acquaintances, and to people I think might take a special interest in the activities it describes, which are those of an unusual and wholly admirable neighborhood association called Cuando.

The members of this group—young Puerto Rican men and women living in the East 1st Street area of Manhattan—have been working for two years to improve the horrendous condition of the neighborhood, especially as it affects the young. They began modestly, but now the logic of the mess has brought them to a number of projects they can neither abandon nor—without help—fulfill. The most important of these is a full-fledged, non-tuition, libertarian school (or tutorial cooperative), staffed at present by two full-time teachers and one assistant. Eight children attend the school. (There will soon be more.) All are from broken and impoverished homes. A 14-year-old boy and several 10-year-olds are unable to read, though they are actually of good intelligence. *In one short month*, all of the children are responding (some few spectacularly) to their sudden medication of common decency and close relations with concerned adults.

Since I seem to be talking about eight children, let me describe my own larger interest in Cuando. I think others may share it. It's simply this: that in the context of federal, state, and city ministrations, this local, almost powerless organization is blazingly rational and correct. It is correct to move *humanly* against dehumanization. It is correct to create havens of safety in an environment that is appallingly unsafe. It is correct to band together and try to fill, *directly*, the fundamental needs of communal life.

These actions, obviously, are responses to crises. But they are more than that, for they form a pattern of a particular kind. I mean that they are the *type* of truly functional decentralized responsibility. They are libertarian and sensitive. They are political in the fundamental (to me, most valid) sense that the organized activity exists exclusively, and visibly, for the purpose of meeting common needs. All this, certainly, is writ small, yet it can be classed among the impulses that keep alive the idea of non-violent social revolution. I am not claiming that Cuando itself is the seed of anything. (One can hardly claim even that it will exist a year from now!) I *am* saying, however, that Cuando possesses a rationality which, in kind, and in the present condition of political life, is irresistibly attractive. It is a tiny beacon, and for my own part I want to keep it lit.

That's my long-range interest, and I do certainly urge it on others. It may be, however, that the short, that is immediate, view is far more compelling. The neighborhood is a meat-grinder. We know that heroin is being pushed in the public school. We know—and this is the newest development—that neighborhood addicts are recruiting 12 and 13-year-old kids into robbery gangs. The police know too, and are nearly useless. Nor has anyone failed to observe that the chief products of the public school are ignorance, apathy, and collapse of self. All this is what Cuando is contending with. On the one hand, they're snowed under. On the other hand, their achievements are impressive. (Which is how things are these days.)

I find it impressive:

1. that Cuando exists;
2. that for more than a year they have conducted an after-school storefront Children's Center, staffed by volunteers and paid for out of their own pockets;
3. that for more than two years they have conducted athletic programs and weekend outings (Frank Baez, Melvin Cadiz, Daniel Torres);

4. that they have conducted a successful voter registration drive (David Munoz);

5. that they have initiated clean-up campaigns; have cleared a vacant lot for play; have collaborated with an architect on the design of a mini-park, and are trying to bring it into existence (John Corsale); have agitated (and are) for playground lights, for landlord and NYC responsibility, and for some form of official and community response to the drug problem;

6. that they have held one very successful block festival, and are trying to make it an annual event;

7. that they have formed a school, have recruited students, and have been able to inspire three teachers to take on exhausting responsibilities.

The expenses and labors of Cuando have been borne by the members themselves, all of whom work hard for a living. Now their new school is under way, and the teachers, Barbara Hawkins and Damon Cranz, and their assistant, Teddy Gilliam (all of whom have been working without pay), must soon be given money if they are to go on eating. This is another of the impressive things about Cuando: that they have been able to attract people like these, who without any guarantee of a living have more or less turned themselves over to the community, not only teaching but visiting families and receiving visits from neglected kids, often working far into the evening. Their devotion will be all the more evident if I mention that all have agreed there will be no pay for time already spent, which amounts now to well over a month. Ann Wagner, a lawyer, has worked long and hard for Cuando, similarly without pay. Volunteers from the Catholic Worker have manned the Children's Center. Among others who have helped and encouraged Cuando are: Paul Goodman and David Andree, a psychologist, whose friendship with the original members has influenced much that is happening now; the Reverend William P. Pickett of the Church of the Nativity, who has made space available; Father Daniel Berrigan (to whom many others, also, are indebted); Joe Gilchrist, of the Cornell United Religious Works; Anita Moses, of the Children's Community Workshop School; and Mabel Chrystie Dennison.

Obviously, there is a spirit here that touches others. Perhaps it can be proposed as a model of hope, 1970's style, i.e., the enterprise looks impossible, it won't divert our larger rush to disaster, all powers (including the unions) are either by policy set against it or profoundly indifferent, *and yet* one is moved (even excited) in the presence of Cuando: their endeavor is admirable, their people cheerful, practical, and good, their example invaluable, their labor productive. Hope, then, is this: that under the enduring condition of expecting nothing, one is heartened by the creation of positive good.

Cuando is approaching foundations for long-term (one year! two years!) support. In the meantime, the teachers (and children too, since lunches are provided) must eat, materials must be purchased, trips must be paid for, more children must be reached.

I know that everyone who reads this letter reads, every week, dozens of urgent and truly important pleas for help. I don't know what to say about this, except here's another. I needn't stress that it's urgent. I do want to stress, however, that Cuando is unique. Its concerns are the basic functions of social life. It is a life-support organization—for which reason its claims on our assistance are of the clearest and most legitimate kind.

Cuando is tax exempt. The address is: Cuando, Inc., 39 East 1st Street, New York 10003.

GEORGE DENNISON
East 7th Street

THE PEDESTRIAN

Ray Bradbury

To enter out into that silence that was the city at eight o'clock of a misty evening in November, to put your feet upon that buckling concrete walk, to step over grassy seams and make your way, hands in pockets, through the silences, that was what Mr. Leonard Mead most dearly loved to do. He would stand upon the corner of an intersection and peer down long moonlit avenues of sidewalk in four directions, deciding which way to go, but it really made no difference; he was alone in this world of A.D. 2131, or as good as alone, and with a final decision made, a path selected, he would stride off sending patterns of frosty air before him like the smoke of a cigar.

Sometimes he would walk for hours and miles and return only at midnight to his house. And on his way he would see the cottages and homes with their dark windows, and it was not unequal to walking through a graveyard, because only the faintest glimmers of firefly light appeared in flickers behind the windows. Sudden gray phantoms seemed to manifest themselves upon inner room walls where a curtain was still undrawn against the night, or there were whisperings and murmurs where a window in a tomblike building was still open.

Mr. Leonard Mead would pause, cock his head, listen, look, and march on, his feet making no noise on the lumpy walk. For a long while now the sidewalks had been vanishing under flowers and grass. In ten years of walking by night or day, for thousands of miles, he had never met another person walking, not one in all that time.

He now wore sneakers when strolling at night, because the dogs in intermittent squads would parallel his journey with barkings if he wore hard heels, and lights might click on and faces appear, and an entire street be startled by the passing of a lone figure, himself, in the early November evening.

On this particular evening he began his journey in a westerly direction, toward the hidden sea. There was a good crystal frost in the air; it cut the nose going in and made the lungs blaze like a Christmas tree inside; you could feel the cold light going on and off, all the branches filled with invisible snow. He listened to the faint push of his soft shoes through autumn leaves with satisfaction, and whistled a cold quiet whistle between his teeth, occasionally picking up a leaf as he passed, examining its skeletal pattern in the infrequent lamplights as he went on, smelling its rusty smell.

"Hello, in there," he whispered to every house on every side as he moved. "What's up tonight on Channel 4, Channel 7, Channel 9? Where are the cowboys rushing, and do I see the United States Cavalry over the next hill to the rescue?"

The street was silent and long and empty, with only his shadow moving like the shadow of a hawk in mid-country. If he closed his eyes and stood very still, frozen, he imagined himself upon the center of a plain, a wintry windless Arizona country with no house in a thousand miles, and only dry riverbeds, the streets, for company.

"What is it now?" he asked the houses, noticing his wrist watch. "Eight-thirty P.M. Time for a dozen assorted murders? A quiz? A revue? A comedian falling off the stage?"

Was that a murmur of laughter from within a moon-white house? He hesitated, but went on when nothing more happened. He stumbled over a particularly uneven section of walk as he came to a cloverleaf intersection which stood silent where two main highways crossed the town. During the day it was a thunderous surge of cars, the gas stations open, a great insect rustling and ceaseless jockeying for position as the scarab beetles, a faint incense puttering from their exhausts, skimmed homeward to the far horizons. But now these highways too were like streams in a dry season, all stone and bed and moon radiance.

He turned back on a side street, circling around toward his home.

He was within a block of his destination when the lone car turned a corner quite suddenly and flashed a fierce white cone of light upon him. He stood entranced, not unlike a night moth, stunned by the illumination and then drawn toward it.

A metallic voice called to him:

"Stand still. Stay where you are! Don't move!"

He halted.

"Put up your hands."

"But—" he said.

"Your hands up! Or we'll shoot!"

The police, of course, but what a rare, incredible thing; in a city of three million, there was only one police car left. Ever since a year ago, 2130, the election year, the force had been cut down from three cars to one. Crime was ebbing; there was no need now for the police, save for this one lone car wandering and wandering the empty streets.

"Your name?" said the police car in a metallic whisper. He couldn't see the men in it for the bright light in his eyes.

"Leonard Mead," he said.

"Speak up!"

"Leonard Mead!"

"Business or profession?"

"I guess you'd call me a writer."

"No profession," said the police car, as if talking to itself. The light held him fixed like a museum specimen, needle thrust through chest.

"You might say that," said Mr. Mead. He hadn't written in years. Magazines and books didn't sell any more. Everything went on in the tomblike houses at night now, he thought, continuing his fancy. The tombs, ill-lit by television light, where the people sat like the dead, the gray or multi-colored lights touching their expressionless faces but never really touching *them*.

"No profession," said the phonograph voice, hissing. "What are you doing out?"

"Walking," said Leonard Mead.

"Walking!"

"Just walking," he said, simply, but his face felt cold.

"Walking, just walking, walking?"

"Yes, sir."

"Walking where? For what?"

"Walking for air. Walking to *see*."

"Your address!"

"Eleven South St. James Street."

"And there is air *in* your house, you have an air-*conditioner*, Mr. Mead?"

"Yes."

"And you have a viewing screen in your house to see with?"

"No."

"No?" There was a crackling quiet that in itself was an accusation.

"Are you married, Mr. Mead?"

"No."

"Not married," said the police voice behind the fiery beam. The moon was high and clear among the stars and the houses were gray and silent.

"Nobody wanted me," said Leonard Mead, with a smile.

"Don't speak unless you're spoken to!"

Leonard Mead waited in the cold night.

"Just walking, Mr. Mead?"

"Yes."

"But you haven't explained for what purpose."

"I explained: for air and to see, and just to walk."

"Have you done this often?"

"Every night for years."

The police car sat in the center of the street with its radio throat faintly humming.

"Well, Mr. Mead," it said.

"Is that all?" he asked politely.

"Yes," said the voice. "Here." There was a sigh, a pop. The back door of the police car sprang wide. "Get in."

"Wait a minute, I haven't done anything!"

"Get in."

"I protest!"

"Mr. Mead."

He walked like a man suddenly drunk. As he passed the front window of the car he looked in. As he had expected, there was no one in the front seat, no one in the car at all.

"Get in."

He put his hand to the door and peered into the back seat, which was a little cell, a little black jail with bars. It smelled of riveted steel. It smelled of harsh antiseptic; it smelled too clean and hard and metallic. There was nothing soft there.

"Now if you had a wife to give you an alibi," said the iron voice. "But—"

"Where are you taking me?"

The car hesitated, or rather gave a faint whirring click, as if information, somewhere, was dropping card by punch-slotted card under electric eyes. "To the Psychiatric Center for Research on Regressive Tendencies."

He got in. The door shut with a soft thud. The police car rolled through the night avenues, flashing its dim lights ahead.

They passed one house on one street a moment later, one house in an entire city of houses that were dark, but this one particular house had all its electric lights brightly lit, every window a loud yellow illumination, square and warm in the cool darkness.

"That's *my* house," said Leonard Mead.

No one answered him.

The car moved down the empty river bed streets and off away, leaving the empty streets with the empty sidewalks, and no sound and no motion all the rest of the chill November night.

LAST GASPS

Terrence McNally

A large clock, the kind whose minute hand visibly
"jumps" every sixty seconds.

It is 11:59. Hold there in silence until the minute hand
jumps and it is 12:00.

SFX: The sound of a siren explodes: deafening, urgent, terrifying.

Quick cut to a man in a straight back chair bending over
to tie his shoelaces. His head and body snap up at the sound
of the siren. He sits rigidly in the chair, not moving at all,
his eyes staring straight ahead right into the camera.

He fills his lungs with as much air as he possibly can.

Extreme close-up of man holding his breath. We watch him
in silence until his lungs explode for air. About 45 seconds.
The moment he gasps he falls out of the chair.

Camera holds a beat on the empty chair.

Black.

The clock. It is 11:59.

A SCIENTIST *in his laboratory, experimenting with a mouse.*

Scientist: Hey, now stop wriggling like that, Charley Brown! No one's going to hurt you.

He scrapes at the mouse's stomach with a scalpel.
The clock. The minute hand jumps and it is 12:00.

SFX: The siren sounds.

The scientist looks up from his work. He fills his
lungs with air.
Extreme close-up of scientist as he holds his breath as
long as he can.
We hear him speak as a voice–over while we watch his face:

Scientist (VO): That's it, there it is. We told them it would come to this, dealt them a straight deck. A child could have understood. Facts aren't difficult. Science is clear, science is precise. We warned them, we did our duty, our conscience is clear. How much longer? Not much anyway. The lung sacs will start to collapse and reflexively I'll gasp. So much about reflexes we never really learned. And cancer.

Scientist: We came real close there. Helen. Poor dear sweet Helen. And this. Now. We were trying to help, trying to find solutions. Our conscience is clear. There's almost pain, something very much like it. I was thinking! We just ran out of time, Charley Brown, there just wasn't any more left us.

He has reached his limit. He gasps for air. He falls.

Close shot of the mouse who is motionless now.

Black.

The clock. It is 11:59.
A TEACHER *is talking to her (unseen) students.*

Teacher: Now let's see if one of you can tell me the *name* of the queen who gave Columbus the Nina, the Pinta and the Santa Maria?

The clock. The minute hand jumps and it is 12:00.

SFX: The siren sounds.

The teacher reacts at once.

Teacher: Now quickly, children, you must do exactly as I say.

A Child (VO): Isabella! Queen Isabella!

Teacher: Not now Karen! We are going to play a very new and very wonderful game. We are going to take the deepest breath we ever took in our entire lives and then we are going to hold our breaths just as long as we possibly, possibly can. Now all together. One, two, three!

She inhales.

SFX: Sound of many children inhaling.

The teacher smiles. There is a long pause.

Teacher: Isn't this fun?

*Each time the teacher speaks, it should be clear she is
expelling as little air as is humanly possible.*

Teacher: Don't give up, children. Whoever wins this game will. . . .

She can't finish. Instead, she forces another smile. Silence.

You are all wonderful, wonderful children and I love you very, very much
and I am very proud of you.

Silence.

As long as you can, Timmy. Think of beautiful, happy things and the
game won't be so hard. Think of ————. Jane? . . . Jane gave up and
now she's out of the game but none of us are giving up. Timmy? . . .
Bobby? . . . Susan?

We can imagine the children falling before her eyes. Silence.

It's just us now, Carol. Let's see who wins.

*The teacher gasps for air. She falls. Behind her on the black-
board are written the name "Columbus" and the date "1492."*

Black.

The clock. It is 11:59.

A WRITER *at work at his typewriter. We peer over his shoulder
and can read what he is writing.*

WRITTEN WORDS: *From the terrace of their hotel room,
John and Sarah had a magnificent view of the Aegean Sea.
"If that's Homer's wine-dark sea, then he must have been
drinking green wine," John laughed. "Look at that,"
said Sarah, watching a stream of brown sewage flow
into the limpid water.*

The clock moves to 12:00.

SFX: The siren sounds.

*The writer's hands pause on the keyboard. We hear him take
a deep breath. After a moment, he begins to type again.*

What the writer writes: Since no one will find what I next write, there is no
point in writing it.
(He pauses.)
I loved.
(Another pause.)
Now is the time for all good men to come to the aid of their country.
Now is the time.

*We hear him gasp for air. His hands drop from the keyboard.
Camera holds a beat on what he has written.*

Black.

The clock. It is 11:59.

A NERVOUS WOMAN *is feeding a goldfish in a large round
glass bowl. She talks with a cigarette in her mouth and
chews on the filter.*

Nervous woman: Eat, you stupid fish. Eat, you goddamn stupid goldfish,
it's good for you!

*She sprinkles more food into the bowl while the fish swims
unconcernedly about.*

The clock jumps to 12:00.

SFX: The siren sounds.

*Nervous woman looks up terrified. She inhales, but not as
deeply as she might have liked to. She realizes this
but is frightened to take in anymore air in the room itself.
She runs frantically around the room looking for some place
where there might still be some good air. She opens a drawer,
empties it, inhales a little more. Then she rushes to
the fish bowl, empties it, puts it over her head, and inhales
some more. Next she runs to closet, flings open door, hurls out
clothes, goes into closet and closes the door behind her.*

*Close shot of goldfish on the floor. Motionless.
Silence. Moments pass. A dull thud as she slumps against
the door.*

Close shot of goldfish on the floor. Motionless.

Black.

The clock. It is 11:59.

An ITALIAN GIRL *is talking on the telephone.*

Italian girl: Si, mamma, vengo domani . . . baci a pappa da me . . . dite che vengo subito . . . arrivederci . . . si, ciao.

As she speaks, subtitles are flashed on the screen to tell us what she is saying.

Subtitles: Yes, mama, I'm coming tomorrow . . . Give daddy a kiss from me . . . Tell him I'm on my way . . . See you . . . Yes, bye!

She hangs up. She looks sad.

The clock jumps to 12:00.

SFX: The siren sounds.

She reacts, inhales. Then she goes to phone and dials. There seems to be an endless wait for someone to answer.

Italian girl: Paolo? Non parlare, non parlare, tesoro. Ascoltami. Non c'e tempo.

Subtitles: Paul? Don't speak, don't say a word. Listen to me. There isn't time.

Italian girl: Io t'amo, io t'amo tanto, io t'amo, io t'amo tanto, io t'amo, io t'amo tanto, io t'amo, io t'amo tanto, io t'amo, io t'amo tanto.

Subtitles: (Flashing on and off) I love you. I love you so much. I love you. I love you so much. I love you. I love you so much.

Italian girl and subtitles continue until she runs out of breaths, gasps for air and falls.

Close shot of receiver. There is no sound at all from the other end.

Black.

The clock. It is 11:59.

A BOY *and a* GIRL *in bed, two lovers. They have just finished making love.*

Boy: Hey!

Girl: (After a pause) What?

Boy: I was better.

Girl: (Rolling over to look at him) You thought?

She falls laughing into his arms.

The clock jumps to 12:00.

SFX: The siren sounds.

Boy and girl pull apart. They look at each other.

Boy inhales first.

Boy: When you can't anymore, take air from me.

Girl shakes her head.

Yes!

They kiss. An agonizingly long desperate-tender kiss. It is as if they were trying to suck life from each other's lips . . . or give it. Finally the boy suffocates, his mouth on hers. The girl realizes he is gone, pulls away from him, gasps in air and falls next to him on the bed.

Close shot of their two heads.

Black.

The clock. It is 11:59.

A NUN *saying her rosary.*

Nun: Hail Mary, full of grace, the Lord is with thee. Blessed art thou amongst women, and blessed is the fruit of thy womb, Jesus. Holy Mary, mother of God, pray for us sinners now and at the hour of our death, Amen. Hail Mary, full of grace, the Lord is with thee.

The clock jumps to 12:00.

SFX: The siren sounds.

The nun raises her eyes, holds there a beat, then lowers them, all the while continuing her rosary.

Nun: Blessed art thou amongst women and blessed is the fruit of thy womb, Jesus. Holy Mary, mother of God, pray for us sinners now and at the hour of our death. Amen. Hail Mary, full of grace, the Lord is with thee. Blessed art thou amongst women and blessed is the fruit of thy womb, Jesus.

The nun falls.

Close shot of rosary clenched in her hand.

Black.

The clock. It is 11:59.

A MAN *is sitting at a table writing out little cards. We peer over his shoulder and see what he has written.*

What we read: I am a deaf-mute. If you care to purchase this genuine ivory, original hand-carved by me good luck charm, I will be grateful to you. $5.00.

Man puts down card, picks up good luck charm, looks at it and smiles. He catches sight of his smiling reflection in a mirror, "says" something funny to himself and laughs soundlessly.

The clock jumps to 12:00.

SFX: The siren sounds.

The deaf-mute is standing in front of a mirror "talking" to himself and laughing soundlessly. A moment later and he falls.

Close shot of a large boxful of the good luck charms. The box is clearly marked "Made in Japan."

Black.

The clock. It is 11:59.

A MIDDLE-AGED LADY *is sitting under a hairdryer and doing her nails. She is smoking. Propped in front of her is a "How To Diet" book. As she alternately reads and dabs at her fingernails, she also drinks a coke and eats chocolates. She seems to be enjoying herself.*

The clock jumps to 12:00.

SFX: The siren sounds.

The middle-aged lady freezes, comprehends, then inhales.

Extreme close shot of her face. We hear her as a voice-over while we watch her face.

Middle-aged lady (VO): I was having my hair done. I was doing my nails and having my hair done. I was reading about a diet and smoking L&Ms and drinking a Coke and eating chocolate covered cherries . . . ciliegge, cherries are ciliegge in Italian . . . and doing my nails and having my hair done. My mind won't move. I can't think. I'm all alone and I'm having my hair done for Margaret's party. Think. Think of something. I'm having my hair done. I can't think of anything else. I was having my hair done. Ciliegge, cherries are ciliegge in Italian.

She gasps for air. Her body tenses.

Long shot of her under the hairdryer, looking as if she's been electrocuted.

Black.

The clock. It is 11:59.

A BLACK MAN. *He is putting shells into a rifle.*

Black man: From me to you, Charley, this one's from me to you. And this here one's from my ma, Rebecca. Hell, you remember big ol' Becky. And this here lil' thinga mabob's from my pa. Timon. Pinky Timon.

The clock jumps to 12:00.

SFX: The siren sounds.

The black man looks up from loading the rifle, inhales, runs to window and throws it open.

Black man: You bastards. You crazy stinking stupid rotten white bastards. I was gonna get me one of you first. How am I gonna do that now? Huh? Answer me that? How am I gonna get me one of you first?

Before he can fire, his lungs burst and he falls, the rifle in his hands.

Close shot of his finger still on the trigger. He slowly pulls it and the rifle fires. Pow!

SFX: Rifle blast.

His finger stops moving, the rifle is still.

Camera starts to pan back. We see the BLACK MAN *full-length. Then the* MIDDLE-AGED LADY, *the* DEAF-MUTE, *the* NUN, *the* LOVERS, *the* ITALIAN GIRL, *the* NERVOUS WOMAN, *the* WRITER, *the* SCHOOL TEACHER, *the* SCIENTIST *and* THE MAN IN THE CHAIR. *They are all in the positions where they fell but we have the impression of a battlefield.*

Camera holds on this silent, bloodless tableau for several beats.

The clock reads 12:01. Then it jumps back to 12:00. Then it jumps back to 11:59.

Silence.

Fade out.

THE INDIVIDUAL AND SOCIETY

J. Krishnamurti

We were walking along a crowded street. The sidewalks were heavy with people, and the smell of exhaust from the cars and buses filled our nostrils. The shops displayed many costly and shoddy things. The sky was pale silver, and it was pleasant in the park as we came out of the noisy thorough-fare. We went deeper into the park and sat down.

He was saying that the State, with its militarization and legislation, was absorbing the individual almost everywhere, and that worship of the State was now taking the place of the worship of God. In most countries the State was penetrating into the very intimate lives of its people; they were being told what to read and what to think. The State was spying upon its citizens, keeping a divine eye on them, taking over the function of the Church. It was the new religion. Man used to be a slave to the Church, but was now a slave of the State. Before it was the Church, and now it was the State that controlled his education; and neither was concerned with the liberation of man.

What is the relationship of the individual to society? Obviously, society exists for the individual, and not the other way round. Society exists for the fruition of man; it exists to give freedom to the individual so that he may have the opportunity to awaken the highest intelligence. This intelligence is not the mere cultivation of a technique or of knowledge; it is to be in touch with that creative reality which is not of the superficial mind. Intelligence is not a cumulative result, but freedom from progressive achievement and success. Intelligence is never static; it cannot be copied and standardized, and hence cannot be taught. Intelligence is to be discovered in freedom.

The collective will and its action, which is society, does not offer this freedom to the individual; for society, not being organic, is ever static. Society is made up, put together for the convenience of man; it has no independent mechanism of its own. Men may capture society, guide it, shape it, tyrannize over it, depending upon their psychological states; but society is not the master of man. It may influence him, but man always breaks it down. There is conflict between man and society because man is in conflict within himself; and the conflict is between that which is static and that which is living. Society is the outward expression of man. The conflict between himself and society is the conflict within himself. This conflict, within and without, will ever exist until the highest intelligence is awakened.

We are social entities as well as individuals; we are citizens as well as men, separate becomers in sorrow and pleasure. If there is to be peace we have to understand the right relationship between the man and the citizen. Of course, the State would prefer us to be entirely citizens; but that is the stupidity of governments. We ourselves would like to hand over the man to the citizen; for to be a citizen is easier than to be a man. To be a good citizen is to function efficiently within the pattern of a given society. Efficiency and conformity are demanded of the citizen, as they toughen him, make him ruthless; and then he is capable of sacrificing the man to the citizen. A good citizen is not necessarily a good man; but a good man is bound to be a right citizen, not of any particular society or country. Because he is primarily a good man, his actions will not be anti-social, he will not be against another man. He will live in co-operation with other good men; he will not seek authority, for he has no authority; he will be capable of efficiency without its ruthlessness. The citizen attempts to sacrifice the man; but the man who is searching out the highest intelligence will naturally shun the stupidities of the citizen. So the State will be against the good man, the man of intelligence; but such a man is free from all governments and countries.

The intelligent man will bring about a good society; but a good citizen will not give birth to a society in which man can be of the highest intelligence. The conflict between the citizen and the man is inevitable if the citizen predominates; and any society which deliberately disregards the man is doomed. There is reconciliation between the citizen and the man only when the psychological process of man is understood. The State, the present society, is not concerned with the inner man, but only with the outer man, the citizen. It may deny the inner man, but he always overcomes the outer, destroying the plans cunningly devised for the citizen. The State sacrifices the present for the future, ever safeguarding itself for the future; it regards the future as all-important, and not the present. But to the intelligent man, the present is of the highest importance, the now and not the tomorrow. What *is* can be understood only with the fading of tomorrow. The understanding of what *is* brings about transformation in the immediate present. It is this transformation that is of supreme importance, and not how to reconcile the citizen with the man. When this transformation takes place, the conflict between the man and the citizen ceases.

CITY PEOPLE
A Photographic
Essay

The Urban Reader has shown that every city person has his own unique way of "seeing" the urban scene around him. Some perceive it in terms of numerical statistics, some in terms of poetic images. Here in this section we present the *photographer's* vision, that insight into the city focused through the camera lens. The collection represents the work of many city photographers from all parts of the country, each of whom has something special to say in pictures. A good look at a photograph will connect you to its subject and its artistic composition. More than that, it will bring you inevitably to the visual concepts of the invisible photographer himself.

The photographs in this section, taken together, present an essay of the people. It takes place visually just as the urbanization of America took place. Space in the empty, unpeopled landscape of the first photograph is peopled slowly at first, in ones, then twos, then threes, then more and more rapidly as the crowds get larger, until that landscape is just about consumed by a swarm of individuals whose faces are barely seen. There are quantitative and qualitative changes as the process takes place, but the beauty of the human image is never lost. Men together, celebrating art shows, the rodeo, or Chinese New Years, share a humanity seen individualized or paired in the earlier pictures. By the clicks of the shutter the people are brought before us.

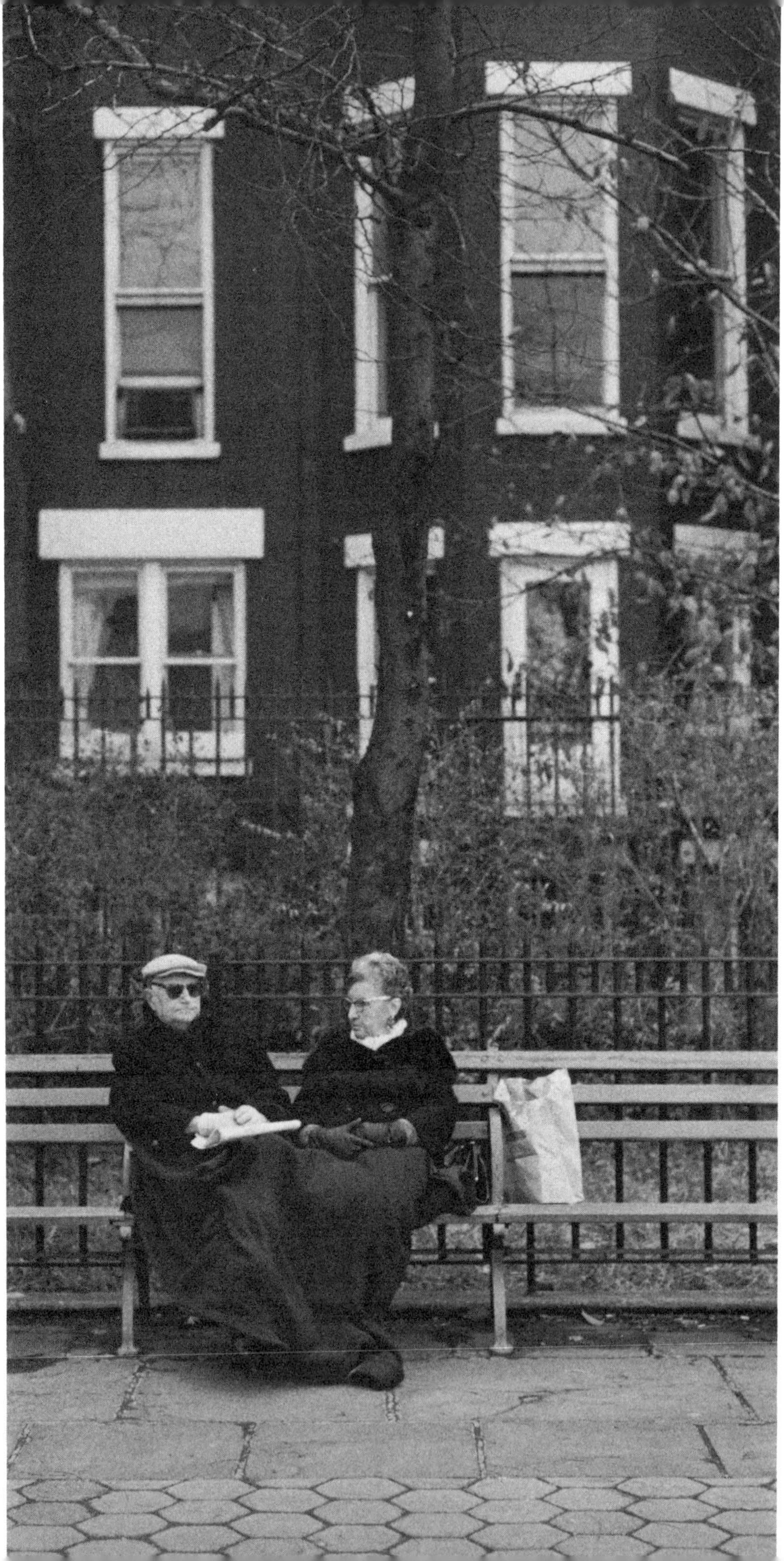

SELECTED BIBLIOGRAPHY

PRELIMINARIES

COUSINS, A. N. and H. NAGPAUL. *Urban Man & Society*. New York, 1970.

GEEN, ELIZABETH, et al., eds. *Man and the Modern City*. Pittsburgh, 1963.

KRAMER, P. and C. HOLBORN, eds. *The City in American Life*. New York, 1970.

MCKELVEY, B. *The City in American History*. New York, 1969.

MUMFORD, LEWIS. *The Culture of Cities*. New York, 1938.

SARTRE, JEAN-PAUL. "American Cities," in *Literary and Philosophical Essays*. New York, 1955, pp. 114–25.

VON ECKARDT, WOLF. *The Challenge of Megalopolis*. New York, 1964.

WAKSTEIN, A. M. *Urbanization of America: An Historical Anthology*. Boston, 1970.

WEBER, MAX. *The City*. Trans. by D. Martindale and G. Neuwirth. Glencoe, Ill., 1958.

WHITE, MORTON and LUCIA. *The Intellectual Versus the City*. Cambridge, Mass., 1962.

LIFE STYLES AND CITY PSYCHES

BOOKS

COX, HARVEY. *The Secular City*. New York, 1965.

LARNER, JEREMY, ed. *The Addict in the Streets*. New York, 1965.

MILLER, HENRY. "Soiree in Hollywood," in *The Air-Conditioned Nightmare*. New York, 1940, pp. 247–58.

SCHNEIDER, WOLF. "Asphalt and Boredom," in *Babylon Is Everywhere, The City as Man's Fate*. New York, 1960, pp. 319–27.

SIMMEL, GEORGE. "The Metropolis and Mental Life," in *Man Alone*. Eds. Eric and Mary Josephson. New York, 1962, pp. 151–65.

ARTICLES

"Exposure to Urban Life Held Aid to Psychic Life," *The New York Times*, May 26, 1970, p. 22.

KOHL, HERBERT and JAMES S. HINTON. "Names, Graffiti, and Culture," *The Urban Review*, III (April, 1969), 24–37.

MITCHELL, HOWARD E. "The Urban Crisis and the Search for Identity," *Social Casework*, L (January, 1969), 10–15.

THOMPSON, HUNTER S. "The Motorcycle Gangs: Losers and Outsiders," *The Nation*, CC (May 17, 1965), 522–26.

WOLFE, TOM. "Radical Chic: That Party at Lenny's," *New York*, III (June 8, 1970), 26–56.

THE PHYSICAL ENVIRONMENT:
URBAN ECOLOGY

CALDWELL, L. K. *Environment: A Challenge to Modern Society*. New York, 1970.

CREIGHTON, R. L. *Urban Transportation Planning*. Glencoe, Ill., 1969.

DE BELL, G., ed. *The Environmental Handbook*. New York, 1970.

GORDON, MITCHELL. *Sick Cities*. New York, 1963.

HELFRICH, H. W., JR. *Environmental Crisis: Man's Struggle to Live with Himself*. New Haven, Conn., 1970.

KEROUAC, JACK. "Manhattan Sketches," in *The Moderns*. Ed. LeRoi Jones. New York, 1963, pp. 266–77.

UDALL, STEWART L. "Cities in Trouble: Frederick Law Olmsted," in *The Quiet Crisis*. New York, 1964, pp. 159–72.

HOUSING: WRECK AND RENEW

BOOKS

BERMAN, D. S. *Urban Renewal: The Bonanza of the Real Estate Business*. Englewood Cliffs, N.J., 1969.

EDITORS OF FORTUNE MAGAZINE. *The Exploding Metropolis*. New York, 1958.

JACOBS, JANE. *The Death and Life of Great American Cities*. New York, 1961.

MUSEUM OF MODERN ART. *New York City: Architecture and Urban Renewal*. New York, 1970.

REYNOLDS, M. J. *Housing the Poor in American Cities*. College Park, Md., 1969.

ARTICLES

BERKELEY, ELLEN PERRY. "MUSE," *Architectural Forum*, CXXIX (September, 1968), 87–88.

"Lost City of the Poor," *Architectural Forum*, CXXIX (July–August, 1968), 37.

"Rehabilitation on a City Street," *Architectural Forum*, CXXIX (October, 1968), 62ff.

SHIPLER, DAVID K. "Troubles Beset Public Housing Across Nation," *The New York Times*, October 12, 1969, p. 1ff.

MINORITIES: STRANGERS AND COUSINS IN THE PROMISED LAND

BIRMINGHAM, STEPHEN. *Our Crowd: The Great Jewish Families of New York*. New York, 1967.

CLARK, KENNETH B. *Dark Ghetto*. New York, 1965.

DRAKE, ST. C. and H. R. CLAYTON. *Black Metropolis: A Study of Negro Life in a Northern City*. New York, 1945.

GREBLER, L., et al. *Mexican American People: The Nation's Second Largest Minority*. New York, 1970.

HANDLIN, OSCAR. *The Newcomers*. Cambridge, Mass., 1959.

HARRINGTON, MICHAEL. "The Rejects," in *The Other America*. New York, 1963, pp. 19–38.

KRINSKY, F. and J. BOSKIN. *Mexican Americans: An Awakening Minority*. New York, 1970.

LEWIS, OSCAR. *La Vida*. New York, 1965.

MEIER, AUGUST and ELLIOTT M. RUDWICK. "Negroes in the Urban Age: The Rise of the Ghetto," in *From Plantation to Ghetto: An Interpretive History of American Negroes*. New York, 1966, pp. 189–220.

SHERMAN, RICHARD B., ed. *The Negro and the City*. Englewood Cliffs, N.J., 1970.

STEFFENS, LINCOLN. *The Shame of the Cities*. New York, 1904.

WITTKE, C. *The Irish in America*. New York, 1970.

ECONOMICS: BIG MONEY FOR WHOM?

BOOKS

GANS, HERBERT J. *The Urban Villagers*. New York, 1962.

JACOBS, JANE. *Economy of Cities*. New York, 1969.

RIIS, JACOB A. *How the Other Half Lives: Studies Among the Tenements of New York*. New York, 1914.

SMITH, W. and C. BLANCHE. *The Great Hunger*. London, 1962.

STURDIVANT, FREDERICK D., ed. *The Ghetto Marketplace*. New York, 1969.

ARTICLES

GAVIN, JAMES M. "Can Industry Manufacture Social Solutions?," *Saturday Review*, LII (May 24, 1969), 21–22.

LOWE, JEANNE R. "Race, Jobs, and Cities: What Business Can Do," *Saturday Review*, LII (January 11, 1969), 27ff.

RASKIN, A. H. "A Union with Soul," *The New York Times Magazine*, March 22, 1970, pp. 24–25ff.

SILBERMAN, CHARLES E. "The City and the Negro," *Fortune*, LXV (January, 1962), 89ff.

YOUNG, WHITNEY M., JR. "The Split-Level Challenge," *Saturday Review*, LII (August 23, 1969), 16–18.

POLITICS AND POWER STRUGGLES

BOOKS

CONNERY, R. H., ed. *Urban Riots: Violence and Social Change*. New York, 1969.

HAYDEN, TOM. *Rebellion in Newark*. New York, 1967.

JACOBS, PAUL. *Prelude to Riot: A View of Urban America from the Bottom*. New York, 1968.

LESTER, JULIUS. *Revolutionary Notes*. New York, 1969.

LINDSAY, JOHN V. *City*. New York, 1970.

OPPENHEIMER, MARTIN. *The Urban Guerrilla*. Chicago, 1969.

ARTICLES

BARON, HAROLD M. "Black Powerlessness in Chicago," *Trans*-action, VI (November, 1968), 27–33.

LYMAN, STANFORD M. "Red Guard on Grant Avenue," *Trans*-action, VII (April, 1970), 21–34.

MOORE, J. W. and R. GUZMAN. "The Mexican-Americans: New Wind from the Southwest," *The Nation*, CCII (May 30, 1966), 646–8.

TYLER, GUS. "Can Anyone Run a City?," *Saturday Review*, LII (November 8, 1969), 22–25.

EDUCATION:
UP AGAINST THE CLASSROOM WALL

BOOKS

ASHTON-WARNER, SYLVIA. *Teacher*. New York, 1964.

COLEMAN, JAMES S., et al. *Equality of Educational Opportunity*. Printed by the U.S. Government. Washington, D.C., 1966.

DENNISON, GEORGE. *The Lives of Children*. New York, 1969.

GOODMAN, PAUL. "The Universal Trap," in *Compulsory Mis-Education and The Community of Scholars*. New York, 1962, pp. 19–42.

HENTOFF, NAT. *Our Children Are Dying*. New York, 1967.

HERNDON, JAMES. *The Way It Spozed To Be*. New York, 1969.

KAUFMAN, BEL. *Up the Down Staircase*. Englewood Cliffs, N.J., 1965.

KOHL, HERBERT. *36 Children.* New York, 1967.

KOZOL, JONATHAN. *Death at an Early Age.* Boston, 1961.

MOORE, G. A., JR. *Realities of the Urban Classroom.* New York, 1967.

POSTMAN, NEIL and C.WEINGARTNER. *Teaching as a Subversive Activity.* New York, 1968.

SEXTON, PATRICIA CAYO. *Education and Income.* New York, 1961.

ARTICLES

HATCH, H. RICHARD. "Children As Urban Planners," *The Urban Review,* II (December, 1967), 24–5.

KOCH, KENNETH. "Teaching Children to Be Poets," *The New York Review of Books,* XIV (April 9, 1970), 17–29.

"School is Not a Place, But an Activity," an Interview with John Bremer, *Media and Methods,* VI (January, 1970), 30–34ff.

THE ARTISTS AT WORK

MUSIC

GARLAND, PHYL. *The Sound of Soul.* Chicago, 1969.

HUGHES, LANGSTON. *The Weary Blues.* New York, 1926.

JONES, LEROI. "The City," in *Blues People.* New York, 1963.

KEEPNEW, ORRIN and BILL GRAUER. *A Pictorial History of Jazz.* New York, 1955.

KEIL, CHARLES. *Urban Blues.* Chicago, 1966.

STEARNS, MARSHALL. *The Story of Jazz.* New York, 1956.

ART

"Art in the Ghetto," *Harvard Art Review,* III (Winter, 1968–9), entire issue.

BINZEN, BILL. *Tenth Street.* New York, 1968.

FRY, E. M. *Art in a Machine Age.* New York, 1969.

HARRIS, N. *The Artist in American Society.* New York, 1970.

LITERATURE

poetry

CRANE, HART. "The Bridge," in *The Complete Poems of Hart Crane.* New York, 1958, pp. 3–62.

ELIOT, T. S. "The Love Song of J. Alfred Prufrock" and "The Waste Land," in *Complete Poems and Plays.* New York, 1962, pp. 3–7 and 37–55.

GINSBERG, ALLEN. "Waking in New York," in *Planet News 1961–1967*. San Francisco, 1968, p. 69.

LAWRENCE, D. H. "City Life," in *D. H. Lawrence: Selected Poems*. New York, 1947, p. 115.

WHITMAN, WALT. "Once I Pass'd Through a Populous City" and "Crossing Brooklyn Ferry," in *Complete Poetry and Selected Prose*. Boston, 1959, pp. 82 and 116–20.

fiction

SHORT STORY COLLECTIONS

BARTHELME, DONALD. *City Life*. New York, 1970.

CAHILL, TOM and SUSAN, eds. *Big City Stories by Modern American Writers*. New York, 1971.

CATHER, WILLA. "Paul's Case," in *The Bedside Book of Famous American Stories*. New York, 1936.

GASS, WILLIAM H. "In the Heart of the Heart of the Country," in *In the Heart of the Heart of the Country*. New York, 1968.

JONES, LEROI. *Tales*. New York, 1967.

MALAMUD, BERNARD. *Idiots First*. New York, 1963.

MICHAELS, LEONARD. *Going Places*. New York, 1970.

NEUGEBOREN, JAY. *Corky's Brother*. New York, 1969.

POE, EDGAR ALLEN. "The Masque of the Red Death" and "The Cask of Amontillado," in *Complete Stories and Poems*. New York, 1966.

ROTH, PHILIP. "Goodbye, Columbus," in *Goodbye, Columbus and Five Short Stories*. New York, 1963.

STEIN, GERTRUDE. "Melanctha," in *Three Lives*. New York, 1936.

NOVELS

ALGREN, NELSON. *The Man with the Golden Arm*. New York, 1947.

BALDWIN, JAMES. *Go Tell It on the Mountain*. New York, 1970.

BELLOW, SAUL. *The Adventures of Augie March*. New York, 1953.

CRANE, STEPHEN. *Maggie, A Girl of the Streets*, in *Complete Novels of Stephen Crane*. New York, 1967.

DOS PASSOS, JOHN. *U.S.A.* Boston, 1960.

DREISER, THEODORE. *An American Tragedy*. Cleveland, 1948.

———. *The Financier*. New York, 1912.

———. *Sister Carrie*. New York, 1927.

ELLISON, RALPH. *The Invisible Man*. New York, 1953.

FARRELL, JAMES T. *Studs Lonigan*. New York, 1938.

FITZGERALD, F. SCOTT. *The Great Gatsby*. New York, 1925.

GARDNER, LEONARD. *Fat City*. New York, 1969.

HIMES, CHESTER B. *If He Hollers Let Him Go.* New York, 1955.

MAYFIELD, JULIAN. *The Hit.* New York, 1957.

MILLER, WARREN. *The Cool World.* New York, 1959.

NORRIS, FRANK. *The Octopus.* New York, 1928.

————. *The Pit: A Story of Chicago.* New York, 1928.

RECHY, JOHN. *City of Night.* New York, 1963.

ROTH, HENRY. *Call It Sleep.* New York, 1934.

SINCLAIR, UPTON. *The Jungle.* New York, 1906.

WALKER, T. MIKE. *Voices from the Bottom of the World, A Policeman's Journal.* New York, 1970

WEST, NATHANAEL. *Miss Lonelyhearts & The Day of the Locust.* New York, 1962.

drama

ALBEE, EDWARD. "The Zoo Story," in *The American Dream & The Zoo Story.* New York, 1959.

BULLINS, ED., ed. *New Plays from the Black Theatre.* New York, 1969.

CORSO, GREGORY. "Standing on a Street Corner," in *The Evergreen Review Reader.* New York, 1962.

HANSBERRY, LORRAINE. *A Raisin in the Sun.* New York, 1958.

autobiography

BROWN, CLAUDE. *Manchild in the Promised Land.* New York, 1963.

HUGHES, LANGSTON. *The Big Sea.* New York, 1940.

KAZIN, ALFRED. *A Walker in the City.* New York, 1951.

MALCOLM X. *The Autobiography of Malcolm X.* New York, 1963.

SCHULBERG, BUDD, ed. *From the Ashes, Voices of Watts.* New York, 1967.

THOMAS, PIRI. *Down These Mean Streets.* New York, 1967.

essays

ALGREN, NELSON. *Chicago: City on the Make.* New York, 1951.

BALDWIN, JAMES. "Fifth Avenue, Uptown: A Letter from Harlem," in *Nobody Knows My Name.* New York, 1961, pp. 53–64.

BELLOW, SAUL. "Skepticism and the Depth of Life," in *Arts and the Public.* Eds. J. F. Miller, Jr. and P. D. Herring. Chicago, 1967, pp. 13–17.

JONES, LEROI. "City of Harlem," in *Home, Social Essays.* New York, 1966.

KAZIN, ALFRED. "The Writer and the City," *Harper's Magazine,* CCXXXVII (December, 1968), 110–27.

RECHY, JOHN. "Chicago, Savage City," in *The Moderns.* Ed. LeRoi Jones. New York, 1963.

THE FUTURE: A BAD TRIP?

BOOKS

BENET, STEPHEN VINCENT. "By the Waters of Babylon," in *Selected Works of Stephen Vincent Benet.* New York, 1937.

CLARKE, ARTHUR C. *The City and the Stars.* New York, 1953.

HELLMAN, H. *The City in the World of the Future.* Philadelphia, 1969.

KEROUAC, JACK. "CITYcitycity," in *The Moderns.* Ed. LeRoi Jones. New York, 1963, pp. 250–65.

ARTICLES

DOXIADIS, CONSTANTINO A. "Life in the Year 2000," *NEA Journal* (November, 1967),??.

GANS, HERBERT J. "Report from the Center for Urban Archaeology," *The Urban Review*, III (November, 1968), 16–17.

KENNISTON, KENNETH. "How Community Mental Health Stamped out the Riots (1968–78)," *Trans*-action, V (July–August, 1968), 21–29.

ACKNOWLEDGMENTS

The editors gratefully acknowledge the following writers, publishers, and agents who have granted permission to reprint copyrighted selections in this book.

Appleseed Music Inc. for "There Once Was a Young Man Who Went to the City" adapted and arranged by Fred Hellerman, Copyright © 1960, 1966 Appleseed Music Inc.

The Architectural Forum for "Deghettoization, Choice of the New Militancy" by Clarence Funnyé from *The Architectural Forum*, April, 1969. Reprinted by permission of the publisher.

Avatar for "Drop City: A Total Living Environment" by Albin Wagner. Reprinted with permission of *Avator*.

AVCO Embassy Records Corp. for "Beautiful People," Words and Music by Melanie Safka, copyright, 1967, Avco Embassy Music Publishing, Inc., Kama Rippa Music Inc. and Amelanie Music Publishing. Used by permission.

Alma Bagu for "On the Rim of Belonging" from *The Center Forum*, September, 1969. Reprinted by permission of the author and Center for Urban Education.

Ballantine Books, Inc. for "Eco-tactics." Copyright 1970 by Garrett de Bell. A Ballantine Book/Friends of the Earth Book.

Barricade Music, Inc. for "Outside of a Small Circle of Friends," words and music by Phil Ochs. Copyright 1966, Barricade Music, Inc.

Beacon Press: for "Coming to the City" from *In the Midst of Plenty* by Ben H. Bagdikian. Copyright 1964 by Ben H. Bagdikian. Reprinted by permission of the Beacon Press.

——————— for "Journey to Atlanta" by James Baldwin from *Notes of a Native Son*. Reprinted by permission of the Beacon Press. Copyright 1948, 1955 by James Baldwin.

Caroline Bird for "The Single Girls of the City: Why They Don't Want to Be Wives" from *New York Magazine*, January 27, 1969. Reprinted with permission of the author and publisher.

The Black Panther Party for "The Black Panther Party Platform and Program. What We Want, What We Believe." Reprinted by permission of Brenda Highson, Ministry of Information, Harlem Branch, and the Black Panther Party.

Changing Times for "What's Gone Wrong in Our Big-City Schools?", July 1969. Reprinted by permission from *Changing Times*. Copyright 1969 by The Kiplinger Washington Editors, Inc.

Frank Chin for "Food for All His Dead." Copyright © 1962 by Frank Chin. First Published in *Contact* and reprinted by permission of the author's agent, Dorothea Oppenheimer.

San Francisco Chronicle for "Take a City to Lunch" by Arthur W. Hoppe, *San Francisco Chronicle*, August 18, 1968. Copyright 1968 Chronicle Publishing Company. Reprinted by permission of the author and publisher.

City Lights Books for "By Air, Albany–Baltimore" by Allen Ginsberg. Copyright 1969 by Allen Ginsberg. Reprinted by permission of City Lights Books and the author.

Delacorte Press: for "The San Francisco Weather Report" or "Gee, You're So Beautiful That It's Starting to Rain" by Richard Brautigan. Reprinted from *The Pill Versus the Springhill Mine Disaster* by Richard Brautigan. Copyright 1968 by Richard Brautigan. A Seymour Lawrence Book/Delacorte Press. Used by permission. First published by Four Seasons Foundation in its Writing series edited by Donald Allen.

_____ for "Adam" by Kurt Vonnegut, Jr. Copyright 1950, 1951, 1953, 1954, 1955, 1956, 1958, 1960, 1961, 1962, 1964, 1966, 1968 by Kurt Vonnegut, Jr. Reprinted from *Welcome to the Monkey House* by Kurt Vonnegut, Jr. A Seymour Lawrence Book/Delacorte Press. Used by permission.

The Dial Press, Inc. for permission to quote from *Revolution For The Hell Of It* by Abbie Hoffman.

Farrar, Strauss & Giroux, Inc. for "My Life with R. H. Macy" by Shirley Jackson. Copyright 1949 by Shirley Jackson. Reprinted with the permission of Farrar, Straus & Giroux, Inc. from *The Lottery* by Shirley Jackson.

Mitchell Goodman for "Snow on the City Three Days Before Christmas," copyright Mitchell Goodman. Reprinted by permission of the author.

Grove Press for permission to quote from Introduction by Warren Tallman to *New American Story* edited by Donald Allen and Robert Creeley. Copyright © 1965 by Donald M. Allen.

Toni Hall and *New Schools Exchange Newsletter* for "Wanted: Teaching Job in City School," from "People Seeking Places" in *The New Schools Exchange Newsletter*, February 4, 1970. Reprinted by permission of the author and publisher.

Handy Brothers Music Co., Inc. for permission to reprint the lyrics to "Saint Louis Blues" by W. C. Handy.

Harcourt Brace Jovanovich, Inc., for "the hours rise up putting off stars and it is" by e. e. cummings. Copyright, 1923, 1951, by e. e. cummings. Reprinted from his volume, *Poems 1923–1954*, by permission of Harcourt Brace Jovanovich, Inc.

Harper & Row, Publishers, Inc.: for adaptions from *Where Do We Go from Here: Chaos or Community?* by Martin Luther King, Jr. Copyright © 1967 by Martin Luther King, Jr. Originally appeared in *The New York Times Magazine* under the title "Abolish Poverty Directly." Reprinted by permission of Harper & Row, Publishers, Inc.

_____ for Abridgement of "Tactics for the Seventies" in *The Professional Radical, Conversations with Saul Alinsky* by Marion K. Sanders, and Saul Alinsky. Reprinted by permission of Harper & Row, Publishers, Inc.

_____ for excerpts from *The Artist's Voice* by Katharine Kuh: from pp. 53 & 55 by Stuart Davis, from p. 107 by Morris Graves, from pp. 243–244 by Mark Tobey. Copyright © 1960, 1961, 1962 by Katharine Kuh. Reprinted by permission of Harper & Row, Publishers, Inc.

_____ for "The Ethics of Living Jim Crow" from *Uncle Tom's Children* by Richard Wright, Copyright, 1937 by Richard Wright. Reprinted by permission of Harper & Row, Publishers, Inc.

Hill and Wang, Inc., for "Last Night in Newark" by Ted Joans from *Black Pow-Wow*. Copyright © 1969 by Ted Joans. Reprinted by permission of Hill & Wang, Inc.

Holt, Rinehart and Winston, Inc. for passages from *Two Blocks Apart* edited by Charlotte Leon Mayerson. Copyright © 1965 by Holt, Rinehart and Winston, Inc. Reprinted by permission of Holt, Rinehart and Winston, Inc.

Jerry Kamstra for "The Grim Plight of the Urban Indian" from The San Francisco Sunday Examiner & Chronicle, December 7, 1969. Reprinted by permission of the author and publisher.

Jonathan Kozol for "Teaching Life at an Early Age in the Slums" from *The New York Times*, June 15, 1968. Reprinted by permission of the author.

Krishnamurti Writings, Inc., Ojai, California for permission to reprint "The Individual and Society" and "Life in a City" from *Commentaries on Living* by J. Krishnamurti.

Liberator for "Quietus" by Charlie Russell from *Liberator*, Vol. 4, no. 11 (November 1964). Copyright © by *Liberator*. Reprinted by permission of the publisher.

The Macmillan Company: for "Meeting the Angels" by Cal from *The Bikeriders* by Danny Lyon. Reprinted with permission of The Macmillan Company. Copyright © 1968 by Danny Lyon.

————————————— for permission to quote from *The Secular City* by Harvey Cox. Copyright by Harvey Cox © 1965, and for permission to quote from *Urban Behavior* by E. Gordon Ericksen, copyright 1954 by the Macmillan Company.

Herbert Woodward Martin for permission to reprint "Dialogue" and "Observation to the Empire State Building," copyright © 1971 by Herbert Woodward Martin.

Harold Matson Company, Inc.: for "The Pedestrian" by Ray Bradbury. Copyright 1952 by Ray Bradbury. Reprinted by permission of Harold Matson Company, Inc.

————————————— for a portion of "El Paso del Norte" by John Rechy. Copyright © by John Rechy, reprinted by permission of the Harold Matson Company, Inc.

McGraw-Hill Book Company for "On Watts" by Eldridge Cleaver from *Soul on Ice*. Copyright © 1968 by Eldridge Cleaver. Used with permission of McGraw-Hill Book Company.

William Morris Agency, Inc., for "Last Gasps" by Terrence McNally. Copyright © 1970 by Terrence McNally. Reprinted by permission of William Morris Agency, Inc., on behalf of author.

Music Sales Corporation for "There Was a Rich Man and He Lived in Detroitium" by Woody Guthrie and the notation for "Skinnamalinkadoolium." From *Hard Hitting Songs for Hard-Hit People* by Alan Lomax, Woody Guthrie, Pete Seeger Copyright © 1967 Oak Publications. All Rights Reserved. Used by permission.

The Nation: for "First Year at Federal City" by David Swanston from *The Nation*, May 12, 1969, reprinted with permission of the author and publisher.

National Review for "Urban Dilemma" by M. Stanton Evans from *National Review Bulletin*, October 10, 1967.

Negro Digest for "Vive, Noir!" by Mari Evans from *Negro Digest*, September/October, 1968. Reprinted with permission of the author and publisher.

The New American Library, Inc., for permission to quote a passage from *Easy Rider* by Peter Fonda, Dennis Hopper and Terry Southern. Copyright © 1969 by Raybert Productions, Inc. Reprinted by arrangement with The New American Library, Inc., New York.

New Directions Publishing Corp.: for "They Were Putting up the Statue of Saint Francis" by Lawrence Ferlinghetti from *A Coney Island of the Mind*. Copyright 1958 by Lawrence Ferlinghetti. Reprinted by permission of New Directions Publishing Corporation.

————————————— for "The Nose of Sisyphus" by Lawrence Ferlinghetti from *Routines*. Copyright © 1963, 1964 by Lawrence Ferlinghetti. Reprinted by permission of New Directions Publishing Corporation. Caution: Professionals and amateurs are hereby warned that the play, being fully protected under the copyright laws of the U.S.A., the British Empire, including the Dominion of Canada, and all other countries of the world, are subject to royalty. All rights, including professional, amateur, motion picture, recitation, tape or phonograph recordings, lecturing, public reading, radio broadcasting, television, and the rights of translation into foreign languages are strictly reserved. Permission for any such use must be secured from the author's representative, New Directions, 333 Sixth Ave., N.Y., N.Y. 10014.

_____ for "I Went to the City" by Kenneth Patchen from *Hurrah For Anything-Doubleheader.* Copyright © 1958 by Kenneth Patchen. Reprinted by permission of New Directions Publishing Corporation.

_____ for "Ancient Gentility" by William Carlos Williams from *The Farmers' Daughters.* Copyright © 1950 by William Carlos Williams. Reprinted by permission of New Directions Publishing Corporation.

Newsweek for "Slums: Instant Renewal" from *Newsweek,* April 24, 1967. Copyright Newsweek, Inc., 1967.

The New York Review of Books for "Mini Schools: A Prescription for the Reading Problem" by Paul Goodman, *The New York Review of Books,* January 4, 1968. Reprinted with permission from *The New York Review of Books.* Copyright © 1967 The New York Review.

The New York Times: for "The Sounds of the City" by James Tuite, 8/6/66; for "City Starts Drive on Lead Poisoning" by John Sibley, 10/19/69; for "Obituary of of a Heroin User Who Died at 12" by Joseph Lelyveld and Charlayne Hunter, 1/12/70; for "Once Upon a Time—A Fable of Student Power" by Neil Postman, 6/14/70 from *The New York Times Magazine*; for "38 Who Saw Murder Didn't Call Police" by Martin Gansberg, 3/27/64. Copyright © 1964, 1966, 1969, 1970, by The New York Times Company. Reprinted by permission.

Harold Ober Associates Incorporated for "Ballad of the Landlord" by Langston Hughes from *Montage of a Dream Deferred.* Copyright Langston Hughes. Reprinted by permission of Harold Ober Associates Inc.

Office of Economic Opportunity for permission to reprint "An Anglo's Barrio" by Genevieve Ray from *The VISTA Volunteer* magazine, July, 1969, Vol. 5, No. 7.

Richie Orange for "Harlem" from *Whereas,* literary magazine of Queens College of the City University of New York, Winter, 1969. Reprinted by permission of the author.

Porter Sargent Publisher for "I Was Born" by Byron Rushing from *The Black Power Revolt,* edited by Floyd B. Barbour. Copyright 1968 by F. Porter Sargent. Reprinted with permission of the publisher.

Frederick A. Praeger, Inc., for "Alternatives to Urban Public Schools," by Kenneth B. Clark from *The Schoolhouse in the City* edited by Alvin Toffler. Reprinted with permission of the publisher.

Prentice-Hall, Inc., for "Letter from a Polish Immigrant" from *Immigration as a Factor in American History* edited by Oscar Handlin. Copyright © 1959. Reprinted by permission of Prentice-Hall, Inc., Englewood Cliffs, N.J.

Random House, Inc.: from *The Poorhouse State,* "Barbara Dugan's Story" by Richard M. Elman, Copyright © 1966 by Richard M. Elman. Reprinted by permission of Pantheon Books, a division of Random House, Inc.

————————————— excerpt from *The Death and Life of Great American Cities* by Jane Jacobs. Copyright © 1961 by Jane Jacobs. Reprinted by permission of Random House, Inc.

————————————— Prologue from *Down These Mean Streets* by Piri Thomas. Copyright © 1967 by Piri Thomas. Reprinted by permission of Alfred A. Knopf, Inc.

————————————— for permission to quote from *The New Radicals* edited by Paul Jacobs and Saul Landau.

Paul R. Reynolds, Inc., for permission to quote from Introduction by Richard Wright to *Black Metropolis* by St. Clair Drake and Horace R. Cayton.

G. Schirmer, Inc., for permission to reprint "Gee, Officer Krupke" from "West Side Story" lyrics by Stephen Sondheim. Copyright © 1957, 1959 Leonard Bernstein & Stephen Sondheim. Used by permission of the publisher, G. Schirmer, Inc.

Charles Scribner's Sons: for permission to quote from *The Great Gatsby* by F. Scott Fitzgerald.

————————————— for permission to reprint "The City" from *Words* by Robert Creeley. Copyright © 1962, 1963, 1964, 1967 Robert Creeley.

————————————— for "Only the Dead Know Brooklyn" (Copyright 1935 by F-R Publishing Corp.; renewal copyright 1963 Paul Gitlin) which first appeared in *The New Yorker*, is reprinted by permission of Charles Scribner's Sons from *From Death to Morning* by Thomas Wolfe.

The Sterling Lord Agency: for "The Last of the Irish Immigrants" by Jimmy Breslin published in *New York Magazine*, March 17, 1969. Copyright © 1969 by Jimmy Breslin. Reprinted by permission of The Sterling Lord Agency.

————————————— for "Uncle Tom's Cabin: Alternate Ending" by LeRoi Jones from *Tales*. Copyright © 1967 by LeRoi Jones. Reprinted by permission of The Sterling Lord Agency.

————————————— for "Why We're Against the Biggees" by James S. Kunen. published in *The Atlantic*, October, 1968. Copyright © 1968 by James S. Kunen. Reprinted by permission of The Sterling Lord Agency.

————————————— for "The Flight from City Hall . . . One Mayor Who Isn't Running Again" by Fred Powledge published in *Harper's Magazine*, November, 1969. Copyright © 1969 by Fred Powledge. Reprinted by permission of The Sterling Lord Agency.

Stranger Music, Inc., for *Stories of the Street* written by Leonard Cohen. Copyright © 1967, 1969 Stranger Music, Inc. Used by permission. All rights reserved.

The Swallow Press for "Clark Street" by Barbara Harr. Reprinted from *The Mortgaged Wife* (Copyright 1970) by permission of the Swallow Press, Chicago.

Time, The Weekly Newsmagazine, for "The Conglomerate of Crime," August 22, 1969. Reprinted by permission from *Time*, The Weekly Newsmagazine; Copyright Time, Inc. 1970.

Trans-action *Magazine* for permission to reprint portions of "The Culture of Civility: Deviance and Democracy in San Francisco" by Howard S. Becker and Irving Louis Horowitz, April, 1970. Copyright by *Trans*-action Magazine, New Brunswick, New Jersey.

Ernest van den Haag for permission to reprint portions of "Ending the Welfare Mess" from *National Review*, December 17, 1968. Reprinted by permission of the author.

TRO for permission to reprint *The Bourgeois Blues*, words and music by Huddie Ledbetter. Edited with new additional material by Alan Lomax. Copyright © 1959 by Folkways Music Publishers, Inc. Used by permission.

The Village Voice: for permission to reprint the letter "The Cuando Community: Beacon in a Dark City" by George Dennison, *The Village Voice*, June 4, 1970. Reprinted by permission of The Village Voice. Copyrighted by The Village Voice, Inc., 1970.

_____ for articles by Jack Newfield "Lead Poisoning: Silent Epidemic in the Slums," September 18, 1969, and "Young Lords Do City's Work in the Barrio," December 4, 1969. Reprinted by permission of The Village Voice. Copyrighted by The Village Voice, Inc. 1969.

The Wall Street Journal for permission to reprint "Aiding the Poor" by Lee Berton, January 4, 1968, and "Undercover Cops" by David Brand, September 10, 1968. Reprinted by permission of *The Wall Street Journal*.

Wesleyan University Press for "I Am Thinking of Chicago and of What Survives" by Lou Lipsitz. Copyright 1965 by Lou Lipsitz. Reprinted from *Cold Water* by Lou Lipsitz, by permission of Wesleyan University Press.

The World Publishing Company: for "Chicago, August 24–29" by Norman Mailer from *Miami and the Siege of Chicago*. Reprinted by permission of The World Publishing Company. Copyright © 1968 by Norman Mailer.

_____ for permission to cite definitions from *Webster's New World Dictionary*, Second College Edition. From *Webster's New World Dictionary of the American Language*, Second College Edition. Copyright 1970 by The World Publishing Company, Cleveland and New York.

Sincere thanks to the following artists, photographers, and agencies for permission to reprint the art and photography in this book.

BILL BINZEN: pp. ii–iii, 1.

MARVE H. COOPER: 1st, 3rd, and 4th pages following p. 144; p. 145 (top).

DESIGN PHOTOGRAPHERS INTERNATIONAL: W. E. Barksdale: p. 130 (bottom); Edith Marshall: p. 99; Walter Vecchio: p. 401.

JAMES ALLEN GARDNER: pp. 67, 144, 160, 397.

MARIO JORRIN: pp. 12 (top), 91, 126, 331.

MAGNUM PHOTOS: Elliott Erwitt: p. 13 (bottom left); Leonard Freed: p. 177, 396 (top); Burk Uzzle: p. 13 (top left).

MOBILIZATION FOR YOUTH: Donald Blumberg: p. 400; Miguel Luis: p. 248.

MONKMEYER: Sam Falk: p. 72; Merrim: pp. 236 (top), 389.

NEWARK NEWS: p. 251.

WILLIAM H. OLIVER: p. 12 (center left), p. 13 (bottom right).

THE RECORD: Al Paglione: p. 112.

HOWARD PETRICK: p. 93 (top right).

PHOTO RESEARCHERS: Al Lowry: p. 2; Arthur Tress: p. 14.

WALTER RABETZ: p. 386.

BETTY RITTER: p. 13 (top right).

MAURICE SCHELL: pp. 19, 20, 236 (bottom), 384–385, 387, 391, 392 (top and bottom), 396 (top), 398, 399 (bottom).

HARVEY SILVER: pp. 18, 130 (top), 271, 283, 323.

LAURENCE SIMON: pp. 3, 48, 92 (bottom left and right), 93 (bottom), 99, 280, 358, 388, 390, 399 (top).

SOCIETY HILL PLAYHOUSE: p. 12 (bottom left).

BOB SPIEGELMAN: p. 278.

MARY TEREH: p. 145 (bottom).

ARTHUR TRESS: pp. 110, 111 (top and bottom), 148, 395.

UNITED PRESS: p. 393.

WIDE WORLD PHOTOS: pp. 12 (center right), 300, 394.

CHRIS YOUNG: pp. 92 (top), 93 (top left).